Exotic Cinema

This book is dedicated to my initially reluctant but eventually enthusiastic travel companion, Chris. Here's to many more exotic adventures!

Exotic Cinema

Encounters with Cultural Difference in Contemporary Transnational Film

Daniela Berghahn

EDINBURGH
University Press

Edinburgh University Press is one of the leading university presses in the UK. We publish academic books and journals in our selected subject areas across the humanities and social sciences, combining cutting-edge scholarship with high editorial and production values to produce academic works of lasting importance. For more information visit our website: edinburghuniversitypress.com

© Daniela Berghahn, 2024

Grateful acknowledgement is made to the sources listed in the List of Illustrations for permission to reproduce material previously published elsewhere. Every effort has been made to trace the copyright holders, but if any have been inadvertently overlooked, the publisher will be pleased to make the necessary arrangements at the first opportunity.

Edinburgh University Press Ltd
13 Infirmary Street
Edinburgh EH1 1LT

First published in hardback by Edinburgh University Press 2024

Typeset in Monotype Ehrhardt by
Cheshire Typesetting Ltd, Cuddington, Cheshire

A CIP record for this book is available from the British Library

ISBN 978 1 4744 7421 4 (hardback)
ISBN 978 1 4744 7422 1 (paperback)
ISBN 978 1 4744 7423 8 (webready PDF)
ISBN 978 1 4744 7424 5 (epub)

The right of Daniela Berghahn to be identified as the author of this work has been asserted in accordance with the Copyright, Designs and Patents Act 1988, and the Copyright and Related Rights Regulations 2003 (SI No. 2498).

Contents

List of Illustrations vi
Acknowledgements vii

Introduction 1
1. Locating Exoticism 18
2. Ethnographic Salvage and Cosmopolitan Exoticism 59
3. The Spectacle of Cultural Difference: The Tourist Gaze and the Exotic Gaze 101
4. 'The Past Is a Foreign Country': Nostalgia and Exoticism 139
5. Exotic Appetites 175

Filmography 210
Bibliography 214
Index 239

Illustrations

1.1	*The Snake Charmer* (Jean-Léon Gérôme, 1879), courtesy of Clark Art Institute, clarkart.edu	24
1.2	*Exotic Landscape* (Henri Rousseau, 1908), creative commons	25
1.3	*African Woman with Child* (Albert Eckhout, 1641), creative commons, photo © John Lee, National Museum of Denmark	27
1.4	*Water* (Deepa Mehta, 2005)	48
1.5	*The Assassin* (Hou Hsiao-Hsien, 2015)	49
2.1	*Ten Canoes* (Rolf de Heer and Peter Djigirr, 2006)	74
2.2	*Atanarjuat: The Fast Runner* (Zacharias Kunuk, 2001)	79
2.3	*Embrace of the Serpent* (Ciro Guerra, 2015), courtesy of Peccadillo Pictures. All rights reserved	81
2.4	*Tanna* (Martin Butler and Bentley Dean, 2015), courtesy of dir. Martin Butler and Bentley Dean, 2015, with J. J. Nako as Cultural Director, showing Marie Wawa and the late Mungau Dain, © Phillippe Penel	91
3.1	*The Best Exotic Marigold Hotel* (John Madden, 2011)	119
3.2	*Eat Pray Love* (Ryan Murphy, 2010)	120
3.3	*Hotel Salvation* (Shubhashish Bhutiani, 2016)	130
3.4	*To the Ends of the Earth* (Kiyoshi Kurosawa, 2019)	134
4.1	*Indochine* (Régis Wargnier, 1992)	147
4.2	*Viceroy's House* (Gurinder Chadha, 2017)	152
4.3	*In the Mood for Love* (Wong Kar-wai, 2000)	155
4.4	*The Road Home* (Zhang Yimou, 1999)	163
5.1	*Eat Drink Man Woman* (Ang Lee, 1994)	184
5.2	*The Scent of Green Papaya* (Tran Anh Hung, 1993)	195
5.3	*Dumplings* (Fruit Chan, 2004)	201

Acknowledgements

This book marks the end of a long journey, and I would like to thank those friends and colleagues who have accompanied me along the way. Their unwavering support and steadfast encouragement has sustained me at every stage of this project.

This book has benefited immensely from the intellectual generosity and constructive feedback I have received from Manishita Dass, Randall Halle and Song Hwee Lim. They have generously given of their time to discuss initial conceptualisations, challenged my arguments and provided helpful comments on chapters. I am truly grateful for their insightful suggestions, which have improved the book immeasurably. My warm thanks also go to those who acted as important interlocutors at various stages. Stella Bruzzi's incisive feedback, enduring interest and friendship over the years have meant a lot to me. Rachel Dwyer, the late Thomas Elsaesser, Olivia Khoo, Deborah Shaw, Rosie Thomas and James Williams have kindly shared their expertise, thereby offering me a wealth of insights and complementary vantage points on exoticism in world cinema. I have profited enormously from the writings of two outstanding experts on exoticism, Graham Huggan and Charles Forsdick. The thought-provoking questions they posed when I met them at research events have prompted me to refine some of the conceptual stakes of this project and bring certain ideas into focus.

Throughout the research and writing of this book, my colleagues in the Department of Media Arts and the School of Performing and Digital Arts at Royal Holloway, University of London, have been incredibly supportive. Two periods of sabbatical leave allowed me to devote myself entirely to researching and writing. The excellent leadership of my Heads of Department, Jonathan Powell and Barry Langford, has fostered a strong research culture and a congenial environment for the genesis and completion of this book. Amongst the many colleagues whose creative and critical work I value highly and who make it a great pleasure to work with them, I am especially indebted to the intellectual camaraderie and friendship of Manishita Dass, Olga Goriunova and John Hill. Warm thanks also go to the students on my Exotic Cinema module for their enthusiastic endorsement of the films we study together and for making this such a deeply rewarding and enjoyable course to teach.

A Research Fellowship and a subsequent Research Grant from the Humanities and Arts Research Institute at Royal Holloway provided funding for the organisation of an international conference and two research symposia, entitled 'Exoticism in Contemporary Transnational Cinema: Music and Spectacle', 'Reassessing the Contemporary Exotic' and 'Visual Alterity: Seeing Difference, Seeing Differently'. I should like to extend my sincere thanks to everyone who contributed and especially to Anna Morcom, who co-organised the first two events. In their inspiring keynotes, Rachel Dwyer, Charles Forsdick, Randall Halle, Song Hwee Lim and Laudaan Nooshin opened up new perspectives on contemporary exoticism. The fascinating contributions of numerous other speakers and the lively discussions highlighted the multi-disciplinary relevance of exoticism as well as the contestations surrounding this mode of cultural representation. These events, including a full list of all speakers, artists, discussants and detailed abstracts, are documented on the project website: www.exotic-cinema.org.

I owe a debt of gratitude to Laura Rascaroli, Paul Cooke, Stephanie Dennison, Lydia Papadimitriou and Yannis Tzioumakis for inviting me to present parts of this project at the ECREA Conference in Copenhagen, at the Annual Lecture of the Centre for World Cinemas and Digital Cultures at Leeds University and at the Liverpool Film Seminar. These events afforded me with welcome opportunities to discuss my research with engaged and critical audiences. Several conversations and interviews with Vincenzo Bugno, Head of the World Cinema Fund, Maryanne Redpath, curator of the former NATIVe programme at the Berlin International Film Festival, and with J. J. Nako, the Cultural Director of *Tanna*, have offered useful insights into the creative and institutional contexts of some of the films analysed in this book.

At Edinburgh University Press, my warmest thanks go to Gillian Leslie for commissioning this monograph (already my second book with her at the helm of Film Studies at EUP). Gillian's instantly positive response to my original proposal has been a great source of encouragement throughout. I also gratefully acknowledge the two anonymous readers, whose thoughtful feedback and endorsement of the book proposal has been just as crucial at the outset as Sam Johnson's and Lel Gillingwater's tremendous editorial support at the end. Chris Jennings of PagetoScreen deserves full credit for enhancing the public visibility of this research by developing the website www.exotic-cinema.org, which combines beautiful design with functionality. Most importantly, it will allow me to continue sharing my thoughts on decentred exoticism in transnational cinema long after submitting the book manuscript. Thanks are due to the School of Performing and Digital Arts for funding the website.

Some of the ideas I present in this book were previously published in somewhat different and much condensed form as journal articles. Sections of Chapter 1 appeared in *Studies in World Cinema* (2021); parts of Chapter 2 in *Alphaville: Journal of Film and Screen Media* (2017, vol. 14); and parts of Chapter 4 in *Transnational Screens* (2019, vol. 10: 1). I am grateful to the editors of these journals, Laura Rascaroli, Eva Jørholt, Armida de la Garza, Ruth Doughty and Deborah Shaw, for providing feedback on earlier versions of the material now included in this book and for granting permission to draw on this material here. I am most grateful to the directors Martin Butler and Bentley Dean and the cultural director J. J. Nako for granting me permission to use the beautiful image from their film *Tanna* on the front cover of this book. I should also like to thank Peccadillo Pictures, the Clark Art Institute and the National Museum of Denmark, who were so kind as to give me permission to reproduce the images for which they hold the copyright.

Finally, I would like to give my heartfelt thanks to my friends outside the world of academia, Petra Pinger, Benno and Birgit Paffrath and Wilfried Müller, who have received no mention yet. Their close friendship has sustained me in many different ways, not just over the past few years but for most of my life. My deepest gratitude goes to my husband Chris and to our daughters, Zoë and Hannah. Thank you for making my life so much richer and happier through your presence and love.

Introduction

To be writing a book about exoticism in contemporary transnational cinema at a time when calls for decolonising the curriculum are proliferating, may seem utterly 'non-pc'. Campaigns like Rhodes Must Fall and the broad support and momentum which the Black Lives Matter movement has gained since 2020 have led to a heightened sensitivity for the many expressions of white supremacy, racial discrimination and their historical origins in European empires, colonial rule and slavery.[1] What contribution can a book about contemporary exoticism in transnational cinema possibly make to these important and topical debates, being ostensibly situated at the other end of the spectrum?

I propose that this book contributes to the urgent agenda of decolonising the film studies curriculum in three ways: first, because its focus on world cinema de-Westernises the canon; second, because many of the films discussed in this book invite us to reassess Western values and epistemes; and third, because it interrogates regimes of visuality, such as the imperial, the ethnographic and the exotic gaze, which have colonised our minds and our ways of looking.[2] While the historical origins of these scopic regimes have received considerable scholarly attention, their persistent legacies in the present remain underdeveloped in critical analysis – and yet they continue to shape our encounters with cultural difference on contemporary screens. Encounters with strangers are meetings, Sara Ahmed argues, that normally involve an element of surprise and conflict and that constitute identities through negotiating the boundaries between Self and Other. Exoticism can be conceived of as a particular discursive framework that structures such encounters and that transforms the objective fact of cultural difference into the imaginative construction of the exotic Other.[3] Inevitably, encounters that occur in the present, 'reopen . . . past encounters' (Ahmed 2000: 8). The encounter with the exotic Other reopens past intercultural encounters, notably those of exploration and discovery, ethnography and colonialism, and the attendant asymmetries of power and privilege that characterise them.

Due to its colonial and imperial legacies, Eurocentric origins and ethnic essentialism, exoticism is a highly contested discourse on cultural difference that regularly sparks controversies. In the essay 'In Defence of Exoticism', Ron Shapiro sums up the prevailing pejorative attitude with acerbic cynicism, noting that, 'to speak of the exotic ... is to condone all manner of European imperialisms and colonialisms, and to deliberately condemn the so-called "subaltern" to continued misery' (Shapiro 2000: 41). Yet Shapiro is actually one of the relatively few scholars to challenge postcolonialism's unforgiving stance, when he argues that exoticism is not 'necessarily false and evil' or 'beyond the pale of responsibility and political correctness', but instead 'part of the ordinary mental process of the construction of alterity' and, therefore, occupies a rightful place in the imaginary construction of cultural difference because 'the imagination and political policies' (Shapiro 2000: 42, 47) need to be kept separate.

Although I will pursue a different line of argument, I, too, set out to critically reassess the cultural value and aesthetic paradigms of certain *contemporary* manifestations of exoticism. With a few notable exceptions (dating back two decades), such as Graham Huggan's *The Postcolonial Exotic: Marketing the Margins* (2001), Rey Chow's *Primitive Passions: Visuality, Sexuality, Ethnography, and Contemporary Chinese Cinema* (1995), Olivia Khoo's *The Chinese Exotic: Modern Diasporic Femininity* (2007) and the anthology *"New Exoticisms": Changing Patterns in the Construction of Otherness* edited by Isabel Santaolalla (2000), contemporary exoticism has attracted far less scholarly interest than historical forms.[4] This lack of critical attention presents an unfortunate obstacle if we seek to understand contemporary Western societies' insatiable appetite for the exotic, be it in the shape of ethnic cuisine, global adventure travel, ethno-chic, world music and the intriguing proliferation of cinematic exoticisms since the 1990s. The premise of this study is that global interconnectedness has resulted in cultural homogenisation which, in turn, has led to a growing interest in cultural difference. In a social context in which alterity has become a prized commodity, exotic cinema has gained popularity at the box office and garnered prestigious awards on the film festival circuit.

Exotic Cinema aims to advance scholarly debates about the representation of cultural difference in contemporary cinema. It demonstrates that in a world of transnational networks and flows, exoticism can no longer be merely conceived of as a projection of exotic fantasies of the Other from one centre, the West, but that it emanates from multiple localities and is multi-directional in perspective. It, therefore, offers a timely and useful critical lens for the study of cinema in a globalised world. Taking a transnationally comparative approach that draws mainly on case studies from contemporary world cinema and global art cinema, the book challenges prevalent negative connotations of exoticism. It illustrates the concept's aesthetic versatility and argues that exoticism in contemporary transnational cinema is decentred and, therefore, does not simply perpetuate the same binary logic of its old Eurocentric precursor, nor does it pursue the same ideological agendas. Whether or not contemporary exoticism in its decentred form is ideologically retrograde ultimately depends on the object of exotic desire. As several of the case studies will demonstrate, decentred exoticism is harnessed to new humanitarian and ethico-political objectives which have little in common with the concept's tainted colonial legacy. Nor is the visual and sensuous pleasure which exotic cinema affords inevitably divorced from a critical engagement with Othered cultures since exotic codes of representation can be deployed strategically to dislodge established modes of essentialising and objectifying the Other and, in so doing, decolonise the gaze. By pursuing these lines of inquiry in depth, this book seeks to encourage a radical reappraisal of exoticism and stimulate its readers to critically reassess this prominent mode of cultural representation.

While there is a significant body of scholarship on *historical* manifestations of exoticism with several recent publications in the fields of cultural geography, cultural studies, postcolonial studies, social anthropology, religious studies, history of art and music, in film studies, exoticism (not to be conflated with Orientalism, as I demonstrate in Chapter 1) has remained under-researched.[5] To be sure, there are numerous studies on Otherness in cinema, yet these are predominantly about Hollywood and cover a much broader typology of Others and ethnic stereotypes than this book, which is specifically interested in the aesthetics of exoticism in world cinema.[6] Its decentred approach to exoticism builds on Ella Shohat and Robert Stam's agenda-setting *Unthinking Eurocentrism: Multiculturalism and the Media* (1994), which makes a compelling case for replacing Eurocentric regimes of visuality with polycentric multiculturalism. Rey Chow's *Primitive Passions* (1995) about autoethnographic practices of Fifth Generation Chinese filmmakers and Olivia Khoo's *The Chinese Exotic: Modern Diasporic Femininity* (2007) about exoticised visualisations of diasporic Chinese femininity in film, fashion and other forms of popular culture, have also shaped my thinking about the construction of the Self as an exotic Other in transnational cinema. The novel contribution to this field of inquiry which the present study aims to make rests on its global scope and transnationally comparative perspective; its attention to exoticism's aesthetic paradigms (a departure from prevalent discussions of ethnic stereotyping); and its focus on world cinema and its transnational circulation (rather than on Hollywood or European colonial cinema).

I conceptualise 'exoticism' in three ways: as a discursive construction of cultural difference; as an aesthetic mode of visual alterity; and as a critical framework that is pertinent to the analysis of cinema in a globalised world.[7] The focus on exoticism as an aesthetic category invites comparisons with Rosalind Galt's *Pretty: Film and the Decorative Image* (2011) and Sianne Ngai's *Our Aesthetic Categories: Zany, Cute, Interesting* (2012), two recent studies which critically reassess received ideas about aesthetic modes of representation that are charged with a high degree of ambivalence and perceived to possess little cultural value. These 'minor taste concepts', which are imbricated in the aesthetics of popular culture, commerce and consumption, Ngai and Galt argue, 'are rarely seen as worthy of close examination', being regarded as too insignificant and superficial (Galt 2011: 9–10). Like Galt, who recuperates the pretty from its alleged insignificance, I propose that exoticism, despite the ideological contestations surrounding it, merits critical re-evaluation since it is uniquely relevant to understanding the transnational appeal of world cinema. *Exotic Cinema* does not attempt to give an exhaustive account of exoticism in contemporary film; instead, the selection of case studies aims to crystallise distinctive aesthetic paradigms and illustrate prominent themes.

A key question I address in this book is how contemporary exotic cinema negotiates the historical legacy of exoticism's white supremacist assumptions, which continue to reverberate in the present. What happens when those cultures and ethnicities that have for centuries been the object of the exotic gaze become both the subject and the object? To what extent do postcolonial diasporic and world cinema filmmakers perform autoethnography by prioritising Western constructions of the exotic Other? What are the power implications of this practice? Is it a calculated artistic choice or, as W. E. B. Du Bois, Frantz Fanon, Rey Chow and others have suggested, the inevitable consequence of having internalised the memory of past objecthood? Does exoticism in world cinema transform hegemonic discourses on Otherness and thus constitute a form of postcolonial resistance? Which new manifestations of exoticism genuinely transcend the binary logic of their old Eurocentric precursors and which ones merely repackage it? How does decentred exoticism challenge Western values and systems of knowledge? How does exotic cinema repurpose familiar exoticist tropes in order to advocate new ethical and political agendas and advance cosmopolitan connectivity?

This book examines why exoticism is central to thinking about the global dynamics of (world) cinema and its transnational circulation and reception. I conceive of the exotic gaze as being both anchored in the cinematic text and elicited in the spectator. The films' transnational (or transcultural) circulation and reception is a prerequisite for the exotic gaze to manifest since exoticism is invariably 'a perspective "from the other side"' and, as such, premised on the outsider status of the beholder (Forsdick 2001: 21). Exoticism can only fully function if the outsider remains outside, if he or she lacks an in-depth knowledge of the Other culture. 'Knowledge is incompatible with exoticism,' Tzvetan Todorov notes, 'but lack of knowledge is in turn irreconcilable with praise of others; yet praise without knowledge is precisely what exoticism aspires to be. This is its constitutive paradox' (Todorov 1993: 265). Todorov's observation goes a long way in explaining exoticism's predilection for surfaces that dazzle, camouflage and ensure the pleasurable consumption of cultural difference. Thus, exotic cinema's sumptuous style, which shifts the attention from deeper layers of meaning to the surface of the text, helps compensate for the hermeneutic deficits that arise when 'films from elsewhere' circulate transnationally. In this way, exoticism plays a vital role in facilitating world cinema's transnational reception.

A detailed analysis of exotic cinema's aesthetics and its critical reception aims to sharpen our understanding of the workings of contemporary exoticism in a globalised cultural sphere, where the positions of cultural insiders and outsiders and the local and the global, have become increasingly fluid. As I propose in Chapter 1, the practice of self-exoticism in contemporary world cinema is reliant on the filmmakers' positionality at the interstice, which compels, or perhaps rather, enables them to see themselves and their own cultures through Western eyes and assume the role of cultural translators and mediators.

The Issue of Positionality

If decolonising the curriculum makes it imperative to consider how our location and identity shape our perspective, then this is perhaps the right moment to reflect upon my own positionality, which is inevitably compromised by the blind spots that come with my white European heritage. My position as a located subject makes me an outsider in relation to the films and their cultural and socio-political contexts. I thus meet an essential prerequisite for the elicitation of the exotic gaze with all the hermeneutic gaps this entails. Conversely, I am conscious that the critical insights which I offer are inflected, on the one hand, by the social privileges I enjoy as a white European woman in full-time employment at a British university, and, on the other hand, by my cultural and linguistic limitations in relation to the films I analyse in this book. I speak three languages, but all of them are European. Therefore, I rely on subtitles and wonder what may get lost in translation. Even if I understand the dialogue, I still miss out on many of the cultural, historical and social meanings and subtexts since the cultures from which these films originate are not my own. My access to scholarship and film reviews is equally limited, which gives my critical investigation of the decentred exotic an undeniably Western bias. In fact, I have consulted almost exclusively English-language scholarship. Though this is in keeping with prevalent scholarly practice, I share Will Higbee and Song Hwee Lim's concerns about its inherent pitfalls, since wielding the 'hegemonic language of English while pronouncing on transnational films that are often polyphonic in their linguistic use' and marked by multiple asymmetries of cultural, economic and symbolic capital, potentially undermines the ambitious projects of developing 'a critical transnationalism' and decolonising film studies (Higbee and Lim 2010: 18). At the same time, much of the scholarship that has shaped my thinking about contemporary exoticism, despite being in English, is written by scholars of the Global Majority, to use a term that is beginning to supersede designations like 'BAME', 'People of Colour' and 'ethnic minorities' which distort the real ratio between white and non-white people inhabiting the world (Campbell-Stephens 2020).[8] Yet most of these academics were educated and are teaching at prestigious universities in the United States and Europe, whereby their position as multiply located subjects complicates their ability to decolonise and de-Westernise film studies and to compensate for the blind spots arising from my own positionality. Are we not all looking through Western eyes, if 'the West', as Saër Maty Bâ and Will Higbee (2012: 1–2) propose, is not 'a fixed geographical location' but 'an ideologically inflected mode of being in and seeing, perceiving and representing the world' that has become ineluctable?

For all these caveats, what has drawn me to exoticism is my long-standing personal and scholarly interest in cultural difference. For well over a decade, I researched migrant and diasporic European cinemas and here, in particular, the self-representation of those filmmakers who, usually together with their families, have migrated from South Asia, the Maghreb and Turkey to the old Europe and who, mostly in the second generation, gained access to the means of film production and thus self-representation. As much as this research was deeply embedded in the socio-historical contexts of migration and diaspora cultures, issues of film aesthetics and the notion of a distinctive diasporic optic were equally important cornerstones of my critical analysis. Initially, my interest in migrant and diasporic cinema coincided, to some extent, with my own migratory experience from Germany to England, originally planned as a temporary sojourn, that has by now lasted more than thirty-five years. Similarly, my interest in the exotic has a personal dimension to it. It has been triggered by my love of exotic travel and my husband's persistent challenging as to why I would find certain destinations like Vietnam, India, Borneo, Costa Rica, South Africa or Namibia more exotic than the Cornish coast or the Greek islands. 'Because everything looks different, smells different, tastes different. It's new and more exciting', used to be my spontaneous response, long before I embarked upon researching exoticism. At around the time when I thought about shifting the focus of my research from migrant and diasporic to exotic cinema, I attended one of the annual NECS film and media studies conferences, in Milan. I was intrigued to observe how my fascination with the exotic was already so deeply embedded in my subconscious that it featured in one of my dreams. There was a baby giraffe in our living room! The giraffe was beautiful with its brown eyes, long lashes and distinctive pattern. It bent its long, elegant neck down towards me so that I could reach its head and gently stroke its soft, delicate nose (in the same way in which I frequently stroke the nose of our blue-eyed spotted snow Bengal cat, Asima). Rather worryingly, the baby giraffe already reached up to the ceiling. Very soon, it would grow much taller and, therefore, surely would not make a good pet. Perhaps our garden with its tall oak tree would be a more appropriate habitat? But, no doubt, the giraffe would soon outgrow the garden too, I worried in my dream. Upon my return home from Italy, the following day, I came across an antique print in a window display at Sanders of Oxford, a shop that sells antique maps and prints, which featured a giraffe. It was a plate from an ethnographic atlas entitled 'Zones of the Earth: Productions of the Torrid Zone', showing a giraffe in a landscape populated by a zebra, a leopard, a vulture, a snake twirling round a palm tree, and several other animals, as well as people native to the torrid zone, carrying spears and other weapons. I could not resist and bought the hand-coloured lithograph straightaway. Together with 'Productions of the North Frigid Zone' from the same ethnographic atlas, which shows a whale, a reindeer, a polar bear, and Inuit in traditional garments against the backdrop of towering icebergs, it now hangs in my study.[9] The dream, coupled with the serendipitous find of the giraffe print, confirmed my decision to pursue the study of exoticism in contemporary world cinema.

Films from Elsewhere: Transnational Cinema, World Cinema and Global Art Cinema

As the attentive reader will have noticed, my attempt to delineate the field of my research and the corpus of films I examine suffers from a certain degree of slippage between the terms 'transnational', 'world' and 'global art cinema'. Perhaps the neutral description 'films from elsewhere' would be the most appropriate term because it is less loaded than these 'baggy monster concepts' (Stam 2019: 1). Moreover, it highlights the ontological instability of the exotic gaze which depends on the positionality of the beholder. Nevertheless, in the title of this book, I use the term 'transnational' for a constellation of cinemas that – in profoundly different ways – transcend the national and traverse cultures and borders of various kinds. Although I privilege world cinema over films made by Western majority culture filmmakers, the latter also feature to illustrate differences between Eurocentric and decentred forms of exoticism. In other words, the elasticity of the term 'transnational' proves useful, while at the same time potentially jeopardising the concept's critical purchase.

For example, Deborah Shaw (2018: 295) includes diverse types of cinema under the concept of 'transnational cinema', ranging from 'low budget non-English language art film supported by a European funding body and exhibited and distributed through a film festival circuit' to 'global Hollywood productions' that are transnational on account of their global reach, multinational 'modes of production, distribution and exhibition' and the international profile of cast and crew. Shaw's conceptualisation of the transnational includes what Dudley Andrew and other scholars refer to as global cinema, whose ultimate goal it is to 'saturate every place in an undifferentiated manner' (Andrew 2010: 80). This, Andrew argues, distinguishes global cinema from world cinema, which is invested in cultural difference. Similarly, Mette Hjort (2010: 13) acknowledges that 'transnational' is often used 'as shorthand for a series of assumptions about the networked and globalized realities' of our contemporary situation, but she ultimately advocates transnational as a term of virtue by distinguishing between strong and weak, marked and unmarked forms of transnationality. Offering a typology of cinematic transnationalisms, she rates those most highly that resist the forces of globalisation and cultural homogenisation and that exhibit a commitment to the 'pursuit of aesthetic, artistic, social and political values' (Hjort 2010: 15). Hjort is not alone in wanting to reserve the label 'transnational' for films that are at the other end of the spectrum from global Hollywood. In the field of transnational cinema studies, there is a tendency amongst scholars to favour non-English language films, be they European or world cinema. Hence, Higbee and Lim (2010: 17) even wonder whether transnational cinema, a term that has gained wide critical currency since the late 1990s, risks 'becoming a replacement for existing terms such as "world cinema"'. In Chapter 1, I examine the concept of world cinema in relation to exoticism and cultural translation in detail, but for now, I want to provide a rationale for choosing 'transnational film' in the title of my book. It is, however, not my intention to map this theoretically complex and porous terrain, a task that has been undertaken so rigorously and brilliantly by others.[10]

'Transnational' foregrounds the crossing of borders in the films' circulation and reception. This is also a constitutive dimension of exotic cinema, which needs to be watched across borders (though not necessarily national ones) in order for exoticism to be decoded by the spectator. Most of the case studies are examples of what Hjort theorises as 'cosmopolitan transnationalism'. This particular subcategory is characterised by the filmmakers' 'multiple belonging[s] linked to ethnicity and various trajectories of migration . . . which becomes the basis for a form of transnationalism that is oriented toward . . . strengthening certain social imaginaries' (Hjort 2010: 20). Although the construction of the exotic Other is not necessarily the kind of imaginary Hjort had in mind, it is, nonetheless, a prevalent one which is underpinned by the filmmakers' transnational perspective. Diasporic filmmakers, such as Ang Lee, Tran Anh Hung and Mira Nair, to mention but a few that feature in this book, spent their formative years at film schools in the West, where they became acquainted with the aesthetic sensibilities of the European New Waves as well as Hollywood. The visual and narrative idioms of their films are inflected by the traces of Western aesthetic principles. This is not to say that they imitate them in a crude mimetic fashion, but present they are, nevertheless. Perhaps more surprisingly, even Fifth Generation Chinese filmmakers, who grew up in a country hermetically sealed off from the West during the Cultural Revolution, eventually, when they entered the Beijing Film Academy, had the opportunity to study not just classic Chinese cinema but also Soviet and Hollywood films, alongside modernist classics by European auteurs to which they had access in controlled screenings at the China Film Archive (see Andrew 2010: 78).[11] The same certainly holds true for other world cinema auteurs whose aesthetic education occurred in more liberal socio-political contexts than that of the People's Republic of China (PRC) in the immediate aftermath of the Cultural Revolution. 'There is no entirely non-Western place left', the Cuban American writer and video artist Coco Fusco (2012: 191) asserts in an interview, published in the anthology *De-Westernizing Film Studies*, since colonialism, neo-liberal capitalism and transnational media flows have made it impossible 'to get rid of ways of thinking, ways of seeing, ways of speaking, and ways of understanding' that attest to Western hegemony. Concurring with Fusco, Black British artist and critic John Akomfrah (2012: 260) observes: 'The question of geography is of very little value in evaluating what one means by "Western".' Without wanting to downplay the significant impact of the hegemonic West on non-Western film cultures, it would be short-sighted to conceive of this process in unilateral terms. Instead, it is necessary to acknowledge that the cinematic exchanges between filmmakers, producers and studios around the world are much more dynamic and have been multi-directional for a very long time.[12] This notion of cinematic cross-pollination renders phrases like 'seeing themselves through Western eyes', which I use, and the binarism of Western and non-Western filmmakers a useful but ultimately inadequate shorthand for referencing forms of cultural difference whose multi-layered complexity deserves a more nuanced conceptualisation. At the same time, these considerations make the project of de-Westernising and decolonising film studies a noble, but in practice difficult to achieve, ambition.

Furthermore, many of the exotic films considered in this book are the result of transnational collaborations, such as the long-lasting collaboration between Hong Kong director Wong Kar-wai and the Australian-born cinematographer Christopher Doyle, who has created the alluring Asian look that has become a trademark of Wong's films. Similarly, most of the Indigenous films discussed in Chapter 2 are the product of transnational, or as I argue, cosmopolitan collaborations between First Nations and filmmakers from the Global North or Global South. And finally, it goes almost without saying, that literally all of the exotic films considered in the present study are transnational co-productions, usually involving production companies and film funding bodies from several countries and made with transnational audiences in mind. Wong Kar-wai's films, which Stephen Teo (2005: 153) describes as 'box-office poison in Hong Kong', are a pertinent example. To finance films with major Asian stars and high production values, Wong pursues a global strategy by securing multinational funding sources and pre-selling his films especially to Asian markets. But even films with far more modest budgets, such as *El abrazo de la serpiente* (Embrace of the Serpent, Ciro Guerra 2015), discussed in Chapter 2, need to tap into funding sources from several countries' (Columbia, Argentina, Venezuela, the Netherlands and Germany) commercial, national, regional and film festival funds to secure production and distribution costs.

The concept of 'transnational cinema' overlaps to a significant extent with 'world cinema' since both are premised on spatial mobility and the crossing of borders, while the prefix 'trans' also denotes the process of transformation that occurs in the transnational reception of 'films from elsewhere' (see Chapter 1). Put simply, 'There are currently two popular ways of understanding world cinema. The first regards it as the sum total of all the national cinemas in the world, and the second posits it against US or Hollywood cinema' (Dennison and Lim 2006a: 6). Yet both the first, polycentric model, originally espoused by Ella Shohat and Robert Stam (1994) and further developed by Lucía Nagib (2006; Nagib et al. 2012) and others, and the second, binary model, raise issues and further questions, which Stephanie Dennison and Song Hwee Lim (2006a) summarise and unravel in their introduction to *Remapping World Cinema*. Neither do I wish to reiterate their insightful arguments here nor adjudicate between these two positions. Nagib (2006: 35), one of the main proponents of the polycentric model, defines world cinema as a 'cinema of the world' that has no centre and no Other. In the attempt to abolish the persistent binarism between 'the West and the Rest', which asserts Hollywood's centrality, Nagib situates world cinema on a map in which Hollywood takes its place as one amongst equals. By contrast, Shekhar Deshpande and Meta Mazaj (2018: 6) conceive of polycentrism not as a cinematic landscape without a centre but as 'an uneven and constantly shifting multiplicity of power centres that gain prominence at different points in history and different topographic zones', including Hollywood, European, Indian, Asian and Nigerian cinemas. These power centres exhibit high levels of cinematic activity, supra-national spheres of reach and influence and the presence of scholarly perspectives on their own cinemas that challenge and decentre dominant Western academic discourses and theories.

Although I am mindful of the reasoning behind such inclusive conceptualisations, in the present context, I nevertheless endorse an understanding of world cinema that excludes hegemonic Hollywood and privileges films from the Global South. First, in order to promote the agenda of de-Westernising film studies, with all the caveats this entails. Second, because I aim to investigate how the decentring of exoticism in contemporary world cinema differs from Eurocentric exoticism in mainstream Western cinemas. And third, since these new exoticisms manifest themselves most clearly in films that are rooted in local cultures and imaginaries (notwithstanding their transnational aspirations) rather than in those that originate in global Hollywood. To be more specific, the kind of world cinema that features prominently in this book is also known by the name of 'global art cinema' and largely excludes mainstream genre films. These, Dudley Andrew (2010: vii) suggests, primarily address local audiences, remain within the confines of the cultures out of which they arose and 'do not participate in the cultural economy of world film and certainly do not belong to anything one would label global art cinema'. Although Andrew's observation is valid overall, Bollywood's crossover appeal and the cult following which certain Asian horror and martial arts films enjoy far beyond the borders of Japan, South Korea and Hong Kong, tell a different story.[13] Moreover, popular genre films may be perceived as global art cinema in the process of transnational circulation and reception. Global art cinema's transnational address, Rosalind Galt and Karl Schoonover (2010: 10) aver, rests on 'art cinema's stake in art', which ensures its 'visual legibility' and translatability, enabling it to reach culturally diverse audiences. It is the kind of world cinema that has been discovered at European film festivals in Cannes, Locarno, Venice and Berlin from the 1970s onwards, when new programme strands were inaugurated that showcased films from outside Europe by the likes of Satyajit Ray, Glauber Rocha, Yasujiro Ozu, Akira Kurosawa and, in subsequent decades, Abbas Kiarostami, Hou Hsiao-Hsien and Zhang Yimou amongst many others (see de Valck 2007; Andrew 2010: 75–80). Film festivals in Europe and the United States have played a pivotal role 'in upgrading the term "world cinema" into a quality label' (Elsaesser 2005: 504). In this way, they have been instrumental in the creation of world cinema auteurs and in the construction of a world cinema canon, affording visibility and granting cultural kudos to productions that might otherwise have gone unnoticed in the West. 'Global art cinema' refers specifically to films made by world cinema auteurs who are recognised and revered in the West through their presence on the film festival circuit, where they have won prizes and prestige. The term expands 'art cinema's foundational Eurocentrism' (Galt and Schoonover 2010: 4) with its emphasis on authorial vision and high-cultural aspirations by pushing the boundaries of art cinema to include aesthetic traditions originating outside Europe. Through the dynamics of cross-cultural exchange and aesthetic hybridisation, these novel impulses have revitalised and reinvigorated Western cinematic traditions.

The Chapters

Exotic Cinema aims to contribute to the buoyant field of transnational and world cinema studies by offering the first sustained account of a prominent aesthetic mode, namely exoticism. It thus complements the extensive body of work on realism in world cinema.[14] Each chapter, with the exception of the final one, brings exoticism into dialogue with cognate frameworks that conceptualise cross-cultural encounters with the aim of shifting the terms of the debate into a direction that opens up new lines of inquiry beyond the prevalent ideological contestations surrounding exoticism. To be sure, the emphasis I place on examining its aesthetic dimension does not imply that I am trying to eschew the concept's problematic socio-political implications. Aesthetics is all too often dismissed as pure taste, sensibility and a preoccupation with form. However, Jacques Rancière (2000: 9) contends that 'aesthetic acts . . . [are] configurations of experience that create new modes of sense perception and induce novel forms of political subjectivity'. The close readings of around twenty films in this book will hopefully prove Rancière's point.

The first chapter, 'Locating Exoticism', theorises the key concepts, 'the exotic' and 'exoticism', and develops a critical framework for the textual and contextual analysis of the subsequent chapters which investigate how the encounter between Self and Other and the construction of Self as Other is (re)configured in contemporary transnational fiction films. It brings exoticism into conversation with Orientalism, (auto)ethnography, cultural translation and postcolonial transformation, and compares the principles and structures that underpin these encounters with cultural difference and their artistic representations. One of the issues this chapter addresses is why certain films are decoded as exotic, whereas others are experienced as merely strange or bewildering by transnational spectators. By analysing a small number of paintings and films that are regularly cited as paradigmatic examples of exoticism, I aim to illustrate some of the distinctive features of this aesthetic category. Chapter 2, 'Ethnographic Salvage and Cosmopolitan Exoticism', examines four Indigenous films, *Atanarjuat* (Atanarjuat: The Fast Runner, Zacharias Kunuk, 2001), *Ten Canoes* (Rolf de Heer and Peter Djigirr, 2006), *El abrazo de la serpiente* (Embrace of the Serpent, Ciro Guerra, 2015) and *Tanna* (Martin Butler and Bentley Dean, 2015). It explores how the project of ethnographic salvage, once the prerogative of Western ethnographers, has been taken up by Indigenous filmmakers who aim to recuperate and preserve their own cultural memory. By exploring the conceptual convergences between exoticism, local authenticity and cosmopolitanism, I aim to rehabilitate what I term 'cosmopolitan exoticism' through demonstrating how contemporary Indigenous cinema appropriates familiar exotic tropes (for example, the Noble Savage, the 'primitive', the South Sea paradise) only to put them at the service of new cosmopolitan goals. These include empowering marginalised Indigenous communities, demanding the atonement of colonial guilt and calling 'the white man' to responsibility for the looming environmental catastrophe he has caused. Whereas these Indigenous films demonstrate that certain forms of exoticism can contribute to the project of decolonising the lens, several of the case studies in Chapter 3,

'The Spectacle of Cultural Difference: The Tourist Gaze and the Exotic Gaze', are intended to illustrate what exactly makes exoticism so 'non-pc'. One of the answers is that exoticism's highly aestheticised visual style is a form of spectacle which substitutes a deep engagement with cultural difference with seductive surfaces, offering pleasure instead of prompting critical interrogation. Thus, by fetishising alterity, mainstream Eurocentric films about white Western tourists in the Global South, including *Eat Pray Love* (Ryan Murphy, 2010), *Hector and the Search for Happiness* (Peter Chelsom, 2014), *The Best Exotic Marigold Hotel* and its sequel (John Madden, 2011, 2015) obscure disparities of power and white privilege. A comparison with thematically similar global art films, *Tabi no owari sekai no hajimari* (To the Ends of the Earth, Kiyoshi Kurosawa, 2019), *Mukti Bhawan* (Hotel Salvation, Shubhashish Bhutiani, 2016) and Bollywood films about Indian tourists abroad probes the limits of the exotic gaze by scrutinising the subtle differences between the exotic and the tourist gaze. Chapter 4, '"The Past Is a Foreign Country": Nostalgia and Exoticism', considers the close affinities between the two concepts. Both spring from a disenchantment with the present and mobilise distance, be it spatial or temporal, to enable an imaginative investment that replaces historical accuracy and cultural authenticity with the construction of a sanitised and embellished past and an idealised alterity. Although exoticism is generally associated with far-away lands, it is also about a longing for the bygone days, which explains why the majority of exotic films are set in an idealised past. Using Régis Wargnier's *Indochine* (1992), Gurinder Chadha's *Viceroy's House* (2017), Wong Kar-wai's *Fa yeung nin wah* (In the Mood for Love, 2000) and Zhang Yimou's *Wo de fu qin mu qin* (The Road Home, 1999) as case studies, the chapter distinguishes between imperialist nostalgia and exotic nostalgia films. Whereas the former glamorise the imperial power and control of European empires, the latter engender a universal longing in the spectator for a time and place when intensity of feeling was still possible. Through an aesthetics of sensuous indulgence, a concept that I develop in the chapter, exotic nostalgia films valorise systems of knowledge and a way of life that call the hegemony of the West and global capitalism into question. The final chapter, 'Exotic Appetites', examines how exotic food films use cooking, eating and gustation as a trope for diverse human appetites and desires, ranging from carnal desires, a nostalgic longing for close affective bonds within the family and community, a slower pace of life and a recovery of the senses. The pursuit of sensory stimulation and indulgence has always been one of the chief driving forces behind exotic quests and conquests and continues to feature prominently in contemporary exotic cinema.

Drawing on theories of multisensorial cinema and synaesthetic perception, I examine the means through which films including *Yin shi nan nu* (Eat Drink Man Woman, Ang Lee, 1994), *Mùi du du xanh* (The Scent of Green Papaya, Tran Anh Hung, 1993), *An* (Sweet Bean, Naomi Kawase, 2015) and *The Lunchbox* (Ritesh Batra, 2014) invite spectators to experience films somatically with their bodies and, thereby, rediscover the visceral intensity and sense knowledge deemed to still exist in Other cultures. In this way, exotic food films hold out the promise of a panacea for white Western culture's alleged anhedonia, while at the same time depicting a non-threatening form of Otherness. A notable exception is Fruit Chan's *Gau ji* (Dumplings, 2004), a generic hybrid between food film and horror movie, about cannibalistic practices in urban Hong Kong. Oscillating between the alluring and the abject, it brings to the fore exoticism's inherent ambivalence.

Notes

1. The Rhodes Must Fall campaign called for the removal of statues of the imperialist British mining magnate and politician Cecil Rhodes at South African universities and at the University of Oxford.
2. What exactly decolonising and de-Westernising the film studies curriculum entails is a hotly debated question. While some advocates are in favour of rewriting the canon by side-lining 'male, pale and stale' (Muldoon 2019) voices, others call for a fundamental reconsideration of who is teaching, what the subject matter is and how it is being taught. The interlocking projects of decolonising and de-Westernising the curriculum are driven by a sense of recuperative social justice that demands for hitherto marginalised voices and perspectives to take centre stage in scholarly debates and canons. When it comes to critically reassessing the film and screen studies curriculum with the aim of de-Westernising it, the question arises, where exactly is the West? Although the dichotomy between the West and the non-West is deeply entrenched in public discourses, scholarly debates increasingly reflect an awareness that 'theories that conceived of the West and the East, the coloniser and the colonized, the center and the periphery, as Manichean oppositions locked in perpetual struggles of domination on the one hand and subordination or resistance on the other' are being replaced by conceptualisations that acknowledge 'the mutual entanglements and imbrications, collisions and compromises' (Ramaswamy 2014: 4) of the West and the non-West. Similarly, Lim (2021) reminds us in relation to world cinema that 'the binary of Western and non-Western [has become] untenable . . . [since] the ex-colonies have been and continue to be westernised'. Furthermore, postcolonial diasporas have brought what Mary Louise Pratt (2008) has famously theorised as the colonial 'contact zone' right to the heart of the metropole. Saër Maty Bâ and

Will Higbee (2012: 1–2) and the authors who have contributed to the edited collection *De-Westernizing Film Studies* (2012) propose that 'the West' is not 'a fixed geographical location' but 'an ideologically inflected mode of being in and seeing, perceiving and representing the world'.
3. Staszak (2009: 43) explains the distinction between cultural difference, 'which belongs to the realm of fact and otherness [which] belongs to the realm of discourse', noting that Otherness is invariably the result of a 'discursive process' by which a dominant group ('Us' or 'Self') stigmatises a real or imagined difference of a dominated group ('Them' or 'Other'), thereby legitimising various forms of domination or discrimination.
4. Agzenay (2015) covers a broad historical sweep from antiquity over the Renaissance to the present day so that the analysis of *contemporary* postcolonial literature falls somewhat by the wayside. Root (1996), though engaging with exoticism, examines related cultural phenomena through a different critical framework, namely cultural appropriation.
5. For a selection of recently published studies on historical forms of exoticism in these fields see *inter alia* Schmidt (2015) in cultural geography; Rangarajan (2014) in cultural studies; Agzenay (2015) and Hartley et al. (2022) in postcolonial studies; Grijp (2009), Kapferer and Theodossopoulos (2016) in anthropology; Childs (2013), Foster (2020) and Sund (2019) in history of art; Locke (2009) and Sheppard (2019) in music. Altglas (2014) in religious studies has a contemporary focus.
6. For studies exploring ethnic stereotyping in Hollywood cinema, see *inter alia* Bernstein and Studlar (1997), Ginneken (2007), Kaplan (1997a), King (2010), Marchetti (1993), Richardson (2010). Naficy and Gabriel's edited collection (2017) privileges non-Western media.
7. Based on these considerations and the distinction between 'the exotic' and 'exoticism' I make in Chapter 1, strictly speaking, the title of the book ought to be 'Exoticist Cinema'. However, I have decided to forsake terminological accuracy and follow common parlance in the title and elsewhere in the book.
8. 'Global Majority is a collective term that first and foremost speaks to and encourages those so-called, to think of themselves as belonging to the majority on planet earth. It refers to people who are Black, African, Asian, Brown, dual-heritage, indigenous to the global south, and or, have been racialised as "ethnic minorities". Globally these groups currently represent approximately eighty per cent (80%) of the world's population, making them the global majority' (Campbell-Stephens 2020).
9. Both prints are archived at the Horniman Museum in London; available at <https://www.horniman.ac.uk/object/2011.43.9/> and <https://www.horniman.ac.uk/object/2011.43.1/> (last accessed 13 May 2022).
10. Monographs and anthologies about world cinema, such as Nowell-Smith (1996), Hill et al. (2000), Dennison and Lim (2006b), Badley et al. (2006), Chaudhuri (2005), Nagib (2011, 2020), Nagib et al. (2012), De Luca (2013), Deshpande and Mazaj (2018), Ďurovičová and Newman (2009)

and Stone et al. (2018), include many chapters on transnational cinema; for transnational cinema see Ezra and Rowden (2006), Stam (2019), Rawle (2018), De la Garza et al. (2020). Many of the most influential essays in the field have been published in the journal *Transnational Cinemas* (now called *Transnational Screens*).
11. Andrew (2010: 80) makes the interesting point that Zhang Yimou, once a rebel in the PRC and revered as a world cinema auteur in the West, crossed the line 'to become the architect of state-sanctioned blockbusters' with *Ying xiong* (Hero, 2002) and *Shi mian mai fu* (House of Flying Daggers, 2004) that assemble stars from along the Pacific Rim, command huge budgets and have all the trappings of global cinema.
12. Much scholarly attention has recently been paid to the creative and commercial interactions between Asian and Hollywood cinema; see Hunt and Wing-Fai (2008), Cousins (2004); in addition, see Lim (2011) on intra-Asian trajectories and intertextuality.
13. For Bollywood's crossover appeal, see Dudrah (2012), Smith (2017) and Virdi (2017); for Asian genre cinema's transnational following, see Hunt and Wing-Fai (2008) and Lim (2011); Sexton (2017) explores the allure of Otherness in transnational cult film fandom.
14. Exoticism is neither the most prevalent aesthetic mode nor the one to have received the most critical attention in relation to world cinema. Certainly, as far as global art cinema is concerned, realism is the privileged mode of representation. The relationship between realism and exoticism is complicated and the two are by no means mutually exclusive, as the hybrid aesthetics of Mira Nair's *Salaam, Bombay* (1988), discussed in Chapter 1, illustrates. Publications about the affinity between realism and world cinema include Elsaesser (2009), Nagib (2011, 2020), De Luca (2013) and, in relation to global art cinema, Galt and Schoonover (2010: 15–17). In addition, there are countless studies about realism in specific national cinemas and about specific filmmakers.

CHAPTER 1

Locating Exoticism

'Never has it been so difficult to delineate the exotic as it is today', observes Peter Mason (1998: 1) in *Infelicities: Representations of the Exotic*. 'Perhaps there was once a time when names like Samarkand or Nepal had an exotic ring to the West, before the voyages of exploration had seriously diminished the capacity for wonder.' For Mason, the experience of the exotic is a thing of the past. He is not alone in mourning the loss of exotic horizons but is in the good company of literally every critic and scholar who has written on the topic, several of whom I will draw on in this chapter. Their lament arises from the fact that the forces of globalisation have profoundly changed the geospatial dynamics and the configuration of Self and Other by facilitating new intercultural encounters, as well as processes of cultural hybridisation and homogenisation.

Mass tourism to the far-flung corners of this world, mass migration, the global circulation of mediated images and trade in culturally Othered goods have exponentially escalated and accelerated the erosion of genuine cultural difference. Therefore, it has become virtually impossible to experience the wide-eyed wonder which, centuries ago, explorers and ethnographers felt when they first laid eyes upon the colourful plumes of a bird of paradise or a hitherto undiscovered tribe in a remote corner of this world. Diminishing cultural and biological diversity, coupled with 'the awareness of the world "becoming smaller" and cultural difference receding coincides with a growing sensitivity to cultural difference' (Nederveen Pieterse 2015: 45). Contemporary interest in the exotic, be it in the shape of world cinema and world music, ethno chic, ethnic fusion food, Booker-prize winning postcolonial novels and global adventure travel, reflects a disenchantment with the perceived blandness of white Western cultures to which exotic Otherness represents the antipode. Disillusionment with the societal conditions of the present and a heightened interest in the exotic have always been interdependent. Therefore, exoticism emerges most prominently at moments of cultural crisis; it is ultimately a utopian projection of plenitude and pleasure on to distant places or times, as the following chapters will illustrate.

First of all, it is, however, imperative to define the book's key concepts, 'the exotic' and 'exoticism', and to chart their historical origins and semantic shifts from a neutral descriptor of relative foreignness to the increasingly pejorative overtones which the terms have acquired in the context of postcolonial studies. To probe these contestations, I will bring exoticism into dialogue with cognate concepts, including Orientalism, primitivism, cultural translation and autoethnography. The purpose of this chapter is to examine some of the main strategies exoticism deploys in its discursive construction of the Other. Although I will draw on a diverse range of examples, I can only provide mere snapshots of an aesthetic paradigm that has dominated the cultural imagination of the West in its encounter with cultural difference for centuries. Building on these inevitably eclectic illustrations, I will examine how decentred exoticism in contemporary world cinema negotiates these enduring visual and narrative tropes and why exoticism is central to thinking about the global dynamics in world cinema and its transnational reception.

Etymologically, the 'exotic' is derived from Latin *exōticus* and Greek *exōtikós*, whereby *éxō* means 'outside'. The word's first recorded use in France dates back to 1548, referring specifically to 'diverse exotic and peregrine products' and 'flora and fauna' that were imported 'from faraway, far from Europe, from Asia and Africa, and, later, from the "New World"' (Célestin 1996: 216–17). Introduced into the English language in 1599, during the age of discovery, 'exotic' originally meant 'alien, introduced from abroad, not indigenous'; some fifty years later, its meaning was extended to include 'an exotic and foreign territory, an exotic habit and demeanor' as well as 'a foreigner' or a 'foreign plant not acclimatised' (*OED* cited in Ashcroft et al. 2000: 94–5). During the period of rapid colonial expansion in the nineteenth century, the exotic gained the connotation of 'a stimulating or exciting difference, something with which the domestic could be (safely) spiced. The key conception here is the introduction of the exotic from abroad into a domestic economy' (Ashcroft et al. 2000: 95). Historically, the exotic is inextricably linked to European voyages of discovery and exploration during which the encounter with radical cultural difference in remote corners of the world prompted a mutual sense of astonishment and wide-eyed wonder, although historical records, travelogues and novels of adventure are invariably skewed towards the astonishment experienced by Europeans. It thus follows that 'the exotic is not, as is often supposed, an inherent quality to be found "in" certain people, distinctive objects, or specific places' (Huggan 2001: 13) but instead denotes a particular perception of cultural difference that arises from the encounter with foreign cultures, landscapes, animals, people and their customs that are either geographically remote or taken out of their original context and 'absorbed into a home culture, essentialized, simplified and domesticated' (Forsdick 2003: 48).

'The exotic is never at home', Mason (1998: 14) notes, since the perception of the exotic only emerges in the process of de- and recontextualisation, displacement and domestication. Europe's colonial expositions of the late nineteenth and early twentieth centuries, which combined the display of imperial power with ethnological voyeurism, deftly illustrate these concomitant processes. In the heart of Europe's metropoles, visitors could marvel at carefully reconstructed tribal villages and 'exotic' tribes in their 'natural' or 'primitive' state. In these so-called 'human zoos', a term that betrays the colonialist credo that the natives were less than human and more like animals, the exotic individuals were placed alongside beasts and were usually fenced off by ropes or other barriers or even put in cages (see Blanchard et al. 2008).[1] This is a significant detail that not only demonstrates the humiliation which the spectacularisation of the Other involved but also that the exotic gaze is reliant on the maintenance of cultural boundaries. By bringing the empire home, these mass spectacles relocated the 'contact zone', which Mary Louise Pratt (2008: 4) defines as a space where 'disparate cultures meet, clash, and grapple with each other, often in highly asymmetrical relations of domination and subordination', from the outposts of empires to their very centres. The same applies to the *Wunderkammern*, or cabinets of curiosities, in which travellers, collectors and ethnographers put on display anything from exotic taxidermy, through ostrich eggs and the colourful beak of a toucan, to precious Ming vases, or just fragments of exotic objects, retrieved from remote parts of the world in their stately homes.[2] The 'aesthetics of decontextualisation' (Appadurai 1986: 28), which governed such exhibits, was driven by a fascination with novelty and showed little regard for the objects' geographic provenance or ethnographic accuracy. Instead, the chief principle that governed such eclectic arrays of foreign objects was their perceived exoticism and their capacity to elicit wonder in the beholder. Royals and aristocrats even shipped live exotic animals from Africa, India and other pockets of empires to Europe and kept menageries of zebras, cheetahs, ostriches, llamas and lemurs on the manicured lawns of their extensive estates. Taking the domestication of these wild animals to the extreme, they tamed and rode ostriches and harnessed zebras, instead of horses, to their carriages (see Foster 2020; Simons 2012).

Perhaps the most famous case of the domestication and commodification of an exotic animal is that of Zarafa, a Nubian giraffe that was presented to King Charles X of France as a diplomatic gift by the Ottoman Viceroy of Egypt and the Sudan, Muhammad Ali Pasha, in 1826. The giraffe's daily constitutionals in the streets of Marseille, where she had disembarked from her long journey by land (on a camel's back) and by sea, and her subsequent exhibition in the Jardin des Plantes in Paris, where she lived for eighteen years, were public spectacles that drew huge crowds. Such was the fascination with this elegant foreign creature that it even inspired a fashion trend, *la mode à la girafe*: a particular shade of tawny yellow was named 'giraffe yellow', women wore dresses in giraffe yellow and accessories replicating the giraffe's distinctive pattern, while her horns inspired towering hairstyles amongst fashionable Parisian ladies. France and other parts of Europe were seized by 'giraffomania', which resulted in a veritable explosion of consumer goods, including textiles and prints, wallpapers, ceramics, toys and countless other objects, all of which celebrated the giraffe's exoticism, while at the same time trivialising, domesticating and commodifying it.[3] However, the incorporation of the foreign into the domestic culture can only go so far in order for the exotic to maintain its appeal and be registered as extraordinary.

Colonial expansion resulted in persistent contact with different cultures so that the actual experience of the exotic became flattened with time. What was once novel and exciting became familiar and commonplace, a development which the French anthropologist Claude Lévi-Strauss laments in *Tristes Tropiques* (2011: 38, originally published in 1955) with the words 'mankind has opted for monoculture'. Due to 'the gradual loss of alternative horizons', the real encounter with the exotic was replaced by its discursive construction, namely 'exoticism', which Chris Bongie (1991: 4–5) defines as 'a discursive practice intent on recovering "elsewhere" values "lost" with the modernization of European society'. It is, therefore, necessary to distinguish between the 'exotic', which denotes the imaginary qualities or essence of difference that are projected on to cultures as well as natural environments that are radically different from one's own, and 'exoticism', which designates a *mode of cultural representation* that renders something *as* exotic.

Exoticism deploys narrative tropes and iconographic conventions that have, over many centuries, become established as standard markers of an exoticist aesthetics. Victor Segalen's *Essay on Exoticism: An Aesthetics of Diversity* (2002), which was published posthumously in 1955 in French, the same year as Claude Lévi-Strauss' *Tristes Tropiques*, provides some useful lists of such markers. Rather than purporting to offer an aesthetic theory on exoticism, Segalen's essayistic fragments interrogate his personal impressions of his travels through Polynesia and China between 1903 and 1912. In fact the reference to 'aesthetics' in the subtitle, foregrounds the close relationship between exoticism and perception since, as Tzvetan Todorov (1993: 327) reminds us in his exegesis of Segalen's essay, 'Aesthetics is, etymologically, the science of perception.' It is also worth noting that Segalen uses the word 'diversity' (in the subtitle and elsewhere) not in accordance with its contemporary usage, denoting the intermingling of different ethnicities and cultures, but rather to refer 'to the existence of absolute (if not essential) differences between peoples and cultures in the world' (Segalen 2002: 3), whose gradual erosion and disappearance he grieves. *Essay on Exoticism* constitutes an important attempt to interrogate and challenge the imbrication of exoticism and colonialism (which is at the root of exoticism's negative connotations) and, instead, shift the terms of the debate by attending to the aesthetic value of exoticism. In this respect, Segalen's essay marks the beginning of a critical reassessment of exoticism that also sets the agenda for this book. Several of Segalen's diary entries articulate his iconoclastic intent. For example, an entry written in 1908 and entitled 'Of Exoticism as an Aesthetics of Diversity' reads:

> Clear the field first of all. Throw overboard everything used or rancid contained in the word exoticism. Strip it of all its cheap finery: palm tree and camel; tropical helmet; black skins and yellow sun ... Then, strip the word exoticism of its exclusively tropical, exclusively geographic meaning. Exoticism does not only exist in space, but is equally dependent on time. From there, move rapidly to the task of defining and laying out the sensation of Exoticism, which is nothing other than the notion of difference, the perception of Diversity, the knowledge that something is other than one's self; and Exoticism's power is nothing other than the ability to conceive otherwise. (Segalen 2002: 18–19)

First, Segalen identifies some of the key features of exoticism here, namely, that it is commonly linked to the tropics and its flora and fauna, rather than the cold and inclement regions of the globe. Second, the proposition that exoticism is, in fact, temporal as well as spatial, reinforces the idea outlined above that the fascination with the exotic is motivated as much by the longing to 'escape from the contemptible and petty present' (Segalen 2002: 24) as it is by the utopian quest for the lost garden of Eden. Segalen's exoticism of time, the longing for the 'bygone days' (Segalen 2002: 24), imagined as pure and uncontaminated by industrial capitalism, helps explain the close affinities between exoticism and nostalgia (see Chapter 4). Third, in the above passage, Segalen addresses the ontological instability of exoticism, which inevitably depends on the positionality of the Self in relation to the Other, since nothing is intrinsically exotic, but only becomes so through the relations and negotiations into which it is drawn.[4]

Having identified some of the coordinates of exoticism, it is necessary to continue mapping the conceptual terrain by trying to distinguish between exoticism and Orientalism, albeit without attempting to offer an exhaustive discussion of Edward Said's seminal book *Orientalism* (first published in 1978), or outlining the criticism Said has faced from his contractors and his subsequent defence.

Orientalism and Exoticism: the Power to Dominate and the Pleasure of Difference

Although Orientalism and exoticism are frequently used interchangeably, they are not synonymous. Of the two, exoticism is the more comprehensive concept. It encompasses specific discourses on Othering, notably Orientalism and primitivism, as well as aestheticised cultural translations, such as *chinoiserie* and *japonisme*. Another distinction between Orientalism and exoticism stems from the fact that the two concepts belong to different epistemological traditions; whereas Orientalism dominates scholarly discourses in postcolonial studies in the Anglophone world, in Francophone studies, *exotisme* is the more widely used concept (see Forsdick 2001: 15). Charles Forsdick and David Murphy (2003: 8) attribute the wide currency *exotisme* enjoys in French and Francophone critical discourse and the fact that it is a less compromised term than in Anglophone contexts to the long-standing French reluctance to thoroughly and actively engage with postcolonial theory – and this despite the fact that anti-colonial French-language writers, such as Aimé Césaire, Frantz Fanon, Albert Memmi and Jean-Paul Sartre, played a pivotal role in launching the postcolonial debate. Conversely, the postcolonial triumvirate – Said, Bhabha and Spivak – perpetually cited and anthologised in Anglophone books on postcolonial studies, hold little sway in the Francophone world. This is not to say that the Francophone discourse on exoticism is insensitive to the condition of postcoloniality, but it is certainly more open to less ideologically committed readings of colonial texts and even draws on the positive connotations of *exotisme*.

On the most basic level, the distinction between exoticism and Orientalism revolves around the two concepts' different geographical scope and specificity. Said himself does not attempt a conceptual distinction between exoticism and Orientalism but instead uses the adjective 'exotic' as an attribute of the Orient or the Oriental, noting that the

Orient has been imagined as 'a place of romance [and] exotic beings' and 'exotic sensuousness' (Said 2003: 1, 72).[5] Despite conceding that at times the term 'Orient' has been applied more loosely to 'the Asiatic East as a whole, or taken as generally denoting the distant and exotic' (Said 2003: 74), by and large, he limits its geopolitical scope to the Arab Islamic world of the Middle East. More specifically, the Orient refers to the Anglo-French-American experience of the Arab Islamic world since the late eighteenth century, the starting point of Orientalism. The imaginative geography of exoticism, by contrast, covers a wider and more heterogenous terrain, ranging from Oceania, over Maritime Southeast Asia, to Amazonia and other parts of the New World, as well as comprising the Orient. Most importantly, the natural world with its strange flora and fauna is an integral part of exoticism but, more or less, irrelevant to Orientalism.[6]

This distinction between exoticism and Orientalism becomes instantly evident if we compare three iconic paintings, one Orientalist and two exoticist. Even without knowing that Jean-Léon Gérôme's painting *The Snake Charmer* (1879) adorns the front cover of the Penguin paperback edition of Said's *Orientalism*, almost anyone would spontaneously identify this glittering vision of the East as an Orientalist fantasy: a nude boy

Figure 1.1 Jean-Léon Gérôme's *The Snake Charmer* (1879) illustrates the iconography of Orientalism (courtesy of Clark Art Institute, clarkart.edu).

with a large, slithering python draped round his body is performing to the tune of a flute player in front of a group of armed, turban-wearing men from a variety of different Islamic tribes. The boy, shown from the back, is standing on an Oriental rug. The turquoise blue glistening tiles, rendered in detail and with great precision (including some Arabic calligraphy from the Qur'an), mark the space as an instantly recognisable Oriental setting.

Henri Rousseau's painting *Exotic Landscape* (1908) is one of a series of similarly themed oil paintings in French Naïve or primitivist style which depict wild animals in verdant jungle settings. Since Rousseau never travelled abroad, it is inspired by the careful study of animals in the Paris Zoo, botanical gardens and illustrated books. It shows a group of monkeys picking and eating oranges amidst a lush tropical landscape of leaves, grasses and trees, painted in vibrant shades of green. The ubiquitous palm tree – the generic signifier of exoticism – in the background and a red-breasted bird with blue wings at the centre, complement the overall sense of exotic lushness and abundance. The comparison of Rousseau's and

Figure 1.2 Henri Rousseau's *Exotic Landscape* (1908) encapsulates exoticism's fascination with foreign flora and fauna (creative commons).

Gérôme's paintings also suggests that Orientalism is primarily concerned with *cultural* differences, whereas exoticism also pertains to the *natural* world, although not exclusively so.

If we add the Dutch Baroque painting *African Woman with Child* (1641) by Albert Eckhout, a life-size portrait of a bare-breasted black woman and naked young boy, further distinctions emerge: in contrast to Rousseau's primitivist painting, which is a pure fantasy of the exotic world, Eckhout's portrait bears all the hallmarks of ethnographic accuracy – or so it may seem. In reality, it represents an eclectic mix of exotica from different parts of world, notably Africa and Brazil. The statuesque black woman is wearing a woven cloth and red sash around her waist, and a 'tribal', curiously shaped woven hat on her head. The strings of coral-red and white beads around her neck accentuate her smooth dark brown skin and round breasts. Phallic symbols, such as the (North American) ear of corn which the boy points at the woman's crotch; a white clay pipe, an erotic symbol of female wantonness in Dutch Baroque painting; and a woven basket 'overflowing with a cornucopia of ripe tropical fruit, suggest the fecundity and palpable sexuality of the female figure' (Schmidt 2018: 187). The plants, a wax palm and a papaya tree, both native to tropical South America, a red-headed African love-bird and an indigenous Brazilian tribe in the background of the canvas offer the natural setting for this pseudo-ethnographic portrait of an exotic and erotically alluring woman. What the brief consideration of this third painting illustrates is the close affinity between exoticism and ethnography as well as the fact that Indigenous people and the New World occupy an established place in exoticism, but not in Orientalism.

Another distinction between Orientalism and exoticism revolves around power and pleasure. While Orientalism and exoticism are both concerned with the construction of the Other in relation to the Self, Orientalism is about the power to dominate whereas exoticism is about the pleasure of difference.[7] Orientalism legitimises its 'impulse . . . to *dominate*' (Said 2003: 331; my italics) by asserting the Orient and the Oriental's inferiority in relation to the West. Where the West is described as 'rational, developed, humane, superior', the Orient is imagined as 'aberrant, undeveloped, inferior . . . something either feared (the Yellow Peril, the Mongol hordes, the brown dominions) or to be controlled (by pacification, research and development, outright occupation whenever possible)' (Said 2003: 300–1). This inferiorisation of the Oriental Other served to justify colonial power structures. Thus, in the 'Afterword' to *Orientalism*, written in 1995 in response to the criticism his seminal work incurred, Said (2003: 345) writes:

Figure 1.3 Albert Eckhout's *African Woman with Child* (1641) combines ostensible ethnographic accuracy with an eclectic range of exotica from around the world (creative commons, photo © John Lee, National Museum of Denmark).

no more glaring parallel exists between power and knowledge in the modern history of philology than in the case of Orientalism. Much of the information and knowledge about Islam and the Orient was used by the colonial powers to justify their colonialism derived from Orientalist scholarship.

The symbiosis of knowledge and power, one of the defining features of Orientalism, makes it a prime example of Michel Foucault's discursive formation in as much as the production of knowledge is a means of exercising power. Acknowledging his debt to Foucault, Said (2003: 3), defines 'Orientalism as a Western style for dominating, restructuring, and having authority over the Orient . . . politically, sociologically, militarily, ideologically, scientifically, and imaginatively'.

Without wanting to deny exoticism's complicity with the uneven power hierarchies that characterised the colonial encounter and that continue to shape contemporary cross-cultural encounters between the Global North and South and their cultural representations, I contend that exoticism is more closely aligned with pleasure than with power. Exoticism seeks to reproduce the pleasures of spatial and cultural displacements. Through its use of spectacle and multisensorial aesthetics, it elicits sensorial pleasure in the beholder. Nonetheless, exoticism's orientation towards the pleasures of difference does not automatically rehabilitate it. Rather, the visual and sensuous allure of exoticism serves as a glamorous disguise that potentially detracts from inequities of power by spectacularising racial, ethnic and cultural differences. The sense of entitlement to put the Other on display for the metropole's voyeuristic pleasure derives from exoticism's Eurocentrism, a positionality it shares with Orientalism. Eurocentrism tacitly posits Europe, and the West more broadly, as the norm and, indeed, as universal. Ella Shohat and Robert Stam (1994: 2) define Eurocentrism as 'a form of vestigial thinking' which has its historical roots in the colonising process but 'which permeates and structures *contemporary* practices and representations even after the formal end of colonialism' (italics in original). Eurocentrism obscures its ideological indebtedness to colonialism by embedding and normalising 'the hierarchical power relations generated by colonialism and imperialism, without necessarily even thematising those issues directly'.

Where Orientalism overtly pits the rational, progressive and enlightened West against the irrational, timeless and backward Orient and invariably assigns the Orient to the negative pole, exoticism operates in a more ambivalent way. On the one hand, it marvels at the wondrous difference of the exotic Other with a genuine sense of astonishment and fascination; on the other, it conceives of exotic alterity as a deviation from the Eurocentric norm. In this way, the fascination with the exotic Other ultimately supports the metropole's claim to universality – and to be universal inevitably carries privilege and power. Therefore, the hierarchies underpinning the discourse of exoticism closely mirror the racial discourse surrounding 'white' and 'non-white' people. As Richard Dyer (1997: 1–2) has illustrated so convincingly, the notion of race is only applied to non-white people, whereas

> white people are not racially seen and named, they/we function as the human norm. Other people are raced, we are just people. There is no more powerful position than that of being 'just' human. The claim to power is the claim to speak for the commonality of humanity.

Put differently, the process of Othering invariably entails asymmetries, whereby a dominant group asserts the particularities of its own identity as 'the norm' and, implicitly or explicitly, devalues or even discriminates against those particularities that deviate from what is, arbitrarily, posited as the norm. While it is easy to see how negative and threatening stereotypes of the exotic Other confirm this argument, it is not readily reconcilable with positive valorisations, which are far more prevalent.

Exoticism's Inherent Ambivalence

The construction of Otherness is governed by ambivalence. In 'The Other Question', Homi Bhabha (1994: 95–6) defines ambivalence as a set 'of discursive and psychological strategies of discriminatory power' that simultaneously renders the Other 'an object of desire and derision', delight and fear, pleasure and menace. Exoticism perpetually oscillates between the positive and negative poles, as is deftly illustrated by the figures of the 'Noble Savage', the 'Primitive' and the 'Cannibal' (see Chapters 2 and 5). Fin-de-siècle anthropologists, such as Félix Regnault and Carl Vogt, regarded 'Primitives' or 'Savages' as 'the "pathological" counterpoint to the European' (Rony 1996: 27), who presumably occupied a lower stage of evolutionary development on account of representing the missing link between humans and the animal kingdom. Michel de Montaigne, however, gives value to the ostensibly threatening figures of the Savage or Cannibal. Without condoning the Brazilian Tupinambá tribe's ceremonial eating of their enemies' dead bodies, the French philosopher finds this tradition far less cruel and barbaric than the wartime atrocities and massacres committed in the name of religion in sixteenth-century France. The figure of the Noble Savage goes back to Montaigne's essays 'Of Cannibals' and 'Of Coaches' (written around 1580) and epitomises the utopian propensities of exoticism, which derive from a profound disenchantment with Western civilisation. What makes Montaigne's Noble Savages superior to Europeans is that they 'still enjoy that natural abundance [and that] they are still in the happy state of desiring only as much as their natural needs demand' (Montaigne 1877). Todorov, who identifies the Noble Savage as a key figure of primitive exoticism, provides an extensive overview of travelogues and philosophical writings on the subject. Glossing Denis Diderot's *Supplément au Voyage de Bougainville* (2017 [1772]), he writes that the French philosopher and armchair anthropologist sternly rejects 'the whole idea of a European civilizing mission' because the Tahitian 'savages' would have nothing 'to learn from us, since they are already better than we are' (Todorov 1993: 276–7).

Todorov's validation of the Tahitian 'savages' chimes with the accounts of European explorers, naval officers, writers and artists, such as Louis Antoine de Bougainville, Samuel Wallis, James Cook, Victor Segalen and Paul Gauguin, who travelled to Polynesia and perceived the islanders as the incarnation of Rousseau's ideal of the natural man and the islands as paradise on earth. For them, visions of paradise translated into tropical abundance and, more importantly, 'a general state of polygamy' (Bougainville cited in Célestin 1996: 79).[8] Paul Gauguin's colour-saturated paintings of Tahitian women, portrayed in a natural state of innocence and sensuality, stand in this tradition and encapsulate the fantasy of an alternative way of life, where beautiful exotic women give themselves freely to men.[9] The wealth of exotic erotic literature that was produced by male travellers, such as Antoine de Bougainville, James Banks (who accompanied Captain Cook on the Endeavour), the nineteenth-century British explorer Richard Burton and the French writer Pierre Loti (a pseudonym for Louis Marie-Julien Viaud), to mention but some of the most prominent authors, provide yet another reason for exoticism's tarnished reputation. Loti was a French naval officer and prolific novelist, who in the late 1870s started writing novels set in faraway lands, including Turkey, Tahiti and Japan, that revolve around erotic encounters with exotic women. The women are of interest only insofar as they provide Loti with new impressions and intoxicating sensations that make him feel revitalised. According to Todorov (1993: 314), who devotes a long section to Loti in *On Human Diversity*, the originality of Loti's contribution to the nineteenth-century discourse on exoticism 'lies in the way he makes exoticism coincide with eroticism'.[10] In so doing, Loti establishes erotic desire for the Other as an important affective component of the exotic experience. In a historical context in which foreign lands offered an escape from the moral strictures of European societies, 'elsewhere is customarily sexualized as much as sex itself is exoticized. Regions viewed . . . as both exotic and marginal are presented as deregulated spaces in which travelers can behave . . . in ways that would be deemed inappropriate at home' (Forsdick 2007: 441).[11]

To be sure, the projection of libidinous desires onto exotic locales and people is by no means a thing of the past, as films that imagine the exotic as erotic, including *Kama Sutra: A Tale of Love* (Mira Nair, 1996), *Chinese Box* (Wayne Wang, 1997), *L'Amant* (The Lover, Jean-Jacques Annaud, 1992), *Memoirs of a Geisha* (Rob Marshall, 2005), *Se, jie* (Lust, Caution, Ang Lee, 2007), *M. Butterfly* (David Cronenberg, 1993) and *Trishna* (Michael Winterbottom, 2011), demonstrate. Without wanting to condone these exotic-erotic fantasies, which objectify the exotic Other, they, nevertheless, demonstrate that exoticism is closely linked to pleasure, be it the erotic or the visual pleasure afforded by the heightened aestheticisation that is a hallmark of exoticism. As I will elucidate in Chapter 3, the pleasure derived from contact with the Other is necessarily a *guilty* pleasure, but pleasure it is nonetheless – and, as such, imagines the exotic Other as a source of delight. The tensions at play in the experience of this guilty pleasure are an apt example of what Bhabha has identified as the ambivalent response that invariably shapes the encounter with the Other. I will return to the issue of pleasure, but for now I wish to bring exoticism into dialogue with cultural translation and autoethnography, two concepts that also theorise cross-cultural encounters and that appear to be ideologically far less suspect than exoticism.

Exoticism as Cultural Translation

Cultural translation provides a useful analytical framework that deflects from exoticism's historical and cultural baggage, thereby enabling a deeper understanding of how exoticism – denoting a particular type of cultural translation – negotiates difference. Increased global mobility has made the interaction of different cultures and, concomitantly, processes of cultural translation ubiquitous. When 'the space of boundedness' is disturbed by 'the forces of mobility . . . creative reconfigurations' and dynamic transformations occur (Papastergiadis: 2011, 2–3). The idea that cultures, rather than just languages, could be translated, dates back to the mid-nineteenth century, when social anthropology developed as a discipline. Anthropology's enterprise to observe, comprehend and describe remote, foreign and, indeed, exotic cultures involves the translation of words, ideas, social practices and meanings from one culture to another. Thus, anthropologists are the quintessential mediators who translate local cultures and, by producing ethnographic texts that contextualise and gloss local concepts, make them accessible to cultural outsiders. Where ethnographic texts use the ostensibly objective discourse of social science to make remote and alien cultures intelligible to a target culture, exoticism pursues a similar goal through aesthetic means.

Cultural translation is an interpretative act, which negotiates the complex relationship between the foreign and the domestic – and one of the two invariably dominates. Distinguishing between 'foreignizing' and 'domesticating' translations, Lawrence Venuti (2018: xii) argues that any translation is 'inevitably domesticating' insofar as it seeks to make linguistic and cultural differences of the foreign source accessible. However, the degree to which a translation assimilates the differences of a foreign source to the target language and cultural horizons of the receiving culture varies. The domesticating translation makes the original source conform as much as possible to the culture into which it is translated and, thereby, affirms 'linguistic standards, literary canons, and authoritative interpretations . . . and ideologies' and even fosters a sense of 'cultural narcissism' (Venuti 2018: xiv). The foreignising translation, by contrast, aims to retain as many features of the foreign source as possible so as to preserve its distinctiveness and cultural norms and, in so doing, has the capacity to challenge the dominant social and cultural hierarchies that structure the receiving culture. Venuti stresses that the distinction between the two approaches determines the 'ethical effects' of the translated source on the receiving culture. Does it have the capacity to turn 'the asymmetrical relation built by translation into an interrogation of the culture that receives the source text' or does it reinforce cultural asymmetries? (Venuti 2018: xiv).[12]

By rendering the Other as simultaneously foreign (and therefore fascinating or threatening) and familiar (and therefore relatable), exoticism oscillates between the foreignising and domesticating poles of cultural translation. If, however, we conceive of Venuti's distinction between the two modes of cultural translation as a spectrum rather than a binary opposition, then exotic world cinema and its global reception would appear to be situated closer to the 'domesticating' end since it assimilates the foreign into 'a fabric of dominant/dominating relationships' (Carbonell 1996: 89).[13] Yet conversely, it could be argued that world cinema, especially global art cinema, is an impure cinema that relies on cross-fertilisation and hybridisation and that juxtaposes exoticising and autochthonous modes of representation. Therefore, its position on this spectrum is necessarily fluid. As world cinema travels from its original production context to multiply (dis)located audiences, it elicits domesticating as well as foreignising effects, depending on the receiving cultural contexts.

As the discussion of cinematic exoticisms in the following chapters will illustrate, it would be misleading to conceive of exoticism in monolithic terms. Instead, a taxonomy of different modes of cinematic exoticisms will allow me to locate them on a spectrum that ranges from overt strategies of domestication to those that represent radical cultural difference as utterly perplexing or entirely impenetrable. Whether films that make no attempt to mitigate alterity through embedding it in a familiar context, can be labelled 'exotic' at all, will merit closer analysis in relation to specific cinematic examples and will serve as something like a litmus test in the attempt to develop an aesthetic of contemporary exoticisms in transnational cinema. What is, however, apparent in any debate on cultural translation – be it exoticism, ethnography or literary translation – is that foreignising strategies are regarded as more 'authentic' and therefore supposedly better since authenticity (a much-vaunted yet hard-to-define term) carries moral and cultural value and is generally regarded as a positive attribute (see Chapter 2).

Exoticism's Emphatic Visuality

Exoticism's emphatic visuality is one of its most enduring characteristics. It can be traced to its colonial roots and the constitutive role vision and image-making practices have played in the fashioning of the Self and its Other during the age of European empires – a vast topic which Martin Jay and Sumathi Ramaswamy's anthology *Empires of Vision* (2014) illustrates with impressive detail. From early modern exotic geography through ethnographic photography and early cinema's travelogues to the visual opulence of contemporary exotic world cinema, the scopic regimes of exoticism are not merely an eye-catching accessory but play a vital role in eliciting curiosity in cultural difference. In *Inventing Exoticism: Geography, Globalism and Europe's Early Modern World*, Benjamin Schmidt (2018: 14, 8) demonstrates how, roughly from the turn of the eighteenth century onwards, an exotic geography emerged that invited Europeans to picture an 'enticingly unfamiliar' world as a place 'of desire and delight'. If earlier accounts of the non-European world had emphasised similarity and sameness, between 1670 and 1730, Europe's engagement with the Other began to follow a new tack that simultaneously foregrounded the distinctiveness of Europe and its difference from the rest of the world. The new exotic geography of illustrated maps, prints, books and paintings insistently presented the world in 'highly pictorial and strikingly visual' terms. The distinctive look created a brand identity, which Schmidt (2018: 20) describes as 'the veritable ancestor of *National Geographic*'. According to the motto, seeing is believing, detailed illustrations invited Europeans to see with their own eyes the wonders of the distant world. In fact,

> the very word *discovery* implied an act of revelation or seeing, a process of making visible and viewable that which had been hitherto unseen, and exotic places in particular enticed viewers and lured inquisitive eyes . . . Pictures delivered data from a distance. (Schmidt 2018: 83–4; italics in original)

And yet, the promise of ethnographic authenticity and factual accuracy was a mere pretence since exoticism has never been concerned with verisimilitude but instead with the projection of fantasies of Other cultures and peoples. The natural history prints, for instance, that were an important part of early modern exotic geography, happily mixed and matched flora and fauna from different natural habitats or even different continents, juxtaposing an American scarlet ibis with an African royal python or showing opossums wandering through vistas of Calicut. Palm trees were uprooted from the tropics, where they flourished naturally, only to adorn maps of New England and other northern latitudes, ultimately becoming so ubiquitous that they advanced to the status of a generic signifier of exoticism.

Cinema's prominent role as purveyor of the exotic rests on the natural affinity between visuality and exoticism. Since its inception, cinema and earlier proto-cinematic devices have invited audiences to become armchair travellers who marvel at the wondrous difference of faraway lands, strange peoples and their customs. The birth of cinema in 1895 not only coincided with the height of European empires but also with the new science of ethnography. Early cinema showed a fascination for ethnographic themes in travelogues, scientific research films and colonial propaganda films, projecting images of non-European people, notably Indigenous and 'primitive' tribes, onto the screen. The Lumière brothers were not alone in recognising and utilising the attraction of exoticism from the outset. At the World Fair in Paris in 1900, they entertained some 25,000 people with their *Cinématograph Géant*, projecting moving images and coloured photographs of distant vistas and imperial subjects in their natural habitats onto a gigantic screen. Meanwhile, Raoul Grimoin-Sanson's *Cinéorama* heightened the illusion of mobility and adventurous travel by simulating a voyage in a hot air balloon. Spectators were invited to become passengers inside a capsule that was suspended from a balloon and marvel at aerial views of a landscape projected by ten synchronous projectors onto a gigantic circular screen (see Costa 2006: 247–8). In addition to celebrating France's major technological innovations over the past century, the 1900 Paris Exposition also showcased the country's successful colonial expansion by putting it on display in colonial pavilions and exotic panoramas and dioramas of the Congo and Madagascar or a virtual voyage along the Algerian coast. Four years later, in the United States, the American entrepreneur George C. Hale launched *Hale's Tours and Scenes of the World*, offering spectators an immersive experience of railway travel in carriages that projected vistas of scenic spots not just in North America but also in remote foreign lands, such as China, Ceylon or Samoa (see Rabinovitz 2006).

Early cinema can be regarded as the successor of the colonial exhibitions and human zoos insofar as it made these celebrations of empire portable and mediatised. Films about empire celebrated colonial acquisitions and indulged viewers in the spectacle of foreign lands and exotic peoples, while the cinematic medium neatly contained any potentially threatening difference, thereby conveying a sense of control over alterity. Dudley Andrew (1997: 232) identifies 'the promise of the exotic', as one of cinema's 'clearest distinguishing traits . . . that most clearly separates the medium from theatre'. As the visual medium par excellence, cinema has always relied on the spectacle of the exotic as one of its main attractions.

The spectacularisation of Other cultures at the height of European empires (and beyond) has never been a form of innocent entertainment. As Shohat and Stam (1994: 104) have persuasively argued, the 'spatially-mobilized visuality' of cinema was complicit with the imperial gaze that transformed 'European spectators into armchair conquistadors', affirming their sense of superiority and power by reducing the colonial Other to a 'spectacle for the metropole's voyeuristic gaze'. That the act of looking confers power, whereas being looked at is disempowering, is an insight that has been eloquently made by Laura Mulvey (1975) in her seminal essay on visual pleasure and the gendered scopophilic regimes of classical Hollywood cinema. Of course, it also applies to numerous other contexts, notably ethnographic film and photography as well as the autoethnographic impulse behind the performance of self-exoticism in world cinema, an issue I shall analyse in detail when considering visual pleasure in relation to the transnational appeal of world cinema below.

Visible Evidence, (Auto)ethnography and Self-exoticisation

In late nineteenth- and early twentieth-century social anthropology, visuality served as 'a conduit of scientific knowledge' (Griffiths 2002: 84) that set out to prove how non-Western and, in particular, Indigenous non-European peoples deviated from what was posited as the human norm. Anthropometric photography even provided measurable and, therefore, supposedly irrefutable evidence of evolutionary theories that underpinned white supremacist assumptions. As Alison Griffiths notes:

> Of all the human senses, sight assumed a position of unquestionable dominance in nineteenth-century anthropology; it was tales of what intrepid travellers had *seen* on their trips to the far corners of the earth in the form of drawings, sketches, engravings, watercolours, paintings, and cultural artefacts that thrilled the general public and scientific societies alike and that provided the much sought-after evidence of racial inferiority and so-called barbaric practices. (Griffiths 2002: 88; italics in original)

Thus, the protocols of viewing that governed anthropological practices from exposition displays and native villages at world fairs in Europe and North America, through ethnographic photography to ethnographic film have established looking relations between the white Western spectator and the native Other that invariably assigns the former the status of privileged onlookers and the latter the object of the gaze. Not only was visuality credited with an innate truth-telling capacity that was considered to surpass that of ethnographic writing, it also afforded the pleasure of looking. As a result, the boundaries between scientific knowledge, public education, voyeurism and popular entertainment were fairly fluid.

Crucially, what distinguishes early ethnographic films like those analysed in detail by Fatimah Tobing Rony in *The Third Eye* and by Alison Griffiths in *Wondrous Difference* from the ones at the centre of this book is a significant shift in the regime of looks. In exotic world cinema, the ethnographic Other, muted and objectified for centuries, assumes the position behind the camera and becomes both the subject and the object of the gaze. And yet, as postcolonial critics including W. E. B. Du Bois, Frantz Fanon, Mary Louise Pratt, Fatimah Tobing Rony and Rey Chow have proposed, 'the binary structure of the observer/observed that is classical anthropology's premise and that has become *the* way we approach the West's "other"' continues to manifest itself in the way the West's Others see themselves (Chow 1995: 177; italics in original). Mary Louise Pratt (2008: 7) has termed this process 'autoethnography . . . to refer to instances in which colonized subjects undertake to represent themselves in ways that *engage with* the colonizer's own terms' by constructing their own texts and images 'in response to or in dialogue with those metropolitan representations' (italics in original).

The question as to whether such autoethnographic texts straightforwardly appropriate metropolitan representation or whether they infiltrate them with autochthonous modes of (self-)representation, remains a contested issue. Can the non-Western Other ever apprehend and articulate its authentic Self or is, as Homi Bhabha (2008: xxvii) suggests, 'the Other-ness of the Self [inevitably] inscribed in the perverse palimpsest of colonial identity'? Frantz Fanon (2008: 84), for one, poignantly renders the internalisation of the white man's gaze in *Black Skin, White Masks*, in which he explores how colonialism deforms the minds and bodies of colonised peoples. It includes a famous passage in which he describes an incident on a train journey in France when a young white boy points at Fanon and exclaims: 'Mama, see the Negro! I'm frightened!' At first, Fanon (2008: 84–5) is amused and tries to laugh, but during this pivotal moment he discovers his own blackness and feels 'battered down by tom-toms, cannibalism, intellectual deficiency, fetishism, racial defects, slave ships'. The white boy's remark makes Fanon recall the exotic image of the Bonhomme Banania, which links black identity with the pleasures of consumption. This iconic French marketing campaign for the Banania chocolate drink, launched in 1915 and modified multiple times over the following decades, shows the broadly grinning face of a Senegalese Tirailleur wearing a red fez, and the slogan 'Y a bon banania'.[14] Fanon (2008: 85) describes how he feels imprisoned by these white supremacist images, and yet he cannot help adopting them as his own self-image: 'I took myself far off from my own presence, far indeed, and made myself an object.' Unsurprisingly, the self-image of a bad, mean and ugly Negro of whom the little white boy is afraid, shivering with fear, fills Fanon (2008: 86, 88) with 'shame and self-contempt. Nausea'. However, the ostensibly attractive image of the jolly Bonhomme Banania is no better since it ultimately reduces the black man to an object amongst many other objects, created by the white man and available for white man's consumption.

For Fanon, the black man's cultural alienation extends further. As a well-educated psychiatrist and political philosopher of Martinican descent, he is regarded by the white coloniser as 'different' from the average black man, as 'one of us' despite his black skin. The coloniser's invitation to identify as white complicates the black man's sense of identity, resulting in a destabilised and ambivalent sense of Self, which Bhabha (2008: xxviii) describes as 'the White man's artifice inscribed on the black man's body'. This turn of phrase draws attention to the processes of cultural inscription and translation that seem to forestall any access to an unmediated Self. That is why Salman Rushdie (1992a: 17) refers to himself and other postcolonial diasporic writers as 'translated men'.

Although particularly influential, Frantz Fanon was neither the first nor the last to ponder this profound sense of self-alienation. In *The Souls of Black Folk* (1903), the African American writer W. E. B. Du Bois coined the term 'double consciousness' to describe the conflicted experience of being an American of African descent, who carries 'two souls, two thoughts, two unreconciled strivings; two warring forces in one dark body'. This, Du Bois (1903) argues, results in a 'sense of always looking at one's self through the eyes of others'. The concept of the 'third eye', developed by Fatimah Tobing Rony, a North American film scholar of Sumatran descent, in relation to ethnographic documentaries and ethnographic spectacle articulates a similar idea. Drawing on Du Bois and Fanon, Rony (1996: 4) proposes that people 'marked as an Other', like herself, inevitably see themselves 'reflected in the eyes of others' and are, therefore, endowed with the third eye, which affords them greater acuity of vision. Despite being somewhat cloaked in ethnic essentialism, Rony's theorisation of the third eye yields pertinent insights into the scopic regimes of autoethnography and self-exoticism in world cinema. Her detailed analyses of canonical ethnographic documentaries offer a rich and nuanced account of the iconography of 'primitive exoticism', which continues to reverberate in contemporary Indigenous cinema, as

Chapter 2 will illustrate. Her analysis demonstrates that the third eye is an empowering gaze, that liberates those endowed with it from carrying the burden of ethnographic voyeurism and colonial mastery in perpetuity. Instead, the third eye destabilises these regimes of looking through self-reflexive performative practices, pastiche and parody and, thereby, invests the Other with sovereignty over their own images.

World Cinema as Autoethnography and Cultural Translation

World cinema, like (auto)ethnography, can be conceptualised as a form of cultural translation that situates foreign films in relation to the West. It is a travelling concept that depends on mobility and the crossing of cultural boundaries to come into being, a feature it shares with exoticism. The term world cinema has been coined in analogy to Johann Wolfgang von Goethe's *Weltliteratur* (world literature) by which he meant not only foreign literature, but also the reception of domestic literature abroad as well as his own literary translations (see Birus 2004). However, Goethe was particularly interested in the European reception of the foreign, which points towards the Eurocentric perspective underpinning world literature. The chief attraction which both world literature and world cinema hold for their recipients is the inherent promise to offer windows to foreign worlds that are imagined as profoundly different from the West. According to David Damrosch (2003: 175), 'works become world literature by being received into the space of a foreign culture, a space defined in many ways by the host culture's national tradition and the present needs of its own writers.' Rather than conceiving of world literature as a canon of foreign literary masterpieces, Damrosch describes it as a mode of transnational circulation and reception that *gains in translation*. The same holds true for world cinema, which must travel from its site of origin and be watched by audiences originating from different nations, regions or cultures. In other words, the transnational dimension inherent in the concept of world cinema is constituted in the process of reception as a film moves outside its own national or cultural sphere into another one.

The transnational reception of exotic world cinema is a form of cultural translation that is based on a peculiarly persistent premise that dates back to the time when Western ethnographers asserted their authority to interpret the signifying systems of supposedly subordinate societies. That is why, as Rey Chow (1995: 177) suggests, we still 'cannot write/think/talk about the non-West in the academy without in some sense anthropologizing it'. This also explains why non-Western filmmakers are often expected to act as native informants and interpreters whose role it is to provide authentic accounts of their cultures of origin. Against this background, contemporary world cinema and the global film festival circuit, its prime site of exhibition, can be understood as a new type of 'contact zone', an intercultural space of symbolic exchange and transculturation, catering for cosmopolitan cinephiles and their interest in cultural difference. Pratt (2008: 7) describes the colonial encounters occurring in the contact zone as 'interactive', as the constitution of subjects 'in and by their relations to each other'. If we conceive of world cinema and its transnational exhibition on the film festival circuit (and beyond) as such a contact zone then the interactive exchange occurring in this space is, on the one hand, the expectation of metropolitan audiences to encounter a particular kind of world cinema that corresponds to their (exotic) fantasies of Other cultures and, on the other hand, the creation of 'autoethnographic texts', that is, films made by non-Western filmmakers which 'appropriate the idioms' of 'metropolitan representation' (Pratt 2008: 7). The late Thomas Elsaesser has famously espoused this view:

> World cinema . . . is always in danger of conducting a form of auto-ethnography and promoting a sort of self-exoticization in which the ethnic, the local or the regional expose themselves, under the guise of self-expression, to the gaze of the benevolent other, with all the consequences that this entails. World cinema invariably implies the look from outside and thus conjures up the old anthropological dilemma of the participant observer being presented with the mirror of what the 'native' thinks the other, the observer wants to see. (Elsaesser 2005: 510)

In this oft-cited quote, Elsaesser planted the seed for an exotic-oriented criticism that alleges world cinema filmmakers of pandering to metropolitan tastes. Below and throughout this book, I will reassess the prevalent understanding that self-exoticism in world cinema is a one-directional process that leaves Western hegemony unchallenged.

Whether or not world cinema's autoethnographic practice is a deliberate strategy or an unconscious process is one of the questions that Rey Chow addresses in *Primitive Passions*, an influential book about Fifth Generation Chinese cinema and Chinese visual culture more broadly. She regards fiction films, such as Chen Kaige's *Huang tu di* (Yellow Earth, 1984) and Zhang Yimou's award-winning *Ju Dou* (1990) and *Da hong deng long gao gao gua* (Raise the Red Lantern, 1991), as a new type of ethnography 'practiced by those who were previously ethnographized and who have, in the postcolonial age, taken up the active task of ethnographizing their own cultures' (Chow 1995: 180). Yet rather than challenging the unequal power hierarchies implied in the ethnographer's act of looking,

Fifth Generation Chinese filmmakers actively replicate 'the state of being looked at' in their films (Chow 1995: 180). In contrast to other scholars, who criticise certain world cinema filmmakers for becoming complicit in Western cross-cultural modes of representation such as exoticism and Orientalism when making films about their own cultures, Chow (1995: 180) regards it as the inevitable consequence of bearing the 'memory of past objecthood – the experience of being looked at – which lives on in the subjective act of ethnographizing like an other, an optical unconscious'. If we concur with Chow, then world cinema can never give a 'true' or 'authentic' representation of China, India, Africa or other cultures, since centuries of European cultural hegemony have conditioned non-Western filmmakers to see themselves through Western eyes.

However, Chow's explanation needs to be treated with a degree of caution. One would be hard pressed to discover traces of such autoethnographic regimes of looking in Bollywood and Nollywood melodramas or in Hong Kong martial arts movies, which are not created with metropolitan cinephiles in mind, primarily target domestic and diasporic mainstream audiences and are usually inspired by local cultural traditions.[15] Similarly, Third Cinema and other postcolonial political cinemas that are in dialogue with and explicitly resist centuries of Western hegemony aim to deconstruct the enduring legacies of 'past objecthood' and, thereby – in the words of Teshome Gabriel (1982: 3) – promote the 'decolonisation of the mind', politically as well as aesthetically. But even with regard to popular genre cinema, the notion of an 'original', 'uncontaminated' or 'pure' Other culture that is not deformed by imperial habits of seeing, thinking and representing is an essentialist fallacy, since in a world of global connectivity and hybridisation, cultural purity is a mere fantasy. In fact, the dogmatic insistence on cultural fidelity is incompatible with the multiple processes of cultural translation and multi-directional flows that impact upon contemporary cultures and world cinema.[16] As Stephanie Dennison and Song Hwee Lim (2006a: 4) persuasively argue, it is 'precisely because of the legacy of colonialism and neo-imperialism [that] essentialised notions of both the West and the non-West have become increasingly untenable as their histories, cultures and peoples become inextricably intertwined'.

Another premise of Chow's account is that colonial forms of representation and colonial language have inculcated the colonial subject and their descendants into a particular way of seeing the world and that their minds are held captive. Yet it would be misguided to conceive of the colonial subject simply as 'a *tabula rasa* on which colonial discourse can inscribe its representations' (Ashcroft 2001: 44). The assumption of a passive colonised mind fails to acknowledge the colonised subject's agency, their ability to actively engage with and transform hegemonic modes of representation in subtle ways. It is important to acknowledge that the colonised subject has the ability and agency to withstand imperial ideology by devising alternative modes of self-fashioning and self-representation. Self-exoticism in contemporary world cinema is precisely such a strategy. Rather than conceiving of self-exoticism in reductive terms as a mere imitation of Eurocentric discourses on alterity, I am taking inspiration from Bill Ashcroft's idea of 'post-colonial transformation' when examining how self-exoticism actively engages with and negotiates dominant discourses and even subverts them.[17] Thus, exotic world cinema does not necessarily pander to the tastes of the West but may, conversely, represent a refusal to being absorbed into dominant discourses by actively transforming and, thereby, resisting them. As Ashcroft explains:

> 'Transformation' is contrary to what we normally think of as 'resistance' because the latter has been locked into the party-political imaginary of opposition . . . But post-colonial transformation has been the most powerful and active form of resistance in colonized societies because it has been so relentless, so everyday, and above all, so integral a part of the imaginations of these societies. Resistance which ossifies into simple opposition often becomes trapped in the very binary which imperial discourse uses to keep the colonized into subjection. (Ashcroft 2001: 21)

I am not suggesting here that all of the films I consider in this study are examples of transformative resistance, but theorising resistance in less overtly political terms than, for example, theories of Third Cinema do, allows us to become attuned to more subtle expressions of resistance, such as the return of the exotic gaze through the 'third eye' and 'the Oriental's orientalism' (Chow 1995: 166–72), concepts which I will discuss below.

It is worth emphasising that postcolonial transformation plays an important part in the various processes of cultural translation that shape world cinema (in particular, global art cinema) at every single stage. It begins with the strategic performance of exotic Otherness with which global auteurs seek 'entry into the discursive networks of cultural dominance' (Ashcroft 2001: 19). It also applies to the various mechanisms of transnational film funding and co-production, circulation and distribution, since the selection procedures involved tend to privilege a particular type of global art cinema and transnational aesthetic that promises to appeal to metropolitan cinephiles. For Randall Halle (2014: 129), many Western-led transnational production mechanisms actually 'institute[s] a cycle of Orientalism, offering European (and American) audiences the tales they want to hear'. And finally, cultural translation manifests itself in the transnational reception process in which cultural outsiders are trying to make sense of films whose cultural-historical context and signifying systems are largely unknown to them. Much gets lost in translation while, conversely, new meanings, whether fitting or not, get superimposed. Therefore, transnational reception and cross-cultural analysis are potentially fraught with problems, tempting film critics and scholars to 'read works produced by the Other through the constraints of one's own frameworks, theories and ideologies' (Kaplan 1997b: 266) and, in so doing, become complicit in a new form of cultural imperialism. Sheldon Hsiao-peng Lu even goes so far as to consider the critical reception of Chinese cinema and visual culture in the West as a form of cultural appropriation:

> Previously, it was the role of China specialists to translate and introduce artistic works from China to the Western audience. Now, in a remarkable reversal of fortune, it is the West that points out what is outstanding and characteristically Chinese in artworks from China. The viewers and critics of the home country can do nothing but be astounded by and follow the judgement of the authority of the Western world. Chinese intellectuals are in a stupor, remain aphasic, and are unable to speak and pass judgement on the works of their own country. (Lu 1997b: 128)

To try and prevent the disjunctures arising when cultural outsiders attempt to understand and analyse world cinema is impossible. However, to reserve this right for 'native' critics and scholars would constitute a form of cultural essentialism that ultimately defeats world cinema's main attraction, namely, to offer windows to other worlds. Furthermore, as defendants of cultural translation have argued, such hermeneutic collisions and reconfigurations are actually highly productive interactions that bring about cultural innovation, provided that the power differentials are not too extreme.

Arguably the most dynamic site of cultural translation is the film festival circuit since it is here where the first contact in this cross-cultural encounter usually occurs and where global art cinema's meaning and artistic value is negotiated. Bill Nichols' (1994: 16, 18) evocative description of film festivals as a new type of contact zone where cosmopolitan cinephiles can enjoy 'an abiding pleasure in the recognition of [cultural] differences' reaffirms Chow's argument that the encounter with the non-West is inevitably imagined in ethnographic terms. In fact, Nichols (1994: 17) compares the festivalgoer's experience with that of an anthropological fieldworker (and tourist), who becomes submerged 'in an experience of difference, entering strange worlds, hearing unfamiliar languages, witnessing unusual styles'. Although the encounter with the strange and unfamiliar is one of the principal fascinations that world cinema affords transnational audiences, it invariably triggers the reflex 'to recover the strange as familiar' (Nichols 1994: 18), or to use the term I introduced in relation to the exotic, to domesticate it. This *'domestication, the taming of the new'* (Bordwell 1989: 256; italics in original), is an integral part of the critical reception of artistically innovative films in general, not just the transnational reception of world cinema. It usually takes two forms: either discovering a common humanity that transcends cultural differences or recognising aesthetic forms and patterns familiar from European art cinema in world cinema.

The cultural translation of world cinema corresponds with the de- and recontextualisation of the exotic, whose alluring alterity only manifests itself when it is perceived by someone belonging to a different cultural sphere. Nevertheless, it would be wrong to assume that world cinema per se is decoded as exotic. For example, the documentary realist aesthetics of the Iranian New Wave films, which Nichols uses as a case study in his essay, is far too austere to qualify as exotic. Likewise, we only need to consider films like *Sud pralad* (Tropical Malady, 2004) and *Loong Boonmee raleuk chat* (Uncle Boonmee Who Can Recall His Past Lives, 2013) by Apichatpong Weerasethakul, whose radical alterity make them extremely enigmatic, if not utterly perplexing, for global audiences to appreciate that they lack two essential characteristics of exoticism: first, their extreme alterity precludes domestication, that is, integration into a familiar system of aesthetic and conceptual reference points and, second, they are largely devoid of the visual and sensuous allure that is a hallmark of exotic cinema.

Decoding the Exotic in World Cinema

How then are certain global art films decoded as exotic, while others are simply strange or bewildering? What particular qualities do films as diverse as *Raise the Red Lantern*, *The Scent of Green Papaya*, *Como agua para chocolate* (Like Water for Chocolate, Alfonso Arau, 1992), *In the Mood for Love*, *Three Seasons* (Tony Bui, 2000), *Water* (Deepa Mehta 2005), *Cike Nie Yin Niang* (The Assassin, Hou Hsiao-Hsien, 2015), *Tanna* and *Embrace of the Serpent* possess to elicit the exotic gaze in the spectator? Their common denominator is, as I shall illustrate, that they resonate with the multi-faceted iconography of exoticism. Exoticism functions like a hermeneutic circuit that relies on the appropriation and reworking of established iconographic conventions and narrative tropes in order to be recognised as such. That is why, in the words of Fatimah Tobing Rony (1996: 6), 'the exotic is always already known . . . explorers, anthropologists and tourists voyage to foreign places in search of the novel, the undiscovered. What they find . . . is what they already knew they would find, images predigested by certain "platitudes and commonplaces".' Rony's observation goes a long way in explaining why exotic forms of cultural representation often seem clichéd and stereotypical.

Vibrant colours; ancient rituals and traditions (both real or invented); a sense of pastness or 'primitive' backwardness in relation to the 'progressive' West; iconic costumes like the loincloth, the sari or the cheongsam that essentialise cultural identities; topographies like the Amazon rainforest, the holy city of Varanasi, waterscapes covered in carpets of floating lotus flowers or bustling street markets; sensuality, lushness and abundance, and a sense of enigma and mystery are all, in varying degrees and combinations, essential ingredients of contemporary exoticism. They allow transnational audiences to domesticate the foreign by integrating it into the established aesthetic paradigm of exoticism, which has been made subservient to shifting ideological objectives over the centuries. Since exoticism turns cultural difference into spectacle it is regularly censured because the visual pleasure that spectacle affords is regarded as something like an opiate that anaesthetises the spectator's critical faculties, thereby precluding intellectual interrogation and critical distance (see Chapter 3, where I discuss this issue in more detail). Therefore, exotic cinema is regularly denounced as unethical and exploitative. Assuming the position of moral gatekeepers, exoticism's detractors expect global art cinema auteurs to perpetuate Third Cinema's commitment to postcolonial resistance instead of becoming 'complicit' in exoticising their own cultures, even if this entails potentially forsaking critical or commercial success. Much could be and has been written on this topic and I will investigate this line of argument in the subsequent chapters. But for now, I will examine how global auteurs enhance the transnational appeal of world cinema through practising self-exoticism. To this end, I will consider four films that are widely cited in critical debates about exoticism and that crystallise distinctive features of this prominent mode of representation.

The emphasis exoticism places on sumptuous images and visual splendour shifts the attention from the film's deeper meaning (such as specific historical events, social conventions and interactions articulated in the narrative) to the surface which, in the words of Rey Chow (1995: 150), 'not only shines but *glosses*, which looks, stares, and speaks' (italics in original). Exoticism's deliberate foregrounding of textures and colours, its reliance on the seductive power of beauty, is a strategy of concealment and obfuscation. It invites the gaze of the beholder to glide along surfaces lest these fragile upper layers crumble under the weight of socio-historical injustice. Paradoxically, for all its exuberant visuality, exoticism is premised on '*not seeing*' (italics in original), Roger Célestin (1996: 162) argues, on 'maintaining a certain amount of ignorance', for knowledge might demand taking action against the social injustice that exoticism camouflages so effectively.

It is here, where contemporary decentred exoticism in world cinema parts ways with its old precursor. The heightened aesthetics of exoticism is deployed like bait that lures transnational audiences to take an interest in and empathise with the suffering of the distant Other (see Chapter 2). In *Salaam, Bombay!* (1988) and *Water* (2005), Mira Nair and Deepa Mehta, two diasporic Indian filmmakers working in North America, use the breathtaking beauty of exotic images strategically to alert audiences to the poverty of destitute street children and to the plight of socially ostracised Hindu widows, who are abandoned by their extended families and banished to a widows' ashram. There they eke out an ascetic existence, being forced into begging and prostitution to supplement their keep. Mehta spells out the ethico-political commitment of *Water* in the epilogue, which reads: 'There are thirty-four million widows in India according to a 2001 census. Many continue to live in conditions of social, economic and cultural deprivation as prescribed 2,000 years ago by the *Sacred Texts of Manu*', an ancient Hindu text that stipulates social obligations, codes of conduct, rituals and religious and social laws. Her public indictment of Hindu patriarchal practices, alongside the politically incendiary revelation that the institution of widows' ashrams is implicated in prostitution – even child prostitution – was seen as an act of betrayal in India, leading to public protests and acts of violence by Hindu nationalists and the eventual banning of the film. Similarly, as if to prove the sincerity of the humanitarian impetus behind her film, Nair set up and donated the proceeds of *Salaam, Bombay!* to the Salaam Balak Trust, an Indian NGO that provides shelter, basic education and care for street children in deprived urban areas of Mumbai and New Delhi. The young lay actors of her film were the first to benefit from this initiative (Muir 2006: 61).[18]

Both films mobilise an exotic imaginary of India that revolves around poverty. The indelible link between India and poverty was cemented in the global imagination through Danny Boyle's international box-office hit *Slumdog Millionaire* but, for cinephiles at least, it harks back to the *Apu Trilogy* (1955–9) by the Bengali director Satyajit Ray. When in 1956, *Pather Panchali*, the first part of the trilogy, was nominated for the Palme d'Or at the Cannes Film Festival, Ray brought Indian cinema to the attention of international audiences and was instantly celebrated as an auteur in the West. In India, Ray's film met with mixed responses, winning awards but also courting harsh criticism for exporting poverty, thereby, betraying India's pride and dignity (see Windsor 1998; Robinson 2011). Louis Malle's documentary *Calcutta* (1969), an off-shoot of the French director's seven-part television mini-series *L'Inde fantôme* (Phantom India, 1969), invited audiences to gawk at the unfathomable metropolis, where millions of people live in abject poverty, passively accepting their fate. As in other cultural representations of India, the harrowing portrayal of poverty is juxtaposed with religious festivals and rituals (both serve as a form of distilled Otherness), thereby suggesting that India's vast social disparities (for *Calcutta* also offers glimpses of privileged lifestyles) are rooted in Hinduism and its caste system. Even more influential has been the eye-catching photojournalism of Steve McCurry and Raghubir Singh, whose vibrant photographs of India have been reproduced in the *National Geographic* and in countless other magazines, newspapers, web sites and coffee table books. Not poverty as such is exotic but *photogenic* poverty in the Global South, as popularised by these photojournalists, is. Through invoking the redeeming power of beauty, McCurry and Singh have played a pivotal role in exoticising the imaginary of India as poor and profoundly spiritual. In their iconic chronicles of Indian life, these celebrated photojournalists have been enormously influential in configuring the visual idiom of contemporary exoticism (see Chapter 3). *Salaam, Bombay!* and *Water* inscribe themselves in this legacy.[19]

Nair's multi-award-winning *Salaam Bombay!*, which has been dubbed 'slumdog without the millionaire', blends a gritty *cinéma vérité* style with moments of pure visual poetry that offer respite from the misery governing the lives of orphaned street children, child prostitutes, pimps and drug pushers. What exoticises the portrayal of underdevelopment in Mumbai's red-light district is Sandi Sissel's cinematography with its delicate use of light and ornamental shadows, which momentarily transfigure the bleakness. Drawing on Malle's *Phantom India* for inspiration, Sissel (cited in Muir 2006: 44) comments that 'it was very depressing . . . You could almost *smell* poverty.' In order to make a film that would allow audiences to 'see the humanity of the characters and not be overwhelmed by the poverty', Nair and Sissel decided to clean up some of the locations and use a lot of colour. The film's dominant colour palette of muddy browns and amber in the street scenes is complemented by a cacophony of candy colours, such as the bright fuchsia in Sweet Sixteen's (Chandra Sharma) brothel room, her vermillion sari and the deep red lipstick on her lips. Mira Nair even had the crumbling facades of houses that serve as the backdrop for Chillum's (Raghubir Yadav) funeral procession painted in a spectrum of greens, blues and other cool pastel shades. As the drug addict's white-robed body is tied to a bier and covered with pink petals and orange marigold flowers, life in the bustling streets comes to a momentary halt as women watch and the saturated colours of their saris clash with the pastel shades of house fronts. The whole scene is steeped in soft pink evening light, literally shining light on darkness, and thereby inviting audiences to witness the final passage of Chillum's miserable life through rose-tinted spectacles.

Mehta's *Water* is a dark heritage film that relies throughout on the seductive appeal of beautifully composed, painterly images to convey a moving tale about the suffering of Hindu widows in the holy city of Varanasi in 1938.[20] Its most startling feature is the apparent incongruity between the beauty of the images and the narrative of women's victimisation, which invites empathy while at the same time courting Western audiences' sense of supremacy by casting Indian traditions as archaic and inhumane. The rich colour harmonies establish poignant contrasts between the frugal existence inside the widows' ashram – shot in sombre shades of grey, white and washed-out blue – and the world outside, beckoning in resplendent colours: the carpet of green and pink lotus flowers floating on a lake; the deep azure of the night sky and the shimmering turquoise of the water; the fiery red of hot chilli peppers on sale in the street; women in colourful saris bathing on the steps of the river Ganges; and the saffron and pink powder of the Holi festival. The contrasting colour schemes convey the material and sensory deprivation of the widows' lives. Dressed in plain white saris (the Hindu colour of mourning), and sleeping in communal dorms on the floor, the bereaved women's existence is one of abstinence to which colour represents the antipode. It signifies life and abundance and conjures a déjà vu of quintessential 'Indianness'. So prominent is the spectacle of vibrant colours in these two films that it can be identified as one of the most prominent hallmarks of exoticism's visual plenitude.

Water, like other films discussed in this book, especially exotic food film, speaks to transnational audiences' longing to escape the sensorial atrophy of Western culture by inviting them to see and sense the world of the Other. By combining visual pleasure with 'haptic visuality' (Marks 2000) and other forms of embodied perception, the film engages the spectator in the widows' anguish with visceral intensity. Thus, in the opening scene, the eight-year-old child-bride Chuyia (Sarala Kariyawasam), whose significantly older husband has just passed away, passively submits to the rituals of widowhood. Her young age and innocence prevent her from comprehending what marriage, widowhood and death mean, making her enforced act of renunciation even more poignant. A montage of close-ups shows how, first, the two red wedding bangles on her delicate wrist are broken, then her long dark hair is cut off and eventually her head

Figure 1.4 Deepa Mehta's *Water* (2005) engages the spectator in the anguish of the child-widow Chuyia with visceral intensity.

is tonsured with a sharp razor. For the spectator, looking and listening becomes touching. To convey the cruelty of these ceremonial acts, the sounds of a stone smashing her bangles, the snip-snapping of the metal scissors as they cut through Chuyia's thick curls, the sharpening of the razor blade on a grindstone and then, the abrasive scraping of the blade on her delicate scalp are amplified. As the camera cuts from a close-up of her now almost bald head to her toes, curling in pain on the stone floor, the child-widow's agony becomes palpable to the spectator.

Conversely, the film also captures rare moments of sensuous delight, for instance, when Chuyia makes the oldest widow, Auntie (Vidula Javalgekar), the rare gift of a bright yellow *ladoo*, a sweet she has been craving during many long years of deprivation in the ashram. Smelling and eating the *ladoo* rekindles in Auntie memories of her wedding day when she ate plenty of sweets. To translate the emaciated widow's sensual delight in savouring the *ladoo*, music and colour substitute for taste, which cannot be directly represented in cinema (see Chapter 5). Her reawakening of the senses, shortly before she dies, chimes with one of exoticism's constitutive tropes, namely the 'intensity of Sensation, the exaltation of feeling and, therefore, of living' (Segalen 2002: 61).

An aesthetics of sensuous indulgence (see Chapter 4, where I develop the concept), which combines visual spectacle with embodied perception, is arguably the chief vehicle that allows exotic world cinema to travel and be understood, or misunderstood, as the case may be, by cultural outsiders, who are potentially disadvantaged by a deficit of culturally specific knowledge when trying to understand films from elsewhere. It effectively makes up for hermeneutic obstacles that may occur when films are watched across borders. At the same time, this incomplete understanding of the film's deeper layers of meaning adds a residue of enigma and mystery. Taiwanese director Hou Hsiao-Hsien's first foray into the *wuxia* genre, *The Assassin*, deftly illustrates this. Set in ninth-century China during the tail end of the Tang Dynasty, it tells the story of Nie Yinniang (Shu Qi), a female assassin who is commissioned to kill a series of government officials. Although her martial arts skills are unsurpassed, on several occasions, her heart blocks her from completing her deadly assignments. On the film festival circuit, Hou won the award for Best Director at Cannes, amongst numerous other awards, and *The Assassin* was voted Best Film of 2015 in *Sight & Sound* magazine's film critics poll. Mark Lee Ping-bin's cinematography has been praised for its matchless 'compositional artistry' (Bradshaw 2016) and Wen-Ying Huang's production design for the 'visual extravagance of Oriental fantasies illuminated by brightly colored silk robes . . . and sensual atmosphere' (Young 2015). Yet for all its prodigious beauty, the film's plot has ultimately remained 'obscure' and 'impenetrable' to all but the initiated (Bradshaw 2016).

Figure 1.5 Vibrant colours and painterly image compositions in *The Assassin* (Hou Hsiao-Hsien, 2015) are a hallmark of exoticism.

'It is ravishing to watch – like being caressed by layers of precious silks,' writes Wendy Ide (2015) in *The Times*, but 'it is virtually impossible to unpick fully what is going on.'

This sense of enigma and mystery is due to complex family and political intrigues that are the mainstay of the narrative coupled with the fact that 'there are two actresses playing double roles' (Clarke 2016). The film's narrative thwarts a long list of (Western) spectators' expectations, such as the one-to-one match of actor and character, expository detail on the character constellations and their backstories, as well as *wuxia*'s generic conventions. Hou reduces the customary fast-paced battle scenes, which are the genre's main attraction, to just a few brief moments. Dynamic pace and action are replaced by an eerie stillness and languorous observational distance. These features jointly contribute to the film's impenetrability which, in turn, engenders a sense of enigma that amplifies its exotic allure by confirming the belief that the Other can never be fully fathomed.

The Assassin alongside other critically acclaimed films by Hou, notably *Hai shang hua* (Flowers of Shanghai, 1998), take the distinctive features of an exoticist aesthetic to their extreme and, in so doing, challenge the familiar critique levelled at global art cinema auteurs that they are pandering to the tastes of Western cinephiles, critics and film festival juries by creating exoticised representations of their own cultures. This prevalent criticism conceives of self-exoticism in world cinema as a form of cultural exhibitionism and a unidirectional practice that ostensibly proves the continued subjugation of the Global South under Western hegemony. While this argument cannot be dismissed *tout court*, it is more appropriate to conceive of self-exoticism in terms of multi-directional intercultural exchanges that follow a dialogic structure. Furthermore, we need to be careful not to take a homogenising approach to exotic world cinema and, instead, to attend to the diversity of its artistic expressions and agendas. It is perhaps not surprising that those films which have been internationally most successful in terms of winning critical acclaim and prizes at film festivals, such as Chen Kaige's *Ba wang bie ji* (Farewell My Concubine, 1993, winner of the Palme d'Or at the Cannes Film Festival in 1993 and nominee for Best Foreign Film at the Academy Awards in 1994) and Zhang Yimou's *Raise the Red Lantern* (winner of the Silver Lion in Venice and Foreign Language BAFTA in 1991 and nominee for Best Foreign Film at the Academy Awards in 1992) have attracted the most disparaging criticism for selling exotic images of China in the international film market, for reifying and commodifying Chinese culture, for betraying the Chinese nation and for wilfully surrendering to 'the dominant discourse of First World Culture' and 'Western cultural imperialism' (Lu 1997b: 128–9, see Zhang 2002: 251–3).

Hou's strategic self-exoticism, however, does not necessarily amount to a cultural sell-out or betrayal. Rather, narrative obliqueness, which precludes easy consumption, coupled with a hyperbolic exoticist visual style, represents a form of self-reflexivity that lays bare and deconstructs the parameters of the exotic gaze. This is a strategy Hou also uses in his earlier film *Flowers of Shanghai*, which purposely invokes the narrative and visual tropes of the Chinese exotic but ultimately subverts them.[21] Thus, *Flowers of Shanghai* draws on 'the most exotic of exoticised images of historical China, the cultivated "high-class" prostitutes' only to stage 'the agonizingly slow and unremarkable quality of their lives' (Kaldis 2016: 131).[22] The exotic-erotic-enigmatic Asian woman, frequently represented as a concubine, geisha, prostitute or simply the suffering wife of a much older oppressive husband, is a prominent ethnic stereotype in Asian cinema. It readily homogenises Chinese, Japanese, Korean, Vietnamese and other Asian women and is instantly legible as exotic. It has been deeply entrenched in the Western imaginary of the Orient ever since Pierre Loti conflated exoticism and eroticism. His immensely popular novel *Madame Chrysanthème* (1887) inspired Giacomo Puccini's opera *Madama Butterfly* (1904) and has served as a template of Asian femininity in the popular imagination of the West (see Heung 1997; Khoo 2007: 6).[23]

Set in four 'flower houses', or elegant brothels, in Shanghai's British Concession towards the end of the nineteenth century, the minimalist plot of *Flowers of Shanghai* paints a static and claustrophobic portrait of a quintessentially exotic Chinese milieu. Most dramatic conflicts, such as betrayal and infidelity, remain tantalisingly off-screen so that very little happens. In the secluded world of the flower houses (the sole setting of the entire film), the prostitutes and their clients attend lavish banquets, play games, smoke opium pipes and engage in endless conversations about quotidian events – yet they are never shown in amorous embraces or in the nude. Despite playing with the ethnic stereotype of the exotic-erotic Oriental woman, the film deliberately thwarts audience expectations. Atmosphere and ambience substitute action. The aestheticisation of the unremarkable tapestry of the everyday of a profoundly alien culture is one of the hallmarks of exoticism which betrays its affinity with ethnography (see Chapter 2).

Hou takes the embellishment of the ordinary to the extreme in this exotic period drama. The painterly style combines an excessively lavish *mise en scène*, with low key lighting, persistent colour harmonies between sets and costumes, and a predilection for long takes, with an average shot length of around 2.5 minutes. In a series of languorous slow panning shots and static tableaus, the camera caresses a proliferation of material objects on display, including antique Chinese porcelain vases and tea sets, golden and rose-coloured brocade curtains and upholstery, elegant wooden tables and bed steads. The ornate lattice work and stained glass of the windows prevent daylight from penetrating the interior of the brothels so that night and day become indistinguishable, creating an overall sense of timelessness and stasis. The ubiquitous tall-stemmed oil lamps and large candelabras emanate a soft golden light that enhances the exquisite beauty of the elegantly dressed and coiffeured courtesans.

Such is the overwhelming beauty of images, the entrancing atmosphere of decadence, the sense of an opium-induced reverie that the film implodes the visual codes of Chinese exoticism by pushing them to their hyperbolic extreme. Hou's self-conscious 'indulgence in *chinoiserie* . . . [with its] surfeit of visual details' (Udden 2017: 144) and narrative enigma represents a deconstruction of the exotic gaze and, as such, an *aesthetic* intervention into *critical* discourses on self-exoticism and the transnational commodification of the Other. Instead of replicating the cultural essentialism that underpins the old, Eurocentric exoticism, *Flowers of Shanghai* returns the exotic gaze. The film's hyper-exoticism, Nick Kaldis (2005: 130) suggests, '*embraces* exotic images of China, multiplies them, reproduces them, and fixates on them, smothering the (Western) viewer in an *excess* of Orientalist fantasy' (italics in original).

In sum, Hou's hyperbolic self-exoticism is a paradigmatic case of what Ashcroft has theorised as 'post-colonial transformation' and what Chow (1995: 166–72) has famously called the 'Oriental's orientalism' (bearing in mind the distinction between Orientalism and exoticism I have made above). She sees this strategy encapsulated in an iconic scene in *Ju Dou*, in which the protagonist Ju Dou (Gong Li) exposes her bruised and beaten naked body to the voyeuristic gaze of Tianqing (Baotian Li) – and to that of the spectator. What some film critics have interpreted as Zhang's fetishisation of the victimised and eroticised Oriental woman, is in fact a self-reflexive staging of an exotic stereotype. Rather than being a straightforward appropriation of the visual and narrative tropes of the old, Eurocentric Orientalism, 'the Oriental's orientalism' is first and foremost 'an exhibitionist self-display that contains, in its very excessive modes, a critique of the voyeurism of orientalism itself' (Chow 1995: 171). It is a new critical autoethnography, a performance intended to draw attention to the means of its own construction and, as such, constitutes an aesthetic intervention into the discourse of exoticism and its long history of representation.

Conclusion

This chapter set out to develop exoticism as a critical category and identify some of the most prominent discursive and aesthetic strategies exoticism deploys in constructing the exotic Other and the Self as Other. Perhaps the most salient points to note are that exoticism is a mode of aesthetic perception and representation that is simultaneously anchored in the cinematic text and elicited in the spectator in the process of reception. In order for exoticism to enable the kind of imaginative investment that replaces cultural authenticity with the construction of an idealised (or, conversely, threatening) form of alterity, it needs to traverse cultural borders. Exoticism, like world cinema and its transnational circulation and reception, is premised on mobility. Therefore, the exotic gaze, which transforms the objective fact of cultural difference into the discursive construct of cultural Otherness, is necessarily a view from the other side, reliant on the vantage point of the cultural outsider. Whether these outsiders are explorers or travellers who encounter the Other by journeying to the far-flung corners of the globe and inserting themselves into a foreign culture, or visitors who marvel at imported exotica exhibited in curiosity cabinets or museums, the exotic invariably involves a process of de- and recontextualisation, displacement and domestication. As the story of Zarafa, the giraffe, who was dislocated from the savannahs of Sudan to become a diplomatic gift and eventually a French fashion icon, illustrates, this process is profoundly transformative.

It has been one of my ambitions to open to scrutiny the contestations surrounding exoticism and to ascertain whether the decentring of exoticism in contemporary world cinema represents a form of recuperative transformation. By bringing exoticism into conversation with Orientalism, subtle yet significant distinctions emerge: both are Eurocentric discursive constructions of the Other that are tainted by the looming shadow of empire. Exoticism's denotative scope is wider, encompassing the natural world as well as culture, making Orientalism, alongside primitivism, a sub-category. Where Orientalism seeks to subjugate, exoticism wants to marvel at the Other; where Orientalism is about the power to dominate, exoticism is about the pleasure of difference. Conceiving of exoticism (and the corresponding practices of self-exoticisation and autoethnography) as cultural translation offers a framework for lightening its ideological baggage and shifting the focus of analysis onto more neutral terrain. Cultural translation offers a framework for investigating structural correspondences, such as the mechanisms of de- and recontextualisation, domestication and foreignisation, whose transformative dynamic results in creative reconfigurations and the generation of new meanings. Against this background, world cinema filmmakers emerge as the pre-eminent cultural mediators who interpret and negotiate between different cultures and their epistemes, making cross-cultural understanding possible. Actively pursuing the project of 'post-colonial transformation', these global auteurs acquire Western cultural capital to their own advantage and are adapt at operating within the frameworks of dominant discourses to negotiate and subvert them. Far from being victims of Western hegemony, they are skilful brokers of their own alterity – and self-exoticism is one of their most powerful strategies.

I have tried to delineate the contours and hallmarks of this contested and neglected aesthetic category by considering cinematic and other visual texts that have been identified as incontrovertibly exotic by scholars and critics. What emerged were the following distinctive features: exoticism's eclecticism and indifference to ethnographic accuracy which contravenes its perceived and proclaimed authenticity; its specular structure which serves as a projection surface for utopic desires; its recycling and repurposing of familiar tropes and, perhaps most importantly in the present context, its emphatic visuality which explains its natural affinity with the cinematic medium. In fact, the spectacularisation of the Other in human zoos and at the grand colonial exhibitions, the visible evidence provided by ethnographic photography and documentaries and early cinema's fascination with exotic locations all point to this innate affinity. It also manifests itself in the visual pleasure that exotic cinema, past and present, affords through its vivid chromatic design, visual plenitude, compositional harmony and the overall sensuous abundance it imparts. The visual, alongside other sensorial, pleasures afforded by exotic cinema's sumptuous style compensate for the hermeneutic deficits that arise when world cinema travels and is watched and translated into multiple, locally specific idioms by global spectators.

Exoticism's emphatic visuality is not merely an innocent delight. Rather, it beguiles the beholder to ignore what dark layers of social injustice, domination and exploitation may lie underneath and be purposely obscured. This mechanism of concealment is certainly present in the old, colonial exoticism and continues to operate in Eurocentric exotic films, especially of the kind I consider in Chapter 3. The new, decentred exoticism of world cinema, however, inverts exoticism's tendency to conceal and camouflage by deploying its seductiveness strategically with the aim of engendering spectatorial desire and, in so doing, bring social and historical injustices and a host of humanitarian issues to public attention.

Finally, it seemed imperative for me to interrogate two postulations that have gained wide currency in scholarship on world cinema of the exotic variety. The first hypothesis assumes that imperial habits of seeing and being seen have left an indelible imprint on postcolonial subjectivities. In film studies, this idea has been advanced most prominently by Rey Chow in relation to Fifth Generation Chinese cinema, a quintessentially exotic type of world cinema, when she argues that Chinese directors such as Chen Kaige, Zhang Yimou and others – and by extension world cinema filmmakers more broadly – have been conditioned to see themselves through Western eyes. As I hope to demonstrate in this book, however, world cinema filmmakers are marked by imperial habits of seeing and being seen, but they are not constrained by it. The sheer aesthetic diversity of world cinema seems to suggest that self-exoticism is a strategic choice rather than the inevitable consequence of having internalised the state of being looked at. In fact, Chow's influential concept of the Oriental's orientalism supports my argument that self-exoticism in world cinema is a conscious, deliberate and strategic performance.

The second widely held assumption is that global cinema auteurs exoticise their own cultures to pander to the tastes and expectations of Western critics, cinephiles and festival juries. Although this allegation cannot be dismissed entirely, the intercultural dynamics at play are more complex and do not simply follow the binary logic of centre and periphery that is so deeply entrenched in the popular imagination. Instead, as the above discussion of *The Assassin* and *Flowers of Shanghai* demonstrates, the critical performance of the exotic gaze has the capacity to expose and transform the paradigms by which the West has, for centuries, constructed its Other. It therefore represents a form of resistance and a tactic to decolonise the lens.

Notes

1. A particularly prominent example of this colonial practice was the display of Saartje Baartman, known as 'Hottentot Venus', on the entertainment circuit in so-called 'freak shows' in early nineteenth-century England and France. She became a sensation on account of her large protruding buttocks and the rumoured peculiarities of her genitalia, which are, to this day, preserved and displayed in the ethnographic Musée de l'Homme in Paris! See Hall (1997: 264–9), Gilman (1985: 88–91) and Boetsch and Blanchard (2008). Hobson (2018) traces cultural representations of contemporary black women's bodies back to Baartman's hyper-sexualised and exoticised body. The feature film *Venus Noire* (Black Venus, 2010) by the Maghrebi French director Abdellatif Kechiche tells the story of her humiliation and degradation, albeit not without courting controversy for replicating the ethnographic voyeurism it tries to expose.

2. Greenblatt (1990: 29) discusses these historical *Wunderkammern* or 'wonder-cabinets' in relation to the aesthetic experience of wonder in contemporary contexts, notably curatorial practices in museums.
3. See Majer (2009–10), Sharkey (2015) and Sund (2019: 18), who provide accounts of Zarafa's impact on fashion. Allin's novel (1998) and Rémy Bezançon and Jean-Christophe Lie's animated film *Zarafa* (2012) give fictionalised accounts of the famous giraffe. Sund (2019: 9–10) cites a similar fascination with a 'real unicorn', a rhinoceros named Miss Clara, that was imported to Europe by the Dutch East India Company in the mid-eighteenth century and that also sparked a fashion trend.
4. For an in-depth discussion of Segalen's *Essay on Exoticism* and its significance for discourses on exoticism, see Forsdick (2000).
5. Like most scholars, Clifford (1988: 256) uses the terms interchangeably, when he describes Said's *Orientalism* as 'a critical study of Western knowledge about the exotic'. Similarly, Grijp (2009: 91–6) includes a discussion of Orientalist paintings by Ingres, Delacroix, Fromentin, Gérome and Ziem in a chapter about the search for the exotic in Western art.
6. According to Mason (1998: 167), in eighteenth-century France, the use of the term 'exotic' was confined to that of an epithet qualifying unfamiliar flora or rare objects from foreign places, while the noun 'exoticism' was linked to the discovery of the New World.
7. I owe this felicitous turn of phrase to Song Hwee Lim.
8. Captain Cook, however, adamantly refuted that his crew partook in the natives' polygamous way of life; see Porter (1990: 130) and Connell (2003).
9. Segalen's (2002: 44) diary entry about Tahiti reads: 'The whole island came to me like a woman. And, in fact, I had from women there such offerings as one no longer receives in any country nowadays.'
10. Todorov's (1993: 342–52) chapter on exoticism in *On Human Diversity* includes a taxonomy of ten types of cross-cultural interaction, including tourism, exile and exoticism.
11. In the essay 'The Exotic as a Symbolic System', Foster (1982: 23–5) notes that travellers to foreign lands generally perceive 'exotic milieus [as] quintessentially permissive'. He comments on Gustave Flaubert's journey to Egypt in 1849, where the French writer immersed himself in the delights of coffee houses and brothels, whose 'alternate (and more wondrous?) forms of sexuality . . . are one of the meanings of the exotic'.
12. Despite briefly mentioning 'exoticizing translation' as a third category, Venuti (2018: xiii, 163) does not theorise the concept beyond noting that its superficiality and predilection for ethnic stereotyping tend to elicit 'sympathetic identification . . . and an unreflective response that lacks critical detachment'. These remarks suggest that Venuti fully subscribes to the widespread short-shrift dismissal of exoticism.
13. Cf. Carbonell's (1996: 89) exploration of exoticism and cultural translation, where he notes: 'Exoticism constitutes a semiotic model imposed from *within*

a culture [onto another] from a one-sided, biased perspective' (italics in original).

14. According to Hinrichsen (2012: 63–5), the original poster design showed a racially mixed Antillaise woman with a Madras scarf in lush exotic setting pouring out the allegedly beneficial and nourishing drink, utilising the overtly exotic connotations of France's colonial empire. In 1915, she was replaced by the image of a jolly Sengalese infantryman in uniform, and the drink was promoted as a nourishing drink for soldiers during World War One.

15. It is worth noting that Ashcroft (2001: 32) includes Bollywood cinema amongst his examples of textual resistance, proposing that it appropriates a First World medium, cinema, with the desire for self-empowerment.

16. Elsewhere, Chow (1995: 182–3) makes the point that any form of cultural translation is by its very nature contaminated through cross-cultural exchange. Cultural translation, she argues, is a form of distortion, even betrayal: 'Etymologically, the word translation is linked, among other things, to "tradition" on the one hand and to "betrayal" on the other. The Italian expression *Tradutore, traditore* – "Translator, traitor"' – allows us to grasp the pejorative implication of infidelity that is often associated with the task of translating . . . And yet the word *tradition* itself, linked in its roots to translation and betrayal, has to do with handing over. Tradition itself is nothing if it is not a transmission. How is tradition to be transmitted, to be passed on, if not through translation?' (italics in original).

17. Ashcroft (2001: 10) distinguishes between 'postcolonial' without and 'post-colonial' with a hyphen: 'The hyphen puts an emphasis on the discursive and material effects of the historical "fact" of colonialism, while the term "postcolonialism" has come to represent an increasingly indiscriminate attention to cultural difference and marginality of all kinds, whether a consequence of the historical experience of colonialism or not.' I will use 'postcolonial' without a hyphen in this book, unless I cite Ashcroft directly.

18. See <https://www.salaambaalaktrust.com/> (last accessed 15 May 2022) for information about the Salaam Balak Trust. Cynics might argue that the activities of the Salaam Balak Trust commodify the plight of the street children it supports. In 2007, the trust launched a city walk programme in which deprived urban youth act as tour guides showing tourists areas of social deprivation to 'sensitise participants about street life, street children and Indian society problems; and uniquely engages them in the lives of children in distress. During the walk, the guides share their personal story of survival with the participants and show them the contact points and shelter homes SBT provides'. Available at <https://www.consciousjourneys.com/en/works/salaam-baalak-trust/> (last accessed 15 May 2022).

19. Mehta has acknowledged that Ray's *Apu Trilogy* and the photography of McCurry and Singh have served as blueprints for *Water*; see Hopgood (2006: 145) and Chaudhuri (2009: 11).

20. The original shoot of *Water* in Varanasi in 2000 had to be aborted because 'a mob incited by the Rashtriya Swayamsevak Sangh (an organisation linked to the then-ruling right-wing Hindu nationalist party Bharatiya Janata Party (BJP)) destroyed the set in Varanasi and conveyed death threats to Mehta and her crew' (Chaudhuri 2009: 7). Mehta subsequently shot *Water* in secrecy and under a different title in Sri Lanka, which stands in for Varanasi. The concept of 'dark heritage cinema', derived from 'dark tourism', refers to heritage films about traumatic historical events, notably the Holocaust; see Koepnick (2002), Chaudhuri (2014) and Cooke (2016).
21. Even so, *Flowers of Shanghai*, which alongside Taiwanese funding, received significant transnational production funding from Japan, proved far more successful with transnational audiences than domestic ones. Udden (2017: 142) even asks whether the film was ever intended for Taiwanese audiences. After its nomination for Best Film at the Cannes Film Festival in 1998 and winning the award for Best Art Direction, as well as the Jury Award at the Golden Horse Film Festival in Taipei, it played for two months in Parisian cinemas but only briefly in Taipei.
22. There are numerous other exotic films set in Chinese brothels, including the popular Hollywood film *The World of Suzie Wong* (Richard Quine, 1960) set in 1950s Hong Kong about a prostitute with a heart of gold; *Yim ji kau* (Rouge, Stanley Kwan, 1987) about a doomed love affair between a wealthy young man and a prostitute in a 1930s Hong Kong brothel; the tripartite film *Zuihao de shiguang* (Three Times, Hou Hsiao-Hsien, 2005) contains a segment, 'A Time for Freedom', which revolves around a courtesan's wish to be bought out of the brothel and become her patron's concubine. Like the Hollywood box-office hit *Memoirs of a Geisha*, which is set in a Japanese geisha house before World War Two, these films are invariably set in the past, combine nostalgia with exoticism and depict brothels as refined milieus of conviviality. A common theme is the tension between the professional promiscuity of the prostitutes and their fidelity, loyalty and even love of their favoured client. Lu (2016), who provides a broad overview of the figure of the prostitute in Chinese-language cinema, does not sufficiently develop the important distinction between these idealised Chinese prostitutes of the past and modern-day sex workers in films like *Durian Durian* (Fruit Chan, 2000).
23. David Cronenberg's film *M. Butterfly* (1993), based on a play and screenplay by David Henry Hwang, plays with this stereotype, making the object of the French civil servant René Gallimard's (Jeremy Irons) desire, the opera performer Song Liling (John Lone), a man, mistaken for a woman. Gallimard is either unaware or in wilful denial that traditionally female roles were performed by men at the Peking opera.

CHAPTER 2

Ethnographic Salvage and Cosmopolitan Exoticism

This chapter focuses on one of the most enduring tropes of exoticism, ethnographic salvage. The project of ethnographic salvage was widely pursued by early twentieth-century anthropologists who sought to rescue remote, 'authentic' cultures from the ravages of historical change and, ultimately, from disappearance. The salvage paradigm has been particularly prevalent in anthropological accounts of 'primitive', 'tribal' or 'native' people, who were perceived not only to be at the bottom rung of the evolutionary ladder but also to inhabit a 'time other than the present of the producers of anthropological discourse' (Fabian 1983: 31). This 'denial of coevalness', as Johannes Fabian (1983: 31) puts it in *Time and the Other*, relegates the ethnographic Other to a distinctive temporality that, in its alleged unchanging, static pastness, starkly contrasts with the modern, dynamic time of the anthropologist.[1] Associated in particular with Indigenous peoples, who are posited to exist 'just prior to the present' (Clifford 1989: 74), their contact with and entry into the modern world is feared to jeopardise their cultural authenticity. Nowhere is the idea that contact equals contamination – and the concomitant threat of extinction – more poignantly illustrated than in the recent plea of the famous photojournalist Sebastião Salgado to protect the Amazon's Indigenous peoples from the COVID-19 pandemic in 2020, which was imported by illegal loggers, gold miners and tourists to the region: 'Just in the Brazilian Amazon we have 103 indigenous groups which have never been contacted – they represent humanity's pre-history,' Salgado wrote. 'We cannot allow all of this to disappear' (Salgado 2020).[2]

Nostalgically imagined as the antipode of modernity and global capitalism, indigeneity has gained increased attention in the West, a phenomenon also reflected in the growing visibility and critical acclaim of Indigenous cinema or Fourth Cinema, over the past twenty to thirty years.[3] The term 'Fourth Cinema' was coined by Māori filmmaker Barry Barclay in an influential short essay published in 2003, where he discusses the global 'emergence of feature-length art cinema by indigenous peoples' that reflects a sustained engagement with local cultures rather than national ones (cited in Mackenzie and Westerstahl-Stenport 2015: 8–9).[4] What distinguishes contemporary Indigenous cinema from early twentieth-century ethnographic documentaries, both scientific and popular, and from mainstream films about Native Americans, such as *Dances with Wolves* (Kevin Kostner, 1990) and *The Last of the Mohicans* (Michael Mann, 1992); about Australian Aborigines in *Walkabout* (Nicolas Roeg, 1971) and *Rabbit-Proof Fence* (Phillip Noyce, 2002); and about Māori in New Zealand, such as *Whale Rider* (Niki Caro, 2002), is that they attest to Indigenous communities' successful struggle for self-representation. They bring Indigenous oral storytelling traditions, belief systems and cultural memories on to the screen and to the attention of their own local communities while at the same time targeting national and transnational cinephile audiences.

In this chapter I will explore how films made by Indigenous filmmakers, mostly in close collaboration with majority culture filmmakers, appropriate Eurocentric ethnographic accounts of their past in an attempt to reclaim their cultural memory. In particular, I am interested in unravelling the relationship between local authenticity and exoticism. If, as Salman Rushdie (1992a: 67) has proposed, nowadays local authenticity is 'the respectable child of old-fashioned exoticism', then this may be due to the fact that the local – and especially in combination with the concept of authenticity – is often celebrated as a 'site of resistance to capital and the location for imagining alternative possibilities' that call the imperatives of global capitalism into question (Dirlik 1996: 22). In other words, whereas exoticism carries overwhelmingly pejorative connotations, local authenticity appears to be at the opposite end of the spectrum, being associated with postcolonial resistance and several other positive attributes, as I shall illustrate. Although it may be tempting to simply replace the problematic concept of exoticism by the ostensibly appealing concept of local authenticity, in terms of aesthetics and affective resonance, exotic and locally authentic films exhibit significant differences, as the close analysis of *Atanarjuat: The Fast Runner*, *Ten Canoes*, *Embrace of the Serpent* and *Tanna* will reveal. What these films that are set in the far-flung corners of the earth – the Canadian Arctic, north-western Australia, the Amazon and Melanesia – have in common is that they evoke what Alison Griffiths (2002: xix) describes as the 'iconography of savagery', characterised by 'nudity, spears, decorative feathers [and] animated dancing', which is a staple of ethnographic representations of Indigenous peoples. This familiar codification makes the spectacle of alterity legible and accessible to cultural outsiders. Furthermore, to a greater or lesser degree, the films domesticate Indigeneity's 'wondrous difference' (Griffiths 2002) by embedding it in universal narratives about love, jealousy, revenge or cross-cultural encounters, thereby conforming to one of the distinctive strategies of exoticism outlined in Chapter 1. Yet despite appropriating the visual tropes of ethnographic photography and film, these autoethnographic texts do not perpetuate old imperialist ideologies but instead promote a cosmopolitan agenda.

In conceptualising cosmopolitan exoticism, I argue that the Indigenous films examined in this chapter differ profoundly from their ethnographic precursors, which sought to convey Western knowledge about the ethnographic Other. By contrast, this new type of exotic cinema challenges and decentres Western values and systems of knowledge by assuming what Māori scholar Linda Tuhiwai Smith (2012: 244) terms an 'Indigenizing' perspective that invites audiences to see the world through Indigenous eyes. These films are exotic insofar as they mobilise familiar visual and narrative tropes of the ethnographic Other only to align them with cosmopolitan values, notably the promotion of cross-cultural dialogue, the recuperation of Indigenous cultural memory, the empowerment of hitherto marginalised communities and ecological issues.

The Quest for Authenticity

When, a few years ago, I tried to persuade the World Cinema Fund at the International Berlin Film Festival to collaborate with me on a research project on exoticism in world cinema, I encountered a mixture of enthusiasm and hesitation. Exoticism, even in its decentred, contemporary manifestations in world cinema, was clearly a concept with which the then festival director, Dieter Kosslick, did not want to tarnish the reputation of his festival fund as the following email indicates:

> I am delighted to learn that one of the Berlin Film Festival's initiatives [the World Cinema Fund] meets with such interest amongst the academic community. It is the World Cinema Fund's mission to support films that *portray local cultures authentically* rather than producing films that instill a vague *longing for exotic countries and customs* in European and North American audiences. We have managed to stay true to this distinctive feature of our festival films and we are pleased that you appreciate this. (Berghahn and Kosslick 2016; my italics)

Kosslick's 'clarifying' remark, just like Rushdie's above-cited comment, indicates that 'local authenticity' is increasingly deployed as the politically correct alternative to the ideologically problematic 'exotic'. Though not synonymous, both concepts project a desired elsewhere onto cultures imagined as geographically and/or temporally remote. The preoccupation with and longing for disappearing worlds, and the intention to salvage them, is an integral part not just of the quest for authenticity but also of the exotic. According to Chris Bongie (1991: 6), exoticism is 'a story about loss (the loss of tradition, the loss of alternatives, the loss of the possibility of an "authentic experience")'. The project of ethnographic salvage seeks to rescue the disappearing object by reclaiming it textually.

The growing interest in Indigeneity partly arises from the cultural cachet that authenticity has accrued in contemporary Western societies. Pronouncing something as authentic validates contemporary consumption practices, ranging from locally harvested food over tourism and arts and crafts (see Fillitz and Saris 2012). Authenticity, often put in inverted commas, as if this would dispense with any requirement to define it, literally denotes 'the quality of being authentic', 'genuine', 'true' and 'of undisputed origin' (*OED*). The search for authenticity usually directs us to geographically remote cultures or those on the margins of our own society since authenticity, like the exotic, is deemed to exist somewhere outside the realm of our own experience. It springs from the perception that today's hypermobile world has become deracinated, hybridised, homogenised and therefore 'inauthentic' and, conversely, the belief that supposedly less advanced cultures, especially those with deep attachments to a circumscribed locality and close ties to nature, have remained untrammelled by historical change and cultural hybridisation. 'What counts as "authentic"', Linda Tuhiwai Smith (2012: 142) argues, 'is used by the West as one of the criteria to determine who really is indigenous, who is worth saving, who is still innocent and free from Western contamination.' Graham Huggan (2001: 156, 158) goes one step further, proposing that this 'cult of authenticity', is not so much about salvaging '"authentic" cultures from the threat of dissipation, contingency and loss', as it is about catering to 'dominant culture's needs'. In light of these considerations, authenticity, despite its ostensibly positive connotations, emerges as yet another strategy by which dominant cultures both contain, commodify and control Indigenous cultures.

In the context of postcolonial studies, authenticity has attracted a great deal of attention and criticism. Typically associated with the recuperation of pre-colonial traditions, it becomes entangled in essentialist and nativist positions that valorise stable cultural practices as authentically Indigenous and critique extraneous influences as sources of contamination and hybridisation. Gareth Griffiths (1994: 70–1), for example, cautions against the dangers involved in contemporary claims for an 'authentic voice' since the discourse of authenticity is actually 'an act of "liberal" discursive violence, parallel in many ways to the inscription of the "native" (indigene) under the sign of the savage'. In this sense, authenticity, not unlike exoticism, is a discursive formation imposed by white dominant culture upon those communities it purports to represent and defend. However, Griffiths (1994: 76) concedes, that Indigenous *self-representation* can potentially be a recuperative strategy insofar as it empowers Indigenous peoples to recover 'their own tongues and cultures'. Whether projected from the outside or actively appropriated by Indigenous peoples, 'recuperative autoethnography' (Huggan 2001: 43) runs the risk of fetishising Indigeneity by re-enacting precisely those cultural stereotypes that white settler societies have imposed upon Indigenous peoples. The contemporary cult of authenticity encourages Indigenous filmmakers, writers and other artists to *perform* their supposedly authentic selves (typically imagined as prior to 'first contact') in a bid for audiences beyond their own ethnic and local constituencies. As Mary Louise Pratt (2008: 9) has demonstrated, such autoethnographic texts are never '"authentic" or autochthonous forms of self-representation' since they arise 'in dialogue with metropolitan representations' and, therefore, appropriate 'the idioms of the conqueror'. Consequently, autoethnographic texts are hybrid and, as such, the very opposite of authentic.

The performance of authenticity, while appearing to be a route to enhanced visibility and emancipation, can be a trap since it encourages Indigenous communities to capitalise on their cultural heritage, their ancient customs and traditions, thereby becoming fetish objects instead of agents of socio-political change. By actively participating in the project of ethnographic salvage and preserving the relics of a vanishing world, Indigenous filmmakers run the risk of getting stuck in a de-historicised past instead of using the access to self-representation, over which they have struggled so long, as a means to articulate the political goals of the present. Preserving the past instead of changing the future is potentially a form of disempowerment that denies Indigenous filmmakers, writers and other artists a culture that is alive and changing.

The construction of the Indigenous Other as inherently authentic goes back to the imperial narratives of classic anthropology which were as much concerned with providing supposedly scientifically accurate accounts of native tribes as with negotiating Self–Other relations. The alleged authenticity of Indigenous people, which situates them outside global networks of exchange, continues to shape the Indigenous imaginary until the present day. It functions simultaneously as an object of nostalgic desire and as a currency in the marketplace of cultural difference.⁵ For example, for a work of art to qualify as authentic, it simply needs to be genuine or original, whereas Indigenous art needs to meet an additional criterion. 'It needs to be made by the Indigenous community to whom it is attributed in accordance with traditional practices, a form of nativism that does not apply to artworks of white majority cultures' (Grijp 2012: 138). In the context of cinema, ethnographic documentaries about Indigenous peoples are widely perceived as authentic, regardless of authorship. Thus, Robert Flaherty's 'documentary' about an Inuit family, *Nanook of the North* (1922) has become a 'touchstone for ongoing debates concerning questions of authenticity – and the depiction of racial and cultural difference'. In fact, 'Flaherty's reputation as "ontological realist" [André Bazin] stems as much from the status of the Ethnographic Other as inherently authentic' (Geiger 2005: 119, 117) as from the tacit equation of ethnographic realism and authenticity.⁶

The films under consideration in this chapter foreground their ethnographic credentials as an overt strategy to assert their claim to local authenticity. In contrast to early twentieth-century ethnographic documentaries,⁷ whether scientific or commercial, or Flaherty's fake documentary *Nanook of the North*, in contemporary Indigenous films, the impetus to preserve and recuperate ancient traditions arises from *within* Indigenous communities themselves. In press notes, the making-of documentaries and interviews, Indigenous filmmakers like Zacharias Kunuk and Peter Djigirr explain that through their films they want to pass on their cultural memory to the next generation while at the same time making their heritage known to global audiences. This is typically achieved through cross-cultural collaboration with non-Indigenous directors, scriptwriters and cinematographers who act as cultural mediators and translators, being attuned to metropolitan tastes and expectations. Consequently, they are more adept at accessing funding opportunities outside the 'media reservations' (Ginsburg 2003: 828), with their forbiddingly small production budgets, to which Indigenous artists are all too often confined.

According to Maria Rovisco (2012), the kind of cross-cultural creative collaborations and modes of production which enable hitherto marginalised social groups to gain access to self-representation, are a constitutive feature of cosmopolitan cinema. In the broadest sense, cosmopolitan cinema is defined as reflecting a cosmopolitan outlook through the representation of marginalised Others, such as ethnic minorities, migrants, and other socially and politically disenfranchised groups, and through promoting engagement with other cultures via film on an institutional level, for example through designated funding initiatives and film festivals (see Mulvey et al. 2017: 3). In order to understand what constitutes a cosmopolitan outlook, it will be necessary to define cosmopolitanism and explore how it relates to exoticism.

Cosmopolitanism and Exoticism

What cosmopolitanism has in common both with the ethnographer's quest for remote, authentic cultures and exoticism's fascination with alterity is a positive disposition towards cultural difference. But whereas exoticism depends on the maintenance of cultural boundaries lest cultural difference be preserved, cosmopolitanism has been described as a form of 'cultural ambidexterity – the condition of inhabiting two [or more] distinct cultures' (Dharwadker 2011: 140). Both concepts have experienced revived scholarly interest in recent years since the dynamics of globalisation have profoundly changed the configurations of Self and Other, necessitating a critical reassessment of these partially overlapping concepts. Thanks to its greater interdisciplinary relevance and its undeniable appeal (for who would not want to be a 'citizen of the world'?), cosmopolitanism has attracted significantly more scholarly attention than exoticism, a concept whose pejorative overtones have inhibited the same kind of extensive scholarly engagement.

According to Ulf Hannerz (1996: 103), cosmopolitanism is 'an orientation, a willingness to engage with the Other. It entails an intellectual and aesthetic openness toward divergent cultural experiences, a search for contrast rather than uniformity.' It requires certain cultural competencies that enable the cosmopolitan to manoeuvre within different environments and access and interpret unfamiliar systems of meaning. These skills exceed those of the average tourist or the mere consumer of global exotica – and explain why cosmopolitanism is often denounced as elitist.[8] In many respects, the cosmopolitan's positive disposition towards the different cultures is not dissimilar from that of the ethnographer who observes, tries to interpret and understand other cultures or, indeed, the '"exot" ... a traveller in exotic worlds, living, collecting and recording exotic difference' (Kapferer 2013: 819).

At first glance, these considerations seem to suggest that exoticism, denoting a particular mode of aesthetic perception and representation, and cosmopolitanism, referring to 'an intellectual and aesthetic stance of openness toward divergent cultural experiences [and] an appreciation of cultural diversity', exhibit significant overlap, making a clear demarcation of the terms difficult (Cohen and Vertovec 2002: 13). Yet at closer inspection it transpires that cosmopolitanism is a far more polymorphous concept than exoticism. Cohen and Vertovec differentiate no less than six rubrics:

> (a) a socio-cultural condition; (b) a kind of philosophy or world-view; (c) a political project towards building transnational institutions; (d) a political project for recognizing multiple identities; (e) an attitudinal or dispositional orientation; and/or (f) a mode of practice or competence. (Cohen and Vertovec 2002: 9)

Such is the complexity of the term that scholars have felt the need to narrow it down by prefacing it with modifiers such as 'discrepant' (Clifford 1992), 'rooted' (Appiah 2005), 'visceral' (Nava 2007), 'vernacular' (Bhabha 1996; Werbner 2006), 'aesthetic' (Urry 1995), 'decolonial' (Mignolo 2011), and countless more. Clearly, this is not the place to trace the scholarly debates that have surrounded this proliferating concept in recent years in depth. Instead, my primary concern here is to identify how exoticism and cosmopolitanism intersect.

Whereas cosmopolitanism's empathetic engagement with cultural difference is anti-essentialist, exoticism's discursive construction of Otherness relies on cultural essentialism. Another important distinction arises from the different ideological premises with which these concepts are customarily associated. Cosmopolitanism is closely allied to the project of European Enlightenment and, in particular, to the German philosopher Immanuel Kant, who postulated the normative ideal of a cosmopolitan order and a universal civic society in a series of essays written around the time of the French Revolution.[9] Kant's moral cosmopolitanism is based on the premise that reason is a capacity shared by all human beings and that this universal quality makes them members of a single moral community. As equal members of such a universal brotherhood of mankind, all human beings should enjoy the same rights, freedom and equality.[10] This ethico-political imperative also informs contemporary conceptualisations of cosmopolitanism, which emphasise the need for solidarity and the obligations we have towards the distant Other, the respect for human dignity and diversity and a commitment to promote universal equality amongst all world citizens (see Appiah 2006; Skrbiš and Woodward 2013).

Evidently, the ethic precepts of cosmopolitanism are incompatible with ideologies that promote racial difference as a justification for hierarchies of power, such as slavery and colonial exploitation. It is here where exoticism – at least in its old colonial and imperialist forms – and cosmopolitanism fundamentally differ. For centuries, exotic spectacle and the fascination it arouses has served as a decoy to conceal inequities of power between the West and its Others. Although contemporary exotic cinema has not entirely succeeded in diffusing its colonial legacy, it has nevertheless come a long way in dissociating itself from the tainted discourses of colonialism and imperialism with which it has been entwined by aligning itself with various cosmopolitan agendas. According to Maria Rovisco (2012: 149), contemporary cosmopolitan cinema is defined as a 'cross-cultural practice [and] a mode of production' characterised by 'particular aesthetic and ethico-political underpinnings' that has arisen in the contemporary context of multi-directional global mobilities and border crossings. Indebted to Anthony Kwame Appiah's notion of cosmopolitanism as a moral obligation towards the perils of the distant Other, with whom we share neither kinship nor citizenship, Rovisco proposes that cosmopolitan cinema aims to promote a deeper understanding of different cultures, while at the same time engendering greater sensitivity and active solidarity with the plight of distant Others.[11] She takes further cues from Appiah (2005: xiii), who argues that cosmopolitan ethics takes seriously

> the value not just of human life but of particular human lives, which means taking an interest in the practices and beliefs that lend them significance. People are different, the cosmopolitan knows, and there is much to learn from our differences.

Thus, cosmopolitan cinema facilitates the process of learning from our differences by giving those whose access to the public sphere is severely limited the opportunity to speak for themselves. What this means in concrete terms is that those communities hitherto silenced, marginalised or excluded altogether from self-representation are empowered by becoming active collaborators or even the chief agents in the construction of their own images.

In what follows, I will examine how the four films negotiate between exotic and cosmopolitan sensibilities and the discourse of (local) authenticity. I will pay particular attention to the authenticating and legitimising accounts that are provided in the films' extensive paratextual materials, such as press kits, DVD bonus materials and accompanying books, as they construct elaborate narratives of the ethnographic fieldwork that underpinned the making of these films. Furthermore, the Indigenous crew and cast's enthusiastic endorsement of the cross-cultural collaboration with majority culture filmmakers invalidate potential charges of cultural appropriation. By comparing *Atanarjuat* and *Ten Canoes* with *Tanna* and *Embrace of the Serpent*, I aim to illustrate that cosmopolitan exoticism is not a monolithic mode of representation. Rather, in terms of their aesthetic strategies, the films occupy different positions on a broad and fluid spectrum ranging from the ethnographic realism with which the austere living conditions of the Inuit in the Canadian Arctic are depicted to the exotic spectacle that conjures up visions of an abundant South Sea paradise.

The Transnational Turn of Indigenous Cinema: *Atanarjuat: The Fast Runner* and *Ten Canoes*

When *Atanarjuat* won the Caméra d'Or at the Cannes Film Festival in 2001, it was widely celebrated as a watershed for Indigenous cinema.[12] It was the first Indigenous-language film to be awarded the prestigious prize, and it went on to sweep up a string of other national and international awards, becoming Canada's highest grossing film in 2001 (see Bessire 2003: 832). Although sharing a commitment to collective authorship and the preservation of Indigenous language and cultural memory with other Indigenous films, what accounts for *Atanarjuat*'s transnational resonance and critical acclaim is its ambivalent status as both autoethnographic document and art film. The transnational appeal of this Arctic epic is, in no small measure, due to what Harald Prins (1997: 244) has called the 'paradox of primitivism' to denote the deployment of familiar primitivist imagery with the aim of gaining access to global exhibition and distribution channels and, thereby, an international arena to promote political goals. This form of strategic exoticism, which mobilises tropes of colonialism and exploration but puts them in the service of a cosmopolitan ethics, underpins, to a greater or lesser extent, all four films under consideration in this chapter. However, before developing this idea in more detail, it is necessary to examine what exactly made this Inuit-produced film, with a run time of nearly three hours and a fairly obscure plot, so exceptionally successful both with local Inuit audiences in Nunavut, where it was shot, as well as with North American and transnational cinephiles.

In contrast to most Indigenous films that target local Indigenous communities and are primarily instruments of political advocacy or intended to strengthen Indigenous communities' sense of identity and social cohesion, *Atanarjuat*'s crossover appeal was part of a skilful strategy that combined a commitment to local authenticity with a degree of multicultural fluency. Although promoted as an Indigenous production by the Igloolik Isuma production company, it actually involved the collaboration of Inuit director Zacharias Kunuk and the late scriptwriter Paul Apak Angilirq with non-Indigenous creative partners, notably the director of photography Norman Cohn. Not unlike the Australian, Hong Kong-based DOP Christopher Doyle, who has created a distinctive 'Asian aesthetics' that resonates with transnational audiences, Cohn, too, acted as cultural mediator by making the sublime Arctic landscape and the crisp northern light the

ETHNOGRAPHIC SALVAGE AND COSMOPOLITAN EXOTICISM 69

film's chief attraction. This is reflected in a number of international film reviews, that laud *Atanarjuat*'s 'singular beauty' (Campbell 2001), 'terrific [look] due to the exceptional light so near the North Pole' (Nesselson 2001) and its 'dozen distinct shades of white' (Scott 2002), which invite cultural outsiders to experience a sense of wide-eyed wonder just like explorers did when they first set foot on the vast expanse of ice and snow close to the Arctic Circle. Whereas many low-budget Indigenous films are made solely in Indigenous languages, the screenplay of *Atanarjuat* was written in two versions, one Inuktitut and the other English. This enabled Isuma to top up the modest ring-fenced funding allocated to Indigenous filmmaking by attracting additional funding, not normally accessible to Indigenous productions which tend to rely on advocacy organisations, regional or state public bodies, or are entirely self-funded (see Ginsburg 2003: 829; Knopf 2008: 317). Bigger budgets readily translate into higher production values that make it possible for Indigenous films to be appreciated for their artistic merits rather than solely as ethnographic documents or as instruments of political advocacy.[13]

Atanarjuat represents a marked step change from earlier phases of Indigenous filmmaking which has gained momentum since the 1960s throughout the American continent, New Zealand, Australia and parts of northern Europe. Indigenous self-representation on screen is part and parcel of an encompassing political movement that James Clifford has termed 'Indigènitude' in analogy to the *négritude* movement of the 1950s, an alliance of black activists who recognised commonalities of culture, history and political potential, when they embarked on a process of recovering their shared experiences of colonial and postcolonial histories.

'Like *négritude*, Indigènitude is a vision of liberation and cultural difference that challenges, or at least redirects, the modernizing agendas of nation-states and transnational capitalism' (Clifford 2013: 16). It manifests itself in different forms and projects of activism, including the revival of local traditions, the renewal of Indigenous languages and concrete political goals, notably sovereignty and land claims. The vast Inuit-governed region of Nunavut in north-eastern Canada, which was created in 1999, is a particularly significant achievement. These important political struggles culminated in the United Nations Declaration of the Rights of Indigenous Peoples in 2007, which formalised Indigenous peoples' demands for political inclusion globally.

The establishment of film and video training workshops where Indigenous communities acquire the skills of visual self-representation is but one aspect of the gradual empowerment of Indigenous peoples around the world. The increased affordability and availability of media technologies, such as portable video cameras and VCRs, has put Indigenous peoples in control of their own images. It has allowed them to 'talk back on their own terms to those who might have presumed to speak for them' (Ginsburg 1995: 68). The collectively authored and produced projects that arise from such workshops are mainly geared towards local audiences and offer counter-narratives to official reports on national media by reflecting Indigenous perspectives on territorial disputes over Indigenous land, human rights abuses and similar politically sensitive matters. Notwithstanding their overtly local origins and themes, some of these Indigenous films enter transnational exhibition via Indigenous film festivals or festival strands. There are now over sixty-five festivals worldwide that showcase Indigenous cinema (see Córdova 2012: 73). Some of the better-known ones include The Smithsonian Institution's Native American Film and Video Festival, the Latin American Indigenous People's Film Festival, imagineNATIVE Film + Media Arts Festival and permanent sections at international film festivals, for example at Sundance, Morelia and Amiens.[14]

Atanarjuat was developed by the world's first majority Inuit-owned film and video production company Igloolik Isuma Productions, which was co-founded by the director Kunuk, cinematographer Cohn, screenwriter Apak and actor Paul Qulitalik in 1990. The company's ambition was to 'actively decolonize media production in the Arctic' (Bredin 2015: 33), initially through community-based film and video production in the Inukitut language and, after *Atanarjuat* garnered prizes and a significant box-office revenue of USD3.7 million, through other feature-length films.[15] Based on a traditional Inuit legend and set in Igloolik in an unspecified past, long before European explorers arrived in the Arctic, the narrative spans several decades. It tells the story of Atanarjuat (Natar Ungalaaq), whose father Tulimaq (Stepehn Qrunnut and Felix Alaralak) is denied his rightful place as the tribal chief due to the intervention of an evil shaman who helps Kumaglak (Apayata Kotierk) and, subsequently his son Sauri (Eugene Ipkarnak), usurp power. The feud between the two families is carried over into the next generation, when Atanarjuat wins a fierce head-punching contest with Sauri's son Oki (Peter-Henry Arnatsiaq) and marries the beautiful young woman Atuat (Sylvia Ivalu), who had been promised to Oki. Five years later, when Atanarjuat and Atuat are expecting their second child, Atanarjuat sleeps with Oki's sister Puja (Lucy Tulugarjuk) and takes her as his second wife. But Puja is lazy and treacherous. She commits adultery with Atanarjuat's elder brother and then complains to Oki that Atanarjuat has allegedly tried to kill her. The old tensions between the two families flare up and Oki, planning to assassinate Atanarjuat, accidentally stabs Amarjuaq (Pakak Innuksuk), who is sleeping next to his brother in a tent. Atanarjuat escapes and, in the film's most iconic sequence, runs naked and barefoot at superhuman speed across the ice, eventually leaving Oki and the other attackers behind. He finds refuge with the shaman Qulitalik (Pauloosie Qulitalik) and his family, who hide and nurse him back to strength. Equipped with magic amulets and supported by the shaman's spiritual power, Atanarjuat embarks on his long journey home, during which he encounters and overcomes shape-shifting evil spirits and other obstacles. Eventually, he is reunited with his family. In a significant departure from the ancient legend, the narrative ends on a peaceful note: instead of taking revenge on Oki for killing his brother and raping his wife Atuat, Atanarjuat decides to stop the vicious cycle of murder and revenge. Oki and Puja are expelled from the community. The spiritual balance and order that was disrupted by the evil shaman's curse two generations ago is restored at last.

Ten Canoes is in many respects the southern hemisphere's companion piece to *Atanarjuat*. It is the first Australian feature film entirely shot in Aboriginal languages without subtitles (though the international release version comes with a voice-over narration in English). It garnered numerous prizes, including the Un Certain Regard award at the Cannes Film Festival and several top prizes at the Australian Academy of Cinema and Television Awards, and it became Australia's top grossing film in 2006. It is the tenth film by white Australian filmmaker Rolf de Heer and was developed in close collaboration with the Ramingining Aboriginal people in the Northern Territory, many of whom appear in the movie and who are credited as de Heer's creative collaborators. The impetus came from David Gulpilil, a well-known Aboriginal actor, who wanted to make a film with de Heer about his people.[16] Gulpilil is also the film's voice-over narrator and cultural mediator, offering insider knowledge about the Yolngu people's customs and belief systems, alongside metanarrative reflections on the profound differences between Yolngu and Western storytelling traditions. In a direct address to cultural outsiders he remarks: 'I am going to tell you a story. It's not your story. It's my story. A story like you've never seen before', affirming at the end of the film, that 'it is a good story all the same.' In this way the storyteller endorses the benefits of encountering radical cultural difference on screen and, by implication, the unique opportunities cosmopolitan cinema affords. Conceding that Western audiences may find the large number of characters and their hard-to-pronounce names confusing, he comments: 'Too many names to remember', while the main characters are facing or smiling directly at the camera in static close-ups that are reminiscent of the portraiture of early twentieth-century ethnographic films and Nanook's camera-facing smile in Flaherty's paradigmatic film.

If it had not been for de Heer's reservations, as far as Gulpilil and the Ramingining people were concerned, *Ten Canoes* should have been devoted in its entirety to the ancient tradition of goose-egg gathering and canoe making. In an attempt to satisfy the expectations of Western producers and audiences, de Heer felt, there had to be an element of dramatic conflict. And so a compromise was found: *Ten Canoes* skilfully interweaves two narrative strands: one is filmed in black and white, takes place in 'the distant past, tribal times' and revolves around a goose-egg hunt and the making of ten bark canoes (*Ten Canoes Press Kit*). It serves as a narrative frame in which Dayindi (played by Gulpilil's son Jamie) reveals that he covets one of his older brother's wives. In order to prevent him from breaking tribal law, his brother Minygululu (Peter Minygululu) tells him 'an ancestral story that will take a very long time to tell, all through the next days of canoe making and swamp travelling and goose egg gathering' (*Ten Canoes Press Kit*). This cautionary tale is the other narrative strand and shot in colour. It is set in the mythical past, revolves around Ridjimiraril (Crusoe Kurddal) and his three wives, one of whom is coveted by his younger brother Yeeralparil (also played by Jamie Gulpilil). As in *Atanarjuat*, the arrival of a stranger disrupts the peaceful existence of the Yolngu people who live amidst the verdant water landscape of Arnhelm Land. When one of Ridjimiraril's three wives disappears, the stranger is, mistakenly, blamed for her abduction. In keeping with tribal laws, revenge and bloodshed follow. Ridjimiraril is wounded by a spear and a bad spirit enters his body. Even the Sorcerer's (Philip Gudthaykudthay) magic cannot save him. In a scene just as memorable as Atanarjuat's four-and-a-half-minute run across the ice, Ridjimiraril rises and performs his own death dance, before he collapses and dies. Yerralparil is now free to marry Munandjarra (Cassandra Malangarri Baker), his brother's widow, and order is restored. Dayindi has learnt his lesson and realises that patience and time will present him with a suitable wife.

What makes the storylines of *Atanarjuat* and *Ten Canoes* obscure and occasionally somewhat tedious for cultural outsiders to watch is the large number of characters, whose family relationships and positions in the tribal communities can only be fully discerned by watching the films multiple times. These mythic tales revolve around universal human experiences that should offer transnational audiences an opportunity to relate to and identify with the characters. This, at least, is the intention of the filmmakers, as stated in countless interviews, press kits and other publicity materials. 'Our legend', Kunuk comments, 'is a universal story about love, jealousy, murder, revenge, forgiveness – the same for everybody everywhere ... It was shot, acted, edited in our own style. Everything is authentic. The audiences really get the story' (cited in Krupat 2007: 620). However, for all their alleged universality *Atanarjuat* and *Ten Canoes* self-consciously reference the interpretative obstacles cultural outsiders experience. Thus, the narrative voice-over in the opening sequence of *Atanarjuat* announces: 'I can only sing this song to the one who understands it' – in other words, Inuit viewers. Film reviews and scholarly essays attest to the film's obscurity. A review in *Sight & Sound*, for instance, compares the experience of watching *Atanarjuat* to 'kayaking without a paddle' since the film 'describes a whole world closed to the outsider, who is obliged to take up the position of an ethnographer cracking alien codes' (Matthews 2002: 36). Although the films' extensive paratextual materials ostensibly seek to mitigate the hermeneutic challenges posed by *Atanarjuat* and *Ten Canoes*, their narrative opacity heightens the sense of wonder and astonishment which the encounter with such extreme alterity elicits in the transnational spectator.

The films' casting and the performance style of lay actors precludes the kind of audience identification that the universality of the narratives was meant to mobilise. In the case of *Ten Canoes*, actors were chosen neither for their looks nor for their acting abilities but because of their real-life kinship relationships or because they could make claims to being the nearest descendant of the ancestors they play (*Ten Canoes Press Kit*). These creative choices result in an ethnographic performance style and one-dimensional characters, each identified by just one distinctive trait (for example, the fastest runner (Atanarjuat), the disloyal wife (Puja) or the ever-hungry honey eater (Birrinbirrin)) that provoke a stance of detached observation rather than emotional identification.[17] More than half a decade earlier, Robert Flaherty identified precisely these limitations and opportunities afforded by working with Indigenous actors. In an interview with the BBC in 1949 about the making of *Nanook of the North*, he commented: 'I don't think you can make a good film of the love affairs of the Eskimo ... because they never show much feeling in their faces, but you can make a very good film about Eskimos spearing a walrus' (Flaherty cited in Raheja 2007: 1159). Flaherty's racist observation about the facial expressions of the 'Eskimos' (as Flaherty designated Inuit people) is indicative of the hermeneutic gaps of cross-cultural translation rather than the Inuit's lack of emotional expressivity. Even so, spectators of *Atanarjuat* and *Ten Canoes*, who are not part of the represented communities, may also struggle to relate to the protagonists on an affective level. Despite revolving around fiction film themes, such as love, sexual

Figure 2.1 *Ten Canoes* (Rolf de Heer and Peter Djigirr 2006) draws on the visual language of ethnographic documentaries.

rivalry and jealously, they have all the trappings of ethnographic documentaries. It is not their supposedly universal themes that make these films intriguing but the detailed insights they give into radically different cultures. They are widely praised by critics for their local authenticity as well as for their 'cosmopolitan commitment' (Krupat 2007: 262) to challenging transnational audiences to adopt an Indigenous perspective with all the cultural barriers and interpretative obstacles this inevitably entails. Situated at the interstice of ethnography, education and entertainment, *Atanarjuat* and *Ten Canoes* demand of their transnational audiences a willingness to engage with the radically different cultures they depict on a level that goes far beyond the easy consumption of the commodified exotic.

That is why the release of both films was accompanied by extensive paratextual sources that enable cosmopolitan cinephiles to undertake the research necessary for a more informed understanding. *Atanarjuat* comes with a 240-page companion book that includes a bilingual screenplay (in Inuktitut and English), alongside interviews and an ethnographic commentary on the legend of Atanarjuat, the Inuit and shamanism, authored by Bernard Saladin d'Anglure (2002), a Canadian anthropologist and student of the famous Claude Lévi-Strauss. Similarly, *Ten Canoes* is accompanied by an illustrated forty-two-page press kit that comprises, amongst other source materials, a hand-drawn map, reminiscent of an ethnographer's notebook, of Arnhelm Land and the Arafura Swamps where the film is set, a historical account of the Yolngu tribe's origins and their past and present life, and some information about the different languages spoken in the region and in the film. The DVD bonus materials include a documentary, *The Balanda and Bark Canoes* (Rolf de Heer and Tania Nehme, 2006) about the making of the feature film and about subsequent community projects engendered by *Ten Canoes*, which benefited the Ramingining community both economically and culturally (see *Ten Canoes Press Kit*: 19). Such a wealth of resources is not merely a tacit acknowledgement that these films are, indeed, hard to understand for cultural outsiders but it also confronts audiences with their own ethnocentrism by tasking them to learn about Inuit and Aboriginal cultures and to acquire the necessary cultural competencies to fully appreciate these films as ethnographic documents.

Cosmopolitan collaboration and locally authentic films

The publicity materials that accompanied the films' release read like accounts of ethnographic fieldwork, a promotional strategy already deployed successfully by Robert Flaherty, when he made *Nanook of the North* in the 1920s (see Rony 1996: 99–126). The narratives about the making of these films invariably serve to attest their local authenticity and to celebrate a mode of film production, characterised by non-hierarchical structures, a profound respect for Indigenous cultures, collectivity and a spirit of adventure. The filmmakers lived together with the Indigenous cast and crew for weeks or months, often in rough and highly challenging conditions; they consulted the last surviving elders who still possess a living memory of certain customs (such as making igloos or canoes) and of now extinct languages; they drew on ancient legends and myths and translated Indigenous oral storytelling traditions into narrative forms more or less accessible to cultural outsiders; they studied old black-and-white photographs, which early twentieth-century ethnographers had taken, and used them as inspiration for the *mise en scène* and cinematography; they cite the source materials of their research by inserting original ethnographic photographs at the beginning or end of the films in order to authenticate what are, arguably, Indigenous fiction films posing as autoethnographic documentaries.

The project of autoethnographic salvage, to which all four films under consideration here are committed, is a form of recuperative cultural memory work that relies to a significant extent on European anthropological discourses and sources. For example, Kunuk and his team consulted the sketches of Captain George Lyon, who took part in a British expedition led by William Edward Parry to explore the Northwest Passage at the beginning of the nineteenth century, as visual source material for the recreation of traditional clothes, hunting weapons, kayaks and seal skin tents in *Atanarjuat* (Knopf 2008: 319). Similarly, *Ten Canoes* was inspired by black-and-white glass plate photographs of the Yolngu people, taken by Donald Thomson, an Australian anthropologist who worked in central and north-eastern Arnhelm Land during the 1930s. Some of his photographs of the canoeists in the swamp are meticulously recreated in the film's static black-and-white cinematography. This re-appropriation of colonial accounts could be perceived as a form of cultural contamination that potentially calls the films' avowed authenticity into question if it were not for the fact that the Indigenous communities themselves enthusiastically endorse and authorise these anthropological texts and images as integral to their own cultures. According to *Ten Canoes*' press notes, 'some of [Donald Thomson's] photos have made their way back to Raminging, and there . . . they've been consumed by the culture, become part of it. There's such a concept as "Thomson Time", which is fondly remembered (*Ten Canoes Press Kit*: 9). Precisely because Indigenous peoples around the world have been expropriated of their artefacts and records of their ancient cultural practices, have they been forced to rely on documents and images created by white Western explorers and scientists as a means of reclaiming their forgotten histories. However, in so doing, they challenge and, thereby, decolonise Eurocentric modes of representation while at the same time being in constant dialogue with them.

Where exactly is the borderline between cultural appropriation and cosmopolitan collaboration? And how does the creative intervention of majority culture filmmakers impact on the films' authenticity, which, as outlined above, is tethered to notions of cultural purity, in itself a highly problematic concept? The creative involvement, or even control, of non-Indigenous directors, cinematographers and other creative personnel in Indigenous productions raises concerns about cultural appropriation. As Deborah Root has convincingly argued, cultural appropriation is based on inequities of power and a sense of entitlement to represent Other cultures in a particular way. 'The key issue [about cultural appropriation] is how a culture comes to be aestheticized by people who have no stake in that community and in particular by those who exercise authority over the culture or people being rendered exotic' (Root 1996: 30). Perhaps that is why cinematographer Norman Cohn and director Rolf de Heer both refute the importance of bloodline and descent in relation to Indigenous filmmaking, claiming instead some sort of elective Indigeneity. New York-born and bred Cohn argues that being Inuit 'is not a matter of blood quantum. It is not about who your grandparents were or what your skin looks like. It is about how fully you embrace Inuit culture and embrace Inuit perspectives' (cited in Evans 2010: 34). Cohn's professed elective kinship takes us down a treacherous path, replacing bloodline and descent with cultural essentialism. And where does this leave Inuit people who do not uphold their ethnic heritage? Do they automatically forsake their entitlement to being 'authentically Inuit'? Meanwhile, Rolf de Heer pursues a different legitimising strategy. He disavows his creative ownership of *Ten Canoes* and emphasises the collective endeavour behind the production. Peter Djigirr, the Australian-Aboriginal co-director of *Ten Canoes*, in turn, attests to the pivotal role de Heer and his predominantly white crew have played in salvaging Indigenous culture. In an interview, Djigirr states:

> We come from this land. People, Balanda [white person/s], always come, miners and that, and we always say no to them, no mining, because we don't want to lose our culture. White man's ways will just destroy us [. . .] If we can do this movie, all them Balanda [white people] put us down, but you people [the film crew] just come to lift us up, to teach them because we don't want to lose our culture, you know [. . .] It's really important this movie get done [. . .] We gonna show this film, and then they can recognise, all them white mens [*sic*] . . . that's nicer. (*Ten Canoes Press Kit*: 21)

Despite the fact that de Heer and other members of the team, including DOP Ian Jones (who was also the DOP of *Rabbit Proof Fence*), are 'Balanda' who have historically posed a threat to Aboriginal culture, Djigirr credits them with having preserved Yolngu culture and increased its visibility and public recognition. His testimony mounts a challenge to the widely held perception that ethnographic salvage is a form of cultural appropriation in which cultural outsiders select particular aspects of a dying culture deemed worth preserving, thereby becoming the 'owners and interpreters of other cultures' (Root 1996: 74). Yet Djigirr, on the contrary, identifies de Heer and his crew as important accomplices in the cosmopolitan endeavour of rescuing Aboriginal cultural memory from oblivion by making a film not *about* but *with* the Yolngu people that reflects their perspective, cosmology and sensibilities. Admittedly, the cross-cultural collaboration during the production of *Atanarjuat* was less extensive since only the cinematographer is not Inuit. But even so, the filmmakers' avowed intention to engage non-Indigenous audiences and challenge them to see the world through Inuit eyes, coupled with the fact that they succeeded in securing funding from various national and commercial Canadian organisations that were prepared to promote the cosmopolitan cause of enabling the self-representation of hitherto marginalised communities, speak to the goals of cosmopolitan filmmaking.

Ten Canoes and *Atanarjuat* reflect cosmopolitan cinema's distinctive ethical stance and promote an aesthetic and intellectual openness towards cultural diversity and difference. But can they also be designated exotic? Is the films' ethnographic realism and aesthetic austerity compatible with the alluring qualities of exotic spectacle that instils desire for the Other in the beholder? Or is not their focus on a particular locality, discrete cultural practices and detailed evocation of material culture and everyday practices premised on a different affective relationship with the spectator than the exotic? Where the exotic gaze is driven by desire, the ethnographic gaze is directed by a quest for knowledge. Another fundamental issue concerns topography. Can the Arctic ever be exotic or 'is exoticism "willingly" tropical', as Victor Segalen (2002: 13) muses in his pioneering essay on the subject. Watching *Atanarjuat* engenders awe and astonishment in the viewer but certainly not desire. To be sure, Cohn's cinematography spectacularises the majestic expanse of ice and snow and the nuanced shades of glaring Arctic light that is sometimes bluish, sometimes golden or pink. The tone-in-tone chromatic in which the Inuit people's seal skin and fur clothes merge with the many shades of white all around them is a sensorially impoverished aesthetic that stands in stark contrast to the sensuous indulgence, commonly associated with exoticism. The minimalist colour palette of white and cream that dominates the *mise en scène* intimates that the Inuit are living in perfect harmony with nature, while at the same time making the harshness of this inhospitable environment and the relentless struggle for survival palpable – or so it may seem to cultural outsiders. This notion is reinforced by the long and slow sequences tracking the Inuit traversing the ice, which viscerally capture the fierceness of the terrain and the patience and resilience required to exist there. Close-ups of the Inuit's tattooed faces alternate with close-ups of everyday chores, such as the preparation and consumption of raw caribou meat that needs to be bashed for a long time before it is tender and edible. The film's quasi-documentary realist style, slow observational stance and the depiction of everyday rituals are alien and anything but alluring. The film's critical reception testifies to the unmitigated alterity of *Atanarjuat*, which is invariably tethered to notions of 'authenticity' rather than 'exoticism': 'For non-Inuit at least, the impression of authenticity derives partly from the film's bewildering otherness', writes Peter Matthews (2002) in *Sight & Sound*. Lucas Bessire (2003: 835) praises the film for its 'painstakingly accurate' depiction of local customs and 'tribal authenticity', while Russell Meeuf (2007: 737) notes that the film relies 'heavily on a notion of localism concerned with cultural authenticity'.[18]

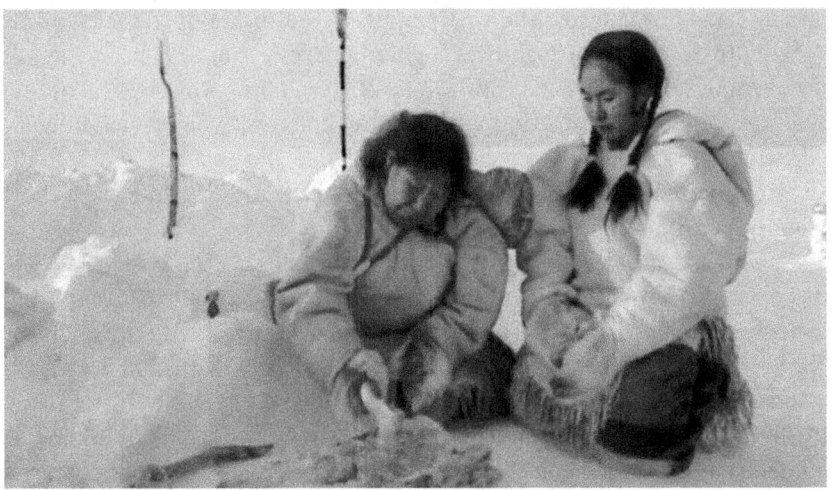

Figure 2.2 *Atanarjuat: The Fast Runner* (Zacharias Kunuk, 2001) depicts the daily rituals of Inuit life in beautiful shades of white.

Similarly, *Ten Canoes* could be more accurately described as a locally authentic than an exotic film because it represents cultural difference without spectacularising alterity. Both films eschew the commodification of Indigenous culture, instead asking cultural outsiders to relinquish the objectifying exotic gaze and see the world through Indigenous eyes. Whereas *Atanarjuat* dispenses with any form of cultural translation that would make this strange Inuit legend more accessible, *Ten Canoes* assigns the storyteller the role of cultural interpreter and commentator in order to achieve the film's intended dual address to cultural insiders and outsiders. The fact that both films have primarily been lauded for their authenticity, which according to James Clifford (2013: 198–9) is 'an anthropological category', would seem to imply that they are first and foremost valued as 'ethnographic objects' rather than as 'works of art' whose 'cultural value is measured by . . . aesthetic and formal qualities'. But conversely, the award of the Caméra d'Or to *Atanarjuat* at the Cannes Film Festival 2001 indicates that Clifford's distinction between anthropology and art is rather more fluid.

The Convergence of Cosmopolitan and Exotic Sensibilities in *Tanna* and *Embrace of the Serpent*

Tanna and *Embrace of the Serpent* also occupy an ambiguous position on the fluid spectrum of ethnographic verisimilitude and exoticism; however, they are more obviously fictionalised narratives that make greater concessions to the tastes and expectations of cultural outsiders, blending local authenticity with readily recognisable exotic tropes. The casting of Indigenous lead actors who conform to Western notions of physical beauty and storylines that place individualised characters, who invite audience identification, rather than collectivities or one-dimensional types at the centre, are important strategies that domesticate alterity and make these films appealing to transnational audiences.

Tanna is located on the eponymous remote South Pacific island which, as part of the Vanuatu archipelago, gained independence from French and British colonial rule as late as 1980. This is also the decade in which the film is set. *Tanna*'s iconography of lush tropical forests, gushing waterfalls and Indigenous tribes clad merely in grass skirts and penis sheaths, though reminiscent of ethnographic documentaries, is actually a fiction film. The film's narrative was inspired by a song Martin Butler and Bentley Dean, two Australian filmmakers who made a number of award-winning documentaries about Australia's Aboriginal history together, heard on Tanna Island when researching another documentary. Together with John Collee, whose scripts include mainstream films like *Master and Commander* (Peter Weir, 2003) and *Happy Feet* (George Miller, 2006) and 'in collaboration with the Yakel people', they developed the script (*Tanna Press Kit*). The plot revolves around Wawa (Marie Wawa), a young girl from the Yakel tribe, who falls in love with the chief's grandson, Dain (the late Mungau Dain). When an intertribal dispute escalates, Wawa is promised in marriage to a man from the Imedin tribe as part of a peace deal. Dain and Wawa reject the custom of arranged marriage and elope together. The only place where the star-crossed lovers can find refuge is with an Indigenous Christian community, whose way of life is presented as a monstrous form of cultural hybridity and, therefore, no alternative for Dain and Wawa. But with nowhere to go on the small island, they eventually poison themselves with mushrooms and die together in eternal embrace on top of a roaring, fire-spitting volcano.

Embrace of the Serpent is the third feature by the Colombian director Ciro Guerra and was nominated for an Academy Award in 2016. It is a visually stunning film whose cinematography recalls the daguerreotype photographic plates of the Amazon and its Indigenous people taken by early twentieth-century explorers who inspired the film. Though not acknowledged by the director or DOP, David Gallego, it may also be indebted to 'the master of the massive jaw-dropping monochrome' (Jones 2021), as Sebastião Salgado has been dubbed on account of his extensive black-and-white photography of Amazonia, its breathtaking panoramas and portraits of its Indigenous people. The narrative is loosely based on the travel journals of two scientists, the German ethnographer Theodor Koch-Grünberg (called Theo in the film and played by Jan Bijvoet) and the American ethnobotanist Richard Evans Schultes (Evan, played by Brionne Davis), who travelled through the Amazon during the first half of the twentieth century. In the film's fictionalised account of these journeys, they are both looking for the sacred Yakruna plant. Theo, who is weakened by a tropical disease, hopes the flower's healing properties will save his life. Evan, ostensibly interested in the plant's hallucinogenic effect, is actually looking for a disease-resistant rubber tree which the United States badly needed for the war effort. Yet rather than placing these Western ethnographers at the film's narrative centre, *Embrace of the Serpent* tells the story from the perspective of the Amazonian shaman Karamakate (meaning 'the one who tries'), whose young and old selves are played by two different actors (Nilbio Torres and the late Antonio Bolivar). Karamakate's muscular body, covered merely by a loincloth and a majestic necklace, and his dignified poise evoke the iconography of the Noble Savage. This last survivor of the Cohiuano tribe, however, lacks the innocence and utopian promise associated with this archetypal figure since contact with Western civilisation has made him a profoundly conflicted character, angry and mistrustful of foreign intruders. Nevertheless, the young and old Karamakate agree to escort Theo and later Evan up the Amazon River in a wooden canoe. The two journeys, set more than

Figure 2.3 In the figure of Karamakate, *Embrace of the Serpent* (Ciro Guerra, 2015) salvages the memory of Amazonia's wise warrior-shamans, who are now extinct (courtesy of Peccadillo Pictures. All rights reserved).

thirty years apart, convey in time-lapse fashion the increasing devastation Spanish and Portuguese *conquistadors*, Roman Catholic missionaries and rapacious Columbian rubber barons have wrought on the Amazonian wilderness, having shown neither respect for the natural resources nor for the traditions and beliefs of the Indigenous people whom they converted to Christianity, enslaved and worked to death on the rubber plantations. A scene set in a mission serves as a further indictment of the corrupting influence of the West on Indigenous communities; it dramatises how the Christian sacrament of the Holy Communion has become creolised, culminating in a cannibalistic orgy.

Like *Atanarjuat* and *Ten Canoes*, *Tanna* and *Embrace of the Serpent* are borne out of the collaborative practices of cosmopolitan filmmaking. The publicity materials surrounding *Tanna*'s release suggests that the co-directors and co-producers, Butler and Dean, were merely the facilitators, who enabled the Yakel tribe to bring their own story on to the screen and, eventually, to the attention of international film festival audiences. Martin Butler's statement in the film's press kit describes the making of the film as a truly cosmopolitan encounter that matches Ulf Hannerz's characterisation of genuine cosmopolitanism, cited above:

> For seven months we lived together [with the Yakel tribe], exchanging food, stories, ceremonies, laughter, pain and adventures. Bentley's children played with theirs, learning their language and way of life. One day the men sung a deeply moving song about two lovers who dared defy the ancient laws of arranged marriage, some 20 years earlier. They said the young lovers' story changed the course of Kastom [traditional system of laws, beliefs, songs and social structures] on the island. *Tanna* is a cinematic translation of that song – which is at its heart a story of the universally transformative power of love. (*Tanna Press Kit*)

Rather than claiming creative ownership, Butler and Dean assume the role of cultural translators, who possess the equipment, technological knowhow and cultural competencies to translate Indigenous culture and oral history into the cinematic style and language global audiences are accustomed to, albeit without sacrificing its authenticity. When I approached Butler and Dean in 2016, requesting an interview with them, they adopted the same self-effacing stance and suggested that I interview J. J. Nako, the film's cultural director and a member of the Yakel tribe, instead.

The emphasis on shared creative ownership in the film's publicity campaign is particularly salient in the context of Indigenous cinema which is inextricably linked to a sense of colonial guilt. The cosmopolitan sensibilities of the contemporary moment demand a heightened sensitivity to a long history of colonial violence and exploitation and the need for atonement. For a white majority culture filmmaker to appropriate an Indigenous story, therefore, creates a sense of unease and raises serious ethical questions, as testified for example by the controversies surrounding the globally successful film *Whale Rider* (Niki Caro, 2002), which is based on a Māori story written by Witi Ihimaera but directed by Niki Caro, a Pākehā filmmaker.[19] In particular, these revolved around issues of cultural appropriation and the erasure of the specificities of gender and leadership rules in Māori culture, which were subordinated to a universal feminist agenda, in a bid for global audiences (see Joyce 2009: 240). However, Indigenous self-representation, the alternative approach, is, as some critics have argued, not necessarily 'a solution to the problem of cultural exploitation' on account of its inherent ethnocentrism and essentialism (Davis 2007: 6; see Fee 1995). Advocates of cross-cultural collaborative filmmaking perceive genuine intercultural dialogue and cooperation not only as an ethically sound middle way but as the *only* way. They argue that the radically different storytelling traditions of Indigenous communities make their narratives (and, by implication, films based on Indigenous oral history) inaccessible to metropolitan audiences – an argument deftly illustrated by the obscure storyline of *Atanarjuat*.

In an extended interview with *Cineaste*, Ciro Guerra also highlights the need for cultural translation and close collaboration. When he started working with the Indigenous peoples of the Amazon, he realised that the 'anthropologically accurate film' which he had originally planned to make had to be 'contaminated with Amazonian myth' in order to make the film 'feel more like an Indian tale'. But then he worried that 'the film would become incomprehensible for an audience [as] it's such a different way of storytelling' (Guerra cited in Guillén 2016). One example Guerra discusses is the different temporality that shapes the experience of the Amazonian Indigenous people: 'Time to them is not a line, as we see it in the West, but a series of multiple universes happening simultaneously' (*Embrace Press Kit*). In order to convey this alternative sense of time, 'we translated the script together with them. And during the process of translation, they rewrote the script. They put a lot into it. They made it their own' (Guerra cited in Prasch 2016: 94). This alternative sense of time is reflected in the fluid transitions between the narrative strand revolving around Theo's and Evan's journeys in 1909 and 1940, which convey simultaneity rather than temporal progression.

The film's cosmopolitan orientation is further reflected in the director's avowed intention to spark 'curiosity in the viewers, a desire to learn, respect, and protect this [Indigenous] knowledge which I think is invaluable in the modern world' (*Embrace of the Serpent Press Kit*).

In order to equip transnational audiences with a better understanding of non-Western regimes of knowledge, the press kit of *Embrace of the Serpent* includes a glossary of some eighteen terms, which are explained in detail, for example: 'Caboclo: Name given to "acculturated" natives who work for the whites. The literal translation of the word is "traitor"', and 'Mambe: Mixture of coca leaves, minced to a fine powder, and ashes of leaves of yarumo, a plant that activates and empowers the energetic and nutritional properties of the coca leaf.' Such a glossary (similar ones can be found in the press notes of *Tanna* and *Ten Canoes*) coupled with the film's multilingualism, is a strategy designed to create an aura of authenticity, be it real or staged.

The concept of 'staged authenticity', originally developed by Dean MacCannell in the 1970s with reference to the social space of tourist settings, is especially pertinent to *Tanna*. It creates the seductive fantasy of the inhabitants of Tanna Island leading a timeless existence that is virtually indistinguishable from the legendary pasts reconstructed in *Atanarjuat* and *Ten Canoes*. MacCannell (1973: 589–90) proposes that the tourist's quest for 'authentic experience' stems from 'the shallowness [and] inauthenticity' of modern society, which explains the fascination with 'the sacred in primitive society'. Yet tourists rarely have access to what the anthropologist Erwin Goffman has described as 'back region' knowledge. Instead of becoming participants, they remain outsiders for whom supposedly authentic rituals are performed or 'staged'.

Ethnographic filmmaking has traditionally accommodated this curiosity to get a 'back region' glimpse of radically different cultures. The ethnographic aesthetics of *Tanna* and the other films under consideration here, coupled with the emphasis placed on cross-cultural collaboration with Indigenous people, taps into this representational tradition while at the same time catering to metropolitan audiences' interest in local authenticity. *Tanna*'s aura of ethnographic verisimilitude is further reinforced by the fact that the film is based on a true tragic love story that changed marriage customs on the island. Moreover, like in an ethnographic documentary, the first-time actors are performing their real selves: 'The chief played the chief, the medicine man played the medicine man, the warriors played the warriors', cultural director Nako comments (*Tanna Press Kit*). In contrast to *Atanarjuat* and *Ten Canoes*, however, the lead actors Marie Wawa and Mungau Dain were cast on account of their good looks. In fact, Dain, who tragically died aged twenty-four a few years after starring in *Tanna*, was nominated for the leading role by the Yakel people, who considered him to be the best-looking man in the village (Ives 2019).

ETHNOGRAPHIC SALVAGE AND COSMOPOLITAN EXOTICISM 85

Most film critics appear to have accepted the premise of authenticity on which the promotion, and arguably the success, of *Tanna* are based. Reviewers have lauded the film for its 'captivating simplicity' (Rooney 2015) but also for its 'consummate visual achievement', the untrained cast's 'magnetic' performances and its 'warm, shimmering vitality' (Buckmaster 2015). Surprisingly, nobody has raised any objections to *Tanna*'s overtly exoticist representation. Even when Nako and the lead actors, Mungau Dain and Marie Wawa, attended the Venice Film Festival in 2015 in their traditional tribal attire, nobody suggested that the cast and crew were merely staging an exotic fantasy to please global festival audiences. The film's positive reception stands in stark contrast to the critical comments exoticism, even in its postcolonial decentred forms, customarily incurs.

Salman Rushdie's above-cited distinction between exoticism and local authenticity provides a plausible explanation for the critics' surprising leniency vis-à-vis *Tanna*'s exoticism. While local authenticity is perceived as 'good' since it gives a voice to various marginalised communities and since it is associated with various cosmopolitan, humanitarian and political causes, exoticism is 'bad' due to its Eurocentric imperialist legacy. But how would our response to *Tanna* change if we found out that the fantasy that there is still a remote place on earth untouched by the homogenising forces of globalisation, is actually a skilful invention – a form of 'staged authenticity'? The film's plot and *mise en scène* purposely construct the fiction that the Yakel people are 'the last keepers of *Kastom*' and adhere to 'the old ways of life'. For example, money does not appear to be legal tender in this pre-capitalist society, instead the Yakel and Imedin tribes trade with kava and pigs; when Wawa's father is fatally wounded in an attack, he is not taken to a nearby hospital but cured by spiritual healing practices. Similarly, the Yakel people are never shown with mobile phones but use drums and a conch shell to communicate via long distances. Lamont Lindstrom, an anthropologist specialising in Melanesia who has lived on Tanna Island for many years, takes issue with the film's 'staged authenticity'. According to Lindstrom:

> A freelance photojournalist in the early 1970s convinced people from the community to take off their clothes to boost the appeal of his photographs. Ever since, men here (especially when paying tourists come around) sport traditional penis wrappers, and women wear bark skirts ... In real life, Yakel is a popular tourist site, located only a few kilometres up the hill from Lenakel, Tanna's main town centre ... Most everyone on Tanna, young and old alike (including folks in Yakel), carries mobile telephones these days ... And those penis-wrapper-wearing Yakel men are the island's outstanding global travellers. They have starred in a variety of reality television series that have brought them to the UK, France, USA, and Australia ... the

Tannese are extremely savvy about the West's romanticism for "ancient cultures" and cannily position themselves within the international tourism marketplace accordingly. (Lindstrom 2015)[20]

I tried to verify these allegations in an interview with the film's cultural director. Despite wearing Western clothes during the interview, Nako asserted that the Yakel people's dress code was entirely authentic, not a costume put on to please the tourists or film festival audiences in Venice and elsewhere. However, he confirmed that the Yakel people do, indeed, have mobile phones, as well as access to Vanuatu's public health system, thereby undermining the myth of the tribe's complete self-sufficiency and rejection of all modern technologies. 'We need support from the Westerners, but we also need to protect our culture. Whatever protects our culture, we accept. Whatever destroys our culture, that's what we keep away' (Berghahn and Nako 2016). Does this revelation of partially 'staged authenticity' make us feel cheated? Do we now regard *Tanna* as ethno kitsch or as a clever form of tourist destination marketing? The film's cultural director does not see it this way, asserting instead that the film has given his people public visibility on a global scale, shown audiences around the world a different way of life and has even advanced a political objective, namely the recognition of the Tannese Indigenous communities and their laws of *Kastom* by the Vanuatu government (Berghahn and Nako 2016). In this way, the making of *Tanna* and its (trans)national circulation have advanced the cosmopolitan agenda of empowering a hitherto disenfranchised community.

Embrace of the Serpent is motivated by a similar cosmopolitan impetus. By making this film, the Colombian filmmaker Ciro Guerra assumes the role of custodian of Indigenous collective memory, a role that can be ascribed to cosmopolitan as well as exoticist sensibilities. The director's intention is made explicit in the intertitles which accompany the explorers' ethnographic photographs at the very end of the film: 'This film is dedicated to all the peoples whose song we will never know', a reference to the Indigenous peoples of the Amazon, most of whom were annihilated. In an interview, the director states that the film aims to rescue 'the memory of an Amazon that no longer exists' and to 'create this image in the collective memory, because characters like Karamakate – this breed of wise, warrior-shamans – are now extinct. The modern native is something else, there is much knowledge that still remains, but most of it is now lost' (*Embrace of the Serpent Press Kit*).

On the one hand, the endeavour to salvage the collective memory of Amazonian Indigenous peoples is the kind of atonement for past collective guilt which is in keeping with the human rights regime of cosmopolitan memory politics. This kind of cosmopolitan memory, Daniel Levy and Natan Sznaider (2011: 205) argue, derives from the 'expanded global awareness of the presence of others and the equal worth of human beings' and the willingness to preserve 'memories of past human rights violations'. On the other hand, the preservation of Indigenous collective memory is precisely the kind of salvage operation which, according to Chris Bongie (1991: 46), has always been one of exoticism's primary objectives:

> The project of exoticism is to salvage values and a way of life that had vanished, without hope of restoration, from post-Revolutionary society (the realm of the Same) but that might, beyond the confines of modernity, still be figured as really possible.

Exoticism understood as a 'salvage operation [is] a revolt against the ravages of modernity' (Shapiro 2000: 46), which explains why temporal and spatial remoteness frequently coalesce in the exotic imagination. Nowhere is this more apparent than in representations of so-called 'primitive' cultures, a term formerly used by anthropologists to describe Indigenous peoples.

Primitivism is a particular form of artistic exoticism that emerged in Western fine arts at the beginning of the twentieth century. It is inspired by non-Western influences, particularly artefacts from Africa, Oceania and Indigenous peoples in the Americas, and reflects a deep yearning for authenticity (see Grijp 2009: 10, 13). Like exoticism (the more encompassing concept), primitivism projects Western fantasies that encapsulate everything modern civilisation is deemed to have lost: a close attachment to the land and nature, sexual plenitude, a deep spiritual connection to the universe, the lived experience of the sacred and a strong sense of community. It is thus not surprising that cultures perceived as primitive have elicited the very same instinct to salvage and recuperate in ethnographers and ethnographic filmmakers which Bongie (1991) and others have identified in relation to the exotic. Owing to an ascribed antithetical relationship to modernity, primitivised cultures hold a particular appeal in times of crisis and disenchantment with modernity since they are imagined as 'uncontaminated' by Western civilisation (and therefore more authentic). The fascination with the primitive has inspired Western thinkers across the centuries to reflect upon the shortcomings of their own societies. The 'primitive', to which Rony (1996: 10) refers as 'fascinating cannibalism', is, however, an ambivalent concept, denoting a 'mixture of fascination and horror'. If the primitive is constructed as the pathological opposite of the European, then it is also its utopian Other. The utopian propensities of primitivism are encapsulated in the myth of the Noble Savage, who is constructed as 'authentic, macho, pure, spiritual, and an antidote to the ills of modern industrialized capitalism' (Rony 1996: 194). Yet both variants of the ethnographic Other, imagine Indigenous people as stuck in the evolutionary past and closer to nature in comparison with the more 'civilised' West.

From today's vantage point, shaped by a combination of post-imperial guilt, an acute awareness of ecological destruction and a deep nostalgia to recuperate a world and a way of life which technological progress and global capitalism have destroyed, the ethnographic Other holds out an unadulterated utopian promise. *Tanna* and *Embrace of the Serpent* articulate this idea by reconfiguring the primitive as a form of active resistance and as an ecological consciousness that has the capacity to save the planet and humanity. As Theo's Indian servant Manduca (Miguel Dionisio Ramos) puts it, 'If we can't get the whites to learn, it will be the end of us. The end of everything.' Karamakate fears it may be too late already but hopes he might be wrong. This remark is one of the many interesting inversions of the civilising mission, which has been an integral part of the old imperial exotic. The new exoticism, by contrast, challenges these long-established hierarchies of knowledge and power insofar as it encompasses forms of reciprocity and inversion.

Constructing and reversing the exotic gaze

In what follows I will examine, first, how the aesthetic strategies of *Tanna* and *Embrace of the Serpent* construct the island of Tanna and the Amazon rainforest and its native inhabitants as exotic and, second, how the processes of reciprocity and inversion, dramatised in the two films, align the visual pleasure exotic spectacle affords with cosmopolitan sensibilities. As already indicated above, exotic texts build on an intertextual system of already familiar reference points that make them legible as exotic. Brown-skinned, bare-breasted women in grass skirts and men covering their nudity with *namba*s (*Tanna*) or loin cloths (*Embrace*), have been an integral part of ethnographic exoticism since the middle of the seventeenth century when the Dutch painter Albert Eckhout travelled to Brazil where he painted native Indians and established an 'iconography of savagery' (Griffiths 2002: xix; see Chapter 1). Karamakate in *Embrace of the Serpent* stands in this iconographic tradition but, as noted above, complicates the myth of the Noble Savage since he has witnessed 'The horror!' (to cite Kurtz's dying words in *Heart of Darkness*) which 'civilisation' has brought to the Amazon, rendering him a profoundly conflicted and disillusioned man. Intertextual references to *Heart of Darkness*, Joseph Conrad's paradigmatic text about the transformative power of cross-cultural encounters deep in the African jungle, abound and have been noted in numerous film reviews. Other obvious exotic antecedents regularly cited by critics are *The Mission* (Roland Joffé, 1986) and Werner Herzog's Amazonian adventure films *Aguirre, der Zorn Gottes* (Aguirre, the Wrath of God, 1972) and *Fitzcarraldo* (1982). In fact, the scene in which Evan plays Joseph Haydn's *The Creation* on his gramophone and Karamakate listens appreciatively, is reminiscent of a scene in which Fitzcarraldo (Klaus Kinski) plays Caruso on top of the steamer in the middle of the jungle.[21] Such correspondences notwithstanding, a comparison between Herzog's and Guerra's Amazonian adventure dramas provides interesting insights into the changing representational strategies of exoticism. The reification of Amazonian Indigenous peoples, who are reduced to de-individualised and largely hostile inhabitants of an impenetrable jungle, coupled with the predominance of German dialogue in Herzog's films, stand in stark contrast to the nine different languages spoken (including Indigenous languages such as Tikuna, Bubeo and Huitoto) in Guerra's film and the overall attention to ethnographic detail. Whereas in the 1970s and 1980s Herzog's construction of Amazonia satisfied audience expectations, in the twenty-first century, when global eco- and adventure tourism has made the Amazon an accessible destination, a higher degree of verisimilitude has become *de rigueur*, at least in arthouse cinema.

Both the Amazon and the South Sea islands are mythic landscapes, steeped in a long history of Eurocentric imaginative projections that instantly identifies the films' topographies and their inhabitants as exotic. Consistent with exoticism's ambition to salvage idealised forms of cultural difference threatened by extinction, both Amazonia and the South Pacific are imagined as vanishing paradises. The West's enthralment with the Amazon has taken vastly different forms over the centuries, ranging from the conquistadors' quest for the legendary El Dorado over Claude Lévi-Strauss' search for the unspoilt earthly paradise and, conversely, a green hell that drives Western explorers to insanity. In contemporary cultural representations, ecological and humanitarian concerns about the destruction of the Amazon rainforest and the catastrophic consequences this has for its Indigenous inhabitants, for biodiversity, species extinction and, indeed, our survival on planet earth dominate.[22] *Amazônia*, a recent touring exhibition which showcases Sebastião Salgado's spectacular black-and-white photography of the Brazilian Amazon rainforest and its Indigenous peoples, is in keeping with the contemporary cosmopolitan agenda of ecological salvage. Several of the exhibition's accompanying textual displays state the urgency of saving the Amazon. The exhibition's final appeal, in the words of Sonia Guajajara, the Executive Coordinator of the Association of Brazil's Indigenous Peoples, is the most powerful one: 'The Amazon is on fire, putting indigenous lives, biodiversity and the global climate at great risk. If we lose the Amazon, we lose the fight against climate change.'[23]

By contrast, the imaginary attributes of the mythic landscape of the South Seas have remained remarkably static since Cook, Bougainville, Diderot, Segalen, Gauguin, Flaherty, Murnau and other Western travellers and artists created a textual and visual paradigm that conjures visions of an authentic life, a state of innocence coupled with uninhibited sexuality and lush tropical nature. In his brief essay 'Cinema and Exploration', André Bazin (2005: 155) discusses 'the gradual formation of a mythology' surrounding the South Seas in films such as *Moana* (Robert Flaherty, 1926), *Tabu: A Story of the South Seas* (Friedrich W. Murnau, 1931) and *White Shadows in the South Sea* (W. S. van Dyke, 1928), observing: 'We see the Western mind as it were taking over a far-off civilization and interpreting it after its own fashion.'[24] The South Pacific islands are a utopian imaginative topography that offer the promise of an escape from the loathsome present and an exciting encounter with the elsewhere. Murnau's *Tabu* epitomises the idea of a vanishing paradise. The first part, entitled 'Paradise' captures the last glimpses of mankind's Edenic state, whereas the second part, 'Paradise Lost', depicts the expulsion from the Garden of Eden, when the romantic couple encounter the encroachment of civilisation and the corrupting forces of money and alcohol.

Tanna's exoticism inscribes itself in this enduring legacy. Although most critics have dubbed it a 'Romeo and Juliet' story set in the South Pacific, in terms of its iconography and, indeed, narrative conceit of star-crossed lovers *Tanna* betrays far more conspicuous similarities with Murnau's *Tabu*. In fact, Butler and Dean initially considered giving their film the title *Taboo* (see Dunks 2016: 29). Dain's crown of fern fronds and Wawa's garland of leaves recall the almost identical natural attire of Matahi (Matahi) and Reri (Anne Chevalier) in *Tabu* and are a staple of visual representations of the South Pacific. Tannese children and the star-crossed lovers frolicking amidst ferns and fronds and a native heralding a call to all villagers by way of a conch shell are further references to what can be regarded as the cinematic urtext of the South Sea genre.

While these cinematic precursors lend *Tanna* and *Embrace of the Serpent* their exotic credentials, the spectacle of pristine nature is arguably the films' main attraction for contemporary audiences. Shots of luxuriant

Figure 2.4 Wawa and Dain's exotic attire and the lush tropical nature in *Tanna* (Martin Butler and Bentley Dean, 2015) evoke the iconography of the South Sea paradise (courtesy of dir. Martin Butler and Bentley Dean, 2015, with J. J. Nako as Cultural Director, showing Marie Wawa and the late Mungai Dain, © Phillippe Penel).

tropical forests with a variety of ferns, palm trees (both traditionally part of the iconography of the exotic) and a myriad of other plants convey the idea of natural abundance. The absence of roads, electricity cables or telephone masts suggests that on the remote island of Tanna time has stood still. Placing the islanders within nature but outside history is another topos of the exotic imagination. The sounds of wilderness, birdsong, cicadas, gushing waterfalls, a rumbling volcano hurling fiery lava into the sky and the growl of a Jaguar allow metropolitan audiences to immerse themselves in soundscapes they could hardly experience at home. Panoramic vistas of breathtaking natural beauty and the extended aerial shot at the end of *Embrace of the Serpent*, which first races upwards and then glides contemplatively over the vast expanse of the meandering Amazon River and the immensity of the rainforest, elicit a sense of awe at the grandiose spectacle of sublime nature.[25]

At the same time, *Embrace of the Serpent* taps into the popular image of Amazonia as 'a storehouse of natural wonders, one that the "global community" must protect to avoid widescale environmental calamity' (Viatori 2009: 117). Such environmental concerns have also been linked to cosmopolitanism, namely the need for tackling the global challenges our planet is facing – climate change, the loss of biodiversity and ecosystems, and water shortages (see Held 2011: 170). Once again, the affinities between cosmopolitan and exotic sensibilities become apparent when we consider the film's ecological agenda in relation to Renato Rosaldo's (1989: 69–70) concept of 'imperialist nostalgia', a particular type of nostalgia that I explore in detail in Chapter 4. 'Imperialist nostalgia revolves around a paradox': just like colonisers mourned the disappearance of the cultures they have transformed or even destroyed, nowadays 'people destroy their environment, and then they worship nature.' Especially representations of the unspoilt wilderness and of putatively primitive societies encapsulate this longing for stability in a world of rapid change and hypermobility. *Embrace of the Serpent* spectacularises the sublime Amazon landscape to celebrate its splendour and ineffability while at the same time conjuring up apocalyptic visions of an ecological cataclysm. Cast as nature's disempowered saviour, Karamakate possesses the shamanic knowledge of how to live in harmony with nature, but in order to avert environmental destruction and species extinction, he has to communicate his knowledge to the white man.

Although the shaman's ominous warnings, 'The jungle is fragile and if you attack her, she strikes back' and 'You bring hell and death to Earth', articulate the film's conservationist stance explicitly, more importantly, Ciro Guerra and the director of photography David Gallego rely on the alluring power of exotic images and their immanent mystery to convey this idea. Several of the film's most captivating scenes are highly evocative, yet their symbolic meaning remains ultimately opaque, or rather, mysterious in the sense of resisting rational explanation. *Embrace of the Serpent* illuminates this distinctive feature of exoticism by creating fluid transitions between mimetic realism and an alternative, oneiric reality that reflects the myths and spiritual beliefs of the Amazonian Indigenous peoples. Enigmatic dreamlike sequences convey the shaman's view of the natural world, a world animated by ancestral spirits and governed by laws only he understands. Yet what are spectators who are not conversant with Indigenous myths to make of the image of the serpent that devours its young ones in the film's opening sequence? What does the serpent's embrace referenced in the film title signify?[26] Is it the Amazon itself which, according to Amazonian mythology, was created when 'extraterrestial beings descended from the Milky Way . . . on a gigantic anaconda snake' which then became the river Amazon (Guillén 2016)? Or is it Theo, to whom the disillusioned Karamakate says 'You are the serpent' (possibly a reference to the serpent in the Garden of Eden), shortly before a prowling jaguar (perhaps the shape-shifting shaman himself), previously identified as the harbinger of Theo's imminent death, devours the serpent? When, in the film's final sequence, Karamakate offers Evan *caapi* made from the last surviving Yakruna flower (in order to impart his ecological consciousness to the white man so that he can save the planet), he explains that this is 'the embrace of the serpent', his gift to him. Equally arresting is the haunting image of young Karamakate's eyes being transformed into two brilliant white glowing orbits and his open mouth into a dazzlingly bright star, before the camera cuts to an infinite firmament of stars. By blurring the boundaries between myth and reality, *Embrace of the Serpent* transports its viewers into a dreamlike world of mystery and cosmic wonder, where the limitations of Western routines of cognition and scientific knowledge become apparent.

This is not the only way, however, in which *Embrace of the Serpent*, as well as *Tanna*, challenge the presumed superiority of Western epistemes and evolutionary progress on which older forms of exoticism are based. Instead, the films' decentred perspectives encompass 'the potential reflexivity or reciprocity within exoticism', which according to Charles Forsdick (2001: 14), is an integral part of exoticism but one all too easily overlooked by its critics. For example, both films tackle the notion of Indigenous peoples' presumed backwardness head-on. *Tanna* reconfigures it as a form of deliberate resistance when Chief Charlie says: 'We have always fought to keep *Kastom* strong. The colonial powers, we have resisted. The Christians – we resisted. The lure of money – we resisted that also. We are the last keepers of *Kastom* and we are few.' *Embrace of the Serpent* reflects a similar disdain for the values of capitalism by showing that the heavy suitcases and boxes full of objects, which the ethnographers have brought to the Amazon, are nothing but a useless burden. As Deborah Shaw (2016) notes: 'There is no superior white saviour here, only white men who must be humbled, corrected and taught how to see and recognize the flaws in their culture and the strengths in the culture of the Amazonian people.' Admittedly, this kind of culture critique has its own exotic appeal since it is precisely what metropolitan audiences and critics expect of the Other, to resist Western hegemony, to take pride in their cultural difference and to mount a critique against rampant capitalism and everything else deemed wrong with the West. The fact that the Indigenous people in these films are represented not as 'being stuck in the past' but as people who have actively chosen to resist modernity, commands our respect. Conversely, Theo's paternalistic attempt to deprive his Indigenous hosts of the achievements of scientific progress in order to preserve their native ancient knowledge, when he demands his compass back, meets with Karamakate's harsh criticism. 'You can't deny them knowledge', he reprimands Theo for trying to freeze the Indians in a static past.

Another example of how *Embrace of the Serpent* reverses the exotic gaze is the scene in which the German scientist Theo performs a

Schuhplattler, a traditional dance from the Alpine region, much to the delight of the Indigenous people whom he entertains in this way. Since Indigenous dance typically serves as an icon of alterity, the dance scene self-consciously plays with exotic iconography by Othering the white European man. In a similar vein, *Tanna* directs the exotic gaze at the British monarchy, challenging the Eurocentric assumption that arranged marriage is symptomatic of the islanders' backwardness, when Wawa's father shows his daughter photos of Queen Elizabeth and Prince Philip and suggests that theirs has also been an arranged marriage, and a happy one, too.[27] By projecting the practice of arranged marriage – perceived as a signifier of alterity in the West – onto British royalty, the film makes the cultural assumptions underlying the exotic gaze transparent for metropolitan audiences. The reversal of the exotic gaze draws attention to the fact that positing the Western romantic ideal of love marriage as the universal norm is misguided by suggesting that amongst the highest echelons of British society arranged marriage is practised, too. Somewhat inconsistently, however, *Tanna*'s narrative trajectory does not quite carry this idea through. Rather than valorising the equality of both matrimonial practices, the film's melodramatic conclusion and affective resonance ultimately advocate the superiority of romantic love as the basis of marriage.

Embrace of the Serpent eschews the dichotomies typical of imperial exoticism. In contrast to dominant regimes of representation that cast white explorers, anthropologists and botanists, who were deeply implicated in the project of scientific colonialism, as bearers of knowledge, Guerra's film portrays Theo and Evan as lacking the knowledge necessary for them to succeed with their expeditions. The Amazon is a mythical place in which dreams, visionary revelations and ancestral knowledge are believed to reveal the right path. Therefore, Theo and Evan are entirely dependent upon the help and knowledge of the native shaman. Since lack of knowledge (alongside other alleged deficits), has been a prominent theme in the depiction of the non-West in colonialist and Eurocentric discourses, the reversal of this trope contributes to the film's decolonising perspective (see D'Argenio 2018). However, *Embrace of the Serpent* purposely avoids a simplistic reversal of old imperialist binaries and, instead, reimagines the encounters between Indians and white explorers as a mutual rapprochement and exchange. For example, an intertitle at the end of the film acknowledges the fact that Western explorers have played a crucial role in preserving Indigenous memory, stating that their travel 'diaries are the only known accounts of Amazonian cultures'. In fact, Guerra regards Koch-Grünberg and Schultes, whose diaries were read by influential people, as the beginning of an ecological movement that developed, with a strong focus on the Amazon, in the 1970s (Guillén 2016).

The reciprocity underpinning the intercultural dialogue between the white scientists and the shaman is dramatised in numerous scenes. For instance, Evan helps the old Karamakate, who suffers from memory loss, remember aspects of his culture by showing him detailed drawings of necklaces and photographs in Theo's travel journals. Evan and Karamakate re-enact symbolically, and thereby acknowledge, the hostilities that have for centuries divided their people. When Evan tries to stab Karamakate, the shaman admits to having killed Evan (since he sees the two men as identical, or Evan as a revenant of Theo) some fifty or a hundred years ago (a reference to the Indian's different sense of time and their belief in shape-shifting). On the other hand, Evan and Karamakate share what they revere most in their respective cultures: Joseph Haydn's music and the sacred Yakruna plant whose hallucinogenic powers are visualised in a mesmerising spectacle of colours that suddenly bursts onto the screen, unexpectedly disrupting the nuanced palette of shades of grey. The exchange of these gifts symbolises the reconciliation of hitherto hostile cultures.

Conclusion

In this chapter, I set out to re-examine and rehabilitate the contested concept of exoticism by bringing it into dialogue with cosmopolitanism and local authenticity, the politically correct avatar of exoticism, thereby demonstrating how fundamental shifts in the geospatial dynamics of globalisation have transformed the exotic imaginary and its ideological underpinnings in Indigenous cinema. As the analyses of the four films have shown, the project of ethnographic salvage, once the exclusive pursuit of Western ethnographers, has become central to the cosmopolitan sensibilities of the contemporary moment. Much of the agency has been transferred to Indigenous filmmakers for whom ethnographic salvage translates into the recuperation and maintenance of Indigenous cultural memory. The filmmakers aim to preserve Indigenous memory for the next generation while, at the same time, claiming a space in their countries' national histories, where they have been hitherto silenced or forgotten. The impetus behind these films, which, to a greater or lesser extent, were borne out of cross-cultural collaborations between Indigenous and majority culture filmmakers, speaks to the cosmopolitan aspiration to atone postcolonial guilt and to decolonise the lens.

The construction of Self and Other in the four films considered here avoids the binary logic of the old imperial exotic and, instead, imagines encounters with cultural difference as a reciprocal process that challenges or even inverts long-established hierarchies between the West and its ethnographic Others. While the notion of local authenticity is central to the films' genesis and the publicity surrounding them, they occupy different positions on the spectrum of ethnographic realism and exotic spectacle.[28] *Atanarjuat* and, albeit to a lesser degree, *Ten Canoes*, mount the most radical resistance to the exotic gaze, whereas *Tanna* and *Embrace of the Serpent* appropriate it with the aim of transforming hegemonic discourses on the exotic Other. Yet regardless of their different aesthetic approaches, all four films capture the attention of global audiences through their exquisite cinematography, which spectacularises the breathtaking beauty of unspoilt nature while at the same time promoting a diverse range of humanitarian and ecological issues: to rescue from oblivion the collective memory of Indigenous peoples; to empower disenfranchised communities to attain a voice; and to draw attention to the depletion of natural resources and ensuing ecological disaster. They are shrouded in a sense of melancholia in which the threat of environmental destruction blends with that of Indigenous extinction. In this way, the project of salvaging Indigenous memory is extended to salvaging the world's natural habitats which are vitally important for the planet's survival.

While all four films promote cross-cultural dialogue by inviting transnational audiences to engage with Indigenous cultures that are radically different from their own and to see the world through Indigenous eyes, *Embrace of the Serpent* goes one step further by explicitly calling the presumed superiority of Western values and regimes of knowledge into question. The cross-cultural collaborative mode of production, coupled with the ethico-political agendas of cosmopolitanism they articulate make the films discussed in this chapter paradigmatic examples of a cinema in which contemporary interest in locally authentic and exotic cultures converges with cosmopolitan sensibilities.

Notes

1. The anthropologists' customary use of the present tense in their observational accounts, which Fabian refers to as the 'ethnographic present' (Fabian 1983: 80), is more than a disciplinary convention, he argues. It goes hand in hand with excluding the ethnographic Other from participating in the dialogue with the anthropologist and foregrounds the assumption of an unchanging existence. According to Clifford (1989: 73–4), '"ethnographic

presents" are actually pasts. They represent culturally distinct times ("tradition") always about to undergo the impact of disruptive changes', caused by external influences.
2. Antonio Bolivar, who played the old Karamkate in *Embrace of the Serpent*, tragically died of COVID-19 when the virus was introduced to the Amazon by tourists in 2020.
3. 'Indigeneity' and the adjective 'Indigenous' refer to 'first peoples' such as Aborigines in Australia, Māori in New Zealand, and the 'Indian' tribes of North and South America, who were already present when colonial settlers arrived. The term denotes 'societies that are relatively small-scale, people who sustain deep connections with a place [and whose identity is shaped by] comparable experiences of invasion, dispossession, resistance, and survival' (Clifford 2013: 15).
4. The term 'Fourth World' was coined in 1974 by George Manuel, a Shuswap Indian and president of Canada's National Indian Brotherhood. In *The Fourth World: An Indian Reality* (1974), co-authored with Michael Posluns, he identifies the commonalities of Indigenous peoples around the world, namely a shared history of subjection to colonial settlers as well as a worldview that emphasise a reverence for the land and the importance of communal networks. Columpar (2010: 1–28) provides a useful overview of the emergence of Indigenous cinema as a transnational phenomenon.
5. Dior's 2019 advertisement for their fragrance range Eau Sauvage illustrates how the authenticity of Indigenous peoples is leveraged as a marketing tool. The promotional video featured Johnny Depp and two actors of First Nations descent and promised to take viewers on 'an authentic journey deep into the Native American soul in a sacred, founding and secular territory'. Despite having been made in collaboration with Native American consultants, it was harshly criticised for its racist stereotyping and cultural appropriation. Dior had to remove the video from social media (Singh 2019).
6. Rony (1996: 103) describes 'the myth of authentic first man' in *Nanook of the North* by identifying certain archetypal features, including 'a society ignorant of guns or gramophones: a society of man the hunter, man against nature, man the eater of raw flesh'.
7. Griffiths (2002: xxix) uses the term 'ethnographic film' to designate 'a set of cinematic practices' deployed by 'anthropologists, commercial and amateur filmmakers alike' to render native peoples. She does not use the term to refer to specific significatory practices or films based on anthropological fieldwork, but to designate the 'looking relations between the initiator of the gaze and the recipient'. For Griffiths, ethnographic film is not a distinct genre, but 'a way of using the cinematic medium to express ideas about racial and cultural difference'.
8. In *Cosmopolitan Cinema*, Chan (2017: 1–17) proposes that cosmopolitanism is an inherently ambivalent concept, whose ethical aspirations for social justice

and equality are undermined by its implicit celebration of a life of privilege that is reserved for the prosperous few.
9. Kant's key essays on cosmopolitanism are 'Idea for a Universal History from a Cosmopolitan Point of View' (1785); 'On the Common Saying 'This May Be True in Theory But it Does Not Apply to Practice' (1793); 'Toward Perpetual Peace: A Philosophical Sketch' (1795, revised 1796); and 'International Right in The Metaphysics of Morals' (1797). All are collected in Reiss (1970).
10. Fine and Cohen (2002: 145) are not the only scholars to have pointed out that Kant's cosmopolitan ideals are profoundly Eurocentric and even explicitly racist, leading them to conclude: 'Kant's views on race would not discomfort the average Nazi.' Similarly, Mignolo (2011: 332) notes that Kant's ideal of 'cosmopolitan conviviality and perpetual peace' is severely tainted by the ethnic and racial hierarchies he endorsed, whereby 'all non-European civilizations (even the South of Europe) were deficient in relation to the standards set by France, England and Germany'. To overcome cosmpolitanism's historical Eurocentrism, Mignolo advocates a decolonial cosmopolitanism that is based on dialogue, alliances and collaboration between different civilisations who, at different scales, share the repercussions of colonial racism and patriarchy.
11. Appiah continues a line of argument that can be traced back to Kant's normative ideal which, in effect, 'was no more than a recognition of the fact that the peoples of the earth have entered in varying degrees into a universal community and it has developed to the point where a violation of rights in one part of the world is felt everywhere' (Fine and Cohen 2002: 142).
12. Two noteworthy earlier Indigenous feature films, popular with mainstream audiences, are *Smoke Signals* (Chris Eyre, 1998), with an all-Native American creative team, and *Once Were Warriors* (Lee Tamahori, 1994), about an Auckland-based Māori family. Unlike the films discussed here, both are set in the present.
13. *Atanarjuat* was produced on a budget of CAD1.9 million.
14. The NATIVe festival strand at the International Film Festival in Berlin was short-lived; it closed in 2019 after just seven years.
15. These included *The Journals of Knud Rasmussen* (2006), which tells the story of Arctic colonial exploration from an Inuit point of view, while *Inuit Knowledge and Climate Change* (Zacharias Kunuk, Nunavut, 2010) provides a new angle on the negative effects of climate change on the Arctic region, foregrounding local Indigenous knowledge. Kunuk and Cohn's latest film, *One Day in the Life of Noah Piugattuk* (2019), is set in 1961 and captures a key moment in recent colonial history of the Inuit people, when they were forced by the Canadian government to abandon their self-sufficient way of life and move to a modern settlement.
16. Gulpilil originally intended to co-direct the film but for various reasons decided against it and the role of co-director fell to Peter Djigirr.

17. These characters are types, rather than stereotypes, as defined by Dyer (1996: 13, 16): 'The type is any character constructed through the use of a few immediately recognizable and defining traits, which do not change or "develop" through the course of the narrative and which point to general, recurrent features of the human world.' Whereas types make Otherness instantly recognisable, 'the role of stereotypes is to make visible the invisible . . . and to make fast, firm and separate what is in reality fluid.' In the mediated encounter with alterity on screen, Halle (2021: 41) suggests, the use of types is 'an easy and efficient way to quickly render otherness visible, to demarcate both identity and alterity'.
18. For an overview of the film's critical reception, cf. Krupat (2007) and Evans (2010: 86–100).
19. 'Pākehā' is the Māori language term for New Zealanders of European descent and, more broadly, any fair-skinned New Zealander who is not of Māori or Polynesian heritage.
20. Connell (2003: 571–3) offers an illustrative account of other 'spectres of inauthenticity' and 'invented traditions' on the Melanese islands (to which Tanna belongs) in the wake of the islands' decolonisation.
21. The gramophone also functions as a metonymy for Western civilisation in several other films, most notably *Nanook of the North*, where Nanook, who has supposedly never seen a gramophone or record before, tries to eat the record. In *Out of Africa* (Syndney Pollack, 1985), *Un barrage contre le Pacifique* (The Seawall, Rithy Panh, 2008) and *Indochine* gramophones introduce a flair of European sophistication to these putative outposts of progress in Kenya and Indochina, where white women attempt to restage European life in the colonies, dancing to the sound of European waltzes and tangoes in their opulent homes or colonial clubs or hosting lavish dinner parties. These scenes seem to show us that the characters have actually not 'gone native' but have retained strong connections to the places whence they came.
22. For cultural imaginaries of Amazonia, see Whitehead (2002), Slater (2002), Vieira (2020) and Russell (2020); for the South Sea islands, see Connell (2003) and Childs (2013). In his discussion of the South Sea islands, consisting of different archipelagos (Polynesia, Micronesia, Melanesia), Connell (2003: 567) details how Melanesia has hitherto been imagined in rather negative terms as 'an area of violence, taboo and danger' and 'a land out of time, the Stone Age par excellence', whereas Polynesia and Micronesia were imagined as a tropical paradise.
23. See *Amazônia* exhibition in London. Available at <https://www.sciencemuseum.org.uk/what-was-on/amazonia> (last accessed 23 June 2022).
24. Originally, the film *Tabu* was the joint project of Flaherty and Murnau. However, Flaherty envisaged a more documentary-style film that was true to the contemporary situation of Polynesia. Murnau, by contrast, wanted to create a romanticised fantasy that constructed a utopic image of a primitive world, in which innocence, sensuality and natural beauty prevail until

the destructive impact of civilisation heralds the romantic couple's expulsion from paradise. Flaherty and Murnau parted ways over their different approaches and only Murnau is credited as its director. Tragically, Murnau died in a car accident one week before the film's premiere in New York City in 1931.
25. Vieira (2020) proposes that the extensive use of aerial footage is part of 'a post-Anthropocentric Amazonian aesthetics' that elicits admiration and wonder in the spectator.
26. Guerra offers a full explanation of the mythological references and of the film's title in an extended interview in *Cineaste* (Guillén 2016).
27. The reference to Queen Elizabeth and Prince Philip is not as far-fetched as it may seem, since the Queen and Prince Philip visited Tanna Island in 1974. The royal visit resulted in the development of a religious sect, the Prince Philip Movement, on the island, whose followers believe that he is a divine being.
28. See Chapter 3 for an in-depth discussion of exotic spectacle.

CHAPTER 3

The Spectacle of Cultural Difference: The Tourist Gaze and the Exotic Gaze

A scene in the British comedy *The Best Exotic Marigold Hotel* shows seven retirees, who have turned their backs on the wet British weather and the long NHS waiting lists, on a bus to Jaipur, where they will start a new life in an Indian retirement home, the titular Best Exotic Marigold Hotel. Muriel (Maggie Smith) anxiously asks Graham (Tom Wilkinson), a retired judge who is sitting next to her: 'Do you think it'll be alright?', whereupon he replies: 'Don't ask me, I'm probably as scared as you are.' Then, after some reflection and a brief pause, he adds with optimism: 'It'll be extraordinary.' The cacophony of noise and spectacle of colour, the chaotic traffic of tuk-tuks amidst teeming crowds, the odd cow in the street, and the hustle and bustle of street markets that awaits the retirees in Jaipur instantly confirms Graham's prediction. The quest for the extraordinary, the purposeful departure from the ordinary and the familiar, propels travellers and tourists to suspend their everyday lives, normally for a limited time, and experience places and cultures different from their own. What is perceived as extraordinary, or indeed exotic, is in the eyes of the beholder. The crossing of cultural boundaries transforms one person's everyday into another person's exotic.

This chapter examines the relationship between the tourist and the exotic gaze by focusing predominantly on popular mainstream tourist films. It represents an attempt to set the record straight, since it would be disingenuous to undertake a critical reassessment of exoticism and its cultural value while deliberately omitting those manifestations of exoticism in contemporary (transnational) cinema that have contributed to the concept's tarnished reputation: its white supremacist assumptions, its cultural essentialism, and the spectacularisation and commodification of cultural difference. Since I am primarily interested in exoticism as an aesthetic category, I will pay close attention to the visual regimes of exoticism, notably its vivid chromatic design, alongside other spectacular qualities. Both regularly court suspicion in the West for being associated with excess and indulgence. Therefore, the visual pleasure they produce is, for reasons I shall delineate, regarded as a form of *guilty* pleasure. In short, this chapter addresses the allegedly irredeemable aspects of exoticism that make the concept so unequivocally 'non-pc'. To this end, I will compare the exotic and the tourist gaze in mainstream British and American films about touristic encounters in the Global South. *Eat Pray Love*, *Hector and the Search for Happiness*, *The Best Exotic Marigold Hotel* and its sequel have received scant scholarly attention, presumably on account of their perceived banality and indefensible representational politics. Due to their similar thematic concerns (old age and a woman's transformative journey), the Indian arthouse film *Hotel Salvation* and the Japanese–Uzbekistan co-production *To the Ends of the Earth*, have been cited as companion pieces to *The Best Exotic Marigold Hotel* and *Eat Pray Love*. An analysis of these films, alongside a brief consideration of Bollywood tourist films about Indians abroad, will allow me to further probe the limits and (ir)reversibility of the tourist and the exotic gaze.

To be sure, the tourist gaze is by no means limited to films about travel and tourism; instead, 'the textual construction of the spectator as virtual tourist' (Corbin 2014: 315) also occurs in films that do not thematise tourist experiences but that, nevertheless, mobilise touristic instincts and activate the spectator's pleasure in the inherent Otherness of people and places. The *James Bond* franchise with its glamorous foreign settings and the epic fantasy trilogy *The Lord of the Rings* (Peter Jackson, 2001–3), whose sublime landscapes enthralled millions of spectators and had an unprecedented impact on New Zealand's tourism, are apt examples. Even so, in this chapter I will examine films explicitly concerned with travel and tourism. Unlike Sue Beeton's *Film-Induced Tourism* (2005), Rodanthi Tzanelli's *The Cinematic Tourist* (2007), Stefan Roesch's *The Experiences of Film Location Tourists* (2009) and Alfio Leotta *Touring the Screen* (2011), to mention but a few books that examine the impact of cinema on tourism and destination marketing, I will pursue a different route and investigate the textual construction of the tourist and the exotic gaze without actually attending to the effect that films like *Eat Pray Love* have had on tourism in Bali (which was significant) or the influence of *The Best Exotic Marigold Hotel* on outsourcing 'the third age in the third world' (Ciafone 2017: 155).

To begin with, I will briefly outline how the emergence of tourism and the tourist gaze in the nineteenth century was inextricably linked to the production of images. The simultaneous development and expansion of transportation systems, notably railways and steamships, and new technologies that produced and projected images of foreign places led to a 'spectacle-oriented touristic consciousness' (Kirby 1997: 42). Travel lectures alongside guidebooks were indispensable in plotting itineraries of future journeys. Yet surprisingly, far from seeking to discover genuinely new, hitherto unseen places, tourists wanted to travel to destinations already familiar from images which had shaped their travel fantasies and which planted structures of touristic desire in their hearts and minds.

Tourism is a quintessentially modern experience, relying on the distinction between work and leisure. The rise of the leisure class and collective organised tourism, which was no longer the preserve of social elites, coincided with the birth of photography in 1840 (Urry and Larsen 2011: 14). But it was not until Eastman Kodak introduced the lightweight and affordable Brownie in the late 1880s that picture-taking became an integral part of the tourist experience. Until then, photography had by and large been the domain of professionals, whereas the user-friendly Kodak Brownie empowered amateurs to produce and consume their own images. Photography and travel became mass cultural practices and 'a means of appropriating the world through images' (Gunning 2006: 27). Travel images, whether in the form of photographs, postcards or travel lectures accompanied by lantern slides were crucial to the emerging tourist industry. Not only did they document the traveller's experience but they also incited the desire to travel or, conversely, served as a substitute for armchair travellers who lacked the financial means or motivation to explore foreign lands. Jointly, the expansion and affordability of new transport systems, innovations in image technology and the beginnings of organised tourism led to the making of 'the mobile, modern world' in which professional photographers, filmmakers and tourists captured images of distant places, brought them home and exhibited them in 'spectacular displays that taught the art of gazing at the world with touristic curiosity' (Urry and Larsen 2011: 165).

The birth of cinema in 1895 and the enormous popularity which travelogues, foreign views and scenics enjoyed, attests to the symbiotic relationship between the spatial mobility of travel and the moving image.[1] Panoramas, phantom rides and other early travel films functioned as machines for virtual travel that put 'the whole world within reach' (Gunning 2006: 33), as the promotional tagline used by many exhibitors of the early cinema of attractions promised.

The Tourist Gaze and the Exotic Gaze

The tourist gaze, a concept that has gained wide critical currency since John Urry introduced it in the 1990s, denotes a socially and culturally constructed way of seeing 'that orders, shapes and classifies, rather than reflects the world' (Urry and Larsen 2011: 2) by producing imaginary geographies. Given that tourism relies to a significant extent on the appeal of foreign places and cultures, the tourist and the exotic gaze have much in common. First, both are relational concepts, dependant on the deictic stance of the beholder. What is perceived as extraordinary or exotic depends on the socio-cultural background of the gazing subject. Like other scopic regimes (such as the male gaze, famously theorised by Laura Mulvey (1975)), the tourist gaze is constituted 'in relationship to its opposite, the non-tourist forms of social experience and consciousness' (Urry and Larsen 2011: 3).

Second, the tourist and the exotic gaze could be described as déjà vu experiences. Despite promising the excitement of discovering something new, paradoxically, they cite and recycle familiar iconographies and vistas that make supposedly unchartered territories instantly recognisable. In contemporary culture, professional tourist photography and other mediated images in tourist brochures or on websites, televised travel shows, in documentaries and feature films prompt travellers and tourists (a distinction to which I shall return) to go in search of views, most of which have been reproduced multiple times before. They want to see them with their own eyes and take pictures or videos, replicating the same view once more.[2]

Third, the tourist and the exotic gaze are aesthetic modes of perception that are governed by principles of selection and composition, creating beautiful images that are 'aesthetically more compelling than those seen through mere human vision. They overpower human vision by being more theatrical, better lit, sharper and more highly coloured than seeing itself' (Urry and Larsen 2011: 174). Although what is regarded as beautiful, picturesque or photogenic has changed over time, it typically conforms to approved models. For example, eighteenth-century scenic tourism and the Grand Tour, practised by the upper classes, can be regarded as an important precursor of the tourist gaze. It promoted the idea of aesthetic connoisseurship and the well-trained eye. Devices such as the *camera obscura* and the Claude Glass, named after the French landscape painter Claude Lorrain, were used to capture, or rather construct, scenic views. Unlike photography, the *camera obscura* and the Claude Glass did not actually produce images but merely served as aids for facilitating aesthetic appreciation and drawing. Claude Glasses were small, convex mirrors which travellers used to gaze at a beautiful or picturesque view. Rather than looking directly at the countryside, travellers turned their backs on it and, instead, marvelled at the compressed and composed reflection in the mirror. The delicate golden tint of the glass enhanced the harmony of colours and the overall unity of the image, lending the composition a painterly quality (see Gunning 2010: 35). By giving it perspective and frame, the Claude Glass tamed nature and turned it into landscape. It transformed experience into aesthetic perception.

In the contemporary context, the *National Geographic* has played a pivotal role in establishing an aesthetic template for the visual representation of the exotic and locating it in the Global South. It also deftly illustrates what Susan Sontag (1979: 112) has described as 'photography's democratising notion of beauty', no longer limited to classical ideals of proportion and perfection, but instead a beauty that 'has been revealed by photographs as existing everywhere'. Famous for its award-winning photojournalism, the American magazine with a global circulation of around 6.7 million, together with its television channels, website, the magazine *National Geographic Traveller* and upmarket global adventure tours, *National Geographic* has provided a globally recognised blueprint for the exotic as well as the tourist gaze. As Catherine Lutz and Jane Collins demonstrate (1993: 95), the *National Geographic* invariably renders the strange as beautiful and, until the 1970s at least, pictured 'a world without blemish or handicap . . . [by] virtually eliminat[ing] the ill, the pockmarked, the deformed, or the hungry'. Even when a growing demand for authenticity required a more balanced approach that showed the coexistence of the 'beautiful *and* ugly, [the] ordered *and* disordered' (Lutz and Collins 1993: 114; italics in original), *National Geographic*'s eye-catching photojournalism has continued to beautify the world by making the everyday, and even poverty and human suffering, look photogenic. Central to *National Geographic*'s beautification of the world are the use of nuanced and vibrant colour palettes and well-proportioned image compositions that, despite their ostensible documentary realism, are overtly aestheticised.[3]

Fourth, the heightened aesthetics of the tourist and the exotic gaze instantiate what Sontag (1979: 121) has theorised, in relation to photography, as 'an acquisitive relation to the world'. She argues that photography, though purporting to merely document reality, actually has the capacity to transform reality into an object of beauty. Ultimately, it is the pleasure elicited by 'the aestheticizing tendency' (Sontag 1979: 119) that arouses the desire for appropriation:

> Whatever moral claims made on behalf of photography, its main effect is to convert the world into a department store or museum-without-walls in which every subject is depreciated into an article of consumption, promoted into an item for aesthetic appreciation. Through the camera people become customers or tourists of reality . . . Bringing the exotic near, rendering the familiar and homely exotic, photographs make the entire world available as an object of appraisal. (Sontag 1979: 119–20)

Sontag establishes a direct link here between aesthetic pleasure and the desire it stimulates for the consumption of the beautiful object. Echoing Sontag's observations about photography's acquisitive impetus, Urry (1995: 132–6) proposes that the gaze is not only central to tourist activity but, in fact, a form of consumption in itself. The tourist gaze holds out the promise of intense pleasures that are 'either on a different scale or involving different senses from those customarily encountered' (Urry and Larsen 2011: 4). The tourist industry promises to fulfil these anticipated pleasures by converting them into commodified experiences. In a similar vein, the exotic gaze can transform cross-cultural encounters into commodities by spectacularising and fetishising cultural difference and, thereby, capitalising on the commercial appeal it holds for transnational audiences, tourists and consumers more broadly.

Notwithstanding the many correspondences, the tourist gaze is more encompassing in terms of its object scope than the exotic gaze. It includes domestic as well as foreign landmarks anywhere in the world, be it the Empire State Building or the Taj Mahal, or typical landscapes such as the Alps or the African savannah, and particular signs that make a locality instantly recognisable, such as the colourful classic cars against the backdrop of Havana's colonial architecture. It is obvious that, from a Western vantage point, the Taj Mahal and the nostalgic charm of Havana would be both exotic and touristic attractions, whereas the other sights would not. It thus follows that exoticism serves as a particular lens for the tourist gaze. But whereas tourism inevitably results in cultural homogenisation, exoticism depends on the maintenance of cultural boundaries lest novelty and a sense of astonishment be preserved. Yet ironically, global tourism destroys the very commodity it sells and therefore continually needs to search for and promote new, supposedly undiscovered destinations. The recent rise of slum tourism, which according to Ana Mendes (2010: 478) was significantly driven by the global box-office success of Danny Boyle's multi-Academy-Award-winning film *Slumdog Millionaire* (2008), suggests that, where there are only few new horizons to discover, tourists' attention is channelled away from the beautiful and desirable cultural Other and, in the name of cultural authenticity, directed to its dark and ugly underbelly. Zoya Akhtar's Hindi-language musical drama *Gully Boy* (2019) which, like *Slumdog Millionaire*, is set in the Dharavi slums of Mumbai, dramatises such a visit when a group of British tourists, equipped with cameras, mobile phones and selfie-sticks, descends upon the Indian protagonist's overcrowded home. His business-savvy grandmother demands 500 rupees extra, in addition to the slum tour ticket for which the tourists have already paid, to grant them access. With a sense of resignation, the Indian family succumbs to the voyeuristic gaze of the intruders, whose feigned admiration for the efficient use of space barely camouflages their sense of relief that they themselves do not have to live in such cramped conditions.

As the above considerations demonstrate, both the tourist gaze and the exotic gaze use beautiful and, therefore, seductive images that promise to deliver pleasurable or exciting experiences. This even applies to the portrayal of abject poverty in films like *Salaam, Bombay!* and *Slumdog Millionaire*, which combine elements of documentary-style realism with the tropes and visual grammar of exoticism. By making poverty picturesque, these films attenuate the moral unease spectators might otherwise feel about child exploitation, the misery of eking out an existence in the back alleys and slums of Mumbai and the social inequalities between the Global North and South in general.

Spectacle as Guilty Pleasure

While it is obvious that the voyeuristic spectacle of poverty is ethically indefensible, spectacle in itself, regardless of the object put on display, is generally viewed with profound suspicion – at least in the West. To be sure, the pioneers of cinema saw things differently. The early 'cinema of attractions' was celebrated for 'inciting visual curiosity and supplying pleasure through an exciting spectacle' (Gunning 2011: 73). But as soon as it began to compete with narrative cinema (roughly from 1906 onwards), narrative was accorded priority over spectacle. Despite cinema being a visual medium, spectacle is perceived as a form of excess that disrupts narrative coherence and progression (see Bukatman 2006; Lewis 2014). That is why Hollywood blockbusters, action films and musicals are often dismissed as 'empty spectacle'. Spectacle, a term derived from the Latin *spectare* (to view, watch) and *specere* (to look at), commands the spectator to look rather than think, reflect and analyse. It addresses the senses rather than reason. Spectacle's colourfulness, opulence and flamboyance – in short, its indisputable sensuality – are perceived as threatening and transgressive and feared to disrupt the inherent logic of the narrative system and, indeed, the stability of its meaning. Its fascination with surfaces makes spectacle per se, but especially the spectacle of cultural difference ideologically suspect since, as detailed in Chapter 1, seductive surfaces are alleged to distract from and obscure uncomfortable truths. The heightened aesthetics of beautiful images, such as those created by the exotic and the tourist gaze, purportedly harbour deception, whereas gritty realism's aesthetic of austerity and its typically sparse visual style is perceived to reveal the truth. Finally, the pervasive suspicion which has suffused critiques of spectacle centrally revolves around its inherent power dynamics. In contrast to the active act of looking, which confers power and control onto the looking subject, the passive state of being looked at is disempowering. The object of the gaze – whether it is the male, the exotic or the tourist gaze – generates visual pleasure and desire in the subject: the desire to control, to possess or to consume. The critique levelled at the consumable visual pleasure that spectacle affords is, by Marxist critics indebted to the Frankfurt School, linked to the commodification of popular culture, which starkly contrasts with the emancipatory power that high culture and autonomous art are believed to have.

The spectacularisation of cultural difference is a prime example of commodity fetishism. In the context of today's 'booming "alterity industry"', commodity fetishism represents 'the postmodern version of exoticist mystique' (Huggan 2001: vii, 18), one of the distinctive features of earlier forms of exoticist representation. Huggan (2001: 19) identifies three aspects of commodity fetishism in relation to the postcolonial exotic: 'mystification (or levelling-out) of historical experience; imagined access to the cultural other through the process of consumption; reification of people and places into exchangeable aesthetic objects'. In this way, exotic modes of representation construct an economy of desire for the consumption of the cultural Other.

The above considerations would seem to suggest that the pleasures derived from the spectacle of cultural difference are ethically unsustainable. Its glossy surfaces please the eye, engulf the senses and, supposedly, invite passive consumption rather than active critical engagement, thus precluding any form of intellectual interrogation and political resistance. As Dana Polan (1982–3: 137, 140) puts it, spectacle is 'a command to "look here" that needs no cognitive assent other than the initial fact of looking . . . it blocks, ignores, shuts out, other forms of cognition . . . Spectacle works to convert the critical into the merely watched and watchable'. It seduces, instils desire and gives pleasure – *guilty* pleasure.

The sense of guilt arises for two reasons. First, exotic spectacle fetishises the Other and, in so doing, 'licenses an unregulated voyeurism' (Hall 1997: 268). According to Freud, voyeurism is driven by a disavowed desire for illicit pleasure which, ultimately, cannot be fulfilled. Second, the notion of guilty pleasure is linked to the consumption of cultural artifacts with mass appeal. The sense of guilt does not derive from moral transgressions but instead from the fact that these popular artifacts offer easy enjoyment without edification or intellectual effort. Wedded to long-established cultural hierarchies, this line of argument is indebted to a philosophical debate that reaches back to Aristotle, Plato, Immanuel Kant and, most influentially, Theodor W. Adorno and Max Horkheimer's (1997: 144) critique of 'mere pleasure' in their important essay 'The Culture Industry': 'Pleasure always means not to think about anything, to forget suffering even where it is shown. Basically it is helplessness. It is flight; not, as is asserted, flight from a wretched reality, but from the last remaining thought of resistance.' Adorno and Horkheimer's profound mistrust of pleasure is based on the distinction between the emancipatory power of high art and the simple gratifications of mass culture. Their critique posits an uncritical passive consumer who is incapable of recognising – or indeed resisting – the guilty pleasures popular culture affords. Yet their argument has been challenged. For instance, Sandra Ponzanesi (2014: 47) contends that spectators, and consumers of culture more broadly, do not simply 'succumb to [popular] entertainment' and suspend their 'critical awareness', but are 'cosmopolitan critical participant[s]', capable of actively deconstructing and interrogating the processes of meaning-making and seduction. Rosalind Galt (2011: 11) reminds us that 'consumerism and aesthetic seduction' are an integral part of cinema. Meanwhile, Slavoj Žižek (2006: 12) urges us to indulge in the guilty pleasure of watching films widely dismissed as artistically insignificant, 'charmingly commercial' or outright 'trash' and take them seriously. But why? Žižek does not provide an answer. Perhaps the cultural iconoclasm he endorses signals an attempt to liberate audiences in the West from the prevailing Protestant attitude towards pleasure that needs to be reassessed against the background of globalised media cultures. As Bollywood cinema, with its spectacular song-and-dance sequences that interrupt narrative progression and afford multiple opportunities for spectatorial pleasure, illustrates, the distrust in the pleasures of spectacle originates from a distinctly Western set of attitudes and values that can be traced back as far as the Enlightenment. In the context of popular Hindi cinema these interruptions, a concept theorised by Lalitha Gopalan in her book *Cinema of Interruptions* (2002), do not constitute a negative stalling of the narrative development but, instead, 'pleasure pauses'. Ranjit Kumar introduces this alternative term in response to Gopalan to emphasise that these interruptions, though by no means devoid of a narrative or structural function, mainly serve to heighten the spectator's visual and aural pleasure. While some are integrated into the diegesis, others, including song sequences set against the backdrop of idealised tourist settings, transport spectators into an alternative world where they can enjoy 'a pleasurable interlude to the film's narrative' (Kumar 2011: 40).[4] The pleasure pauses of Bollywood cinema are, however, a special case, whose structural characteristics differ from the spectacle in the other films under consideration in this chapter and elsewhere in the book.

The implicit assumption that spectacle and narrative are somehow antithetical has been superseded by approaches that demonstrate how narrative, character and spectacular modes of address in cinema are deeply intertwined (see Tasker 2004; Hall and Neale 2010). Rather than eclipsing narrative, spectacle momentarily shifts the balance between narrative and spectatorial address, amplifying the spectator's affective response and providing a different route to accessing meaning. The case studies that follow aim to illustrate how the spectacle of cultural difference works in tandem with narrative tropes to assert white power and privilege.

White Privileged Tourists: *Eat Pray Love*, *The Best Exotic Marigold Hotel* and *Hector and the Search for Happiness*

'Tourists dislike tourists' (MacCannell 2013: 10) and most tourists deem themselves to be travellers, which is a more aspirational term since it invokes the positive images of heroic explorers, intrepid adventurers or curious ethnographers. Whereas tourists are mere 'sightseers' and, as such, 'satisfied with superficial experiences of other peoples and other places' (MacCannell 2013: 10), travellers aspire to a deeper engagement with other cultures and societies. Todorov describes the tourist as 'a visitor in a hurry' (Todorov 1993: 344), equipped with a camera and in search of the typical, which the locals are eager to provide in exchange for money. As early as the 1960s, Daniel Boorstin (1961: 84) laments the disappearance of the active inquisitive traveller and the rise of the passive, pleasure-seeking tourist. This distinction between travellers and tourists, which assigns the tourist to the inferior position, contrasts with that of tourists and vagabonds, proposed by Zygmunt Bauman. It is important to note, however, that Bauman uses the concepts not in a sociological sense but instead as metaphors of contemporary life, which he sees as characterised by a heightened sense of mobility and transience, fluidity and inconsequentiality.

> The tourists stay or move at their hearts' desire. They abandon the site when the new untried opportunities beckon elsewhere. The vagabonds know that they won't stay in a place for long, however strongly they wish to, since nowhere they stop are they likely to be welcome. The tourists move because they find the world within their (global) reach irresistibly *attractive* – the vagabonds move because they find the world within their (local) reach unbearably *inhospitable*. The tourists travel because *they want to*; the vagabonds because *they have no other bearable choice*. (Bauman 1998: 92–3; italics in original)

The figure of the vagabond comprises the migrants and refugees, who are clamouring at the gates of European and of other prosperous nations. The vagabond is the 'the *alter ego* of the tourist' (Bauman 1998: 94) just as the destitute is the alter ego of the rich. For Bauman, the distinction between tourists and vagabonds reflects the principal division of postmodern society, where some are forced to move around and others possess the freedom to actively determine their itineraries. Tourists are the ultimate figures of privilege, endowed not only with choice but also with the financial means to travel and the leisure time to do so.

In the case studies discussed in this chapter, tourists (who conceive of themselves as travellers) combine these privileges with that of being white. White privilege, Richard Dyer argues, is the enjoyment of advantages and positions of dominance and power that are systematically bestowed upon white people irrespective of their individual efforts or achievements. So ubiquitous is white privilege in the West, that it is invisible, or so it may seem, to those who enjoy it and who are oblivious to their particularity. This is due to the tacit 'equation of being white with being human [which] secures a position of power. White people have power and believe that they think, feel and act like and for all people . . . they construct the world in their own image' (Dyer 1997: 9). Consequently, white privilege creates a blind spot and a profound insensitivity to the asymmetries inherent in cultural difference.

The journeys on which the American writer Liz Gilbert in *Eat Pray Love*, the group of retired British seniors in *The Best Exotic Marigold Hotel* and the wealthy psychiatrist in *Hector and the Search for Happiness* embark are as much impelled by a sense of disenchantment with their privileged lives as by a profound sense of entitlement that the world out there is theirs for the taking. They believe that contact with exotic cultures will serve as a panacea for their discontent, marital problems and anhedonia. What distinguishes these privileged tourists, however, from the idealised figure of the knowledge-seeking traveller is that their engagement with foreign cultures is ultimately self-indulgent since their journeys of quest are actually not about discovering India, Tibet, Africa, China or Indonesia but about finding themselves through the revitalising and exciting contact with the exotic Other.[5]

Rarely is the white privilege of speaking for humanity as a whole made more explicit than in Liz's (Julia Roberts) voice-over in the opening sequence of *Eat Pray Love*. The film adaptation of Elizabeth Gilbert's best-selling memoir of her year-long journey, *Eat Pray Love: One Woman's Search for Everything across Italy, India and Indonesia* (2006), begins with a montage of aerial shots of gentle waves lapping a beach, lush green palm trees and terraced rice paddies in Bali, intercut with shots of Liz cycling amidst this quintessentially exotic scenery.[6] The sound of local gamelan music gives way to Liz's voice-over reflections on the human condition, or rather, what she perceives it to be. She gives an account of what her friend, a psychologist from Philadelphia, told her when she was counselling a group of Cambodian refugees who had recently arrived in the city after having experienced harrowing boat trips, starvation, genocide and years in refugee camps.

> So guess what all these refugees wanted to talk about to my friend Deborah, the psychologist: 'I met this guy in a refugee camp . . . I thought he really loved me, but when we got separated on the boat, he took up with my cousin . . . now he keeps calling and says he really loves me.' This is how we are.

By suggesting that regardless of race, colour, class and the vastly different experiences that shape people's lives, we are all the same, Liz, a journalist in her thirties who is going through a marriage crisis, trivialises the trauma and existential plight of the Cambodian refugees. What is more, she makes her own relationship problems the measure of all human suffering. Her voice-over encapsulates the film's premise that the experience of a broken heart unites humanity and that, therefore, the quest of a white, affluent woman to regain her zest for life after a divorce by learning to eat (in Italy), pray (in India) and love again (in Indonesia), is a universal quest. The fact that all the countries she visits start with the letter 'I' underscores the egocentricity of Liz's voyage of self-discovery. 'White people discovering themselves in brown places' has become a fashionable form of tourism and neo-colonialism, which is less overt than that of 'the old colonials in their pith helmets trampling over the Empire's far-flung outposts', Sanip Roy (2010) observes sarcastically.

> At least they were somewhat honest in their dealings. They wanted the gold, the cotton, and laborers for their sugar plantations. And they wanted to bring Western civilization, afternoon tea and anti-sodomy laws to godforsaken places riddled with malaria and beriberi.

The new breed of colonials are white Western tourists, like Elizabeth Gilbert, who go on long journeys to faraway places but mostly socialise with other tourists or expats, while the locals supply local colour and an opportunity for white tourists to do good by becoming the saviours of brown people.

As if to give Gayatri Chakravorty Spivak's (1995: 33) oft-cited remark that 'white men are saving brown women from brown men' a feminist twist, *Eat Pray Love* assigns this role to a white woman. Liz uses her network of rich American friends to raise enough money for Wayan (Christine Hakim), a Balinese healer who, after divorcing her abusive husband lost her home, to build a comfortable house for herself and her daughter. Rumya Sree Putcha (2020: 451–61) regards Liz's benevolence as a manifestation of a popular form of contemporary tourist practice, known as 'voluntourism' or 'mission trips', a form of 'charitable imperialism ... which is predicated on entrenched Orientalist notions of those in the global South as eternally destitute'. Equally problematic is Liz's encouragement of the Indian teenage bride Tulsi (Rushita Singh), whom she meets in the Indian ashram, to accept the arranged marriage her parents have planned for her and relinquish her ambition to go to university. Tulsi's acceptance of her fate reinforces the idea that freedom of choice is the privilege of the tourist, as defined by Bauman, whereas the vagabond (or subaltern in this instance) is denied the autonomy of determining her own destiny. This ideological dilemma is barely touched upon and remains unresolved in the film. Instead, it creates a welcome opportunity for the spectacle of a Hindu wedding.

Ethnic weddings feature prominently in exotic cinema since they are colourful rituals that function as moments of cultural display and serve as a form of distilled cultural Otherness. Rituals encapsulate 'two primary features of exoticism – living close to the sacred or supernatural and living with the past' (Lutz and Collins 1993: 91). Therefore, rituals offer glimpses of something that Western societies are deemed to have lost, a connection with the sacred through religion and a connection with the past through lived tradition. Moreover, the transformation of cultural difference into beautiful images contains the potential threat of alterity. In *Eat Pray Love*, Tulsi's richly embroidered red-and-golden sari and veil, the abundance of golden jewellery, including a large ornamental nose ring and earrings with which her body is festooned, serves as an index of cultural Otherness. The scene showcases a cornucopia of bright orange marigold flowers and distinctive rituals of a Hindu wedding which audiences have come to expect from similar scenes in countless Bollywood films that culminate in a wedding, including *Kuch Kuch Hota Hai* (Karan Johar, 1998), *Vivah* (Sooraj Barjatiya, 2006) and diasporic wedding films, such as *Monsoon Wedding* (Mira Nair, 2001), *The Namesake* (Mira 2007) and *Bride and Prejudice* (Gurinder Chadha, 2004): the application of a bindi on the bride's forehead, the exchange of flower garlands between bride and groom (*jaimala*), the couple taking seven steps around the holy fire (*saptapadi*) and an exuberant wedding dance that unites the newly-weds with their families and guests.

The soundtrack of the Hindu wedding scene foregrounds exoticism's propensity for cultural eclecticism. 'The Long Road' is performed by the American musician Eddie Vedder and Nusrat Fateh Ali Khan, a famous Pakistani singer of qawwali, who has popularised this form of devotional music globally. Qawwali is linked to Sufism, a particular form of Islamic mysticism; however, qawwali wedding songs are played at Indian weddings (both Muslim and Hindu) and have evolved into secular music. The qawwali-inspired song is followed by the cheerful tune of a brass band and, as soon as Tulsi's wedding gives rise to Liz's memories of her own wedding dance, the music switches to 'Celebration' by Kool and the Gang. Similar instances of musical bricolage occur throughout *Eat Pray Love*. In Italy, Liz is relishing a bowl of pasta bolognese to the tune of an aria from *The Magic Flute* by Wolfgang Amadeus Mozart. Why, one cannot but wonder, an aria by an Austrian composer, when Italian operas by Giacomo Puccini and Giuseppe Verdi are just as famous and more fitting for an alfresco meal in one of Rome's piazzas? The musical score accompanying Liz's sojourn on Bali, 'S Wonderful' by João Gilberto and 'Samba da Bênção' by Bebel Gilberto, is similarly incongruous with the setting. Their Brazilian provenance may either highlight the centrality of Liz's encounter with the Brazilian Felipe (Javier Bardem), with whom she falls in love on Bali, or simply serve as a generically exotic soundtrack that is globally recognisable.[7]

Eat Pray Love's musical bricolage stands in stark contrast to the espoused value of local authenticity that supposedly underpins Liz's identity quest and that has become a cornerstone of contemporary tourist practice. The experience of an authentic local culture is widely regarded (and marketed) as invigorating and, indeed, an antidote for white, middle-class problems. The Balinese healer, Ketut (Hadi Subiyanto), who offers his services in the heart of the picturesque tourist town Ubud, assumes the role of Liz's spiritual healer, who helps her regain balance. He is a small man with a perpetual broad smile on his wrinkled face, who exudes warmth and shares his words of wisdom in broken, heavily accented English, which automatically seems to enhance their spirituality. During their first encounter, Ketut reads Liz's hand and predicts: 'You will live on Bali for three to four months and teach me English; and I will teach you everything I know.' But when she returns a year later, now newly divorced, he does not even recognise her at first since hundreds of American tourists have been seeking his spiritual guidance. He is running a thriving business. This reference to the commodification of Ketut's spirituality diminishes its perceived authenticity since what is commonly regarded as authentic is precisely that which has remained unaffected by the global commodification of cultural difference. Although the verbal repartees between Ketut and Liz suggest that their relationship is based on a reciprocal exchange – spiritual healing for English lessons – the English lessons are not dramatised and it is the privileged white American woman who benefits unilaterally from the pop psychology teachings of the Balinese healer ('Sometimes to lose balance for love is part of leading balanced life'). At face value, this seems to suggest that *Eat Pray Love* inverts colonialism's civilising mission by assigning the role of the educator to the exotic Other. What complicates this ostensible inversion of the old colonial power dynamics, however, is the fact that Ketut is simultaneously depicted as an old wise man and a child. His characterisation, therefore, recalls the infantilisation of colonial subjects in colonial discourse that legitimised the civilising mission in the first place. For example, when Liz invites him to come and visit her in the United States, his reply, 'Ketut cannot fly on aeroplane. Ketut have no teeth', suggests that his powers of logical reasoning are as underdeveloped as those of a small child. Ultimately, and for all his commodified spirituality, the spiritual healer and teacher Ketut is cast as endearingly childlike and unworldly, and therefore incapable of inverting the power hierarchies that underpin the encounter between white privileged tourists and the exotic Other.

Similar ambivalences shape the encounters between the white British psychiatrist Hector (Simon Pegg), who is galivanting around the world to learn from other people what makes them happy in *Hector and the Search for Happiness*. Like *Eat Pray Love*, the film is based on a bestselling book, a blend between novel and self-help manual by the French psychiatrist François Lelord. Throughout his journey, Hector jots down his realisations in memorable maxims, such as 'Avoiding unhappiness is not the road to happiness' and 'Happiness is being loved for who you are' that are handwritten across the screen and serve as take-away lessons in life for the spectator. One of the destinations of Hector's journey is a remote Tibetan monastery, perched on the edge of a steep mountain high up in the Himalayas. The stunning scenery is familiar from countless advertisements for tourism to Tibet, while also recalling the convent in *Black Narcissus* (Michael Powell and Emeric Pressburger, 1947), where a group a of British nuns is trying to educate the local Himalayan hill-tribes, only to eventually succumb to the sensuous allure of this exotic location and see their mission fail. The Buddhist monk (Togo Igawa), whose spiritual guidance Hector seeks, imparts his lessons in life in heavily accented English and speaks in riddles ('Higher than that, Hector'), which lends his teachings a certain exotic mystique. Like Ketut, he is portrayed as simultaneously sage and childlike, requiring nothing more than a gust of wind that blows and twirls the colourful prayer flags to be jumping with joy underneath them. Similarly, in 'generic Africa', imagined as a continent with expansive savannas, lions and elephants, as well as violent warlords, Hector learns once again how little it takes to be happy. The African woman (S'Thandiwe Kgoroge), whom Hector meets on a precariously unsafe aeroplane, invites him to enjoy a meal of sweet potato stew and a celebratory dance with her large family. Through this experience Hector realises that you do not have to be rich to be happy, an insight that eases his and any white privileged Westerner's conscience about poverty in 'generic Africa' or other developing countries or continents in the world. To be sure, Hector meets some inspiring teachers on his world-wide quest for happiness, but whether these encounters invert the hierarchies that once underpinned colonialism's civilising mission, is questionable. Hector himself is portrayed as childlike. He identifies himself with the teenage protagonist of the comic book series *The Adventures of Tintin*, who travels around the world with his dog Snowy (whom Hector repeatedly imagines by his side). Therefore, his encounter with the infantilised exotic Other is more like a meeting between equals. What undermines this equality, however, is the highly reductive portrayal of the exotic Other that verges on racism. Although his African hosts are portrayed in positive terms as fun-loving, hospitable and warm-hearted, they are reduced to ethnic stereotypes, that simplify and essentialise 'complex cultural codes to easily consumable visual and verbal cues' (Wiegman 1998: 161). The film's inherent racism manifests itself in the imbalance between the collectivisation of the laughing and dancing Africans and the individualisation of Hector, whose needs they serve. In this way, the interaction between Hector and the Africans replicates the master–servant trope between the white coloniser and the coloured colonial subjects.

The same holds true for the relationship between the seven white British seniors who have decided to spend their golden years in the Best Exotic Marigold Hotel in Jaipur, and the hotel's young proprietor Sonny Kapoor (Dev Patel) and his staff. Not only does the economic differential make India, where they can enjoy a relatively comfortable lifestyle on their insufficient pensions, an attractive destination, but the hotel setting automatically assigns the locals the role of service providers, if not exactly servants. The popular feel-good movie *The Best Exotic Marigold Hotel* and its (less humorous and less successful) sequel *The Second Best Exotic Marigold Hotel* explore what motivated the retirees to travel to India and how they adapt to the new life there. The hotel 'for the elderly and beautiful' (as the advertisement proclaims), an old, colonial-style palace in one of

Rajasthan's most touristy cities, has seen better days and is a far cry from the luxurious retirement home advertised in the photoshopped marketing brochure that attracted the British guests to relocate. The plaster is crumbling, the telephones are broken and pigeons have made their nests in some of the rooms. Lack of funds has prevented the owner from refurbishing the hotel, but his charm and the warm welcome he extends make up for the somewhat basic amenities which lend the place an exotic atmosphere. Sonny uses the humble language of a servant interspersed with malapropisms: 'It is my pride and honour to tell you that the building is 100 per cent shipshape' and 'You have all heard the chimes at midnight and long in tooth have you become. Who knows how many days you have left?' His inadvertent ageism is incommensurate with his entrepreneurial spirit to make a profit out of old people, who are discarded as unproductive and useless in the West. The offensiveness of his unintentional ageism is counterbalanced by Muriel's outspoken racism. Despite not liking foreigners in the first place, she has come to India to get a cheap hip replacement and to avoid the long waiting lists of the British NHS.

Not unlike the British colonisers, the British pensioners make it their mission to rescue the 'natives' from backwardness through the inculcation of Western know-how and business-savvy: the affable retired judge Graham Dashwood, who has returned to Jaipur to find the man whom he loved deeply in his youth, teaches a group of kids playing cricket in the street how to improve their batting technique. Evelyn Greenslade (Judi Dench) coaches the staff of a call centre how to enhance their communication skills and sales pitches when dealing with clients in Britain. Although she has been a housewife for her entire life and would, therefore, seem ill-equipped to act as a business coach for a large company, she is confident that her own experience of being at the receiving end of a rather depersonalised long-distance call from an Indian call centre at the beginning of the film has provided her with just the right expertise to advise the call handlers on how to deliver a more tailored and efficient service. The bigoted Muriel, who initially instructs one of the hotel staff how to sweep the hotel floors properly, eventually succumbs to the magic of the Best Exotic Marigold Hotel, abandons her virulent racism and does everything in her might to save the hotel from bankruptcy by checking the business accounts, striking a financial deal with an investor and becoming the assistant manager. In short, John Madden's neo-colonial fantasy casts the British hotel guests, who inject some entrepreneurial spirit into Jaipur's supposedly ailing economy, as the heroic white saviours of endearing but incompetent Indians. By the end of *The Second Best Exotic Marigold Hotel*, all of the British pensioners are in gainful employment. In keeping with the film's capitalist logic, economic productivity is equated with the mature protagonists' successful rejuvenation.

The revitalisation of the body and senses is one of exoticism's most enduring tropes (see Chapter 1) but the means of achieving this are not usually imagined in terms of the ethos of labour and productivity in foreign lands. In keeping with this trope, the retirees gain a new lease of life through the visceral experience of Indian culture simply by 'donning dupattas, riding in rickshaws, [and] doing yoga at daybreak' (Ciafone 2017: 160). Ultimately, the film's endorsement of cultural assimilation remains rather tokenistic since it is the British seniors who maintain 'the relative upper hand' in their relationship with the Indians and, in so doing, attest to the 'flexible *positional* superiority' that Edward Said (2003: 7; italics in original) has identified as constitutive of the power hierarchies between the West and the Orient. Although exoticism is not devoid of asymmetries of power, 'the impulse . . . to dominate' (Said 2003: 331) the Other is, as outlined in Chapter 1, a feature more distinctive of Orientalism than of exoticism. What lends the films discussed above their exotic allure is not primarily the supremacy of the white Western tourists but the exoticism of place.

Exoticism of place

Despite Evelyn's assertion that 'nothing can prepare the uninitiated for this riot of noise and colour, for the heat and the motion, the perpetual teeming of crowds', the spectator of *The Best Exotic Marigold Hotel* is very well prepared because the bustling and chaotic street life is a staple of the iconography of contemporary India. In *The Best Exotic Marigold Hotel*, the fast-paced montage, hyper-mobile camera and blurred tracking shots capture the kinetic energy of urban life in India and convey a sense of excitement and even danger. How many people, a Western spectator cannot but wonder, lose their lives in traffic accidents here every day? Women in colourful saris balance heavy loads on their heads while emaciated, sacred cows amble fearlessly amidst the incessant flow of rickshaws, tuk-tuks, dusty old cars and mopeds. A cacophony of car horns, bicycle bells and the shouting of street vendors accompanies the visual spectacle. These street scenes, which are juxtaposed with images of building sites and new urban development, epitomise what Christa Knellwolf and Iain McCalman (2002: 1–2) have identified as a hallmark of the contemporary exotic, which 'often involves a clash in some way between modes of traditional life and makeshift adaptations to Western technology' and it is precisely this 'resulting incongruity [which] exerts an attraction of its own'.

THE TOURIST GAZE AND THE EXOTIC GAZE 119

Figure 3.1 The chaotic and colourful street life in *The Best Exotic Marigold Hotel* (John Madden, 2011) is a staple ingredient of the imaginary of India.

Street markets are central to the iconography of the contemporary exotic, while at the same time perpetuating a popular motif of Orientalist paintings. They function as 'cultural marker[s] of locale-ness' (Urry and Larsen 2011: 175) and reflect a dominant trend in today's tourism: 'the touristification of everyday life' (Stors et al. 2019: 6). This recent trend does not invalidate Urry's assertion that tourist practices and the tourist gaze are constructed in opposition to the everyday, since the experience of the mundane and ordinary that contemporary tourists seek in foreign countries stands in stark contrast to their own daily lives at home. Hence, rather than representing a de-exoticisation of tourist practices, the growing interest in the embodied practices of the everyday and tourists' endeavour to 'live like a local' represents a new kind of tourist attraction (Larsen 2008: 27). As prime sites of the commodification and consumption of the exotic Other, street markets feature prominently in travel shows on television, tourist destination marketing and in countless films, especially those set in the Global South. In *Eat Pray Love*, the Brazilian Felipe, who has made Bali his home, introduces Liz to the local produce, describing the taste of the bright red, prickly rambutan, shown in a close-up, as 'it's like an orange made love to a plum' and warns her against sampling the green spiky durian, 'no, no they taste like dirty feet.' As the lovers-to-be wander along, they rub shoulders with locals and tourists. Their route leads them to a small temple, nestled amongst the market stalls. Shot against the hazy light of the golden sun, the altar is laden with *gebogans*, offerings of local fruit that are arranged, layer by layer, to form ornate towers. A Hindu temple priest is giving his blessings. The immediate juxtaposition of the everyday and the sacred adds to the scene's exoticism since it reinforces the contrast between a progressive secular West and an underdeveloped

Figure 3.2 Sacred rituals amidst the hustle and bustle of daily life serve as a form of distilled Otherness in *Eat Pray Love* (Ryan Murphy, 2010).

spiritual East, where religion is imagined as being deeply enmeshed with all aspects of daily life.

In keeping with the trend to go off the beaten track, *The Best Exotic Marigold Hotel* and *Hector* barely show traditional tourist sites. Even though Douglas (Bill Nighy) sets out with great enthusiasm each morning to explore Jaipur's rich architectural heritage and, in the sequel, even becomes a tour guide, only a few of the heritage sites, such as the Palace of the Winds, Panna Meena Ka Kund Step Well and the Kanota Fort, are fleetingly shown. Similarly, neither Hector nor Liz go sight-seeing in Shanghai, Tibet, Africa, Bali or India but instead immerse themselves in the local atmosphere. Liz's sojourn in Italy is more ambiguous in this respect, since in Rome she behaves like an old-fashioned tourist when she visits the Colosseum, the Piazza Navona, the Mausoleum of Augustus and several other well-known attractions. At the same time, she learns a smattering of Italian from a handsome teacher, rents a bohemian apartment from a stereotypical Italian landlady – who espouses the values of family life to the divorcée and forbids male visitors – samples pizza, pasta and ice cream and, quite literally, consumes the Other culture. In her hedonistic embrace of Italian sensuality and culinary delights, she abandons any concerns for her waistline, which have supposedly prevented her from enjoying food (and life) in the United States. As Diane Negra (2001: 89) argues in relation to comparable films, such as *Notting Hill* (Roger Michell, 1999) and *French Kiss* (Lawrence Kasdan, 1995), about white American women travelling to Europe, 'as they Europeanize, they shed the constraints of American whiteness, connecting themselves to the ideologies and lifestyles the films mourn as lost within our own national context.' Negra's assessment of these liberating encounters with a nostalgically imagined Europe suggests that for the films' American tourists, Europe is no less exotic than the far-flung corners of the globe once were for European travellers who turned their back on stifling European civilisation to be revitalised through the exciting encounter with the Other.

This raises the question as to whether Italy in *Eat Pray Love* is exoticised or merely essentialised? Does Italy, from a North American vantage point, appear exotic? So as to distinguish between the exotic and the tourist gaze, two aspects merit closer attention here: differences in visual style and the (ir)reversibility of what is an inherently Eurocentric concept.

Panoramic views and vibrant colours

Sweeping panoramic views and aerial shots that, to repeat the advertising slogan for early cinema's travelogues, 'put the whole world within reach', are a distinctive feature of both the exotic and the tourist gaze. In *Eat Pray Love*, the first shot of Rome shows Liz on a roof terrace overlooking the entire city steeped in golden evening sunlight, as the camera pans from right to left, revealing bridges spanning the river and countless church cupolas. In *The Best Exotic Marigold Hotel*, scenic views of the Lake Palace in Udaipur and the skyline of Jaipur are shot from the perspective of the British residents who assume elevated positions on roof tops and balconies. These point-of-view shots of magnificent settings are the contemporary equivalents of what Mary Louise Pratt (2008: 205, 201) has famously theorised as the 'Imperial Eye/I' and 'the monarch-of-all-I-survey' scene in narratives of exploration and discovery. The monarch-of-all-I-survey scene anchors 'the broad panorama ... in the seer' and conveys a sense of mastery, even ownership, of an exotic landscape seen from above. Through the 'explicit interaction between esthetics and ideology' it conjoins power with pleasure.

Nowhere in contemporary cinema is the imperial protocol of seeing executed more memorably than in *Out of Africa*, set in colonial British East Africa, now Kenya. In an iconic scene, the English aristocrat and big-game hunter Denys Finch Hatton (Robert Redford), invites his lover, the Danish coffee plantation owner Karen Blixen (Meryl Streep), to join him in his yellow biplane and fly across the vast open plains and densely forested mountain ranges with him. The aerial shots alternate with point-of-view shots from Blixen and Finch Hatton's aeroplane, as they behold herds of wildebeest and a flamboyance of pink flamingos, close-ups of

Blixen's face and wide-angle shots that show the yellow de Havilland Moth gliding and swooping in the air, accompanied by gentle yet triumphant orchestral music. The scenic flight is the English adventurer's special gift to Karen. By showing the impressive landscapes and exotic animals to her, he shares with his lover the beauty and wildlife of British East Africa about which he is so passionate. In so doing, he claims ownership of the land. She recognises this and, therefore, reaches out to press his leather-gloved hand in a gesture of gratitude. 'A glimpse of the world through God's eye. This was the way it was intended', Karen Blixen reminisces in a voice-over. In this way the film implicitly endorses the imperial claim to British East Africa as the natural order.

Though far less magnificent than the view from the yellow biplane, the aestheticised vistas of erstwhile imperial grandeur that are incongruously juxtaposed with markers of underdevelopment and poverty, perpetuate the perspective of Imperial Eyes. By perching themselves on hotel roof tops and balconies in third-world cities, the postcolonial globe trotters in *Eat Pray Love* and the *Marigold* franchise emulate the colonial adventurers for whom the discovery of foreign lands was tantamount to taking possession. The panoramic view of Rome in *Eat Pray Love*, though also laying claim to everything it beholds, is more ambiguous because it is set in Europe rather than the Global South.

What further distinguishes the Italian sequence in *Eat Pray Love* from those set in India and Bali are the different colour palettes. Golden hues of sandstone and mellow Mediterranean light dominate the Italian sequence, whereas India and Bali burst with bold saturated colours. Scenes, notable for their chromatic overindulgence, include Tulsi's red-and-marigold wedding, Liz's close encounter with an elephant whose head and trunk are decorated in shades of pink, saffron and vermillion, Bali's lush palm groves and rice paddies in different shades of green and a kaleidoscope of tropical flowers. Even more pronounced are the chromatic contrasts between monochrome England and their protagonists' exotic destinations in *Hector and the Search for Happiness* and *The Best Exotic Marigold Hotel*. In fact, the Ainslies relocate to India, described by Evelyn, as a 'riot of colour and noise', to avoid spending their old age in a British retirement home, evocatively captured in Mrs Ainslie's words as 'a beige bloody bungalow with a sodding panic button'. Meanwhile, Hector's upmarket apartment on London's South Bank is stylishly decorated in neutral shades of white, grey and brown. The overdetermined binarism between a monochrome home and a colourful elsewhere in these films derives from the utopian impulse of colour on which Salman Rushdie comments in relation to *The Wizard of Oz*

(Victor Fleming, 1939). Here, the greyness of Dorothy's (Judy Garland) hometown Kansas City is pitted against the Yellow Brick Road on which she skips along in her sparkly red shoes in the Land of Oz. For Rushdie (1992b: 16), 'this is unarguably a film about the joys of going away, of leaving the greyness and entering the colour, of making a new life' in a different place. The film's best-known song, 'Over the Rainbow', links colourfulness to the experience of displacement and the fulfilment of dreams. 'It is a celebration of Escape, a great paean to the Uprooted Self, a hymn – the hymn – to elsewhere.'

Colour is an integral part of spectacular film genres, such as the musical and the epic, while also contributing to melodrama's aesthetics of excess (see Burgyone 2014; Neale 2002). Not surprisingly, colour has been haunted by the same pervasive suspicion as spectacle itself. In his provocative exploration of colour in Western art and aesthetic theory, *Chromophobia*, David Batchelor (2006: 63–4) proposes that 'in the West, since Antiquity, colour has been systematically marginalised, reviled, diminished and degraded.' Western culture's 'chromophobia' has been associated with 'fear of contamination and corruption' by contact with 'some "foreign" body', be it 'the feminine, the oriental, the primitive'. Since the colourful is coded as alien, it is perceived to pose a threat to 'the higher concerns of the Mind [and] . . . the higher values of Western culture'. The degree of scepticism which colourfulness regularly incurs is due to the fact that colour speaks to the senses that have traditionally been assigned a lower place in the hierarchy of faculties than reason in Western culture. For the French colour theorist Charles Blanc, colour is linked to 'the lower forms of nature' and, although he commends 'oriental artists . . . [as] infallible colourists' (cited in Batchelor 2006: 65) and better at understanding and applying the laws of colour than Western painters, he considers drawing to be a superior form of artistic expression. Pursuing a similar line of argument in relation to the devalued aesthetic category of pretty, Rosalind Galt (2011: 47, 145) details how 'aesthetic theories have linked the colourful with the non-European' and specifically the Orient. She demonstrates that colour is an important feature of the decorative and ornamental but refutes the common denigration of the colourful as merely superficial, cosmetic or devoid of semiotic content by demonstrating that it actually fulfils an expressive function in cinema. Similarly, by defending the exuberant chromatic design of films directed by Chen Kaige, Zhang Yimou, Wong Kar-wai, Fruit Chan and several other Chinese-language film directors, Margaret Hillenbrand (2014: 228) demonstrates that 'chromatic expressionism . . . exploits colour's capacity to make images that draw spectacle and story together in vivid "natural union".' In other words, colour is by no means peripheral to narrative signification but generates meaning via different channels – somatically and affectively.

Vibrant chromatic designs are central to the iconography of exoticism. From a transnational vantage point, they are often perceived as markers of some intrinsic 'Chineseness', or 'Indianness' and, with a few exceptions, all of the films considered in this book are intensely colourful. In numerous films set in India, the Hindu Festival of Colours or Holi Festival, during which people throw brightly coloured powder at each other in the streets to celebrate the arrival of spring, is weaved, somewhat gratuitously, into the plot (for example, in *Salaam, Bombay!*, *Water* and Bollywood movies such as *Mohabbatein* (meaning 'Love Stories', Aditya Chopra, 2000) and *Darr* (meaning 'Fear', Yash Chopra, 1993)). So indispensable is this visual cliché that *Zindagi Na Milegi Dobara* (meaning 'You Only Live Once', Zoya Akhtar, 2011), a tourist film about three Indian friends on a bachelor trip in Spain, features what is supposedly the Spanish equivalent of the Holi Festival, La Tomatina, in the town of Buñol, where revellers throw tomatoes at each other instead of paint. Oddly, in *The Best Exotic Marigold Hotel*, which conjures every imaginable visual cliché of India, the Holi Festival is described in the screenplay: 'Everywhere is a riot of extraordinary colour. People have mixed dust and various pigments into paint . . . which rises on up into the sky like so many multicoloured clouds' (Parker and Moggach 2009: 115), but on screen it is reduced to the glimpse of a colourful parade that causes a traffic jam. Nevertheless, colour was a determining factor for John Madden's decision to shoot the film in Rajasthan, instead of Bangalore, where the book on which the film is based, is set: 'We thought Rajasthan was a more visual area to set the story in, because of the texture and colours and intensity of the place' (Madden cited in Schou 2012). Similar considerations motivated Shubhashish Bhutiani to shoot his debut feature *Hotel Salvation* in Varanasi. He felt attracted to the energy of 'this hyper-coloured place . . . [where] every wall is like blue or pink' (Bhutiani and Bhutiani 2017). Because of its setting and chromatic indulgence, *Hotel Salvation* is reminiscent of Mehta's *Water*, which also relies on colour to mitigate – and exoticise – the grim social reality of impoverished Hindu widows living in an ashram in the holy city in 1938 (see Chapter 1).

The (Ir)reversibility of the Exotic Gaze in Bollywood Cinema

What does Europe, the original producer of the exotic gaze, look like when viewed from the decentred perspective of imperially shaped habits of seeing and being seen? If we conceive of exoticism as an intrinsically Eurocentric mode of aesthetic perception, then what consequences does this have for the possibility of an exotic Europe? Is the exotic gaze reversible or, in the words of Roger Célestin (1996: 181), 'is what is exotic to the exotic the same as what is exotic to me?' Perhaps he poses a rhetorical question here, for elsewhere Célestin (1996: 217) defines the 'hard core of meaning for *exotic* [as] . . . what is not me, what is (very) different from me and my culture'. If what is perceived as exotic merely depends on the positionality of the subject in relation to the object of the gaze, then, anything that is markedly different from the onlooker's cultural sphere would potentially qualify.

What implications do these considerations have for Bollywood films that, as has been proposed by several critics, imagine Europe as exotic (see Dwyer 2002; Schneider 2002; Monteiro 2014)? The globalisation of popular Hindi cinema from the 1990s onwards coincided with a rapidly expanding South Asian diaspora in the West, who feature prominently in films set in the Europe and the United States and who are the chief catalyst for Bollywood's popularity outside South Asia (see Bhaumik 2006: 191). In addition, Bollywood cinema has attracted significant crossover audiences who relish its non-realist aesthetics, its visual exuberance, Indian wedding rituals and easily consumable song-and-dance sequences. But does the depiction of Europe, mainly in the shape of instantly recognisable settings, such as the snow-capped mountains and green valleys of Switzerland, the Eiffel Tower in Paris, the Piazza San Marco in Venice, the red double-decker buses in London, the canals in Amsterdam and other landmarks, prompt the tourist or the exotic gaze? Because the tourist and the exotic gaze share an almost indistinguishable visual grammar, relying on spectacle, beautification, cultural essentialism and a sense of déjà vu, it is necessary to determine how the exotic gaze, understood as a particular prism through which the foreign is perceived, differs from the tourist gaze. Since exoticism functions like a hermeneutic circuit (see Chapter 1), we need to ask: how does the depiction of Europe resonate with exoticism's discursive history?

In Bollywood films, Europe serves primarily as a scenic backdrop for song-and-dance sequences. It was not until the 1990s that travel to European destinations began to feature as one of Bollywood cinema's new attractions. *Dilwale Dulhania Le Jayenge* (The Bravehearted Will Take the Bride, Yash Chopra 1995), credited as the film that made Bollywood a global phenomenon, invents an imaginary geography that portrays 'Europe as the untouched, pure pastoral [and] . . . the site of romance' (Mishra 2002: 253).[8] In *DDLJ*, the young London-based non-resident Indians (NRIs) Simran (Kajol) and Raj (Shah Rukh Khan) cross paths on a Eurorail trip that takes them to Gstaad in Switzerland, where they fall in love. Here, as in other Bollywood films about Indians abroad, iconic settings serve as a stage for song-and-dance sequences that open fantasy spaces where Indian societal norms and moral codes are suspended – if only for the duration of the song. When Simran bursts into song in the Swiss Alps, she smashes a shop window to steal a sexy, red mini-dress which she then wears while dancing and frolicking in the snow, expressing her sexual attraction to Raj: 'The chill in the breeze sets my body afire. I feel like making love to you.' In this respect, the European settings appear to be as liberating as the earthly paradises of the past which European explorers and travellers to exotic destinations presumed to have found when they indulged in sensual gratifications not permitted at home. Yet what makes *DDLJ*'s fantasy of an Edenic Switzerland markedly different is that the protagonists' desire is neither about an erotic encounter with a European Other nor is it dramatised. Instead, it is displaced onto the lyrics of the song. The physical attraction between Simran and Raj remains firmly contained within India's moral universe, which prevails even thousands of miles away from the homeland: when Simran wakes up in Raj's bed oblivious to what happened the night before, he assures her: 'You think I'm an utter larrikin, but I am a Hindustani and I know what a Hindustani girl's *izzat* (honour) is like.' What makes the musical sequence set against the backdrop of a foreign country such a central component of Bollywood's microcosm is that it functions as a 'narrative interstice for the ... confluence of competing pressures of traditional values, nationalist myth, and economic and cultural globalization' (Monteiro 2014: 439). For all its spectacular qualities, it is so much more than 'empty spectacle'.

Since Indians abroad do not mix and mingle with the locals, preferring the company of other Indians, it could hardly be said that Bollywood films stage exotic encounters. Exotic encounters presuppose a degree of proximity and exchange between the Self and the Other and typically entail a transformative experience. Yet this proximity is markedly absent. Thus, in *Dil To Pagal Hai* (The Heart is Crazy, Yash Chopra, 1997), Germany is literally reduced to a theme park with an abundance of flowers and a miniature train. The musical interludes in *Bachna Ae Haseeno* (Watchout Beauties, Siddharth Anan, 2008) invite the spectator on a whirlwind tour around the world, including snapshots of Venice, Rome, Capri and Apulia's iconic *trulli* houses while the Swiss winter landscape comes complete with a husky-drawn sleigh. Yet these fragments of foreignness are devoid of any cross-cultural contact between Indians and Europeans.

In *Queen* (Vikas Bahl, 2013), which like *Eat Pray Love* revolves around a heroine whose journey abroad is prompted by a romantic break-up, the protagonist's European tour is limited to visiting tourist landmarks in Paris and Amsterdam. Her only encounters abroad are with other South Asians, a Pakistani pole dancer and a partially Indian chamber maid. Both have been 'morally tarnished' by permanently residing in Europe, imagined as a morally liminal space.

Zoya Akhtar's *Zindagi Na Milegi Dobara* signals a departure from the prevalent pattern of Europe as a picturesque backdrop for song-and-dance sequences. Songs accompany rather than interrupt the narrative and the film promotes a modern globalised, rather than a traditional, Indian culture. In addition to providing a welcome opportunity for the Spanish Tourist Board's destination marketing, the road trip on which the three Indian friends embark is an integral part of the storyline. It also leads to the heroes' transformation, albeit in the absence of close encounters with local Spanish people. As the young men drive from Barcelona, along the Costa Brava to Seville and Pamplona, audiences are invited to marvel at the stunning scenery, as well as at Arjun's (Hrithik Roshan) well-toned body that is put on display as he reclines on the back of the vintage convertible, accompanied by three wild horses, running alongside the sky-blue Buik Super, and the song 'Khwabon Ke Parinday'. Although the protagonists' exposure to Spanish culture is by and large limited to tourist attractions, such as the Running of the Bulls in Pamplona, flamenco dancing in picturesque town squares and the afore-mentioned Tomatina Festival, it nevertheless promotes their self-realisation. In this respect it is comparable to the Grand European Tour, an educational rite of passage which became a widely established social practice amongst the higher echelons of European society between the seventeenth and nineteenth centuries. Their itinerary usually included cities such as Paris, Florence, Venice, Rome to ensure that the young men of means were exposed to Renaissance art and the cultural legacy of classical antiquity. To be sure, while Arjun, Kabir (Abhay Deol) and Imran's (Farhan Akhtar) adrenaline-fuelled leisure activities, as well as off-screen sexual encounters with available white women (one Spanish, the other Caucasian-Indian) are not educational as such, they are certainly transformative. The London-based, workaholic Arjun ends his work-induced celibacy and falls in love with Laila (Katrina Kaif), the American-Indian scuba diving instructor who also teaches him to live life to the full; Kabir breaks off his engagement to his bossy Indian fiancée and Imran plans to follow his calling and write poetry instead of advertising slogans. Whereas in *DDLJ* the traditional Indian moral universe remains unaffected by the couple's European tour,

ZNMD endorses 'restless consumption as a marker of a life well lived' (Kamble 2015: 11), in other words, the values of global capitalism and Western sexual mores. The transformation, indeed, Westernisation of the Indian protagonists is further underscored in the film's epilogue which shows Arjun and Laila's wedding, significantly, a white wedding, complete with a multi-tiered white wedding cake.

While there can be no doubt that these Bollywood films imagine Europe as a projection surface for collective Indian fantasies of a glamorous lifestyle and pastoral idylls (even Spain's landscapes in *ZNMD* with fields of sunflowers and wild horses can be described as such), the question remains as to whether Europe's imaginary geographies would elicit the exotic gaze in South Asian spectators. As I have argued in Chapter 1 and elsewhere in the book, the exotic gaze in contemporary world cinema is much more than just a fascination with the foreign. Rather, it stages a 'mode of proximity [that] reopen[s] prior histories of encounter' (Ahmed 2000: 13). These prior encounters are inextricably bound up with the histories and legacies of European colonialism. Of course, colonialism entailed a two-way exchange insofar as colonised subjects in India and in other colonies developed an imaginary of Europe that was based on the literature, art and other cultural influences to which they were exposed in the colonial contact zone. But it remains questionable whether the scenic snapshots of European tourist attractions stand in this discursive tradition and actually reverse the exotic gaze. It seems to me (even though my interpretation may be compromised by one of the blind spots that come with my European heritage) that a reversal of the exotic gaze in Bollywood cinema which constructs Europe as exotic is irreconcilable with exoticism's discursive history and its inherent logic of centre and periphery. While this logic accommodates the performance of self-exoticism in world cinema, a decentring of the exotic gaze from the periphery onto the European centre transcends the limits of exoticism. 'It is out of the question', Jean-Francois Staszak (2009: 46) states apodictically, 'to describe Europe as exotic until minds and words are decolonized.' Popular Hindi cinema, despite its transnational audience appeal, is unlikely to make a significant contribution to the important project of decoloniality.

Probing the Limits of the Exotic and the Tourist Gaze: *Hotel Salvation* and *To the Ends of the Earth*

Hotel Salvation and *To the Ends of the Earth*, two tourist films by world cinema filmmakers, provide fertile ground to further probe the boundaries and limits of the tourist and the exotic gaze. *To the Ends of the Earth* is about a Japanese television crew who are shooting a travel programme in Uzbekistan. Kiyoshi Kurosawa's film examines and critiques how the tourist and the exotic gaze are constructed in the media. *Hotel Salvation* explores an unusual (in the West, at least) form of spiritual tourism in the holy city of Varanasi. Bhutiani's subtle comedy about old age has invited comparisons with *The Best Exotic Marigold Hotel* because it is also set in a dilapidated Indian hotel catering to the needs of elderly guests. But whereas the *Marigold* franchise by and large elides death (except for the image of a white heron ascending from the hotel garden into the sky to symbolise Graham's sudden death), Bhutiani's film makes waiting for death its main theme. When Daya (Lalit Behl), an old widower, has a premonitory dream about his life coming to an end, he decides to spend his final days in Hotel Salvation. According to Hindu belief, the souls of those who die in Varanasi on the banks of the River Ganges will not be reborn but will attain salvation. Daya is accompanied on his valedictory journey by his middle-aged son Rajiv (Adil Hussain), who tries to juggle his filial duties with a stressful job as an accountant and spends much of his time answering calls on his mobile phone. In terms of its realist aesthetics and focus on the father–son relationship, *Hotel Salvation* has more in common with *Le Grand Voyage* (Ismaël Ferroukhi, 2004), which charts the long road trip from France to the holy city of Mecca on which an old Muslim father and his young agnostic son embark, than with the mainstream box-office hit *The Best Exotic Marigold Hotel*. Bhutiani and Ferroukhi's arthouse films pit the secular world view of the sons against the deep faith of the fathers. Both culminate in the emotional rapprochement of previously alienated fathers and sons and the subsequent off-screen death of the fathers.

Hotel Salvation's potentially gloomy subject matter is tempered by a heavy dose of irreverence and wry humour that pokes fun at the commodification of the spiritual quest for salvation. The humble, rodent-infested lodgings are a place 'where eternal rest comes as standard but food, cleaning and medicine are considered extras' (Andrews 2017). The consumption of meat and alcohol are forbidden but trying marijuana-laced lassi is strongly recommended by the hotel's proprietor. Rooms are let for fifteen days only, by which time guests should have 'checked out' permanently. If they are still alive, they have to re-register under a false name so as to preserve the hotel's good reputation for arranging salvation in a timely and efficient manner. Vimla (Navindra Behl), however, has been a permanent resident for the past eighteen years after her plan to die together with her husband failed. She has set up home in this transitory place, having decorated her room in a deep shade of fuchsia and acquired a considerable collection of cooking and tea-making utensils. A close friendship develops between Vimla and Daya, while Daya, too, is overstaying his appointed time. Not troubled by the prospect of death, Daya whiles his time away by writing poetry and obituaries, practising breathing exercises and watching a popular television show in the communal room. Fearing Daya's final hour may have come, his granddaughter and daughter-in-law come rushing to the hotel. When they are proven wrong and death is suspended, at least for a while, the family readily replaces the final farewell with some tourist activities, such as a river cruise on the Ganges, taking selfies, sampling ice cream, going shopping and attending a public prayer ceremony.

Michael McSweeney and David Huwiler's cinematography captures the atmosphere of Varanasi by focusing on well-known sites, such as the famous ghats leading down to the Ganges where people wash their clothes and cremate their dead. Despite being cultural outsiders and, therefore, potentially more inclined to film Varanasi through an exotic lens, the North American and Swiss DOPs eschew the kind of idealisation and spectacularisation that characterises the other films discussed in this chapter. The funeral rites, for example, are never shown in full ethnographic detail. In contrast to Mehta's *Water* (see Chapter 1), which elaborates on every aspect of a Hindu funeral ceremony in aesthetically pleasing images, *Hotel Salvation* captures only brief moments, such as the covering of Vimla's face with a cloth and garland of marigolds or the arduous task of carrying the heavy stretcher on which Daya's body rests. The light is hazy, the sky often grey; the yards that sell wood for the funeral pyres suggest that death is a flourishing business in the sacred city. The rooms in the guest house are cramped and the only attribute that makes their shabbiness visually appealing is their colourfulness. By citing the familiar image repertoire

Figure 3.3 A firm believer in salvation, Daya is calmly awaiting his death in *Hotel Salvation* (Shubhashish Bhutiani, 2016).

of dilapidated architecture and chromatic overindulgence that is a visual marker of exotic India, the tourist and the exotic gaze emerge, yet again, as inseparable. Undeniably, colour is important here, inviting comparisons with the Raghubir Singh's colourful photographs of Varanasi in the volume *Banaras: Sacred City of India* (1987), which as Shohini Chaudhuri (2009: 13) illustrates, has also influenced the visual style of Mehta's *Water*. As a photojournalist for the *National Geographic*, Singh, alongside Steve McCurry, has made a name for himself as a visual chronicler of Indian life, albeit one that caters more to cultural outsiders' preconceptions of what this life looks like. Yet *Hotel Salvation* avoids many of these visual clichés. Its exoticism rests primarily on the representational politics that, in a different context, Olivia Khoo (2007: 3) has described as the reification of 'the more positive and successful, enviable and utopic aspects of Other societies'. Certainly, the most enviable cultural difference that is fascinating for transnational as well as Indian audiences, whose belief in salvation is less solid than that of the hotel's residents, is the fearlessness and equanimity with which Daya approaches his final hour. The astounding portrayal of his unshakable belief in salvation and the humorous juxtaposition of spirituality and materialism (making the quest for salvation a profitable business for the hotel patron) plays with and challenges the exotic imaginary of a mystical and deeply spiritual India.

One might, therefore, argue that Bhutiani's film deftly illustrates the performance of self-exoticism which, according to Randall Halle (2010: 304), 'offers Euro-American audiences tales they want to hear, about people fundamentally different from themselves'. Facing up to one's mortality is a universal human experience and, by choosing this theme, the twenty-four-year-old writer-director retrieves the strange in the familiar and, thereby, domesticates the exotic. Halle (2010: 310–12) proposes that global art cinema often exhibits 'an aesthetic and narrative orientation towards European tastes' because supranational film funding mechanisms, notably EU co-funding schemes, function like 'first-world [development] aid' programmes and constitute a form of 'neocolonialist' intervention in the cultural sphere. At first glance, *Hotel Salvation* appears to corroborate Halle's argument, since Bhutiani received project funding from La Biennale de Venezia for the development and production of his debut feature film. Moreover, thanks to his education in London and New York, the Indian writer-director would be well equipped to pander to Western expectations (as the oft-rehearsed criticism goes), being equally at home in the East and the West. However, this argument reiterates the reductive East–West binarism that does not adequately map onto the kind of multicultural global marketplace in which *Hotel Salvation* and similar films circulate. After its premiere at the Venice International Film Festival, Bhutiani's offbeat film pleased critics and cinephiles on the global film festival circuit and in cinemas in South Korea, the United Arab Emirates, the United Kingdom and Spain, though its resonance in India was disappointing. In Japan, where *Hotel Salvation* attracted primarily older audiences, it was screened for 150 days. According to producer Sanjay Bhutiani, what appealed to the Japanese was its 'spiritual, religious and philosophical' message and 'the universal quality of the story', which he also cites as 'the reason why we have managed to take the film to 60 countries' (Bhutiani cited in Nathan 2018). As the film's transnational exhibition and broadly positive reception indicate, cultural patronage is not necessarily as predictable in its creative outcomes and reception as one might anticipate.

Similarly, Kiyoshi Kurosawa's unorthodox tourist film *To the Ends of the Earth*, which was commissioned by Japan and Uzbekistan to celebrate twenty-five years of successful diplomatic relations between the two countries, refuses to conform to expectations. Rather than creating a marketable travelogue about Uzbekistan that pays homage to the beauty and heritage of the country, Kurosawa purposely deconstructs the tourist gaze by 'interrogating the strange and often compromised experience that is cultural tourism in the mass media age' (Kiang 2019). The film charts the journey of the travel show host Yoko, played by popular J-pop singer Atsuko Maeda, and her television crew along the ancient Silk Road, with the cities of Samarkand and Tashkent being the principal attractions. The exotic-sounding names of these locations alone conjure images of Genghis Khan and the Mongol Empire, ancient traders of silk, spices and other exotic goods, and the imposing Islamic architecture of the madrasas and mausoleums for which Samarkand is famous. Yet *To the Ends of the Earth* deliberately defies these expectations and is anything but exotic. The first scene shows Yoko hastily rehearsing her script for a shoot on the utterly bleak and barren Lake Aydar, where, as she explains, beaming a warm smile straight into the camera, she is hoping to catch a mythical fish. Instead of the fabled fish, which never materialises, the local fishermen pull up a net full of rubbish. On another shoot, Yoko and the television crew visit one of Samarkand's local restaurants, where she is supposed to sample *plov*, a local rice dish. The restaurant is basic and devoid of local colour or charm. Yet when the camera crosses the line, the anti-tourist gaze becomes rapidly transformed as a carefully configured view of what a local Uzbekistani restaurant 'should look like' comes into view. There is a huge photograph of one of Samarkand's mosques on a wall in the background, red and golden brocade cushions, Oriental rugs and hand-woven cloths are arranged behind Yoko, who is sitting alone at a table. Wearing a canary-yellow rain jacket and matching clip-on microphone, Yoko looks straight into the camera while eating *plov*. As she performs once again the effervescent enthusiast, she praises the 'exquisite crunchiness' of the undercooked rice and compares it to Japanese 'fried rice' but judges its flavour to be 'more complex'. By turning the camera onto the production team who just care about shooting enough footage but are not genuinely interested in Uzbekistan, Kurosawa sardonically exposes the manufactured nature of the tourist gaze and the superficiality of travel programmes like the one whose production we are invited to witness.

These staged touristic encounters contrast with Yoko's independent explorations of the back streets and markets of Samarkand and Tashkent during her free time. To capture the foreignness of the place and Yoko's sense of frightening disorientation, the Uzbek language is not translated. In the dark alleyways, shot by Kurosawa's regular director of photography Akiko Ashizawa in the visual grammar of the horror genre for which the director is best known, she nearly gets lost and ends up as the only woman on a bus full of men staring at her. Whereas the film crew avoid filming any of the major tourist attractions, Yoko happens upon the Navoi Theatre and opera house (whose seventieth anniversary the film commemorates), as she follows the beautiful sound of music. In pursuit of the opera singer's voice, she wanders from room to room as the camera tracks behind her. Each room is decorated with different stencils that are intricately carved into the white plaster of the walls. Yoko later learns from the production team's local interpreter that the stencils were created by Japanese prisoners-of-war during their long years of captivity after World War Two. So inspired was the interpreter by the beauty of these carvings that he decided to learn the Japanese language. Ironically, the only homage *To the Ends of the Earth* pays to the relationship between the two countries is a reference to their antagonistic history. Notwithstanding Yoko and the interpreter's prompts to return to the Navoi Theatre to shoot a scene there, the crew refuses as they prefer to capture the experience of the everyday, as has become the fashion in travel shows. Their location of choice, Tashkent's grand bazaar turns out to be a massive shopping mall of the kind one can find it anywhere in the world. There is nothing extraordinary here, except for Yoko's exotic attire. Whereas normally she wears hip-and-trendy outfits, during the bazaar shoot, she dons an orange silk blouse with a delicate floral pattern and a cream-coloured silk scarf that is loosely draped around her head.

Through the combination of the Japanese-style clothes and the timid expression on her face, Atsuko Maeda evokes the visual cliché and cultural

Figure 3.4 *To the Ends of the Earth* (Kiyoshi Kurosawa, 2019) deconstructs the manufactured nature of the tourist and the exotic gaze.

stereotype of alluring Asian femininity (see Chapter 1), albeit one with a video camera, filming as she is being filmed. Ironically, or perhaps strategically, it is this particular image which has featured most prominently in the film's publicity, which has been reproduced more frequently than any other one in film reviews. Partly, this represents an attempt to exploit Maeda's fame as a Japanese pop-star-turned-actress; partly, the publicity responds to global expectations of Japanese femininity. Yet Kurosawa consistently subverts the expectations he sets up.

Although *To the Ends of the Earth* has been promoted as 'the story of a woman's transformation' (in the American trailer) and has been compared with Liz's transformation in *Eat Pray Love* in reviews, Kurosawa charts his heroine's journey of transformation in a bleak and foreign land only to subsequently deflate her trajectory with irony in the film's final scene. Disillusioned with her career as a travel show host, Yoko comes to realise in the Navoi Theatre that she wants to become a singer. This is in itself an ironic self-reflexive twist given that Maeda was the biggest star of the teenage pop-idol band AKB48 before becoming an actress. In the film's final scene then, Yoko abandons the film crew in the barren landscape, marred by ugly storage cylinders, the kind of eyesores that would normally be edited out in order not to affront the tourist gaze. As she walks on and climbs uphill on her own, the landscape changes to lush green scenery, until she reaches the top and a magnificent panoramic view opens in front of her. An over-the-shoulder shot with Yoko in the foreground reveals a green valley, with slopes covered in pine forests and snow-capped mountains in the distance. Similarities with the Alpine landscape of *The Sound of Music* (Robert Wise, 1965) are certainly not coincidental, especially since Yoko, not unlike the Trapp family, suddenly bursts into song. Her performance of Edith Piaf's *Hymn à l'amour* in Japanese is at once, on the diegetic level, a passionate love declaration to her fiancé in Japan, 'If you'd want me, I'd go to the ends of the earth with you', while also serving on a meta-diegetic level as an ironic commentary on the fantasies created by travel programmes and tourist films.

Conclusion

It has been my aim in this chapter to explore those aspects which have given exoticism, even in its contemporary forms, such a bad reputation. This might explain why mainstream Western films like *Eat, Pray, Love*, *The Best Exotic Marigold Hotel* and *Hector and the Search for Happiness* have suffered from scholarly neglect. However, this kind of 'censorship' is not helpful in the context of this study, which seeks to delineate the diversity of contemporary exoticisms in cinema and this, inevitably, includes the analysis of films that illuminate why exoticism is such a contested mode of cultural representation. Issues such as white privilege, the relics of imperial protocols of vision and the commodification of cultural difference emerged as central to the ideological contestations surrounding these films.

The close comparison between the tourist and the exotic gaze undertaken in this chapter revealed remarkable convergences: both are forms of aesthetic perception that are dependent upon the deictic stance of the beholder to reveal what makes cultural difference extraordinary. Both gazes involve an element of déjà vu insofar as they cite, recycle or repurpose familiar visual and narrative tropes. Both construct highly aestheticised images whose beauty generates visual pleasure and desire for the Other – the desire to look, to consume or to possess. The exotic gaze functions like a particular lens through which strange topographies and cultures are perceived and, in this sense, it is more specific than the tourist gaze. Not just any foreign view can be discursively constructed as exotic because only those imaginary geographies which are marked by the cultural memory of encounters in the colonial contact zone are legible as exotic. Therefore, topographies and cultures that have never been beheld by Imperial Eyes in the past may be idealised, essentialised and spectacularised but not exoticised. Thus, the imperial logic of centre and periphery that continues to reverberate in the exotic gaze, precludes the exoticisation of Europe.

Through their self-reflexive and ironic engagement with the exotic and the tourist gaze, the global art films *Hotel Salvation* and *To the Ends of the Earth* mount a critique of these mediatised scopic regimes. Bhutiani's film cites the cultural cliché of a profoundly spiritual India while at the same time undermining it when he reveals its commodification. Meanwhile, Kurosawa's film is more radical insofar as it deconstructs both the exotic and the tourist gaze, even though the image of Maeda donning a Japanese costume, which has dominated the publicity and critical reception, has post hoc attempted to exoticise what is anything but an exotic film.

One of the overarching questions of this chapter has been, to put it quite bluntly, what's wrong with spectacle – and especially the spectacle of cultural difference? Why does the pleasure it affords elicit a sense of guilt? In the West, spectacle is typically denounced for being superficial and empty, even though it generates meaning via channels other than narrative. Like exoticism's indulgence in vibrant colours and visual opulence, spectacle beguiles the senses. Its capacity to impart, above all else, sensory pleasure stands in conflict with the priority and higher value accorded to reason, critical reflection and analysis in the West. Therefore, to succumb to the gratification of sensory pleasure, which the exotic gaze affords, is feared to upend Western cultural hierarchies and comes close to 'going native' – a moral transgression, that, though not uncommon in the colonial context, was also burdened by a sense of guilt.

Notes

1. Costa (2006), Friedberg (1993), Kirby (1997) and Gunning (2006, 2010) provide fascinating accounts of how spatial mobility and new moving image technologies emerged around the same time.
2. The déjà vu that underpins the tourist and the exotic gaze, explains why for example, films like *The Sheltering Sky* (Bernardo Bertolucci, 1990) and *Queen of the Desert* (Werner Herzog, 2015) with their sublime desert landscapes, scorching sun, caravans of camels and turban-wearing Arabs can be instantly decoded as exotic. It has become almost impossible to film the Sahara without evoking *The Sheik* (George Melford, 1921) or *Lawrence of Arabia* (David Lean, 1962) whose iconography and narratives of cross-cultural encounters have served as the blueprint for subsequent travel films set in African deserts. For Shohat and Stam (1994: 169) the desert also functions 'as the site of moral liminality' where desires and 'sexual fantasies unthinkable in a contemporaneous American or European setting' can be acted out. This presumed licence

to trespass the moral strictures of Western societies makes the African desert, not unlike other far-flung corners of the world such as the South Sea islands, an unequivocally exotic space. However, global art films by Middle Eastern and African filmmakers, such as *Theeb* (Naji Abu Nowar, 2014) and *Timbuktu* (Abderrahmane Sissako, 2014), depart from the Eurocentric imaginary and address entirely different themes and encounters. *Theeb* is a coming-of-age drama about a Bedouin boy, set during the Ottoman Empire, that spectacularises the Wadi Rum desert. *Timbuktu* explores the threat of jihadist rule to the city's residents. See also Marks' (2006) discussion of desert spaces in contemporary Arab cinema.
3. Steve McCurry, one of *National Geographic*'s most celebrated photojournalists, has played a pivotal role in creating the visual idiom of contemporary exoticism. His enormously popular photographs (he has more than one million followers on Instagram) purport to show Other cultures at their most authentic while actually indulging fantasies of the exotic Other as timeless and unchanging.
4. Gopalan (2002) focuses on three principal types of interruption: the interval, censorship and the song-and-dance sequence. Kumar (2011), in addition, devotes attention to the 'item song', which displaces erotic desire onto a female character that only features in the song sequence.
5. Interesting in this context is a group of films about female sex tourism in the Global South which demonstrate the re-gendering of colonial encounters with the exotic Other. Examples include *Vers le sud* (Heading South, Lauren Cantet, 2005), featuring Charlotte Rampling as an American professor of French literature who travels to Haiti where she pays young black men for sex; *Paradies: Liebe* (Paradise: Love, Ulrich Seidl, 2012) about Austrian middle-aged women travelling to Kenya for sex tourism; and *Die weiße Massai* (The White Masai, Hermine Huntgeburth, 2005), based on the autobiography of a white Swiss woman who falls in love in Kenya with a Masai man, moves to his remote village and marries him, only to become utterly disillusioned by the incompatibility of lifestyles and gender norms. All three films highlight the inequitable relations between the Global North and South. These films place women in neo-colonial contexts, giving licence to their erotic experiences under the pretext of women's liberation.
6. The film was a global box-office hit, grossing USD80.5 million in the United States and USD204.6 million worldwide. The novel remained on the *New York Times* best-seller list for 187 weeks. The film stars Julia Roberts and Javier Bardem, was produced by Columbia Pictures and Plan B Entertainment for USD60 million, and was distributed by Sony Pictures.
7. Similarly eclectic soundtracks are common in other exotic films, regardless of whether or not they are made by world cinema or white filmmakers. The master of exotic film music is unquestionably the Indian composer A. R. Rahman. In India, where has sold more than 200 million albums worldwide and composed the scores of more than 100 Indian films, he 'is credited with

more or less single-handedly revolutionising Indian film music' (Morcom 2015). He conquered the Western world in the late 1990s by fusing musical influences from the East and the West that sound both strange and familiar, because of their blended harmonies, mixture of Indian instruments and lush string sounds and computer-generated bass. In the West his biggest success to date has been the soundtrack for *Slumdog Millionaire*, which garnered a large number of prestigious awards, including two Oscars. Other soundtracks by Rahman for exotic films discussed in this book include *The Hundred- Foot Journey* (Lasse Hallström, 2014), Mehta's *Elements Trilogy*, comprising *Fire, Earth* and *Water* (1996–2005) and *Viceroy's House*.

8. An early precursor of this trend is *Sangam* (Raj Kapoor, 1964), the first Bollywood film to be partly shot in Switzerland.

CHAPTER 4

'The Past Is a Foreign Country': Nostalgia and Exoticism

At the very end of Wong Kar-wai's film *In the Mood for Love*, Tony Leung's character, Chow Mo-wan, whispers a secret into a tiny hole in a wall at the famous ruins of Angkor Wat in Cambodia. As the camera pulls away and circles around Chow, a slow tracking shot explores the texture of the crumbling masonry that is pock-marked by white lichen, inviting the spectator to feel the rough surface, just like Chow does, when he pokes his finger into the small cavity from which a tuft of grass is sprouting. The architectural ruin makes the passing of time visible through bearing the indelible traces of the interminable battle between culture and nature. A series of tracking shots and abrupt cuts reveals the exotic beauty of the temple complex of Angkor Wat, complete with a Buddhist child monk clad in saffron robes. The ruins of Cambodia's most iconic landmark simultaneously represent a quintessentially exotic location and an 'architectonic *chiffre*' (Huyssen 2006: 13; italics in original) of nostalgic longing, encapsulating the concept's dual spatial and temporal dimensions. Although in its original sense, nostalgia (from Greek *nostos*, meaning 'return home', and *algia*, meaning 'pain') refers to intense homesickness and, thus, foregrounds the longing for a distant place, over time, the concept's temporal dimension has come to dominate.[1] That is why Fredric Jameson (1991: 19) famously describes nostalgia as 'a desperate attempt to reappropriate a missing past'. According to Andreas Huyssen (2006: 7), the architectural ruin conjoins the spatiality and temporality of nostalgia and embodies 'the indissoluble combination of spatial and temporal desires that trigger nostalgia'.

In this chapter I will, first, examine the close affinities between nostalgia and exoticism. In so doing, I seek to explain why so many exotic films are set in the past and governed by a nostalgic impulse. Notable examples include 'Raj revival' films (Rushdie 1992a: 87–101) of the 1980s, such as *A Passage to India* (David Lean, 1984) and *Heat and Dust* (James Ivory, 1983), as well as later manifestations, including *Before the Rains*

(Santosh Sivan, 2007), *Out of Africa*, *The Lover*, *M. Butterfly*, *Palmeras en la nieve* (Palm Trees in the Snow, Fernando González Molina, 2015), *Victoria and Abdul* (Stephen Frears, 2017), *Queen of the Desert* (Werner Herzog, 2015) and *Three Seasons*, *Water* and *Lust, Caution*. Second, I will distinguish between 'imperialist nostalgia' (Rosaldo 1989) and what I shall term 'exotic nostalgia films' and explore in what ways their aesthetic strategies and ideological agendas differ.[2] Both combine an elegiac longing for an idealised past, constructed 'as a site of pleasurable contemplation and yearning' (Cook 2005: 4), with the spectacle of alluring alterity. However, as I shall illustrate, they differ in terms of their ideological positions. Cultural representations of nostalgia and exoticism tend to emerge most prominently at moments of cultural crisis and at significant historical junctures. Thus, my chosen case studies are films that engage directly or indirectly with major historical turning points. Régis Wargnier's *Indochine* is set in 1930s French Indochina and ends with the country gaining independence in 1954; Gurinder Chadha's *Viceroy's House* charts the end of British colonial rule over India in 1947; Wong Kar-wai's *In the Mood for Love* reflects the anxieties accompanying the handover of Hong Kong to China in 1997 via nostalgia for British-ruled Hong Kong in the 1960s; and Zhang Yimou's *The Road Home* nostalgically reimagines the Chinese socialist period from the vantage point of 1990s post-socialism, when China sought to integrate a vague vision of future socialism into the economic and social imperatives of global capitalist modernity. And third, I propose that imperialist and exotic nostalgia films speak differently to local and global audiences. To develop this hypothesis, I will invoke the concept of 'enigmatisation', which Linda Chiu-han Lai (2001: 232) has theorised with specific reference to Hong Kong nostalgia films of the 1990s. Hong Kong nostalgia films, she contends, 'produce messages coded in ways that only a local audience can adequately interpret but that, nevertheless, remain comprehensible to an international audience on a more general level'. In other words, nostalgia films grant local audiences the status of a 'privileged hermeneutic community', capable of decoding culturally specific references by virtue of a 'shared textual horizon' and the 'remembrance of a shared popular tradition' (Lai 2001: 232, 241). Whereas Lai does not problematise the concept of 'local audiences', I concur with Arjun Appadurai (1996: 48) who suggests that in a world characterised by accelerated transnational mobility and de-territorialisation, the distinction between local and global spectators has assumed 'a slippery, nonlocalized quality'. I, therefore, conceive of local and global spectators not primarily in geospatial terms, but rather in terms of the culturally specific knowledge audiences bring to the reception of a particular film, regardless of where they actually live.³ Whereas Lai suggests that the transnational reception of Hong Kong nostalgia films results in an interpretative deficit since global audiences are missing certain locally specific nuances of meaning, I argue that, for global audiences, there remains a residue of enigma and a sense of mystery, which is an important feature of the films' exotic allure. In other words, the affective relationship which local and global spectators develop in relation to exotic nostalgia films is different: whereas nostalgia is community building for local viewers, exoticism relies on and reinforces an outsider perspective. 'The exotic gaze', Charles Forsdick (2001: 21) writes, 'is a perspective . . . from outside and across geographical [or cultural] boundaries'. It depends on the maintenance of boundaries to ensure that cultural difference be preserved and perceived. I shall refine and probe this hypothesis when considering *Inchochine*, *Viceroy's House*, *In the Mood for Love* and *The Road Home* by proposing a model of transnational reception that examines how aesthetic strategies, anchored in the cinematic text itself, have the capacity to provoke a nostalgic or exotic response in the spectator.

Correspondences between Exoticism and Nostalgia

Distance and desire are the axes along which exoticism and nostalgia move in their shared quest for a better elsewhere. Both mobilise distance, be it spatial or temporal, to enable an imaginative investment that replaces historical accuracy and cultural authenticity with the construction of an idealised alterity or an embellished past. The famous opening lines of L. P. Hartley's novel *The Go-Between* (1953), 'The past is a foreign country . . . they do things differently there', encapsulates the chronotopic nature of nostalgia. It is simultaneously the longing for a distant place as well as the longing for a distant time, typically one's childhood or what is perceived to be the golden age in the history of a nation.

Both the longing for an irrecoverable past, described by Salman Rushdie (1992a: 12) as 'a country from which we have all emigrated', and the exotic are premised on the experience of loss and nostalgic longing. Chris Bongie contends in *Exotic Memories* that the actual encounter with the exotic ceased to exist at the end of the nineteenth century as the result of cultural convergence and homogenisation on a global scale. Henceforth it has only continued to exist in cultural memory and the discourse of exoticism (see Chapter 1). Colonial expansion and subsequent postcolonial migration resulted in persistent contact between different cultures so that what was once perceived as strange and exotic became familiar. It is precisely this gradual erosion of alternative horizons and the deep sense of nostalgia provoked by cultural homogenisation and hybridisation that generates exoticism, defined as a particular mode of cultural representation and discursive practice that renders something *as* exotic. In this sense, exoticism *constructs* a desired elsewhere, which is nostalgically imagined as geographically and/or temporally remote. Ultimately, exoticism, like nostalgia, is a story about loss – the loss of a different way of life and an irrecoverable past. Both discourses seek to salvage something that has ceased to exist.

Exoticism and nostalgia spring from the perceived deficiencies of the present. They are profoundly suspicious of progress, whatever form it may take at a given historical moment. Growing cultural interest in the exotic invariably arises at moments of cultural disaffection and discontent when it serves as a projection surface for utopian longings. This holds particularly true for the nostalgic fascination with so-called 'primitive' cultures, presumed as 'being stuck in an earlier stage of "culture" . . . when compared with the West' (Chow 1995: 22).[4] Primitivism, and exoticism more broadly, project fantasies of authenticity and abundance onto Other cultures. A similar sense of disaffection with the present underpins nostalgia's imaginative investment in the past, as the process of 'nostalgic distancing sanitises as it selects, making the past feel complete, stable, coherent . . . in other words, making it so very unlike the present' (Hutcheon 2009: 250).

In terms of their spatial dimensions, exoticism and nostalgia invest their utopic desires in remote localities (the distant home and the foreign faraway), however, they differ in terms of their affective trajectories. Interestingly, Svetlana Boym (2001: 10) ignores this distinction since exoticism is beyond the scope of her disquisition on nostalgia. Hence, she attributes European travellers' fascination with 'barbarous' and 'semi-civilised' people and places to the south and east of Europe as an expression of nostalgic longing, a temporality that has resisted the imperative of continuous progress that dominates 'global time'. Citing Heinrich Heine's poem 'Ein Fichtenbaum steht einsam' (A Spruce Is Standing Lonely), about a spruce up in the icy, barren North that dreams about a palm tree in the distant Orient, Boym (2001: 14) identifies the anthropomorphised spruce's yearning as nostalgic, whereas I consider the affective geography mapped in Heine's poem as incontrovertibly exoticist. Not only is the palm tree a generic signifier of exoticism (see Chapter 1) but – from a European perspective – the Orient is the antipode of home. I contend that the spatial trajectory of nostalgia is necessarily homeward bound. In its original sense, which continues to reverberate in the present, it is a form of *Heimweh* or *maladie du pays*, the longing to return to a place that is intimately familiar. Exoticism, by contrast, is outward bound. It is motivated by *Wanderlust* (literally 'the lust to wander') or *Fernweh* (literally 'the painful yearning for faraway places'), two German words that denote the wish to widen one's horizons and to encounter new places and different cultures. Vladimir Nabokov sums up the idea of *Fernweh* nicely when he describes it as 'nostalgia in reverse' (cited in Farley 2020).[5]

Both nostalgia and exoticism have attracted harsh criticism for fetishising and commodifying the past or cultural difference and for offering it up to mass-market consumption on a global scale. Invoking Fredric Jameson's influential critique, critics have not tired of reiterating that the nostalgia film and its close relative, the heritage film, conjure visions of the past in which historical inquiry is displaced by a museum aesthetics that relishes in the recreation of period detail. Likewise, exoticism regularly courts controversy for spectacularising cultural difference and divorcing it from critical interrogation. Far from celebrating the steadily increasing interest in the postcolonial exotic in contemporary societies, which bestows cultural prestige and commercial success onto the works of postcolonial writers, filmmakers and other artists, Huggan (2001: 33) even refers to it as 'a pathology of cultural representation under late capitalism'.

Having charted how nostalgia and exoticism intersect and, despite being primarily interested in the *exotic* nostalgia film, it is nevertheless necessary to introduce its ideologically more problematic counterpart, the *imperialist* nostalgia film. Bongie's (1991: 17) distinction between 'imperialist exoticism', which 'affirms the hegemony of modern civilization over less developed, savage territories' and 'exoticising exoticism', which 'privileges those very territories and their peoples, figuring them as a possible refuge from an overbearing modernity', identifies them as different manifestations of exoticism. Whereas the former serves to assert and legitimise colonial expansion and domination and their neo-colonial inflections in the present, the latter validates Other cultures by projecting those utopic and desirable qualities which are perceived to be lacking in Western societies onto them.

The Imperialist Nostalgia Film

In a much-cited essay, the anthropologist Renato Rosaldo (1989: 107–8) coined the term 'imperialist nostalgia', to which he alternately refers as an 'elegiac mode of perception', a 'mood' and an 'emotion' that 'makes racial domination appear pure and innocent'. He proposes that it revolves around a peculiar paradox:

> Agents of colonialism ... often display nostalgia for the colonized culture as it was 'traditionally' (that is, when they first encountered it). The peculiarity of their yearning, of course, is that agents of colonialism long for the very forms of life they intentionally altered or destroyed ... and then regret ... that things have not remained as they were prior to his or her intervention ... In any of its versions, imperialist nostalgia uses a pose of 'innocent yearning' both to capture people's imaginations and to conceal its complicity with often brutal domination. (Rosaldo 1989: 107–8)

Although Rosaldo conceptualises imperialist nostalgia as a longing for the time *before* colonial expansion and domination, most critics who have adopted the concept and, indeed, the films Rosaldo himself cites as examples, namely *Out of Africa* and British Raj revival films, such as *Heat and Dust* or *A Passage to India*, actually exhibit a deep yearning for the days when Britain was the largest empire in history. Although imperialist nostalgia films are not identical with films of empire, both express a longing for empire. They differ, however, in terms of their narrative focus and gender politics. Films of empire, including Zoltan Korda's *Sanders of the River* (1935), *The Drum* (1938) and *The Four Feathers* (1939), as well as *Rhodes of Africa* (Michael Balcon, 1936), celebrate male courage and bravery and are concerned with the domination and defence of the colonies. Imperialist nostalgia films, by contrast, feminise empire by adopting a female point of view and revolving around domesticity, love and adultery. 'When a text is one of celebration, it is the manly white qualities of expansiveness, enterprise, courage and control (of self and others) that are in the foreground,' Richard Dyer (1997: 184) observes, 'but when doubt and uncertainty creep in, women begin to take centre stage. The white male spirit achieves and maintains empire; the white female soul is associated with its demise.' There is more than a grain of truth in this observation, as cultural anthropologist and historian Ann Laura Stoler attests in 'Making Empire Respectable'. The wives and daughters of colonial administrators, though officially expected to exert a civilising influence, actually brought the colonial enterprise into disarray through their sexuality – both in reality and in fiction. Until the early twentieth century, colonial officials who served the British, French and Dutch empires overseas were not permitted to be married and bring European wives to the colonies. Instead, concubinage, that is the cohabitation between European men and Asian women, was positively encouraged since it 'was considered to have a stabilizing effect on political order and colonial health', keeping

European men out of the brothels (Stoler 1997: 348). The subsequent arrival of large numbers of European women, perceived as the bearers of morality, did not only lead to a more refined, bourgeois lifestyle but also to increased racial tensions. On the one hand, this was due to their opposition to concubinage and growing racial segregation, and on the other, they felt sexually threatened by native men who were stereotyped as being driven by their '"primitive" sexual urges and uncontrollable lust, aroused by the sight of white women' (Stoler 1997: 352). Even though in reality there were very few incidents of rape, white women were afraid and requested more protection from the 'black peril' (Stoler 1997: 353). Nevertheless, in Raj fictions and films, such as *A Passage to India* and the television mini-series *The Jewel in the Crown* (Granada Television, 1984), 'the threat of the dark rapist appears with . . . frequency' and, according to Jenny Sharpe (1993: 3), is symptomatic of a gradual loss of colonial authority. Female sexuality was seen to lead to temptation, adultery and tensions that ultimately destabilise empire. Invariably set at a time of imperial decline, these Eurocentric imperial fantasies simultaneously indulge in a glamorous colonial past and in the exotic allure of Europe's former colonies, with India under the British Raj, British East Africa and French Indochina featuring prominently.

Imperialist nostalgia films typically imagine the intercultural encounter with the colonial Other as interracial desire. Films including *Chocolat* (Claire Denis, 1988), *The Lover*, *Before the Rains* and the recent television series *Indian Summers* (Channel 4, 2015–16) deftly illustrate Robert Young's (1995: 182) argument that 'colonial desire', denoting the sexualised and exoticised discourse of rape, penetration and miscegenation, became 'the dominant paradigm through which . . . [colonialism's] violent antagonistic power relations of sexual and cultural diffusion' was conceived. Other imperialist nostalgia films, such as *Out of Africa*, *White Mischief* (Michael Radford, 1987) and *The English Patient* (Anthony Minghella, 1996), revolve around doomed love affairs between white expatriates unfolding against the backdrop of the African savannah or desert. The visual appeal of these exotic settings, coupled with the glamorous colonial lifestyle, seduces the spectator into complicity with colonialism, thereby obscuring the power structures of colonial domination and exploitation.

Imperialist nostalgia films typically foreground the retrieval of the past through acts of memory, plunging spectators into extended flashbacks that are usually framed by the female protagonists' voice-over narratives and end with their return to Europe, after they have lost their land, their lovers and whatever else was dear to them. Karen Blixen's famous line,

'I had a farm in Africa, at the foot of the Ngong Hills', which introduces the extended flashback that is the film *Out of Africa*, captures this feminised and feminist imperialist fantasy of the white woman who becomes autonomous and empowered in faraway lands most memorably. Of course, the kind of 'women's liberation' celebrated in *Out of Africa*, as well as in *Indochine*, is at the expense of the colonial subjects, even though Karen Blixen, childless and separated from her Danish husband, is portrayed in highly idealised terms as a benefactress of the African people. She deeply cares about her farm workers and sets up a school for Kikuyu children on her estate.

Like Karen Blixen, the nameless protagonist (Isabelle Huppert) of *Un barrage contre le Pacifique* (The Seawall, Rithy Panh, 2008) also loves the land and the local people, but she is neither powerful nor prosperous. The film, which is based Marguerite Duras' semi-autobiographical novel of the same title and directed by the Cambodian filmmaker Rithy Panh, is exceptional insofar as it depicts a French widow in 1930s French Indochina, who tries to eke out a living for herself and her adolescent son and daughter on a concession she purchased from the ruling French colonialists. Her rice paddies are regularly flooded by the encroaching sea that spoils the crops and results in the family's poverty. In contrast to other imperialist nostalgia films, *The Seawall* does not indulge the spectator in the glamour and opulence of the colonial past but centres on those disenfranchised under French colonial rule. Class, more so than ethnicity, determines social inclusion and exclusion. The French widow is shunned and exploited by her wealthy and powerful compatriots but creates mutual bonds of solidarity with the Indochinese locals. Like in *The Lover*, also adapted from an autobiographical novel by Duras and set in French Indochina, the colonial power hierarchies between the French and the Indochinese are inverted, as the impoverished white mothers encourage their daughters to maintain morally dubious liaisons with prosperous Chinese businessmen, in the misguided hope that these relationships might resolve the families' precarity.[6]

Indochine, a Paradigmatic Imperialist Nostalgia Film

Though unequivocally Eurocentric in its perspective and directed by a white French director, Régis Wargnier, I am including *Indochine* as a case study here, since this Oscar-winning international box-office success is a paradigmatic example of the imperialist nostalgia film. As such it serves as a foil that will illuminate the continuities and contrasts between Eurocentric and decentred imperialist nostalgia films. The French film is set between the 1930s and 1954, during a period of growing anticolonial unrest that culminated in French Indochina's independence and its partition into its successor states, Laos, Cambodia, the Democratic Republic of Vietnam and the State of Vietnam. The film constructs the end of the French Empire in South East Asia as a maternal melodrama with overtly allegorical dimensions. The opening scene shows an opulent funeral procession on the Mekong River, which sets the elegiac mood and theme of death and loss that pervades the entire film. Indochinese officiants dressed in white, black or mauve and wearing quintessentially Indochinese *nón lá* conical hats or headscarves emerge from the mist that envelopes the majestic river. They are rowing flower-decorated barges, accompanied by the sound of a chorus chanting a requiem and the steady beat of a drum. The film's protagonist Eliane, played by one of French cinema's most bankable stars, Catherine Deneuve, stands in statuesque stillness on one of the elaborately decorated barges. She is veiled and dressed in black and holds the hand of a little Asian girl, Camille, the orphaned daughter of her friends, Prince N'guyen and his wife, who died in a plane crash. As the exotic procession of wooden barges carrying gold-leaved coffins that are shaded by a pagoda-shaped canvas roof and red and golden Chinese parasols, glides along the river, Eliane's voice-over narrative is heard. She ponders the inseparability of France and Indochina, configured in terms of close friendship and maternal bonds:

> I had no children, she [Camille] had no parents. I adopted her. Prince N'guyen, his wife and I had been inseparable. Such is youth. We had thought the world consisted of inseparable things. Men and women, mountains and plains, gods and humans . . . Indochina and France.

Figure 4.1 *Indochine* (Régis Wargnier, 1992) stages the end of the French Empire in South East Asia as a maternal melodrama.

This list of binary opposites serves to legitimise French rule over Indochina by suggesting that the inequalities between colonisers and colonised, equated with high mountains and low plains and the divine and mere mortals, conform to the natural order. From the film's retrospective vantage point of 1954, however, these imperialist assumptions are revealed as misguided.

The plot revolves around Eliane, a woman in her late thirties or forties, who successfully manages her father's rubber plantation, one of the largest in Indochina. She raises the Annam princess as if she were French, and the two are very close. The strong mother–daughter bond is ruptured when Eliane and Camille (Lin-Danh Pham), now a teenager, become rivals for the affection of Jean-Baptiste (Vincent Perez), a young French naval officer. Eliane arranges for the officer's reassignment to the far north. Camille leaves everything behind to find him at Ha-long Bay, one of Vietnam's most iconic landscapes, featuring an archipelago of thousands of towering limestone karsts covered by lush green tropical vegetation and surrounded by the deep turquoise waters of the bay. The spectacular setting serves as the backdrop for Camille and Jean-Baptiste's romantic reunion. They have a child together but, soon after their son's birth, get separated and imprisoned. Jean-Baptiste is eventually killed by the Communists and Camille emerges from the notorious Poulo-Condor prison transformed by Communist ideology as 'the Red Princess'. She rejects Eliane's offer to restore her estate to her, ready to fight in the Communist anticolonial struggle for independence. Camille prioritises her political commitment to her country's liberation over her role as mother and leaves Eliane to raise her infant son Etienne. As the end of colonial rule approaches, Eliane sells her plantation and, together with her adopted grandson, heads for France. The film ends with Eliane and Etienne (Jean-Baptiste Huynh), now a young man, on Lake Geneva, where he is supposed to be reunited with his mother, Camille. Here, the memorialised past and the present converge as Eliane's voice-over narration finds its addressee. She tells Etienne the story of French Indochina as a family romance. Although Etienne goes to find his birth mother amongst the Vietnamese delegates at the Geneva Peace Conference, he spontaneously decides not to approach her, since he realises 'how ridiculous' it would have been if he had 'jumped on an Indochinese woman, yelling: "Mama"', declaring instead that Eliane is his real mother. Deeply moved by her adopted grandson's acknowledgement, she turns away to regain her composure. The final shot shows Eliane's elegant silhouette from behind, as she is overlooking Lake Geneva. Yet again, she is dressed all in black, the colour of mourning, her eyes shaded by dark sunglasses instead of the black veil of the opening sequence. Momentarily, Lake Geneva, surrounded by high mountains that rise steeply out of the water, looks remarkably similar to Ha-long Bay. It represents a 'phantasmatic Indochina' (Norindr 1996) that haunts Eliane after the Indochina she once knew and loved has ceased to exist. Thus, the film's final tableau of the erstwhile plantation owner, who mourns the loss of her 'homeland' (for Eliane was born in Indochina and self-identifies as 'une Asiate', despite being French through and through) and the privilege and power she enjoyed there, encapsulates the sentiment of the imperialist nostalgia film.

Indochine stages French Indochina's decolonisation as an allegory in which Eliane represents the French nation and Camille, her adopted daughter, Indochina, whose eventual loss Eliane mourns at the end. This family constellation reinforces the colonial trope which imagines the colonised subjects as infants, relying on the protection and guidance of their white father (or mother, in this instance). As Anne McClintock illustrates in *Imperial Leather* (1995: 358), the family trope naturalises systems of domination and control, especially colonialism, by constructing them in terms of domestic genealogies. The film valorises Eliane as the superior mother whom her adopted grandson chooses over his biological mother. By portraying the two women 'as polar opposites – one masculine, Caucasian, and powerful, the other feminine, Asian, dependent and "innocent" – *Indochine* reinstates the essentializing postures of patriarchal and Orientalist thinking' (Heung 1997: 174). Consistent with this Orientalist imaginary, Camille lacks agency – both as a mother and as an anticolonial freedom fighter. Since she is imprisoned for having shot a French officer, she is separated from her infant son, who is first breastfed and nurtured by Indochinese peasant women and then raised by Eliane. Although key historical events, such as the enslavement of peasants, the Yen-Bay uprising and the amnesty of political prisoners in the French colonial prison of Poulo Condor, are briefly referenced, Camille's courageous investment in Indochina's struggle for independence is entirely elided in the film's narrative. *Indochine* is decidedly not a historical epic but an imperial nostalgia film intent on reappropriating the glamorous colonial past through '"postcard" images of colonial life in French Indochina' (Norindr 1996: 138) that are deeply ingrained in French collective memory and that serve, as Fredric Jameson notes, 'as substitutes for any genuine historical consciousness' (Stephanson and Jameson 1989: 18). In the end, Camille is literally erased from the screen and the narrative, while Eliane takes centre stage in the film's final tableau.

Unlike some of the Raj revival films that concede at least a modicum of postcolonial guilt, *Indochine* seems to be in complete denial of the atrocities committed in the name of empire. While Camille is cast as the monstrous mother who abandons her child, Eliane is imagined as the victimised mother who has nurtured the Indochinese 'on the cream of European civilization' (Kempley 1993), only to eventually lose her daughter and be expelled from the country she called her home. In this way, the film manipulates the spectator to lament the colonisers' loss and the end of empire, thereby obscuring colonial guilt.

Viceroy's House, a New Wave of Imperialist Nostalgia

Viceroy's House by the British Asian director Gurinder Chadha is part of a new wave of imperialist nostalgia that has recently seized British screen culture, examples being the BBC documentary series *The Birth of Empire: The East India Company* (BBC, 2014), the drama series *Indian Summers*, set in the Raj's summer capital Shimla in 1932, and the biographical historical drama *Victoria and Abdul* (Stephen Frears, 2017) about Queen Victoria's affectionate friendship with her Muslim Indian servant Abdul. In the streets of London, echoes of empire reverberate everywhere: the celebrated Indian restaurant chain Dishoom recreates the colonial ambience and food of 1930s Bombay cafes, complete with retro washbasins in the dining area, faded advertisements and sepia photographs of bygone days. Like The East India Company, a chain of luxury shops in London that, seemingly oblivious to its toxic heritage, markets itself as 'history-infused tea & coffee sellers', Dishoom is Indian-owned. What makes this latest nostalgia for the Raj different from its precursors is that Indians or Britons of Indian descent capitalise on it by selling 'a commodified dream of the Raj to Britons' (Jeffries 2015).

What exactly has sparked this imperial nostalgia boom in Britain in the first decades of the new millennium? Not unlike in the Thatcher era, the heyday of the Raj revival films, it has been interpreted as a response to the gloom of austerity resulting in a weakening of national pride and self-confidence. Hence the rallying cry of the Brexiteers 'Now let's make Britain great again' – as if leaving the EU would automatically give Britons the Empire back. In fact, in a YouGov poll in 2016, the year of the Brexit referendum, 44 per cent of Britons declared that they were proud of the British Empire, compared with just 21 per cent who regretted Britain's imperial past (see Stone 2016; El-Enany 2020). While this figure had dropped to just 32 per cent by 2020, a third of British people still believed that countries colonised by the British were 'better off overall for being colonised' (Booth 2020), a higher proportion than in any other former colonial nation.

Paul Gilroy offers a more complex explanation of the imperialist nostalgia boom. In *After Empire: Melancholia or Convivial Culture?* (2004) and, more recently, in an article in *The Guardian* entitled 'The best exotic nostalgia boom: Why colonial style is back' (Jeffries 2015), Gilroy suggests that the British have never properly confronted and mourned the atrocities of colonial rule and, as a consequence, suffer from 'postimperial melancholia' (Gilroy 2004: 98). Indebted to the psychoanalysts Alexander and Margarete Mitscherlich's influential study on the West German people's inability to mourn Hitler's death 'and the larger evil of which their love for him had been part', Gilroy (2004: 107) proposes that melancholia is a pathological condition that manifests itself when an individual or a nation wards off the process of mourning.[7] Having failed to work through the loss of empire and the uncomfortable truths about Britain's colonial history, the British people revisit it obsessively. Whereas postimperial melancholia is 'mourning's pathological variant' (Gilroy cited in Jeffries 2015), imperialist nostalgia is a form of outright guilt denial that allows Britons to fleetingly restore the lost greatness of the British Empire and feel proud of their history and national identity Despite having been dubbed 'a British film with a Punjabi heart' (Thorpe 2017), Chadha's film is a fitting example of the most recent recrudescence of Raj nostalgia.

Viceroy's House charts India's transition from being part of the British Empire to Partition and the founding of the two independent nations, India and Pakistan, in 1947. In India, the British-Indian co-production was released as *Partition: 1947*, but it was banned in Pakistan as it was felt to misrepresent Jinnah and the national interests of Pakistan (Bharathi 2017). The film seeks to tell history from above and below by adopting the upstairs–downstairs formula of *Downton Abbey* (ITV, 2010–15) and casting Hugh Bonneville, the amiable Lord Grantham of this popular heritage television drama, in the role of Lord Mountbatten. The narrative revolves around how Mountbatten, and his formidable wife Edwina (Gillian Anderson) manage momentous political change on the Indian subcontinent. The downstairs sub-plot, situated in the servant quarters, tells the story of star-crossed lovers Jeet (Manish Dayal) and Aalia (Huma Qureshi), whose love cuts across India's religious divide between Hindus and Muslims. Only at the very end does this historical epic reveal itself to be a postmemory film in which the British-Indian filmmaker Chadha has a strong personal investment.[8] A series of white-on-black intertitles states: 'The Partition of India led to the largest mass migration in human history. 14 million people were displaced. One million Hindus, Muslims and Sikhs died. This film is dedicated to all those who died and those who survived Partition.' An old black-and-white portrait of an Indian woman appears, accompanied by the text: 'Including this mother who fled Pakistan for India with her children. Her baby daughter starved to death on the road.' The camera zooms out of the photo and the mother becomes part of a family portrait, surrounded by four children. The text reads: 'After 18 months' search, she was found by her husband in a refugee camp and the family was reunited.' As the portrait dissolves and black and white gives way to colour, the children surrounding their mother are transformed into their significantly older selves, while the mother is replaced by Gurinder Chadha. The accompanying text reads: 'Her granddaughter is the director of this film.'

This revelation enables the filmmaker of Punjabi descent to assume the stance of shared victimhood with all the 'political and psychological benefits . . . the honoured place of suffering' entails (Gilroy 2004: 103). The emotional impact of this unexpected disclosure, underscored by A. R. Rahman's stirring soundtrack, stands in stark contrast to the film's opening epigram, 'History is written by the victors'. The director's personal connection turns what looks and feels like a British heritage film into a postmemory film that articulates the trauma of Partition in the attempt to make the nostalgia for the glamour of the Raj ideologically more palatable. While history is written by the victors, the postmemory of suffering, which is the avowed impetus behind this film, is to pay tribute to the victims; but the victims of what exactly? The violence of Partition or that of the British Empire?

Rather than making the suffering of the victims its main focus, the film's cinematography celebrates the grandeur of the British Empire, captured in numerous aerial and wide-angle shots of the imposing Viceroy's Palace, the British Raj's seat of government in Delhi. Everything is on a grand scale, a reference to the vastness and power of the British Empire.

Figure 4.2 The 'mass ornament' of Indian liveried staff in *Viceroy's House* (Gurinder Chadha, 2017) conveys a sense of imperial control.

The pageantry and the 'mass ornament' (Kracauer 1995) of hundreds of liveried Indian staff, dressed in pristine white and vibrant red uniforms, and moving in synchrony and symmetry – at the service of the British Viceroy – afford aesthetic pleasure.

At the same time, the geometry of pattern reduces the people that form them to mere building blocks, 'fractions of a figure' (Kracauer 1995: 78), thereby de-individualising the Indian subjects and intimating the supreme order and control exerted by British colonial rule. This becomes all the more apparent if one compares the symmetry of the *mise en scène* and the geometrical patterns of lines and circles in which the Indian staff in the palace move and stand with the turmoil of Partition, which puts a sudden end to the film's visual splendour. Captured partly in black-and-white footage and partly in colour, the incessant stream of Indian migrants is depicted as an amorphous mass that merges with the colour of the sand and the dust of the roads. The marked change in the film's colour palette, from the vibrant hues of red and orange and crisp white of the uniforms and liveries at the Viceroy's palace to a monochrome muddy brown, diminishes the *mise en scène*'s exotic appeal, given that high colour saturation is one of the hallmarks of exoticism's visual idiom.

While on a narrative level *Viceroy's House* does not call into question the ethical imperative of 'giving a nation back to its people' (in the words of Mountbatten's daughter), on a visual level it exhibits a nostalgic yearning for the grandeur and control of the British Empire. It thus reveals the same sense of ambivalence, or even schizophrenia, which Harlan Kennedy described with exquisite sarcasm in relation to the Raj revival films of the 1980s:

> While our ears and eyes swoon to the éclat of majestic scenery, lovely costumes, and gosh all those elephants, our souls are being told to stay behind after class and get a ticking off for treating our colonial subjects so badly. For carving up other nations and leaving them to put the pieces together. For snobbery, cruelty and oppression ... There's a love–hate relationship with the Empire in British cinema that's totally unresolved. Intellectually, we agree to eat humble pie about our imperial past. Emotionally, the impact of the India movies is to make us fall head over heels in love with the dear dead old days, when even Britain's villainies were Big; when even its blunders and failures had tragic status; and when, if we had nothing else, goddammit, at least we had glamour. (Kennedy 1985: 52)

What distinguishes Chadha's film from the Raj revival films of the 1980s, however, is that it makes the genre's irresolvable tension between nostalgia and colonial guilt more explicit. The director's British-Punjabi background, with its ambivalent cultural and national allegiances, gives her an acute sensibility for the British, Indian and Pakistani perspectives.

Although it was Chadha's avowed intention to reach diverse transnational audiences and to convey a 'message of reconciliation [that would] . . . speak to Pakistanis, to Indians, and to the British' (*Viceroy's House Press Kit*), the film's critical reception indicates that she could not square this circle. A review in the British magazine *The Economist* praises Chadha for filling 'a gap in Britain's collective consciousness and cultural memory' and argues that 'it will be hard for some to maintain a sense of nostalgia and triumphalism for Britain's empire after watching *Viceroy's House*' (R. V. 2017). Conversely, Fatima Bhutto (2017), a member of the politically prominent Bhutto family in Pakistan, describes *Viceory's House* as the product 'of a deeply colonised imagination . . . [and] a sorry testament to how intensely empire continues to run in the mind of some today'. Arguably, these diametrically opposite verdicts result from the film's generic hybridity. The juxtaposition of heritage cinema aesthetics and black-and-white documentary footage of the Partition represents an attempt to temper the nostalgia for the British Empire with a sense of postcolonial responsibility.

In the Mood for Love, an Exotic Nostalgia Film

Unlike *Indochine* and *Viceroy's House*, Wong Kar-wai's *In the Mood for Love* does not engage explicitly with Hong Kong's colonial heritage, nor does it articulate a melancholic longing for a *specific moment* in its past. Instead, the film exudes a nostalgic mood, a diffuse sense of loss whose appeal is as universal as it is locally specific to Hong Kong. Tony Rayns (2015: 43) describes *In the Mood for Love* as a 'requiem for a lost (colonial) time and its values', while Vivian Lee (2009) sees it as part of the 'nostalgia fever' that seized Hong Kong from the late 1980s throughout the 1990s. For Ackbar Abbas (1997), this nostalgia fever is a symptom of the anxieties that accompanied Hong Kong's anticipated handover to China in 1997.[9] Although nostalgia is usually centred on a particular period, Hong Kong's nostalgia lacked such a clearly identifiable object of loss and longing.[10] If there was 'a place and time that clearly stood out' as a reference point then it was Shanghai in the 1920s and 1930s, 'the glamorous decadence of the "Paris of the East" (Huppatz 2009: 15), whose fate as a cosmopolitan capitalist city, taken over by China's Communist regime in 1949, seemed to prefigure Hong Kong's future.

The reference to Shanghai is salient for *In the Mood for Love* in more than one respect. The narrative is set in the 1960s amongst the Shanghainese diaspora, who live cheek-by-jowl in multi-occupancy rooming apartments in Hong Kong. This is where Chow Mo-Wan (Tony Leung Chiu-Wai) and Mrs Chan, née Su Lizhen (Maggie Cheung), meet. When they discover that their respective spouses, who are frequently taking business trips abroad, are having an affair, they spend more and more time together and eventually fall in love with each other. Yet determined not to be like their unfaithful spouses, they ostensibly never consummate their love.

Like the protagonists, Wong migrated with his family from Shanghai to Hong Kong when he was five years old. His childhood memories of a communal way of life, where privacy was scarce and gossip was rife, inform the film's sense of place and narrative. The vanishing glamour of a nostalgically remembered Shanghai suffuses the *mise en scène*; Shanghainese is spoken alongside Cantonese; one of the many songs, 'Hua yang de nianhua', performed by the Shanghainese singer and actress Zhou Xuan in a movie in 1947, is briefly heard on the radio and, more importantly, lent its title to the Mandarin release version of *In the Mood for Love*, which translates literally as 'When Flowers Were in Full Bloom' (Chow 2007: 68).

The most striking visual reference to Shanghainese culture is the dizzying array of no less than twenty-two cheongsams which Mrs Chan wears in *In the Mood for Love*. The dress changes are a marker of temporality, signalling the progression and repetition of time, specifically the time loops that characterise mourning as well as nostalgic recollection. As Stephen Teo (2005: 128) puts it: 'Maggie Cheung stepping out in high heels and cheongsam, handbag over an arm, hair perfectly coiffured, is the single most evocative image of nostalgia in the film.' For Wong, the cheongsam

Figure 4.3 Mrs Chan's cheongsams encapsulate the nostalgic and exotic appeal of *In the Mood for Love* (Wong Kar-wai, 2000).

is a nostalgia object to which he has personal attachments. As he stated in interviews, there was no need for him to research Maggie Cheung's dresses, 'because our mothers dressed like this' (Wong cited in Teo 2005: 11). I would like to propose that Mrs Chan's cheongsams, 'careful replicas of the 1930s Shanghai style created by a reputed tailor' (Lee 2009: 32), simultaneously encapsulate the film's nostalgic as well as its exotic appeal, inviting culturally specific readings amongst local and global spectators.

The cheongsam – exotic or culturally hybrid?

Although the cheongsam is widely regarded in the West as a quintessentially Chinese garment, its evolution since the beginning of the twentieth century suggests that it has absorbed different cultural influences from the East and the West and is thus hybridised. It was brought to China by the Manchu who imposed it upon the Han people (Clark 2000: 65). Originally a male garment, it was adopted by urban educated women in the early Republican period (1911–49) as a signifier of women's gender equality. The cheongsam's transformation into the iconic dress of Chinese femininity occurred in Shanghai in the 1920s and 1930s, where it was worn by 'sing-song girls' (or prostitutes) as well as film stars, who set fashion trends that were adopted by urban cosmopolitan women. When it was abolished under Mao Zedong's Communist regime in the 1950s, which regarded it as bourgeois and incompatible with the ideals of communism, it was preserved as a symbol of Chinese cultural identity in Hong Kong, Taiwan, Singapore, and elsewhere overseas. Since many wealthy Shanghainese migrated to British-ruled Hong Kong, followed by Shanghainese tailors, the cheongsam really came into its own there. 'Under the influence of Western fashion' it evolved 'and became the everyday wear of the colony's urban woman, who wore a very fitted style accessorised with high-heeled shoes to create the fashionable image of slimness and height' (Clark 2000: 23). Internationally, the British film *The World of Suzie Wong* (Richard Quine, 1960), which is set in Hong Kong in the milieu of seedy bars and prostitutes, reinforced the connection between the cheongsam and the sexual allure of the Orientalised woman. During the 1950s and 1960s, the cheongsam had a significant impact on international fashion centres in Paris, Rome and New York on account of its perceived exoticism, while its slim line coincided with fashion trends in Europe.

The fashion revival of the cheongsam during the pre-handover period of Hong Kong has been attributed to the diffuse nostalgia that anchored itself in the glamour of 1930s Shanghai and that led, amongst other things, to the establishment of Shanghai Tang, a luxury emporium that 'produces

Chinese exotica for a global market' (Huppatz 2009: 28). Launched in Hong Kong in 1994, and subsequently in twenty-four other locations worldwide, Shanghai Tang's cheongsam, either ready-to-wear or tailor-made by the store's 'Imperial Tailors', is one of its most popular items. Mainland China eventually re-appropriated the previously outlawed garment and, at the 29th Olympic Games in Beijing in 2008, hostesses were wearing uniforms that paid tribute to the national Chinese dress par excellence.

This brief excursion into the sartorial history of the cheongsam illustrates a number of salient features of the exotic: in a globalised world, unadulterated cultural difference is largely a fantasy and most expressions of exotica, the cheongsam included, are culturally hybrid. Even so, the cheongsam has retained its status as the foremost sartorial icon of Chinese femininity and is actively promoted as such in the global marketplace. In the process of transnational circulation, the cheongsam – not unlike the English manor houses of English heritage cinema – shifts from being an *ordinary* marker of Chinese cultural identity to an instantly recognisable signifier of *exotic* Chinese femininity.

Exoticism and enigmatisation

It is such discrepancies in the interpretation of foreign, or familiar, cultural signifiers that Lai conceptualises as 'enigmatization' (Lai 2001), as discussed above. Maggie Cheung's cheongsams function as a key device of enigmatisation. For local audiences they evoke, first and foremost, nostalgic memories of Hong Kong in the 1950s and 1960s and the impact of Shanghainese fashion and culture during those decades. For global audiences, by contrast, the cheongsam epitomises the exotic and erotic allure of the Oriental woman, constructed as enigmatic, seductive, yet restrained. Its figure-hugging cut emphasises the delicate feminine contours of Maggie Cheung while at the same time constricting her movements, forcing her to keep a perfectly upright posture and to take small, nimble steps. The high Mandarin-style collar, which conceals her décolletage, adds an air of self-discipline to her attire. Not unlike the constrictive corset of the Victorian era, which according to costume historian David Kunzle 'represents a form of erotic tension and constitutes *ipso facto* a demand for erotic release, which may be deliberately controlled, prolonged and postponed' (Kunzle cited in Bruzzi 1997: 44), the tight-fitting cheongsams in *In the Mood for Love* mobilise a similar tension between sexual attraction and its repression.

In fact, the cheongsam is the material embodiment of the film's romantic plot, encapsulating the irresolvable conflict between erotic desire and an old-fashioned moral restraint. Ultimately, the couple's unconsummated love speaks to a universal nostalgia for 'the past as a time when people believed in love' (Teo 2005: 126), a feeling that has presumably ceased to exist in contemporary society. It is also pivotal to the narrative of Stanley Kwan's *Yim ji kau* (Rouge, 1987), another celebrated Hong Kong nostalgia film. The fact that Mrs Chan and Mr Chow's love is, ostensibly, never consummated makes it all the more poignant. The scene showing the couple consummate their passion was shot but deleted by Wong shortly before the film's release and is clearly marked as a narrative elision. A montage of shots showing Mrs Chan running up and down the stairs leading to hotel room 2046,[11] which Chow Mo-wan has rented, seemingly to be able to write undisturbed, but more likely to avoid the neighbour's gossip, captures the moral conundrum accompanying her first visit. A cut to Mr Chow shows him inside room 2046, smoking and waiting for her. When she knocks on the door, the camera does not follow her inside. Instead, a hard cut marks the ellipsis and shows Mrs Chan on the threshold, already leaving. His remark, 'I didn't think you'd come', is followed by her non-sequitur, 'We won't be like them', a reference to their spouses' affair – and perhaps also an oblique statement that, whatever may have happened between them, will not be repeated. Only the crimson billowing curtains in the dimly lit hallway and Mrs Chan's bright red coat function as material correlatives of the couple's desire, gesturing towards a possible passionate encounter off-screen. The emotional reticence surrounding the relationship is in large measure attributable to the film's elliptical editing, which withholds narratively significant information and evokes a sense of mystery. Although I am not suggesting that local viewers are able to resolve the ambiguity surrounding the true nature of the lovers' relationship, for global viewers, the enigma is heightened by their awareness of being cultural outsiders, who can never fully fathom the Other. In this sense, the film's many elisions contribute to its exotic allure.

Conversely, the theme of romantic love whose qualities of renunciation and steadfastness are linked to the past invites comparisons with similar, canonical melodramas, such as David Lean's *Brief Encounter* (1945), Douglas Sirk's *All that Heaven Allows* (1955) and Fei Mu's *Xiao cheng zhi chun* (Spring in a Small Town, 1948). Meanwhile Wong himself mentions early Hong Kong melodramas, featuring the Chinese singer-actress Zhou Xuan, such as *Chang Xiangsi* (An All-Consuming Love, Zhaozhang He, 1947) alongside Hitchcock's *Vertigo* (1958), as sources of inspiration (Teo 2005: 118–19). These various intertextual references go a long way in explaining the transnational appeal of *In the Mood for Love* since they allow for the exotic to be 'domesticated', that is to say, translated and integrated into a familiar context and, thereby, becoming legible. Wong Kar-wai's film is a perfect example of how the exotic is integrated into familiar discursive and aesthetic frameworks, insofar as it deploys the universal theme of love and renunciation, coupled with the genre conventions of melodrama, to temper its foreignness and allow spectators across different cultural backgrounds to marshal diverse repertoires of cinematic reference points in the process of cultural translation.

The film's eclectic musical score, which combines the sad waltz of 'Yumeji's Theme' by the Japanese composer Shigeru Umbeyashi with popular Chinese songs by Zhou Xuan and Latino pop performed in Spanish by Nat King Cole, fulfils a similar function. At the same time this musical mélange blurs the line between exoticism and nostalgia given that tunes like 'Aquellos ojos verdes' and 'Te quiero dijiste' by Nat King Cole were international hits in the 1960s and therefore likely to evoke nostalgia in spectators all over the world.

Exoticism and the aesthetics of sensuous indulgence

Although a sense of enigma is unquestionably an essential feature of exoticism, it cannot fully account for exoticism's allure. Exotic cinema prioritises, as outlined in Chapter 3, spectacle over narrative absorption, even if not throughout then at least in key filmic moments. If Wong Kar-wai has been criticised for privileging visual pleasure and for furnishing stylish images that 'elude narrative justification' (Bettinson 2015: 58), then these critics have either failed to grasp the aesthetic principles of exoticism or have decided to deliberately denounce them. In other words, 'moments of pure visual stimulation' (Gunning 2011: 75), which invite the spectator to indulge in the elaborate visual style of *In the Mood for Love*, have by some critics been misconstrued as shallow MTV aesthetics, as a 'fashion magazine sensibility' (Scott cited in Bettinson 2015: 59) and as aesthetic self-indulgence (Thomson cited in Bettinson 2015: 59). These charges are not dissimilar to those regularly levelled at the museum aesthetics of heritage cinema, namely, an obsession with glossy images that invites spectators to become absorbed purely on an aesthetic level.

Christopher Doyle and Mark Lee Ping-bin's distinctive cinematography coupled with William Chang's retro production design create a self-consciously aestheticised world in which even the banal and quotidian reveal their immanent beauty. The many tableaus in which the colours of door and window frames echo those of Maggie Cheung's cheongsams lend the film an overtly painterly quality. In addition to nuanced colour palettes, the repetition of similar geometric patterns in the wallpaper and the fabric of the dress invite spectators to feast their eyes on carefully composed images and symphonies of colour. The insistent use of frames and visual obstructions (reminiscent of Douglas Sirk's visual style) that are unmotivated by a character's point of view self-consciously emphasise the gesture of display.

Perhaps the most prominent cinematographic device, which invites the spectator to pause and surrender to the visual splendour of images, is what Vivian Sobchack (2006: 347) has termed 'the exhibitionism of slow motion'. It defamiliarises mundane activities, such as Mrs Chan descending the narrow winding staircase to fetch noodles in her pale green and silver thermos at the nearby *daibaitong*, or Mrs Chan and Mr Chow's walk home along the dimly lit streets of Hong Kong. The slower speed transfigures the everyday into moments of intense aesthetic pleasure. Slow-motion cinematography, accompanied by the sad waltz of Yumeji's Theme and Nat King Cole's 'Aquellos ojos verdes', lends these sequences a dance-like quality, while the characters' seemingly weightless, floating movements underscore the ephemeral nature of fading memories.

Visual spectacle alone does not adequately account for the exoticism of Wong's film, which goes far beyond an aesthetic of visual plenitude, provoking instead a multisensory response in the spectator. The camera seems to caress the texture of surfaces, whether it is masonry, pockmarked with greenish-white lichen in Angkor Wat, the crumbling plaster and peeling posters in the alleyways, the smooth reflection of speckled old mirrors, or the glistening wet rain on a streetlamp and on Chow's jet-black hair. The close-ups of these coarse, smooth and wet surfaces emphasise tactile impressions and, as such, would appear to illustrate what Laura Marks has theorised as 'haptic visuality', referring to a particular type of embodied perception that invokes memories of touch. Combined with other forms of synaesthesia (the perception of one sensation by another modality) and intermodality (the linking of sensations from different domains), these close-ups reproduce the multisensorial pleasure associated with exoticism (see Chapter 5). For Marks (2000: 177), however, haptic visuality and exoticism are incompatible. She asserts that 'haptic images refuse visual plenitude [and deliberately] ... counter viewers' expectations of ... exotic visual spectacle'. Her assertion is arguably borne out of her programmatic intent to promote an 'intercultural cinema' of a more experimental, ethnographic type that 'represents sense knowledges not from a position of wealth but of scarcity', which she contrasts with more dominant cinemas, including 'art-house imports' that represent 'sense knowledges [merely] as commodities' (Marks 2000: 239). Yet I argue that Wong's aesthetics of sensuous indulgence depends precisely on the combination of visual spectacle and haptic visuality without commodifying another culture's sense knowledge in the way mainstream cinema often does.

'Sense longing', to use Marks' (2000: 240) evocative term, denoting the pursuit of sensory stimulation and indulgence, has always been one of the chief driving forces behind exotic quests and conquests, be it the importation of spices and stimulants like coffee and cocoa which was part of the colonial enterprise, or the exotic-erotic pleasures which lured countless explorers and travellers to exotic destinations. The encounter with the exotic Other has traditionally been conceived as a revival of the senses that have been dulled by the repetitive humdrum of modernity. Hence, for Victor Segalen (2002: 61), an important early commentator on exoticism, the encounter with the exotic Other elicits intense sensations and a new zest for life. *In the Mood for Love* invites transnational audiences to escape the presumed homogeneity and anhedonia of Western societies by sensing 'how other people sensuously inhabit their world' (Marks 2000: 241).

Paradoxically, however, the quote from the Shanghainese writer Liu Li-Chang, with which the film concludes, appears to contradict the film's numerous haptically charged images: 'He remembers those vanished years as though looking through a dusty windowpane. The past is something he could see, but not touch. And everything he sees is blurred and indistinct.' The lines are worth citing here since the inherent contradiction heightens the sense of enigma while simultaneously identifying *In the Mood for Love* as a nostalgic memory film that emphatically foregrounds 'the imperfect retrieval of memory' (Rayns 2015: 81) as one of its key concerns.

Postsocialist Nostalgia as an Innocent Romance in *The Road Home*

As the comparison between the imperialist nostalgia films *Indochine* and *Viceroy's House* and the exotic nostalgia film *In the Mood for Love* highlights, the former mourn the loss of empire and articulate what Svetlana Boym (2001: xviii, 41, 49–55) has theorised as 'reflective nostalgia' by recovering the patina of its past power and glory on screen.[12] The latter, by contrast, is suffused by a sense of loss and longing for more universal structures of feeling, such as love, innocence and mourning, to which local and global audiences can relate without a deeper, or indeed any, understanding of the films' historical or cultural contexts.

Like *In the Mood for Love*, Zhang Yimou's *The Road Home* is a nostalgic celebration of an old-fashioned kind of love that is loyal and steadfast in the face of obstacles, separation and adversity. The narrative revolves around the pure and innocent courtship of eighteen-year-old Zhaodi (Ziyi Zhang) and the young schoolteacher Luo Changyu (Hao Zheng), who is posted to a remote village school. Set against the backdrop of the stunning rural scenery of northern China in the late 1950s, it is cast as a timeless period of innocence before the rupture brought about by the Cultural Revolution. Significantly, any references to the political context of the late 1950s, namely the Anti-Rightist Campaign that sought to purge alleged 'Rightists' from the Chinese Communist Party, are left deliberately opaque – and were largely missed in the film's cross-cultural reception.[13]

The Road Home, whose Chinese title *Wo de fu qin mu qin* literally translates as 'My Father and Mother', is based on Bao Shi's novel *Remembrance*. Hence, the film's narrative unfolds in an extended flashback, remembered and told in a voice-over narration by the romantic couple's son (Honglei Sun), who returns to his native village in order to perform the burial rites for his deceased father. The widowed Zhaodi (Yulian Zhao) insists that her husband's body be carried all the way from the hospital in the city back to the village, in accordance with a custom that has fallen into abeyance since the Cultural Revolution. The son is anxious about recruiting enough men to carry the coffin and offers payment, only to realise that money, the currency of the new globalised capitalist China, has no place in the village, for such is the loyalty of the teacher's former pupils that they return in large numbers to attend the funeral procession and carry his body along the long road home.

By editing out social hardship and controversial political events, nostalgia conveys a sanitised version of the past. Thus, the young teacher's removal from the village to be interrogated as part of the Anti-Rightists Campaign in the distant city is only alluded to, while the narrative focus remains firmly on Zhaodi, her heartache and longing during the two-year wait until Changyu eventually returns, never to be separated from her for the next forty years. In this way, the depoliticised narrative mythologises the sentimental love story that lives on in the villagers' collective memory. Posters of the global box-office hit *Titanic* (James Cameron, 1997), which took China by storm in spring 1998 (see Noble 2000; Mu 2003), adorn the widow's humble abode. Not only do the film posters serve as a temporal marker of the frame narrative, but they also equate Zhaodi and Changyu's romance with Jack and Rose's sentimental love story on the ill-fated maiden voyage of the *Titanic* in 1912. 'They don't do love like this anymore', *The Road Home* seems to be saying. San Bao's sentimental score of predominantly string and wind instruments with occasional chords of the erhu (a Chinese two-stringed fiddle), imitates James Horner's quieter theme tunes for *Titanic*, whose grandiose score moved audiences all over the world.

To visualise the different structures of feeling that govern the nostalgically remembered past and the mundane present, *The Road Home* inverses an established cinematic convention by rendering the present in cheerless black and white while capturing the socialist past in a burst of vibrant colours, one of the hallmarks of Zhang Yimou's exotic style. The visual contrast between a monochrome present and a colourful past recalls Salman Rushdie's (1992a: 10) observation about the retrieval of the past through memory, that magically transforms 'the faded greys of old family-album snapshots' into 'CinemaScope and glorious Technicolor'.

Old-fashioned romance is by no means the only object of nostalgia celebrated in *The Road Home*. As Emma Yu Zhang persuasively argues, 'the enchanting world of crafts . . . [and of] handmade and homemade things' such as the ceremonial red cloth that Zhaodi weaves on a loom for the rafters in the new schoolhouse or the broken blue-and-white ceramic bowl that is skilfully mended by an itinerant craftsman, embody 'the durability of things . . . that parallels the constancy of human sentiment' (Zhang 2018: 1–8). There is a sense of material scarcity that makes each object, be it the red and pink padded jackets Zhaodi wears, the hand-woven cloths or the red hair-clasp the teacher gives her, precious. The durability of artisanal objects, entirely incommensurate with the short lifespan of commodities in contemporary consumer society, valorises pre-industrial forms of human labour. In this way, the film reimagines a pre-industrial world of rural simplicity and innocence that diverts our attention away from the historical struggles at this specific historical juncture onto the private

Figure 4.4 Zhang Yimou's postsocialist nostalgia film *The Road Home* (1999) reimagines China's communist past as an innocent, rural romance.

lives and, in so doing, gives socialism a human face. The emphasis placed on the villagers' diurnal existence and communal way of life, coupled with the natural rhythm of the seasons whose autumnal hues of golden foliage and shades of resplendent white snow are put on display in sweeping panoramic shots, exoticises the village's authentic way of life and instils a childlike state of wonder in the spectator. At the same time, as Huyssen (2006: 12) suggests, 'nostalgia is never far away when we talk about authenticity' since the authentic represents contemporary 'media and commodity culture's romantic longing for its other'. As the 'privileged lost object of [nostalgic] desire' (Jameson 1991: 19), authenticity manifests itself in a longing for stable origins and an archaic way of life, assumed to be uncontaminated by the flows of global capitalism.

Despite – or arguably because of – its overt depoliticisation, *The Road Home* speaks to postsocialist China's burgeoning nostalgia for Mao's socialist era, which has flourished since the economic reform of the 1990s that initiated a new era of neo-liberal global capitalism. Certainly, amongst the older generation, who experienced China's socialist past, there has been a disillusionment with contemporary materialism and the inequalities of capitalism (see Lu 2005; Zeng 2009: 108; Meng 2020: 27). Postsocialism, conceptualised by Chris Berry (2007: 116) not as the end of socialism but rather as the persistence of certain political structures, 'long after faith in the grand narrative that authorizes . . . [communism] has been lost', has given rise to postsocialist nostalgia films whose narratives centre on ordinary people and depict the past as a time of romance and innocence, infused with a tinge of nostalgia for the good old days. This privatisation of history served as a strategy for Zhang Yimou to deal with the threat of censorship during a period when he had fallen out of favour with China's Communist regime. Furthermore, the past packaged as a love story and marketed as 'an unforgettable journey into the realm of the heart' promised to broaden the appeal of *The Road Home* amongst local and global audiences.[14]

There are two historical moments in China's past that people feel nostalgic about. One is the old, semicolonial Shanghai of the 1920s and 1930s, whose glamorous capitalist lifestyle was abruptly curtailed by the Communist revolution, and the other is the socialist era, which in its idealised form 'may be used as a cure for the excesses of present capitalist commodification' (Lu 2005: 3). Even in films set against the historical backdrop of the Cultural Revolution, which has deeply scarred China's collective memory, the temporal distance of more than twenty years has made a nostalgic recreation possible that reinvents these dark years as a time of innocence and romance in films such as *Xiao cai feng* (Balzac and the Little Chinese Seamstress, Sijie Dai, 2002) and *Shan zha shu zhi lian* (Under the Hawthorn Tree, Zhang Yimou, 2010). The Chinese directors Dai and Zhang both experienced the 'Up to the Mountains and Down to the Countryside Movement', which was instituted by Chairman Mao Zedong during the Cultural Revolution to educate youth from a 'bad class background'.[15] Both filmmakers were able to draw on their personal memories in creating these movies. But whereas *The Road Home* is one of five films which Zhang made during his 'probation period' when he had to practise public self-criticism for having made films critical of China's Communist regime (notably the banned film *Huo zhe* (To Live, 1994) (Brook 2003: 24)), the Sino-French diasporic writer and director Dai was able to be more explicit with his political references, since his book (originally written in French and translated into twenty-five languages, but not Chinese) as well as the film adaptation were banned in China (Balassone 2005). Despite presenting a highly romanticised view of this traumatic period in Chinese history, the Sino-French co-production *Balzac and the Little Chinese Seamstress* is critical of Mao's re-education programme, intended to eradicate bourgeois ideology and instil the values of communism in privileged urban youth. Ironically, it is the Little Chinese Seamstress (Xun Zhou), an illiterate beautiful village girl and the object of the city boys Ma (Ye Liu) and Luo's (Kun Shen) affection, who is educated by them. The exposure to forbidden bourgeois literature, including Balzac's novels, results in her re-education and prompts her to leave the remote mountain village in the Three Gorges region to head for the city.

What these rural romances, unabashed in their rosy view of a largely depoliticised past, have in common is that they are imbued with an aura of prelapsarian innocence. The rose-tinted lens of childhood and youth has the capacity to retrospectively transform any era of the past into a sentimental memory, whether it be the oppressive regime of the former German Democratic Republic in the *Ostalgie* comedy *Good Bye, Lenin!* (Wolfgang Becker, 2003) or The Troubles in Northern Ireland in Kenneth Branagh's semi-autobiographical coming-of-age drama *Belfast* (2021). In *The Road Home*, the eighteen-year-old Zhaodi with her pigtails, baggy trousers and padded peasant jackets, running and skipping across the hills to cross paths with the young village teacher, looks more like a child than a woman. The purity of her childlike affection is reinforced by the absence of any eroticism in the romantic couple's courtship. More importantly, the film portrays 1950s rural China from her point of view which casts the sentimental patina of her pure and ardent love over everything. Thus, the depiction of innocent love seems to confirm

Slavoj Žižek's observation that 'the innocent, naïve gaze of the other that fascinates us in nostalgia is in the last resort always the gaze of the child' (Žižek 1991: 114).

Encapsulating nostalgia's dual spatial and temporal dimensions, *The Road Home* is the story of a homecoming: the son's return to his father and mother after many long years of absence as well as the homecoming of Zhang Yimou. Whereas his previous films, *Hong gao liang* (Red Sorghum, 1988), *Ju Dou* and *Raise the Red Lantern* dazzled international film festival juries, critics and audiences in the West with the exotic spectacle of an ancient feudal China but (with the exception of *Red Sorghum*) were initially banned in Mainland China, *The Road Home* and Zhang's other village school film, *Yi ge dou bu neng shao* (Not One Less, 1999) were popular at home but were not feted as much by critics and audiences abroad.[16] When Zhang submitted the two films to the Cannes Film Festival in 1999, the selection committee was disappointed because, unlike his critically acclaimed Red Trilogy, his latest productions apparently failed to voice any political critique of the Chinese government. In fact, Zhang withdrew both films from the festival because the judges had misread *Not One Less* as pro-government propaganda. In a letter to Gilles Jacob, the director of the Cannes Film Festival at the time, Zhang states:

> I cannot accept that when it comes to Chinese films, the West seems for a long time to have had just the one 'political' reading: if it's not 'against the government' then it's 'for the government'. The naivete and lack of perspective (literally 'one-sidedness') of using so simple a concept to judge a film is obvious. With respect to the works of directors from America, France and Italy for example, I doubt you have the same point of view. (Zhang cited in Rist 2002)

At home, by contrast, the two films transformed Zhang's status from that of a politically suspect, somewhat marginalised director to 'China's semi-official cultural ambassador to the world' (Meng 2020: 18), who was subsequently invited to direct the opening and closing ceremonies of the Olympic Games in Beijing in 2008.

Nostalgia with(out) exoticism and exoticism with(out) nostalgia?

These dynamics of cross-cultural reception are telling in as much as they point towards a formula that promises to ensure the transnational success of Zhang Yimou's (and other Chinese) films. Exotic spectacle, combined with a critical political stance towards the Chinese regime in the guise of thinly veiled allegorical narratives about the patriarchal oppression of victimised beautiful women, finds favour overseas. Although *The Road*

Home eventually succeeded on the international film festival circuit, for Rey Chow (2002: 653), Zhang's postsocialist nostalgia film falls short of the director's previous allegorical narratives of political intent, representing merely an 'aestheticised spectacle of a socialist humanism that has become politically bankrupt'. Her harsh verdict echoes that of transnational critics and festival juries. Zhang Yimou, however, experiences these expectations as too restrictive. He demands the same freedom of choice that Western filmmakers enjoy. And for Zhang this entails making films that have the capacity to speak to transnational as well as domestic audiences and critics.

How does *The Road Home* square this circle? Zhang's rural romance may appeal to Chinese audiences who have retrospectively idealised the PRC's socialist past, yet how does it capture the attention of global audiences? Is this sentimental tale of first love too universal, and therefore all too familiar, to stimulate a sense of enigma and exotic mystique? Furthermore, do the colourful rural landscapes and the idealisation of a seemingly timeless domesticity resonate with a familiar iconography of 'Chineseness' that is legible as exotic for global audiences?

In terms of its iconography, *The Road Home* takes its inspiration from Chinese New Year prints (*nianhua*) (Farquhar 2002). These bold and colourful woodblock prints are produced for a mass market and are one of China's most popular forms of folk art. As James Flath (2004a) outlines in *The Cult of Happiness: Nianhua, Art and History in Rural China*, *nianhua* emerged as a village-based folk art during the late nineteenth and early twentieth centuries in rural north China. Originally intimately linked to the domestic sphere, *nianhua* represented Door Gods, Stove Gods and other deities that are believed to bring happiness and good fortune to one's home. During Mao's era this peasant art form was adapted to disseminate political propaganda and consecrate the revolution. The 'new *nianhuas*' addressed revolutionary themes and represented 'peasants, workers and soldiers: the Maoist trinity' (Barnes 2020: 127–8) instead of traditional domestic deities and the Chinese zodiac.[17] As this popular art form became increasingly politicised, the CCP's ethos of productive labour was promoted by depictions of peasants ploughing and women weaving (Flath 2004b: 139, 143). Both traditional Chinese New Year prints and their revolutionary counterpart have become an integral part of the popular imagination of what constitutes 'Chineseness' in the West. Tapping into the market for post-communist nostalgia that affirms Western capitalism's belief in its own superiority over Eastern communism, the West has appropriated and recycled revolutionary *nianhua* and other icons of the Maoist era and transformed them into what Amy Jane Barnes

(2009) terms 'Commie kitsch'. Commie kitsch, short for Communist kitsch, assimilates the aesthetics of communism, evacuates it of its original meaning and transforms it into ironic icons of global consumerism.

The Road Home draws on the iconography and visual tropes of revolutionary *nianhua*, which espoused simple peasant life as the cradle of communist consciousness. The film satisfies the demand for Communist exotica that appear just as fascinatingly foreign to Western consumers and spectators as the early twentieth-century rural China that features in Zhang Yimou's acclaimed exotic Red Trilogy. The similarities between the visual style of *The Road Home* and new *nianhua* rest on their shared focus on idealised rural settings, domesticity and the fruits of labour, coupled with bold colours. Together, these features engender a sense of simplicity, naïvete and happiness, while also conjuring visions of Mao's socialist utopia.[18] In particular, the tracking shots, showing the teacher and his happy flock of singing pupils traversing the valley of golden poplar trees, Zhaodi weaving the red cloth on a wooden loom and the women laying out dishes of home-cooked food to collectively feed the builders of the schoolhouse, seem to be modelled on the aesthetics and ethos of revolutionary *nianhua*. Similarly, Zhaodi's wholesome country-girl look, with pigtails and brightly coloured baggy clothes, bears a striking resemblance to depictions of peasant girls in new *nianhua* as well as to contemporary commodified appropriations of Commie kitsch by companies such as Dumpling Dynasty (see Barnes 2009: 264). While this visual pastiche of Maoist propaganda art may engender nostalgia for China's communist past in Chinese spectators, global audiences may perceive it as exotic, even though it resonates with an era and imaginary of 'Chineseness' very different from the mythic past of feudal China or the Republican Era.

Therefore, at face value, *The Road Home* appears to be a far cry from Zhang's earlier films *Red Sorghum*, *Ju Dou* and *Raise the Red Lantern* that enthralled global audiences with their overtly exotic *mise en scène* (pagoda-style sweeping roofs, ornate ancestral shrines, opulently decorated interiors and the exuberant colours of dyed cloth in *Ju Dou*) and invented ancient rituals (such as the nightly raising of red lanterns in the concubines' prison-like courtyard in *Raise the Red Lantern*; the ritualistic performance of filial piety at the funeral procession in *Ju Dou*). In other words, the films' visuality is unmistakably aligned with an instantly legible iconography of 'Chineseness'. Add to this the mystery and enchanting beauty of the lead actress Gong Li, 'the poster girl of Fifth Generation Chinese films' (Khoo 2007: 1) and the first actress in the post-Maoist period to gain global recognition. Her transnational appeal rests primarily on her ability to project an image of quintessential Chinese femininity outside her own culture.[19] Though actively rebelling against the patriarchal feudal system through mobilising the subversive power of lust and seduction, Gong Li is invariably defeated by it. Nowhere is this more apparent than in the narrative closures of *Raise the Red Lantern* and *Ju Dou*, which culminate in the heroines' madness and self-immolation. Gong Li invites transnational spectators to empathise with the suffering Orientalised woman and to take the moral high ground when contemplating the alleged barbarity of China's feudal past, which serves as a thinly veiled allegory for the PRC's repressive political regime during the 1990s. As Mary Farquhar (2002) notes: 'Patriarchy is lethal in these films and many commentators have likened the trilogy's old men to China's aging leaders, especially after the crushing of democracy activists [at the Tiananmen Square massacre] on 4 June, 1989.'

While it is hard to conceive of more obviously exotic films than these, their status as exotic *nostalgia films* remains questionable. Except for *Red Sorghum*, these films lack the distinctive temporality of nostalgia films, which Linda Hutcheon (2009: 252) describes as the imperfect and fragmented retrieval of a 'memorialized past' from the vantage point of the present. Marked by the distortions of desire and forgetting, nostalgia is, first and foremost, an intellectual and affective response to the convergence of past and present in the moment of recollection. Stretching nostalgia to its conceptual limits, Chow proposes that it is not so much the endeavour to retrieve a lost past but merely the effect of temporal dislocation, which manifests itself in a film's distinctive temporality rather than in its subject matter. Such films, she argues, are 'nostalgic *in tendency*' only (Chow 1993: 74), without possessing a clearly identifiable object of nostalgic desire. I contend that, in contrast to *The Road Home*, *Ju Dou* and *Raise the Red Lantern* lack nostalgia's intersecting temporality; they neither enact the process of remembering in the present nor do they project an idealised past. That is why they are exotic period dramas rather than exotic nostalgia films.

Conclusion

As I hope to have demonstrated in this chapter, such are the affinities between exoticism and nostalgia that there is a high degree convergence between the two concepts. Although it would appear as if 'the privileged lost object of desire' (Jameson 1991: 19) in nostalgia films is a distant, idealised past, whereas the object of desire in exotic films is a distant foreign place, this ostensibly clear-cut distinction ultimately collapses. Both nostalgia and exoticism project 'utopias in reverse' (Huyssen 2006: 7) that serve as counterpoints to our disenchantment with the here and now. The nostalgically remembered past is invariably modernity's Other and, therefore, as much an idealised elsewhere as the values lost with modernisation and globalisation, which exoticism seeks to recover through its discursive strategies. Nostalgia's valorisation of the rural, of stable origins, of the alleged authenticity associated with the archaic and primitive is borne out of the putative artificiality and anomie of modern societies. Frequently, these nostalgic projections coalesce with the objects of exotic desire, since 'the nostalgic longing for a past is always also a longing for another place' (Huyssen 2006: 7). It is thus not surprising that by far the majority of exotic films, and not just the ones analysed in this chapter, are set in the past. But whereas nostalgia's utopic quest pursues the familiar (the home, a memorialised past), exoticism yearns for the foreign and faraway.

Imperialist nostalgia films, as the term suggests, engage with a particular past, namely the time of Europe's colonial empires. Despite typically deploying certain visual and narrative tropes of exoticism, imperialist and exotic nostalgia films differ from one another in terms of their ideological trajectories. While both types of nostalgia film glamorise the past, imperialist nostalgia films use visually flamboyant images to deflect from colonial guilt. Thus, *Viceroy's House* and *Indochine* contrast the elegance and grandeur of the colonial past with the tumultuous change of anticolonial resistance and independence that is captured only briefly in footage of amorphous crowds of refugees and anticolonial freedom fighters, suggesting that the end of colonial rule results in chaos and, certainly, a loss of aesthetic pleasure. Imperialist nostalgia films invariably stage cross-cultural encounters between European colonialists and colonised subjects. Through inviting audience identification with the colonialists, who in the end lose their power and privilege, imperialist nostalgia films tempt spectators to mourn the end of European empires, even those that are tinged by a sense of postcolonial guilt and ostensibly espouse decolonisation. Rather than offering history lessons, imperialist nostalgia films invoke partial pasts by crystallising precious moments of glamour and glory, while forgetting to reflect upon the legacy of injustice and guilt.

Exotic nostalgia films, such as *In the Mood for Love* and *The Road Home*, substitute nostalgia for a specific historical period with a more universal longing for a place and time when intensity of feeling was still possible, be it Hong Kong in the 1960s or rural China in the 1950s. These films espouse epistemes and experiences that call the hegemony of the West and global capitalism into question. In terms of visual style, however, the exoticism of *In the Mood for Love*, with its spellbinding beauty of images and aesthetics of sensuous indulgence, has little in common with the visual pastiche of revolutionary *nianhua* in *The Road Home*. Yet what makes both films exotic is that they invoke recognisable visual paradigms of exoticism, reminding us that the exotic gaze invariably invokes a sense of déjà vu. This is not to say that spectators need to be able to identify the specific visual style that is being referenced or imitated. Whereas pastiche 'needs to be "got" as pastiche' (Dyer 2007: 3) to be effective and, therefore, requires a certain cultural capital, as Richard Dyer notes, the decoding of exoticism works on a more subliminal level. All that is required of the spectator of Zhang's and Wong's films is that they are attuned to the quintessential 'Chineseness' or simply the cultural Otherness of the films' visual and narrative paradigms and, through this act of recognition, register the films as exotic.

The case studies in this chapter complicate my initial hypothesis that the films' aesthetic strategies evoke a nostalgic yearning for an idealised past in *local* and a desire for an exoticised Other in *global* spectators. At first sight, *The Road Home* seems to bear out the hypothesis of divergent local and global spectatorial responses. On the one hand, it resonates with the postsocialist nostalgia that emerged in China in the 1990s; on the other hand, it caters to the fetishisation of the foreign that arises from the hermeneutic deficit of transnational reception. And yet, *The Road Home* (albeit to a lesser extent than Zhang's *Red Trilogy*) raises the question whether the fault lines that determine a nostalgic *versus* an exotic reception really run across national borders. Is not rather the imaginary of the rural, remote and archaic China that is constructed in these films as much China's internal Other as it is the West's Other? Do these Other-looking spectacular rural landscapes of *The Road Home* and *Red Sorghum*, the lavish interiors of *Raise the Red Lantern* and the ancient craft of dying in *Ju Dou* not appear as fascinatingly foreign, indeed, as exotic to contemporary urban Chinese spectators as they do to transnational audiences? If the exotic gaze is always a gaze from the other side, a gaze that traverses boundaries, then these boundaries are first and foremost cultural and can be as prominent within one nation state as across national borders. The imperialist nostalgia films *Indochine* and *Viceroy's House* prove equally resistant to my initial hypothesis. While there is no doubt that the films have the capacity to evoke nostalgia in some, ideologically so predisposed French and British spectators, it is highly questionable whether they can elicit a similar affective resonance in South East Asian and South Asian spectators. The films' critical reception suggests otherwise.[20]

My initial distinction between local and global spectatorial responses to exotic nostalgia films is further complicated by what Arjun Appadurai terms 'armchair nostalgia' to describe 'nostalgia without lived experience or collective historical memory' (Appadurai 1996: 78). Following this logic, it would be entirely possible to feel nostalgic about a memorialised past in which one has no personal stake. *In the Mood for Love* appears to be an apt example if it were not for the fact that the hybridising dynamics of globalisation problematise the idea that we live in a world of discrete memorialised pasts, one inhabited by us, the other inhabited by them. Wong's film is ultimately a stylish pastiche of both Eastern and Western influences that challenges the notion of a pure, local culture and, by implication, the idea that only a local community of spectators with insider knowledge of 1960s Hong Kong culture can appreciate it in terms of nostalgia. I wish to illustrate this point with a personal anecdote. I remember my own mother wearing cheongsam-inspired silk dresses in 1960s West Germany. Perhaps this is not surprising given the cheongsam's well-documented impact on international fashion trends. One in particular I have never forgotten. It was a beautifully tailored black silk dress with a large bright-turquoise and pale-yellow stylised flower printed diagonally across from the waist to the hemline. And she wore her dark hair coiffured in a style similar to that of Maggie Cheung – elegant, yet fixed with hairspray and, therefore, entirely motionless. For me, watching Wong's film over and over again has been an exotic, but simultaneously also a nostalgic pleasure, because the film's costume and production design, alongside Nat King Cole's Latino pop songs, continuously oscillate between the strange and the familiar.

Notes

1. Although 'nostalgia' is derived from two Greek roots, the term is not originally Greek but was coined in 1688 by the Swiss doctor Johannes Hofer, who diagnosed 'nostalgia' as an illness he observed in Swiss soldiers who fought far away from home and who suffered a range of physical and mental symptoms which he attributed to the experience of intense homesickness (see Boym 2001: 3–12).
2. Nostalgia in Hollywood cinema and in British and European heritage cinema has received a significant amount of scholarly attention; see, for example, Cook (2005), Dika (2003), Dwyer (2015), Hutcheon (2009), Jameson (1991), Lee (2008), Spengler (2009) and Sperb (2016). However, the two sub-categories which feature prominently in contemporary transnational cinema, imperialist and exotic nostalgia films, merit closer attention.
3. In a place like Hong Kong, Abbas (1997: 12) notes, it is problematic to distinguish between the local and the global because of the 'significant proportion of refugees, migrants, and transients, all of whom could claim local status'.

4. See Chapter 2 on primitivism.
5. See Farley (2020) about the untranslatable German words *Wanderlust* and *Fernweh*
6. The distinctive temporal structure of nostalgia only emerges at the very end of *The Seawall*, when the nameless French woman's life and her greatest achievement, the construction of the seawall, is remembered and commemorated by the Indochinese local community.
7. See also Boym's (2001: 55) discussion of the relationship between nostalgia, mourning and melancholia.
8. According to Marianne Hirsch (1997: 22), who developed the concept in relation the children of Holocaust survivors, postmemory is 'distinguished from memory by generational distance and from history by deep personal connection'. Whereas history may elide or even purposely obliterate memories that cannot be reconciled with official (often heroic) accounts of the past, the 'deep personal connection' that underpins postmemory accords a rather different meaning and affective value to events that would otherwise be forgotten or repressed.
9. As Abbas (1997: 3) outlines, 'the long goodbye of Britain to its "last emporium" began in earnest' when, in 1984, Britain and China signed the Sino-British Joint Declaration which provided for the return of Hong Kong to Chinese rule in 1997. It then became a Special Administrative Region of the People's Republic of China with an agreed expiration date of 2046.
10. Hong Kong's nostalgia did not centre on its precolonial past since, Abbas (1997: 2) argues, its 'history has effectively been a history of colonialism'. Hong Kong's status as a British colony differed significantly from that of other colonies insofar as Hong Kong 'has no precolonial past to speak of' before it was ceded to the British in 1841.
11. The room number, 2046, has been interpreted as a reference to the date when Hong Kong's status as a Special Administrative Region of the People's Republic of China ends. *2046* is also the title of the film Wong Kar-wai made after *In the Mood for Love*.
12. See Boym (2001: 41–55) for the distinction between 'reflective' and 'restorative' nostalgia.
13. According to Lam (2005: 401), the Cannes Film Festival selection committee was disappointed by *The Road Home* and *Not One Less*, the two films Zhang submitted in 1999, because they ostensibly failed to voice a political critique of the Chinese government. This seems to suggest that the film's oblique references to the Anti-Rightist Movement got lost in the cross-cultural reception.
14. This is the publicity slogan on Columbia Tri Star's DVD release of *The Road Home*.
15. Zhang Yimou's father had been an officer in the anti-communist Nationalist Army and some of his relatives had fled to Taiwan in 1949. He spent three years working in the fields, followed by seven more years in a textile mill (cf. Rayns 2022: 78).

16. Even so, *The Road Home* won the Silver Bear at the Berlin Film Festival in 2000 and *Not One Less* the Golden Lion in Venice. Significantly, both films also won prizes at the PRC's most prestigious festivals, the Golden Rooster Awards and the Hundred Flowers Awards.
17. The new *nianhuas* are also extensively discussed by Flath (2004b), Hung (2000) and Barnes (2009: 49–51).
18. As Pang (2012) demonstrates, colour also played a pivotal role in late Cultural Revolution narrative films that depicted Mao's socialist utopia of material plenitude and productive peasant life in brightly coloured harvest scenes.
19. Gong Li's transnational appeal has been widely discussed, for example by Berry and Farquhar (2006: 124–9) and Wong (2011).
20. For the critical reception of *Indochine* by Vietnamese critics and scholars, see Norindr (1996), Vann (2008), Chiu (2005); for that of *Viceroy's House* by South Asian critics and scholars, see Bhutto (2017), Irani (2018), Kang (2017) and Rosario (2017).

CHAPTER 5

Exotic Appetites

An elaborate montage sequence at the beginning of Ang Lee's *Eat Drink Man Woman* cuts from a high angle shot of noisy rush hour traffic in Taipei to an oasis of tranquillity, a house in traditional Chinese architectural style. It is tucked away behind a heavy wooden gate adorned with red-and-white Chinese writing and surrounded by lush green trees and shrubs. Another sharp cut reveals two silvery carp moving around in a terracotta tub filled with clear water. Then, suddenly, a pair of hands catches one of them and forces two wooden chopsticks down its throat. An elliptical montage brings a wooden board inside the kitchen into focus, where the same hands descale the fish and slice open the belly with a sharp knife. Blood spills out onto the wooden surface. The hands, shown in close-up, gut, fillet and lightly dust the fish with flour, before immersing it in a wok filled with sizzling hot oil. A series of close-ups of hands rhythmically chopping and finely slicing cuttlefish, radishes and chillies emphasise the dexterity and precision with which master chef Chu (Sihung Lung) uses sharp knives as he prepares an opulent Sunday dinner for his three grown-up daughters. Strips of juicy pork belly are first fried in hot oil and then dipped into a bath of water chilled with ice cubes, suggesting that every aspect of this artisanal cooking process involves several carefully choreographed stages. Next Mr Chu steps outside, into the sunny courtyard of his house. There are dozens of brown earthenware tubs, pots, strings of garlic and a small pen with live chickens. He looks at them closely and affectionately before choosing one to be boiled for the sumptuous meal. As he re-enters the kitchen with the chicken still alive, the camera pans to a pile of frogs crawling about on a wet stone on the kitchen table, awaiting their imminent transformation into a menu item.

This four-minute opening sequence of *Eat Drink Man Woman* illustrates some of the main ingredients of the exotic food film genre. Great emphasis is placed on demonstrating craftsmanship and the haptic nature of cooking, which lends the scene its sensuality. The sound of chopping, sizzling oil, accompanied by gentle Asian music, stimulates an intensely sensorial response in the spectator. The cooking utensils are functional but basic, nothing is automated here. In addition to an astounding number of differently shaped knives (arranged in three long rows along the kitchen wall) the paraphernalia include a bamboo sieve and baskets for steaming, blue-and-white china bowls and an array of pots, pans and ladles. The length of the sequence and the complexity of the recipes conveys the time-consuming nature of the exotic dishes Chu creates, a feature that stands in stark contrast to the deep-fried chicken and French fries his youngest daughter serves in an American-style fast food restaurant elsewhere in Taipei. In this way, the scene foregrounds fundamental differences between the cultural terms of contemporary food preparation with its emphasis on convenience and mass production and Chinese traditional cooking. Mr Chu's locally harvested and home-cooked food reflects a commitment to the old-fashioned values of nurture and care. The time and effort expended on cooking, alongside the local sourcing of the ingredients, some of which come straight from the backyard, also evokes the slow food movement with its tinge of nostalgia and the pledge to salvage traditional foods (see Petrini 2003; Leitch 2012). The copious dishes Mr Chu prepares in this and subsequent sequences (around 100 in total in the course of the film) and their ornate arrangement and display on the dinner table is another hallmark of the exotic food film. Since the art and ritual of cooking occupies a central place in the transnational imaginary of Chinese culture, the film's opening sequence and the numerous other ones that revolve around Chinese gastronomy, resonate with instantly recognisable cultural clichés.[1] 'Given the traditional centrality of cooking to Chinese ritual, medicine and cosmology', Marks argues (2000: 235), 'it is understandable that a sturdy subgenre of Chinese diaspora films . . . deals with food.' She identifies food as the 'oral signifier of exoticism . . . [and] the locus of displaced Western notions of Asian sensuality' and suggests that 'the contemporary longing in Western countries and urban centres for a soothing "return" to the senses has an undeniable cast of neo-Orientalism' (Marks 2000: 236, 240) that is reminiscent of the impetus behind many exotic journeys of exploration and trade from the Middle Ages through to the age of European empires.

Laura Marks' observation goes a long way in accounting for the growing interest in exotic food. The range of ethnic food restaurants in any major city, the marketing of food with an obvious colonial heritage (coffee, cocoa, spices) as locally authentic and the countless travel-cum-food shows on television in which Western celebrity chefs learn from local chefs in India, Thailand, Mexico, or some other distant corners of the world, how to cook exotic meals, testify to this trend. Exotic food represents a non-threatening form of Otherness but, as Elspeth Probyn suggests, 'the hearty appetite for "foreign food" . . . is supposed to hide the taste of racism' (Probyn 2000: 2). Contemporary Western societies' appetite for exotic food is not simply an innocent curiosity about novel, adventurous experiences but deeply entrenched in a colonial mindset. Lisa Heldke (2003: 43) contends that it reduces the cultural Other, to 'a source of materials to be extracted and used to enhance our own cultures . . . [that] divert us from the monotony of sameness' global capitalism has supposedly inflicted upon us. Going to a restaurant and eating an exotic meal is a superficial engagement that makes foreign cultures subservient to our own hedonism and reduces them to consumable commodities and novel sensorial experiences. Similar charges have been levelled at several exotic food films, especially those targeting mainstream audiences. *Tortilla Soup* (Maria Ripoll, 2001), a Hollywood remake of *Eat Drink Man Woman* transposed to a Mexican American milieu, *Woman on Top* (Fina Torres, 2000) with Penelope Cruz as a seductive Brazilian master chef on a US televised cookery programme, and Lasse Hallström's feelgood movie *The Hundred-Foot Journey* (2014), in which an Indian chef spices up French haute cuisine, are only some of the many films that spring to mind.

Whether or not the exotic food films made by world cinema filmmakers, on which this chapter focuses, take an equally reifying approach is one of the issues I shall address. More specifically, this chapter aims to answer four key questions. First, what distinguishes exotic food films from the food film genre in general and ethnic food films in particular? Second, what appetites and objects of desire are obscured by the fetishised depiction of exotic food? Third, through which aesthetic devices do exotic food films convey the sensuality of culinary delights and the sensations of taste and smell? And fourth, what accounts for the transnational appeal of exotic food films? Drawing on examples from diasporic and global art cinema, the following case studies will illuminate dominant themes and distinctive attributes of the genre: the canonical exotic food film *Eat Drink Man Woman* by the American Taiwanese director Ang Lee explores affective and emotional bonds in the family via food. The ritual of preparing and sharing home-cooked meals in the family circle is nostalgically imagined as a social practice that maintains and forges affectionate family ties. *The Scent of Green Papaya* by the French Vietnamese director Tran Anh Hung illustrates how exotic food films typically deploy a multisensorial aesthetics that engenders an experience of sensuous abundance in the spectator. It prompts a synaesthetic response that conjoins the distant senses of vision and hearing with the proximate senses of smell, taste and touch. That food films are frequently about carnal desires is evidenced by countless exotic food films, including the inaugural global food films *Tampopo* (Juzo Itami, 1985) and *Like Water for Chocolate*, and more mainstream fare, including *Chocolat* (Lasse Hallström, 2000), *Woman on Top* and *The Mistress of Spices* (Paul Mayeda Berges, 2005). My case study, however, is a less obvious example. *Gau ji* (Dumplings, 2004) by Hong Kong filmmaker Fruit Chan links the titular iconic Chinese dish to the quest for eternal youth, eroticism and cannibalism. Significantly, the cannibals in Chan's film are not 'primitive savages' in some remote wilderness, as one of the most enduring tropes of exoticism would have it, but instead two sophisticated Chinese women in contemporary Hong Kong. In this way, *Dumplings* challenges the primitivist discourse that is fundamental to the Western distinction between Self and Other.

The Lure of the Foreign in Food Films

Food is ubiquitous in cinema – and often highly memorable, even in films that do not revolve around food. Anyone who has seen the romantic comedy *When Harry Met Sally* (Rob Reiner, 1989) will remember the following two iconic food scenes. In the first, set in a roadside diner, Sally (Meg Ryan) orders 'a Chef's salad with the oil and vinegar on the side and an apple pie à la mode'. She then adds her rather idiosyncratic specifications:

> But I want the pie heated and I don't want the ice cream on top but on the side and I'd like strawberry instead of vanilla if you have it; if not, then no ice cream just whipped cream but only if it's real; if it's out of the can then nothing.

In the second scene, Sally is discussing male sexual performance and female faked orgasms with her friend Harry (Billy Crystal) while eating a plain turkey sandwich on white bread at Katz's Deli in New York. Entirely unexpectedly and much to Harry's embarrassment and the astonishment of the other patrons, she performs the intimate sounds of an orgasm, prompting the elderly lady at the next table to change her order: 'I'll have what she's having', she demands of the waitress. In *When Harry Met Sally*, food features merely as a prop to develop characters and highlight their idiosyncratic traits. Proper food films, by contrast, make food their central symbolic object and charge it with meaning and resonance. According to Annie Bower, food films emerged as a genre during the 1980s, defined by the following characteristics:[2]

> Food ... has to play a star role, whether the leading characters are cooks (professional or domestic) or not. This means that often the camera will focus in on food preparation and presentation so that in closeups or panning shots, food fills the

screen. The restaurant kitchen, the dining room and/or kitchen of a home, tables within a restaurant, a shop in which food is made and/or sold, will usually be the central settings. And the film's narrative line will consistently depict characters negotiating questions of identity, power, culture, class spirituality, or relationship through food. (Bower 2004: 5–6)

Babette's Feast (Gabriel Axel, 1987) and *Like Water for Chocolate* are widely credited as the first fully fledged food films that captured global audiences' imagination at a time when food also received growing attention in other spheres. Feminism and women's studies led to the formation of the new field of food studies; food movements promoted local, organic and fairtrade foods and highlighted the nexus between food and broader social movements; and cookery programmes gained prominence on television. Subsequent decades witnessed a strengthening of the nexus between (predominantly foreign) food and film, as the number of food films steadily increased and culinary film festivals (typically accompanied by food sampling sessions) emerged. These various manifestations of contemporary food faddism speak to a desire for close encounters with Other cultures.

The early food films *Babette's Feast* and *Like Water for Chocolate* set a trend for the genre in decades to come by celebrating the pleasures and transformative effect of *foreign* food. There are by far more films indulging spectators in the gustatory pleasures of foreign cuisines than films about local foodways. In *Babette's Feast* and the thematically similar *Chocolat*, the female protagonists, Babette (Stéphane Audran) and Vianne (Juliette Binoche) introduce the local communities on the bleak Danish coast and in a quiet and colourless French town, to food from elsewhere. Babette cooks a lavish seven-course banquet for a group of pious and abstemious Lutherans. Having lived on a diet of bland food all their lives, the exquisite French dishes awaken their senses. What is more, the puritanical guests suddenly discover that 'spiritual ecstasy can be achieved more readily through the indulgence of the appetites than through self-denial' (Keller 2006: 154). In *Chocolat*, Vianne, who is of French Mayan heritage and has inherited her mother's shamanic healing powers, tempts the local community with exotic chocolate creations, made from Mayan cocoa, and dispenses them as a magical cure to rekindle passion between husband and wife or to heal rifts in fractured families. Not unlike Babette, Vianne relies on the transformative power of foreign food to bring about the pious French community's spiritual renewal by making them receptive to hedonism and carnal pleasures.

In *Like Water for Chocolate*, a Mexican magical realist movie based on a best-selling novel and screenplay by Laura Esquival, the supernatural powers of food are even more prominent. The elaborate meals which Tita

(Lumi Cavazos) prepares absorb her emotional states and induce similar feelings and urges in those who eat them. Thus, the film's signature dish, roast quails in rose petal sauce, is imbued with Tita's sexual attraction to Pedro (Marco Leonardi), the man she loves but was forbidden to marry. Those who partake of the magical meal are instantaneously seized by quasi-orgasmic pleasure. The narrative voice-over explains the unusual effect of the meal as

> a mysterious alchemical process [that] had occurred. Not only Tita's blood [from a wound inflicted by the rose thorns] but her entire being had dissolved into the rose petal sauce, into the quail and every aroma of the meal. That's how she entered Pedro's body, voluptuously and with utter sensuality.

What makes the quails in rose petal sauce a profoundly exotic dish is not just the intense sensuous response it elicits in the dinner guests, but also the fact that Tita has learnt her culinary craft from her surrogate mother, Nacha (Ada Carrasco), who was present at her birth on the kitchen table and who has subsequently taught her how to cook. Nacha and the other kitchen maid are both illiterate Indigenous women who depend upon Tita, a representative of the dominant white upper class, to preserve their cultural heritage. By passing on Nahuatl recipes to the next generation, Tita, her niece Esperanza (Sandra Arau) and her daughter, these women become the custodians of native Indian heritage. Salvaging a culture on the brink of extinction is, as outlined in Chapter 2, a uniquely exotic impulse and, in *Like Water for Chocolate*, it gives an additional dimension to the exoticisation of food.

As these three examples suggest, exotic food films articulate a desire to become Other than oneself, to be transformed through the contact with or consumption of Other cultures. Both bell hooks and Diane Negra attribute the longing for the Other to Western societies' profound identity crises. Negra (2002: 62) argues that 'perceptions of cultural insufficiency [are] related to a sense of exhausted whiteness'. This has, according to bell hooks, led to the cultural appropriation and commodification of the Other, which she captures in the evocative image of 'eating the other', the title of her much-cited essay. In fact, even though the essay gets quoted in literally every article or book on food films, it is primarily concerned with white Western sexual desire for black men or women and only secondarily with exotic food. However, the prevalent conflation of gustatory and erotic pleasures results from the displacement of presumably illicit temptations and interracial intimacy onto the socially acceptable hunger for ethnic and exotic food. This displacement mechanism is certainly one of the reasons behind the popularity of ethnic and exotic food films. Hooks (2015: 21, 28) offers a further compelling explanation in suggesting that the commodification of Otherness has been so successful because it is offered as a new delight, more intense, more satisfying than normal ways of doing and feeling. Within commodity culture, ethnicity becomes a spice, seasoning that can liven up the dull dish that is mainstream white culture.

It reflects 'the longing of whites to inhabit, only for a time, the world of the Other', perceived as more plentiful, abundant, authentic, gratifying and sensuous than one's own. Whereas the 'colonial desire' (Young 1995) for the Other during the age of empire sought to dominate the Other, contemporary desire for the Other, hooks proposes, is borne out of the fantasy that contact with the Other offers pleasure and renewal.

Exotic vs Ethnic Food Films

Both exotic and ethnic food films stage encounters with cultural difference through foodways; however, their narrative premises are markedly different. Whereas exotic food films speak to the desire for transformation through contact with the Other, ethnic food films are about the maintenance and negotiation of one's own cultural identity, in other words, the very opposite of transformation. In *We Are What We Eat: Ethnic Food and the Making of Americans*, Donna Gabaccia comments on the close connection between culinary traditions and ethnic identity. Food, she argues,

entwines intimately with much that makes a culture unique, binding taste and satiety to group loyalties. Eating habits both symbolise and mark the boundaries of cultures. Scholars and ordinary people alike have long seen food habits, both positively and negatively, as concrete symbols of human culture and identity. When we want to celebrate, or elevate, our own group, we usually praise its superior cuisine. And when we want to demean one another, often we turn to eating habits; in the United States we have labelled Germans as 'krauts', Italians as 'spaghetti-benders', Frenchmen as 'frogs', and British as 'limeys'. (Gabaccia 1998: 8–9)

Ethnic food films made by diasporic filmmakers such as *What's Cooking?* (Gurinder Chadha, 2000), *La graine et le mulet* (Couscous, Abdellatif Kechiche, 2007), *Solino* (Fatih Akin, 2002) and *Nina's Heavenly Delights* (Pratibha Parmar, 2006) are usually set in the immigrants' country of residence. Like exotic food films, they represent a form of culinary tourism insofar as they spectacularise the foodways of non-Western communities. While both tend to turn ethnic identities into commodities, ethnic food films pursue specific political goals, as Lindenfeld and Parasecoli (2017: 175–204) persuasively argue in relation to American productions such as *Big Night* (Stanley Tucci and Campbell Scott, 1996), *Soul Food* (George Tillman Jr, 1997) and *Tortilla Soup*. These films hold out the illusion of offering intimate insights into the ordinary, domestic lives of ethnic minorities. Yet the ostensible proximity they create also throws cultural differences into stark relief. In this way, ethnic food films deploy Other foodways to negotiate issues of exclusion, belonging and citizenship.

What's Cooking? illustrates this very well. Directed and co-scripted by British Asian filmmaker Gurinder Chadha, the film uses food to celebrate ethnic diversity and to promote the idea that the United States is a welcoming multicultural society. Set in Los Angeles' Fairfax district, the narrative revolves around four families of Jewish, Latino, Vietnamese and African American descent. On Thanksgiving Day, each family prepares the traditional Turkey and trimmings according to their own, ethnically inflected recipe. Since the preparation of the turkey takes place in modern well-equipped kitchens with mixers, blenders and food processors, where plastic-wrapped turkeys and tinned ingredients are used, cooking lacks any exotic allure. It is altogether too modern and too familiar. A montage sequence blends the serving and eating of the Thanksgiving dinners in all four households. The similarity of the high camera angles, the dissolves and cross-cutting between the four families, who have all congregated around large tables to celebrate Thanksgiving, encapsulates the formerly espoused ideal of the melting pot, which has been superseded by concepts that advocate pluralism and diversity rather than assimilation and homogenisation. Although the turkeys have been prepared in culturally specific ways and the accompaniments vary from household to household, ultimately, they all conform to the North American tradition of a Thanksgiving dinner. Chadha's fusion movie makes the point that, no matter how these families cook their turkeys, no matter where they originally come from, they are all American families and that, no matter what social inequalities and tensions exist, everything will be fine, as long as they eat together.

Conversely, rather than promoting cultural assimilation, other ethnic food films imagine ethnic cuisine as enriching and invigorating white majority culture by introducing Americans in New Jersey to Italian pasta (*Big Night*), Germans in the industrial town of Duisburg to pizza (*Solino*), Parisians in the global gastronomic capital to North African couscous (*Couscous*), Glaswegians to hot Indian curries (*Nina's Heavenly Delights*) and gourmets in rural France to French-Indian fusion food (*The Hundred-Foot Journey*). These films not only negotiate ethnic identities through the meals that are cooked and consumed, they also celebrate immigrant success by featuring chefs who run popular restaurants and achieve status and recognition in their countries of residence. For instance, the Scottish Nina (Shelley Conn), who is of Indian heritage, wins a televised cooking contest, starring on national Korma Television in *Nina's Heavenly*

Delights,[3] while the young Indian chef Hassan Kadam (Manish Dayal) in *The Hundred-Foot Journey* achieves critical acclaim and several Michelin stars for blending French haute cuisine with Indian influences and spices he inherited from his mother before the family had to flee their native Mumbai. His award-winning fusion food encapsulates the premise of *The Hundred-Foot Journey* and that of other ethnic food films that two cultures can be successfully fused through food.

The Way to the Heart Is Through the Stomach: *Eat Drink Man Woman*

While exotic food films are incontrovertibly about the desire for sensuality and transformation, they also speak to other, perhaps less obvious fantasies and longings: a slow pace of life, a sense of innocence, a nostalgia for deep emotional bonds and family ties, all of which are presumed to have either existed in the past or to have survived in cultures that have escaped the impact of globalisation. Like slow cinema and, indeed, the 'slow food' movement and other grassroots movements that seek 'to rescue extended temporal structures from the accelerated tempo of late capitalism' (De Luca and Barradas 2016: 3), exotic cinema, and especially food films, stand in an antagonistic relationship to global capitalism. They reassess its dominant social values, such as the cult of speed and an efficiency-driven lifestyle, the ethos of economic success or the assertion of individual self-fulfilment over obligations towards the family and community, by reflecting life through a different cultural prism.

Ang Lee's film *Eat Drink Man Woman* intersects with these wider societal and cultural discourses by using food as a means for exploring family dynamics at a time of rapid social change. Produced by Taiwanese and American production companies, it is part of the 'Father Knows Best' Trilogy, which includes *Tui shou* (Pushing Hands, 1991) and *Xi yan* (The Wedding Banquet, 1993). All three films, co-written by Ang Lee and James Schamus, dramatise how cultural conflicts between tradition and modernity, East and West, fathers (played by Sihung Lung in all three films) and their grown-up children, are negotiated within the family. While the domestic drama in *Eat Drink Man Woman* is steeped in a sense of nostalgia for 'the lost haven of the family', which according to Anthony Giddens, evokes 'more nostalgia ... than any other institution with its roots in the past' (Giddens 2002: 53), it refrains from conjuring up fantasies of a harmonious, traditional family life, untrammelled by the transformative forces of global modernity. Right from the outset there is a sense that the ceaseless flow, speed and noise of the traffic in Taipei, 'one of Lee's defining images of Taiwanese modernization' (Dariotis and Fung 1997: 209), is encroaching upon Mr Chu's family home, ostensibly a sanctuary of a more traditional lifestyle that is guarded from the outside world by a fortress-like wooden gate. Here, widowed Mr Chu, a first-generation Chinese immigrant and master chef in Taipei's Grand Hotel, is living with his three grown-up daughters. Each Sunday evening, they share an opulent home-cooked dinner, prepared by their father in accordance with ancient Chinese tradition. Although the abundance of food and the time devoted to its preparation is the material manifestation of the abundance of love, nurture and care that holds the family together, it soon transpires that the ritual of commensality is fraught with tensions and devoid of joy. One daughter even refers to the dinner as the 'Sunday torture ritual' behind her father's back. Despite dutifully attending the Sunday dinners, the daughters hardly touch the twelve-course banquet, consisting of traditional dishes from Szechuan, Shandong, Inner Mongolia, Shanghai, Canton and other regions in Mainland China. Most of the ornately presented menu items, including eight jewel duckling, steamed crabs with ginger and imperial palace lamb, are discarded into plastic containers at the end of the evening and given to their neighbour, Jin-Rong (Sylvia Chang).[4] Since Chu's sense of taste is impaired, the beautiful appearance of the food is occasionally somewhat deceptive: the ham is too smoky and the crab paste is missing. The father's loss of taste corresponds with the daughters' lack of appetite; both gesture towards unspoken emotional tensions and the repression of desire. At each of the five ritualistic dinners, a family member is struggling

Figure 5.1 *Eat Drink Man Woman* (Ang Lee, 1994) demonstrates that the art and ritual of cooking occupies a central place in the transnational imaginary of Chinese culture.

to articulate what they really want by making an announcement: Jia-Chien (Chien-Lien Wu), a glamorous and successful executive at an airline company, is planning to move into her new luxury apartment; Jia-Jen (Kuei-Mei Yang) reveals that she has fallen in love with a fellow teacher at her school and just got married; the youngest, Jia-Ning (Yu-Wen Wang), is pregnant and will move in with her boyfriend.

The daughters' attempts to leave the family home are fraught with the conflict between the old Confucian virtue of filial piety and the Western value of pursuing individual happiness. Filial piety, which governs Chinese family relations, entails showing 'gratitude toward one's parents for the care they have given, to respect and love one's parents, and to show duty and devotion to take care of one's parents' (Laine 2005: 106). Ironically, the father and his daughters want the same thing, namely, to get on with their own lives but feel compelled to honour the Confucian virtue of familial interdependence. This dilemma is eventually resolved when Mr Chu confesses that he and Jin-Rong have been secretly in love for a long time and that they are planning to get married. This unexpected revelation abruptly ends the largest Sunday banquet. Chu's surprising choice of wife proves that he is far less traditional than everyone had assumed since Jin-Rong is a recent divorcee and single working mother of the same age as his daughters.

Although the film ends with the dispersal of the family, it nevertheless espouses family love as a core value. In a remarkable twist (also a distinctive feature of the other films in this trilogy), the ending redefines family love in a non-Confucian way by advocating the pursuit of individual desires over submitting to the ethos of filial piety. Only through adapting to change can family love survive, Lee's film seems to be saying. Thus, by the end of *Eat Drink Man Woman*, all family members (except Jia-Chien) have started families of their own. Even Chu, who is in his late sixties or early seventies, and Jin-Rong are expecting a baby. Meanwhile Jia-Chien accepts a job in Amsterdam since she no longer needs to take care of her father. Yet before she leaves, she cooks an elaborate Sunday dinner in the family home that has just been sold, presumably to her. Unlike in the past, when everyone attended dutybound, now everyone except the father sends their apologies. When he criticises the soup for containing too much ginger, father and daughter suddenly realise that he has regained his sense of taste. In a hitherto inconceivable gesture of intimacy, Chu and Jia-Chien hold each other's hands and affectionately call each other 'father' and 'daughter'. Through the liberating transformation of the family structure, a harmonious balance between Western independence and Confucian familial interdependence has been achieved.

In addition to bringing emotional tensions to the surface, food serves as a conduit for love and creating new familial bonds. As Sheng-mei Ma (1996: 195) rightly notes, 'Food, as a "metaphor for love", is poorly produced as the chef can no longer control the right amount of seasoning and is poorly received as the daughters contemplate a move away from the family prison.' The idea that the family home is simultaneously a place of nurture and a prison is reinforced in several shots that portray the family meals through a grid-like wooden screen, suggestive of a cage or prison. A similar ambivalence characterises Mr Chu's culinary artistry. On the one hand, the almost meditative absorption with which he prepares elaborate banquets for his daughters is an expression of his devotion to them; on the other hand, the violence with which he smashes a chicken-shaped clay pot with a heavy axe at the dinner table betrays an undercurrent of aggression. His daughters, who observe this violent act in silence, are wincing at each blow of the axe as it sends tremors across the table. Inside is a piece of roasted meat wrapped in several layers of lotus leaves that are tied together with a thick piece of string, which Mr Chu cuts. This symbolically charged scene poignantly expresses the need to loosen family ties. As Mr Chu cuts the strings, his eldest daughter suddenly gets up from the table and hastily announces that she got married in the morning. Jia-Jen, a devout Christian convert, had to get married in a hurry because pre-marital sex was not an option and she and her boyfriend could not wait any longer. In fact, the title of the film *Eat Drink Man Woman*, which is a reference to a Chinese saying, draws attention to precisely this tension between family (Eat Drink signifying nurture and sustenance) and sexuality (Man Woman), which Mr Chu and his daughters are struggling to reconcile.[5]

Where emotional sustenance and carnal desire do not coalesce, harmony and happiness are impossible to attain, as Jia-Chien's relationship with her ex-boyfriend Raymond (Chit-Man Chan) demonstrates. Besides maintaining a passionate affair with him, she occasionally cooks lavish dinners at his apartment. Cooking is a means of establishing intimate bonds and a link to the past for Jia-Chien. Reminiscing how, as a little girl, she spent many magical moments with her father in the large hotel kitchen while he baked bracelets and a ring 'full of spices and sugar diamonds made from dough' for her. 'I don't have any childhood memories unless I cook them into existence', she explains. Raymond responds to these revelations in a facetious manner, then gets up from the table and declares that he is full, although he has hardly touched the multi-course meal his ex-girlfriend prepared. Once again, the lack of appetite signals an emotional imbalance between the two. On a different occasion, they meet at Raymond's stylish art gallery, where he discloses that he is about to get married and that his fiancée is a talented artist as well as a very good cook. His imminent wedding does not prevent him from suggesting that he and Jia-Chien continue their sexual liaison, regardless. Deeply hurt and without any further comment, she leaves and immediately throws up in the gallery garden. Jia-Chien's intense visceral response to Raymond's disrespectful proposition indicates that the trope of food, taste and appetite (or lack thereof) serves as an index of emotional disturbances and ruptures.

Conversely, Mr Chu appears to have found a perfect match in Jin-Rong, who fulfils his sexual and emotional needs. His cooking skills especially are in high demand in his new family. Jin-Rong is a hopeless cook and, unlike Jia-Chien, whose culinary skills are almost on par with those of her father, no competition in the kitchen. Long before Jin-Rong and Mr Chu announce their wedding plans, he provides Jin-Rong's eight-year-old daughter, Shanshan (Yu-Chien Tang), with elaborate school lunches, which are the envy of her classmates, while he eats the lacklustre lunch boxes Jin-Rong prepared for her daughter. In one scene Jin-Rong, who has found out about the lunchbox exchange, thanks Chu for his generosity of spirit and for putting up with her tough and chewy spare ribs, whereupon he remarks: 'I eat your food happily. After all, I have lost my ability to taste and eating is but a feeling in the heart.'

The complementary nature of this successful food – and, by extension, romantic – exchange serves as the yardstick by which the health and happiness of intimate relationships are measured in *Eat Drink Man Woman*. While cooking and serving the elaborate dinner Jia-Chien has prepared in accordance 'with ancient philosophy', she explains that all food needs to be 'balanced with energy, flavour and nature', whereupon her unappreciative ex-boyfriend responds with a hint of irony: 'Like mixing yin and yang.' An integral part of Taoist philosophy, the duality of yin and yang (literally 'shade and light') is embedded in diverse aspects of Chinese culture, from cosmology over traditional medicine to food and martial arts. The concept of yinyang expresses the belief that everything in the universe – female and male, night and day, moon and sun, earth and heaven – is based on interconnected and reciprocal forces that jointly form a harmonious and dynamic whole (see Wang 2012: 3, 222). The divided circle of the black-and-white yinyang symbol captures the idea of mutual inclusion visually since it integrates a small portion of the opposite element in each of the teardrop-shaped halves. The icon's swirling pattern, which has been compared to two intertwined fish chasing each other, visualises the dynamic and transformative nature of yinyang. The round terracotta pot with the two swimming carp in the opening sequence of *Eat Drink Man Woman* is likely to be an oblique reference to the yinyang symbol. Far beyond the immediate influence of Eastern thought, the yinyang symbol has been appropriated all over the world as a commodified, decorative ornament featuring on jewellery, business cards, advertisements and tattoos, while its complex significance has been reduced to the notion of a balanced lifestyle (see Wang 2012: 201–26). In accordance with the principles of yingyang, foods with a higher water content, such as lotus, cucumber and tofu, are classified as predominantly yin, and foods with a higher energy content, such as duck and beef, and those that are sweet or spicy, cinnamon, ginger and chilli peppers, are predominantly yang. In a perfect Chinese meal, these different energies need to be well balanced since, according to traditional Chinese medicine, 'one's spiritual, physical and emotional wellbeing are all regulated by the balance of yin and yang in the body' (Gao 2017). If then Ang Lee uses the trope of food, appetite and taste as a metaphor for the emotional equilibrium (or lack thereof) that governs family and other intimate relationships, one might argue that Mr Chu's loss of taste and resultant over- or under-spicing corresponds with imbalances in the family dynamics. An insistence on too much proximity and patriarchal control stifles everyone's wish for greater independence and, indeed, the prospect of starting families of their own. Mr Chu's regaining of his sense of taste in the film's final scene confirms that the balance between yin and yang has eventually been restored.

(Re-)constructing Family Ties Through Food

The idea that food is a conduit of love and capable of (re-)constructing familial ties or alternative socialities is also the premise of numerous other exotic food films. *Ramen Teh* (Ramen Shop, 2018) by the Singaporean director Eric Khoo sketches Japan's traumatic occupation of Singapore during World War Two as the historical background for a family-food-melodrama. Masato (Takumi Saitoh), a ramen chef based in Japan, discovers a suitcase filled with memorabilia and his deceased mother's little notebook, after his father suddenly dies. He finds out that his mother, who was of Singaporean Chinese descent, was disowned by her own mother because she married 'the enemy', a Japanese man. To find out more about his family's history and meet his grandmother, he travels to Singapore. By cooking ramen soup, based on a family recipe, he eventually wins over his initially hostile grandmother and family harmony is restored.

An (Sweet Bean, Naomi Kawase, 2015) is a Japanese sentimental feelgood movie that centres on a food stall, where the three protagonists' lives converge over the preparation and consumption of *dorayaki*, a Japanese snack consisting of two small pancakes filled with sweet azuki bean paste. Sentaro's (Masatoshi Nagase) food stall gains in popularity when Tokue (Kirin Kiki), a tottering elderly lady, joins forces with him and replaces the tinned manufactured filling with her home-cooked sweet bean paste. Tokue soaks, boils and stirs the red beans with devotion and remarkable patience. She also listens to the stories they seemingly whisper in her ear. She has a spiritual connection to all things around her, be it the abundance of pink cherry trees, birds, the moon or red azuki beans. Brought and held together by the sweet sticky bean paste, the three social outsiders at the film's narrative centre form a happy three-generational family: Sentaro, a former prison inmate, Tokue, a patient in a sanatorium for people afflicted by leprosy, and Wakana (Kyara Uchida), a teenager neglected by her single mother. By invoking certain cultural clichés commonly associated with Japan, such as the visual spectacle of pink cherry blossoms or the extreme emotional reserve and politeness with which the characters interact, coupled with the notion that there is a profoundly spiritual dimension to the preparation and consumption of food, Naomi Kawase ensures that *Sweet Bean* has an exotic mystique for transnational audiences. Like other exotic food films discussed in this chapter, '*An* is essentially a shrine to "slow food", to time-won wisdoms, and to the traditions being lost to today's hyper-capitalist, factory-model food industry' (Carew 2016: 50).

A similar air of nostalgia envelopes *The Lunchbox* (2014), the debut feature by Indian director Ritesh Batra. The film takes a rare anomaly in Mumbai's highly efficient lunchbox delivery system as its narrative premise. For more than 125 years, some 5,000 *dabbawallahs* (deliverymen) have transported tiered tiffin containers with food prepared by housewives and professional kitchens to the city's office workers. According to a study carried out by Harvard University in 2010 (that is explicitly mentioned in the film by one of the *dabbawallahs*), 'only one in six million lunchboxes is delivered erroneously' (Masukor 2015: 70). In Batra's romance-cum-food-film, it is precisely the *one* misdelivered lunchbox, which connects two lonely and unhappy strangers. Ila (Nimrat Kaur), a young middle-class housewife tries to regain the attention and affection of her unfaithful husband by preparing exquisite lunches for him. By mistake, the four-tiered lunchbox lands on the desk of Saajan Fernandes (Irrfan Khan), a widowed insurance clerk, close to retirement. When Ila discovers the error that occurred, she adds a note to the lunchbox. Soon, the short messages about the food turn into longer letters in which the lonely housewife and the isolated office clerk begin to tell each other things about their lives. Little by little, a tender, innocent romance begins to blossom. Moreover, food has a transformative power, both for the housewife and even more so for the recipient of the lunchbox. The hitherto reclusive and grumpy Saajan starts sharing his lunch with Shaik (Nawazuddin Siddiqui), the new colleague who will take up his position in the claims department after the older man's retirement. While food can reflect the divisions of Indian society, in *The Lunchbox* it serves as the principal connecting device between people of different class, caste and religion. Ila is middle-class Hindu, Shaik is Muslim and certainly poorer and presumably of a lower class than Saajan, whose name suggests that he is of Portuguese Christian descent. Through sharing the food that Ila cooks, Shaik and Saajan develop a quasi-father–son relationship. Food also forges a family-like bond between Ila and Auntie (Bharti Achrekar), her upstairs neighbour. Although Auntie remains invisible throughout the film, the two women have intimate conversations through the open kitchen windows while Ila prepares the contents of the lunchboxes. Occasionally Auntie smells that an essential ingredient is missing and hands it down in a basket on a string, giving Ila advice on how to spice the food, originally to entice her husband, and later, to win the affection of the letter-writing office clerk.

What makes the Indian food in Batra's film exotic for cultural outsiders are not just the home-cooked recipes and the amount of time and effort spent on concocting four different dishes for a routine lunch, but also the shiny tiered tiffin lunchboxes and the various modes of transport (rickety bicycles, commuter trains and pushcarts) that ensure their timely delivery. Batra, who originally intended to make a documentary about Mumbai's 5,000 *dabbawallahs*, tracks the lunchboxes' route from door to desk in considerable detail to make spectators marvel at the efficiency of this 'human-powered-lunchbox-delivery system' (Masukor 2015: 70) while at the same time suggesting that, in India, labour is not yet automated and cheap. By juxtaposing familiar visual tropes of India (monsoon rain, overcrowded trains, chaotic traffic) with the locally specific custom that global audiences will never have heard of before, Batra relies on the exotic appeal of local authenticity. The absence of technology, be it in the tiny, cramped kitchen where Ila prepares everything by hand, over the delivery system and the high piles of paper insurance policies and endless rows of files in Saajan's cluttered office (without a single computer, notwithstanding India's reputation for being at the forefront of IT developments), panders to a nostalgic fantasy of India as a culture being rooted in the past, where there is still a place for courtly, old-fashioned romance.

Embodied Spectatorship and the Lowly Senses of Taste and Smell

In the Western hierarchy of the senses, taste and smell have traditionally been accorded the lowest position and often been associated with non-Western cultures. The lowly sense of smell has been associated with 'primitivism and has served the ends of cultural imperialism in the name of civilizing and controlling the perceived odorous excess of other cultures' (Ferguson 2011: 374). Priscilla Parkhurst Ferguson suggests that the more corporeal a sensual faculty is, the less cultural kudos it enjoys:

> From mastication and swallowing to heartburn and beyond, the corporeality of eating daily reminds us humans of our status as animals and our subjection to the imperative dictates of the body. The inescapable connection with the body and functions that modern societies have come to see as shameful reinforces the lowly placement of taste in the hierarchy of the senses of the Western philosophical tradition. The primacy accorded reason as a defining feature of humans, along with the corresponding distrust of the body as a source of knowledge, and the consequent depreciation of taste, touch, and smell, follows the body itself: the farther from the head, the presumed seat of reason, and the closer to the appetites, the less esteemed and the less 'noble' the sense. Association with the intellectual knowledge of reality elevates sight and hearing. Although taste starts out in a favored location, its sites then descend, philosophically no less than physiologically, into the nether regions. (Ferguson 2011: 374)

Whereas the sense of sight is linked to reason, power and control (see Chapter 3), the sense of taste is associated with the abdication of self-control, with succumbing to one's appetites, unrestrained indulgence, even addiction. Similarly, the olfactory perception of strong scents, aromas or fragrances is considered dangerously sensuous because it can lead to a state of intoxication. While Ferguson's compelling argument holds true for European thought and culture from the Bible to the latter part of the twentieth century, more recently, the privileging of sight and sound as the superior senses has come under critical scrutiny and the pendulum is swinging in the other direction.

Anthropologists and cultural theorists argue that contemporary Western societies suffer from an 'atrophy of sensuous knowledge' and that we 'need to relearn how to inhabit our bodies, appealing to the embodied knowledges of non-Western cultures', an exhortation that implies 'a kind of primitivist longing for another culture's sense knowledge' (Marks 2000: 207). Exotic food films speak to this longing by serving as a bodily provocation that triggers sensorial responses, thereby enabling spectators to experience films somatically, with their whole bodies and, thereby, rediscover visceral intensity and sensual pleasure deemed to still exist in Other cultures.

In film studies, the growing attention to the body has manifested itself in theories of embodied spectatorship that build on perception theories, neuroscience, Maurice Merlau-Ponty's phenomenolgy and on Gilles Deleuze's theories of affect. In contrast to ocular-centric approaches that investigate the gaze and spectatorial identification, theories of embodied spectatorship, such as those proposed by Steven Shaviro (1993), Linda Williams (1991), Laura Marks (2000) and Vivian Sobchack (2004), amongst others, make a case for a holistic spectatorial experience. Film viewing, according to Sobchack (2004: 56, 63), is a 'visceral event' that involves 'our entire bodily being, informed by the full history and carnal knowledge of our acculturated sensorium'. This kind of bodily, multisensorial perception is, in fact, not unique to film spectatorship, but is the normal way of being in and experiencing the world around us (see Atunes 2016: 95). In spite of this, film studies has, until quite recently, overlooked the involuntary interplay between the senses. Laine and Strauven (2009: 249–50) regard what they call the 'synaesthetic turn', which shifts the focus from the cinematic 'image as objectively readable text to the image as subjectively and bodily experiential event' as part of a broader 'synaesthesia fever' that has seized contemporary culture more broadly, and film studies, in particular, at beginning of the twenty-first century. Synaesthesia (from Greek *syn*, meaning 'together' and *aesthesis*, meaning 'perception') refers to the 'union of the senses' (Cytowic 2002) that occurs when the stimulation of one sense triggers the perception in another. Exotic food films offer an exceptionally productive terrain for exploring synaesthesia because they are not merely a feast for the eyes but provoke a rich sensorial experience in the spectator by stimulating a synaesthetic response that conjoins the distant senses of vision and hearing with the proximate senses of smell, taste and touch. They enable spectators to taste food through making inferences and establish intersensory links between sight, hearing and the senses of taste and smell. This strategy is central to all the exotic food films discussed in this chapter.[6] However, what makes *The Scent of Green Papaya* a particularly pertinent case study is that it links synaesthetic perception to embodied memories.

Embodied Memories and Synaesthetic Perception:
The Scent of Green Papaya

For people living in exile or diaspora, sense memories are especially important since they provide a lifeline to their homelands, their pasts and the culture left behind. No longer within reach, the fabric of everyday experiences has become encoded in the senses, and here, specifically, the proximate senses, which are better at storing memories than the visual sense. Memories and their affective charge are actualised in bodily sensations. Thanks to a direct neural pathway between olfaction and the limbic system, in which memory and emotion are anchored, the perception of smell is an enduring storehouse of long-term memories that can be spontaneously activated when a particular smell is re-encountered.

The same applies to the perception of taste, since the olfactory centre in the nose complements the five taste modalities (sweet, sour, salty, bitter, savoury) produced by the taste buds in the mouth. Marcel Proust's widely cited seven-volume novel *À la recherche du temps perdu* (Remembrance of Things Past aka In Search of Lost Time, 1999 [1913]) renders this intimate connection between taste, with its capacity to access the furthest recesses of memory, and the recuperation of the past. The taste of a madeleine, 'the most famous cookie in literary history', as Ferguson (2011: 383) puts it, dipped in lime blossom tea on a dreary November afternoon, demonstrates how taste can bring back to life a long-buried past. As the sensorial stimulation triggers the narrator's involuntary memory, he is transported back to his family's country home in Combray, his favourite walks and the people he encountered while he stayed there as a child. The reference to Proust is particularly relevant in relation to *The Scent of Green Papaya* here, since a similar process of involuntary memory inspired Tran Anh Hung when he wrote the screenplay. 'The smell of green papaya', he remarked in an interview, 'is for me a childhood memory of maternal gestures.' In making a film about the daily rituals and domestic routines of the servant girl Mui at the film's narrative centre, Tran (cited in Blum-Reid 2003: 63) intended to pay homage to his mother and to the 'many years of servitude' that shaped her life, like that of most other Vietnamese women.

Tran, who was born in Vietnam and emigrated with his family to Paris in 1975 at the age of twelve, recreates domestic scenes in *The Scent of Green Papaya* that are inspired by memories of his childhood. Since he was unable to shoot on location in Saigon, he went to great lengths to reconstruct a credible fauna and authentic ambient sound on a soundstage on the outskirts of Paris, importing plants for the lush tropical backyard and even insects, birds and other animals from Vietnam. Set in 1951 and 1961, the film tells the story of Mui (which means 'scent' in Vietnamese), a ten-year-old peasant girl (Man San Lu), who moves to Saigon to work in the household of a moderately prosperous merchant family. Under the tutelage of an elderly housekeeper (Nguyen Anh Hoa), she learns how to cook and serve food and how to keep the house neat and tidy. The family is not a happy one: one of their four children, a daughter the same age as Mui, died, and the husband is unfaithful and absconds with the family savings. His return, illness and subsequent death are conveyed obliquely through close-ups of acupuncture needles being inserted into his back to save his life. Not a single word is spoken. Tran's radical approach to storytelling relies on narrative elisions and a deliberate shift in focus away from narratively significant events to the small and insignificant domestic routines that shape Mui's daily life. The camera foregrounds the sensorial interactions, the pleasure Mui takes in her humble chores and communion with crickets (she keeps one as a pet in a tiny bamboo cage), ants and other small creatures in the backyard. A temporal ellipsis of ten years fast forwards to Mui (Nu Yen-Khe Tran), now working as a maid for Khuyen (Hoa Hoi Vuong), whom she first met and fancied when she was in service at the merchant's house. Now a handsome and wealthy pianist, Khuyen is engaged to be married to a glamorous, Westernised Vietnamese woman (Vantha Talisman). However, their engagement ends abruptly when Khuyen becomes attracted to Mui, whom he teaches reading and writing. The film concludes with Mui no longer serving elaborate meals or polishing her master's shoes but spending her time leisurely reading a book in her lover's luxurious house, surrounded by tropical plants and other exotic paraphernalia. She is pregnant and wears a yellow silk dress, the colour of a ripe papaya. Mui's remarkable transformation corresponds to that of the titular papaya, which is classified as a vegetable in its green state but in its ripened yellow state as a fruit.

In Tran's fragrant film, food preparation is first and foremost a means to convey the intensely sensuous atmosphere of a bygone Vietnamese domesticity. Exotic ambient sounds of birds, crickets, bullfrogs and the heavy downpour of tropical rain take precedence over dialogue. It was Tran's ambition to portray 'a specific rhythm, to find the very movement of the Vietnamese soul' (Tran cited in Cross 1994: 36) rather than rehearse dominant media images of Vietnam that either glamorise the country's colonial past or centre on its war-torn history. That rhythm manifests itself in the juxtaposition of mobility and stasis. Slowly drifting camera movements, which seem to follow the scent (or Mui) wafting round the house are punctuated by static shots that calmly observe the performance of domestic tasks from a medium distance or that attend to other minutiae of daily life. These close-ups convey the texture of food, such as the moist, glistening seeds of the green papaya, which Mui cuts open, before touching the pearly white seeds gently with the tip of her finger. Another extreme close-up reveals the white sap of the papaya tree dripping very slowly onto one of the dark green leaves. The slowness of the drip evokes

EXOTIC APPETITES   195

the viscosity of the milky sap. As a drop lands on the veined surface of the dark green leaf and hardly moves, the 'cinesthetic subject', as Sobchack (2004: 71) calls the spectator who engages with the film with their 'sensible-sentient lived body . . . commutes seeing to touching and back again without a thought'. To convey the texture of the green papaya, Mui is shown and heard hacking away with a large, serrated knife at the hard white flesh, before scraping off the juicy shreds that are the main ingredient of green papaya salad, a typical Vietnamese dish. Since the texture of food is an important aspect of taste, the film's tactile aesthetic captures this sensorial dimension effectively via a crossmodal link between vision, touch and texture. However, for someone who has never eaten green papaya and can, therefore, not rely on their sense memory, the taste and, indeed, the scent of green papaya will remain an exotic mystery.

For the cinesthetic subject to perceive taste and smell that is refracted through the cinematic apparatus, he or she needs to recollect and activate similar sensorial experiences and project them onto the screen.[7] Multisensorial perception is prompted through the combination of audio-visual cues, such as the visible steam rising from a pot of freshly boiled rice, or the sound of sizzling oil followed by a series of close-ups of stir-fried shiny green vegetables and meat. Although the older maid's instructions on how to prepare the stir fry ('The oil has to be hot. Fry the vegetable. Burn it for flavour. Not too much or it gets all soft.') provide

Figure 5.2 The multisensorial aesthetics of *The Scent of Green Papaya* (Tran Anh Hung, 1993) plunges the spectator into a sensorially abundant world of exotic flavours, smells and sounds.

some insights into Vietnamese cuisine, ultimately, they cannot simulate the visceral experience in the spectator. This can only be achieved through activating the spectator's embodied perception synaesthetically or crossmodally. Colour, like the deep green of the fried vegetables, offers important clues here. The phenomenologist Merlau-Ponty suggests that there is a connection between colour and taste which informs our 'alimentary intuition' (see Beugnet 2007: 73). While it is well known that synaesthetes, who possess the rare neurological condition of blending different senses, are able to taste colours or see sounds, people with normal sense perception, too, 'systematically associate specific colours with particular tastes' (Spence et al. 2015: 1).[8] For example, shades of red and pink are consistently linked to sweetness, white is associated with saltiness, yellow with sourness, green with bitterness or sourness, and so on. Similarly, saturated and bright colours are perceived as being of an intense flavour (Saluja and Stevenson 2018; Spence et al. 2015). Whereas synaesthetes who are gifted with chromatic gustation automatically and concurrently *see* a particular colour while *tasting* a particular food, people with normal sensation merely establish crossmodal correspondences between colour and taste. Neuroscientists and psychologists are divided as to whether these consistently occurring taste–colour mappings are due to underlying neural pathways or to empirically observed correspondences based on accumulated sense knowledge. For example, 'the association of green and red to sour and sweet, respectively, comes from our brains having picked up on the environmental regularity that many fruits do indeed transition from green, unripe and sour to red, ripe and sweet' (Spence et al. 2015: 9). Thus, from a scientific perspective, the embodied perception experienced by cinesthetic subjects is based on crossmodal correspondences, even though the perceptual anomaly of synaesthesia has gained wide critical currency and, in film studies, has established itself as the preferred term.[9]

The Scent of Green Papaya and other exotic food films stage the encounter between different acculturated sensoria, namely that of the filmmaker and that of the (transnational) spectator. Given the local specificity of food and flavours, these different sensoria are unlikely to intersect and, therefore, require strategies of sensorial translation. In this process of cross-cultural mediation, sense memory plays a pivotal role. For Tran, the embodied memory of his childhood in Vietnam was the creative impulse behind making the film. For the transnational spectator, who is plunged into a sensorially abundant world of strange flavours, smells and sounds, the encounter with locally specific Vietnamese sense knowledge entails the decoding of audio-visual cues. Since transnational cinesthetic subjects may never have tasted green papaya or fish sauce or Cai Xanh, Rau Muong or any of the other green Vietnamese vegetables, their sense memory is likely to prove inadequate. They will, therefore, try to compensate by sensorially translating the taste of these unfamiliar foods into the familiar idiom of their own domestic cuisine. In other words, to viscerally experience the strange texture and aroma of the stir-fried greens in *The Scent of Green Papaya*, they will have to invoke the *recollected flavour* of similar green leafy vegetables, their crisp freshness, the hint of bitterness and the tough texture of their stalks.

Two features make *The Scent of Green Papaya* an exotic food film par excellence. First, the film deploys an aesthetic of sensuous indulgence (see Chapter 4) which combines modes of synaesthetic perception with the visual pleasure of spectacle. Whereas Marks (2000: 177) proposes that haptic visuality and other forms of multisensorial perception are the preserve of a 'cinema of scarcity' and, therefore, incompatible with visual plenitude, I contend that exotic films in general, and Tran's food film in particular, demonstrate that the two are not mutually exclusive.[10] To be sure, in the cinema of scarcity, which privileges the material qualities of the image over its representational power, haptic visuality and other forms of crossmodal perception are the chief means of capturing and communicating the sense memory of diasporic and other deterritorialised filmmakers. In exotic cinema, these aesthetic strategies are effectively blended with visual spectacle. In fact, it is one of the hallmarks of exotic cinema that it engages the spectator on a multisensorial level and, thereby, engenders a feeling of sensuous abundance. In addition to appealing to the proximate senses, *The Scent of Green Papaya* is a feast for the eyes. Highly patterned and multi-layered image compositions, a colour palette of shades of green, yellow and blue, coupled with an almost excessive use of frames within frames and ornately carved screens that partially block the view contribute to the film's painterly style. There are shots that resemble meticulously composed still lifes replete with exotic objects, such as the carved head of a Buddha, a mosquito coil and, right in the centre, Mui's mask-like face illuminated in golden hues by the light of a paper lantern in the right-hand corner of the frame. The film's pictorial qualities are reinforced through static tableaus, long takes and slow floating camera movements that seem to trace the drift of an exotic scent in the air and invite spectators to succumb to the spell of visual perfection.

A second feature that contributes to the film's exoticism is its affinity with slow cinema. This affinity is not surprising since, as Song Hwee Lim (2014: 40) has persuasively argued, 'a cinema of slowness [is] . . . in part, a form of Western consumption of postcolonial visuality, with its attendant politics of othering and exoticisation.' Although he acknowledges that the specific durational aesthetics is by no means unique to postcolonial visuality, being just as prevalent in European art cinema, it nevertheless coalesces with Western perceptions of Other cultures as being rooted in a timeless past and governed by a pre-modern temporality. For Lim, the cinema of slowness is not exclusively defined by its extremely long takes. In fact, based on the average shot length, *The Scent of Green Papaya* would probably not even qualify as an example of slow cinema. But slow cinema relies on another stylistic parameter, namely 'stillness', understood as both 'stillness of the camera and stillness of diegetic action' which, especially in conjunction with 'silence' (Lim 2014: 81), contributes to an overall atmosphere of slowness. *The Scent of Green Papaya* by and large conforms to Lim's definition (2014: 10) of silence as an 'abstanence of sonic elements . . ., such as diegetic and non-diegetic music, dialogue, and voiceover'. Nevertheless, its soundtrack reverberates with the delicate sounds of nature (chirping crickets, croaking frogs), of cooking (sizzling oil, running water) and of religious rituals (grandma chiming the gong after her prayer at the ancestral altar). These soothing, quiet sounds encourage 'contemplation' in the spectator. Michel Ciment (2003), one of the first critics to have used the term 'slow cinema', regards contemplation as a distinctive response to the cinema of slowness that allows spectators 'to live again in the sensuous experience of a moment revealed in its authenticity'. This kind of mindful immersion in the present moment is achieved through 'a pronounced emphasis on quietude and the everyday' coupled with 'understated modes of storytelling' (Flanagan 2008) and a sense of time passing, or drifting, during which nothing happens. The attention bestowed on narratively insignificant domestic chores is, of course, also a prominent feature of ethnographic filmmaking, reminding us once again that autoethnography is a strategy popular with diasporic and world cinema filmmakers who seek to appeal to transnational audiences.

Cannibalism, Capitalism and Carnal Desire in *Dumplings*

In contrast to the other films discussed in this chapter, which illustrate exoticism's allure and seductiveness, Fruit Chan's *Dumplings* brings the concept's inherent ambivalence to the fore by revealing exoticism's dark and threatening underbelly.[11] This generic hybrid between an exotic food film and a cannibalistic horror movie portrays the gruesome practice of cannibalism through visually enthralling images of beautiful women and exotic food that are accompanied by the revolting sounds of people slurping and crunching human flesh and bones. The film is based on a short story by Hong Kong writer Lilian Lee, 'Mei Yuege's Dumplings' (1999).

Its narrative revolves around Aunt Mei (Bai Ling), who used to work as a gynaecologist in an abortion clinic in Mainland China before setting up a small business that supplies Hong Kong's super wealthy with youth-enhancing dumplings. They are filled with ingredients she imports, hidden in a multi-tiered red-and-white lunchbox, from across the Hong Kong and Shenzhen border. Aunt Mei, who is sixty-four but looks more like thirty, sells the secret of her youth to Mrs Lee (Miriam Yeung Ching Wah), an ageing film star, desperate to restore her youthful looks in order to regain her philandering husband's attention and affection.[12] Initially with disgust, but subsequently with an almost insatiable appetite, Mrs Lee eats Aunt Mei's rejuvenating dumplings that are stuffed with a mix of herbs, vegetables and chopped up human foetuses, obtained from the Chinese abortion clinic. In search of ever more potent ingredients to satisfy her client's demands, Aunt Mei resorts to performing an illegal abortion on a fifteen-year-old girl who was raped by her father. For Mrs Lee, the ingestion of the five-month-old foetus, conceived in incest, proves exceptionally effective, whereas for the teenage girl, whose mother is too poor to afford a safe clinic in China, the abortion is lethal.

Mr Lee (Tony Leung Ka-fai) is not averse to unsavoury food either, as long as it enhances his virility. In the presence of his masseuse-mistress he cracks open an egg and devours a fully developed duck embryo. Upon discovering the secret of his wife's youthful looks and regained libido, Mr Lee also visits Aunt Mei in her small, shabby apartment, decked out with exotic Chinese paraphernalia, and becomes her client and lover. In order to avoid a police investigation into the fatal abortion and her illicit trade, Aunt Mei flees to China where she works as a street vendor selling conventional dumplings. Bereft without her regular purveyor of dumplings, Mrs Lee pays her husband's pregnant mistress a handsome sum of money so as to persuade her to abort her five-month-old foetus in a high-class abortion clinic. She then chops up her husband's fully formed offspring for her own cannibalistic consumption. In a shorter version of the film that is part of the Asian horror trilogy *Three . . . Extremes* (2004), alongside films by Japanese director Takashi Miike and the South Korean Park Chan-wook, Mrs Lee aborts her own baby in the bathtub and then ingests it, literally eating her own flesh and bones.

Described by Tonglin Lu (2010: 187) as 'the portrayal of the most elegant cannibalism of our time', the beautifully handcrafted dumplings do not conform to the familiar iconography of cannibalism. Similarly, the fashionably dressed, attractive protagonists are a far cry from the traditional figure of the cannibal, which serves as an icon of the barbaric Other and as 'an imaginary of absolute alterity (the cannibal as the inhuman other) and one of extreme, violent closeness (cannibalism as the illicit ingestion of a member of one's own species)' (Bachner 2018: 1141). These cannibals are professional women, one a former gynaecologist, the other a former actress, who live in contemporary urban Hong Kong, not 'primitive savages' in some remote jungle who boil humans in cauldrons or even eat their flesh raw.[13]

In the film's first cooking scene, when the audience is still unaware of the actual ingredients of Aunt Mei's youth-enhancing dumplings, Christopher Doyle's seductive cinematography with its carefully calibrated lighting and colour compositions, is unequivocally appetising. In her crammed kitchen space, Mei carefully places slices of ginger in a bowl of water before adding translucent, orange-coloured balls that have the appearance of juicy melon balls, and pops one into her mouth. She continues to chop up the ingredients and, as if she wanted to teach her wealthy client the secret art of dumpling making, explains that she will not use chives because of the strong flavour, but more pak choi and ginger. A close-up shows the pristine white flour snowing onto her kitchen table, while Mei's delicate bejewelled hands knead the dumpling dough. 'Dumplings have existed in China for more than 1,400 years', she expounds. 'I use high-gluten flour for texture and chewiness. I knead it smooth, until it's like a peeled egg, smooth translucent and soft.' Doyle's framing offers a restricted view of the kitchen, evoking a sense of illicit intrusion and mystery. The billowing curtains which partially block the view, both conceal and momentarily reveal the activity in the kitchen, thereby effectively translating Mrs Lee's ambivalence, her curiosity to see and know and yet rather not see and not know what she is about to eat. Served in a small white porcelain bowl with some soy sauce on the side, the white dumplings, with their pale orange stuffing shining through, look fresh, pure and wholesome. And yet, the expression of disgust on Mrs Lee's face, the effort she makes to force the food down and the amplified sound of crunching and swallowing tell a different story. Mei, in an effective sales pitch that includes some well-researched facts about anti-ageing skin care regimes and, bizarrely, the performance of a traditional Chinese song, needs to encourage her to eat the meal: 'Think about the results, not what it used to be.'

Once the spectator is in the know, the depiction of cooking and consuming the dumplings changes from the alluring to the abject, or rather, oscillates between the two. In *Powers of Horror*, Julia Kristeva (1982: 2) identifies 'food loathing . . . [as] the most elementary and the most archaic form of abjection', describing the visceral reactions, such as nausea, vomiting, perspiration and rapid heartbeat this form of horror triggers in the subject. While the 'skin on the surface of milk', 'a wound with blood and pus', the 'acrid smell of sweat, of decay' or the sight of a disintegrating corpse can elicit this extreme form of repugnance, what ultimately characterises abjection, however, is 'not lack of cleanliness or health . . . [but] what disturbs identity, system, order. What does not respect borders, positions, rules' (Kristeva 1982: 3–4). First and foremost, abjection is linked to a collapse of borders, such as the border between the inside and the outside of the body and that between Self and Other. In this respect, the endocannibalism in *Dumplings*, that is the ingestion of one's own species, is a paradigmatic example of abjection. Mrs Lee's transgressive consumption of human flesh rejuvenates her while at the same time making her beautiful face and body diseased: she suffers from itchy skin rashes and, on one occasion while entertaining friends, exudes the odour of rotten fish. Despite its loathsomeness, abjection is 'a terror that dissembles', Kristiva notes (1982: 4), and that may manifest in ambiguous forms.

In *Dumplings*, this ambiguity revolves around the aestheticisation of cannibalism, which collapses the distinction between the beautiful and the monstrous. Thus, as Mei chops up the ingredients, the camera reveals in extreme close-up how the chopping knife slices through the crimson jellied texture of the embryos, which already have two visible dark marks for the eyes. Her hands are smeared with the bloody flesh of the foetuses. Although Mrs Lee has by now developed an appetite for the dumplings, in the spectator the ingestion of the dumplings elicits repulsion, even horror. The camera focuses in an extreme close-up on Mrs Lee's pale

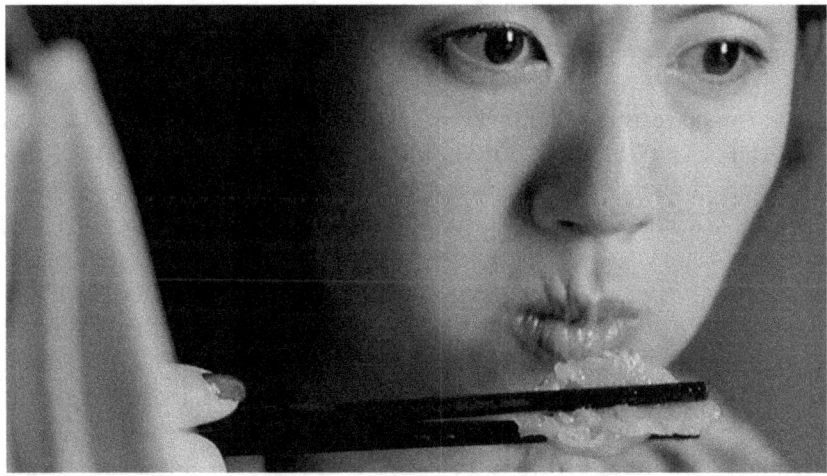

Figure 5.3 The aestheticised cannibalism in *Dumplings* (Fruit Chan, 2004) oscillates between the alluring and the abject.

pink lips, capturing how she bites into the gelatinous foetuses, slowly chews and swallows them.

Doyle's striking use of colour harmonies highlights the visual correspondence between the minced orange-red embryos and Mrs Lee's elegant orange-and-red check silk suit and her colour-matching shoes and designer handbag. As the narrative progresses and Mrs Lee asks for a faster-acting rejuvenating diet, the representation of Mei's culinary skills takes an overtly cannibalistic turn. The five-month-old foetus, conceived in an act of incestuous rape and aborted by Mei in her own bathroom, has a fully developed human shape, with a small penis, ears and even some hair. Yet astonishingly, the actual meal of six dumplings, arranged in a circle on a bed of steamed green cabbage leaves in a bamboo basket, looks exquisitely beautiful and appetising, thanks to the subtle chiaroscuro lighting and the complementary colour scheme of pale red and vibrant green. This stark contrast between the gruesome cannibalistic practices and the deceptively delicious appearance of the dumplings, makes exoticism's inherent ambivalence visible.

The representation of contemporary cannibalism in Fruit Chan's film chimes with an exotic imaginary of China that associates Chinese culture with insalubrious food practices – an imaginary that contrasts with the valorisation of Chinese alimentary culture as a form of art. 'Revulsion for the food eaten by another is a common expression of discrimination and xenophobia', Deborah Lupton (2005: 322–3) proposes. 'Those who eat strikingly different foods . . . may sometimes even be thought to be less human.' The existence of wet markets in China, where people buy live animals including cats, dogs, bats, monkeys, civets, snakes and pangolins (the latter having been alleged to have triggered the outbreak of the COVID-19 pandemic) for consumption, alongside rumours about 'breast-milk treatments for male virility or the ingestion of baked placentas or foetal flesh' (Bachner 2018: 1143) and other repulsive foodways attributed to Sinophone cultures, mark them as Other in the Western imagination. As Glennis Byron notes, around the time of the handover of Hong Kong to China, 'old urban myths about China's supposed cannibalistic practices . . . began to proliferate on the internet'. An article in Hong Kong's now defunct newspaper *Eastern Express* suggested that '"aborted babies [were] sold as health food for $10" . . . and accused Chinese doctors in Shenzhen of foetal cannibalism, of eating and selling foetuses' to benefit clients' general health and the appearance of their skin. Such unsubstantiated rumours were further embellished by 'reports of foetal soup being on the menu in Chinese restaurants' (Byron 2013: 135), which demonised China as the uncivilised, primitive Other that would drag metropolitan

Hong Kong, commonly branded as a unique blend of East and West, tradition and modernity, back to a state of primitivism. *Dumplings* unequivocally links cannibalism to China and its cultural practices. Aunt Mei hails from China, where she performed abortions in support of the Chinese Communist Party's one-child policy, 'serving the people', as she comments in a witty pun. She now imports aborted embryos from the Shenzhen clinic to Hong Kong. Unlike Mrs and Mr Lee, who speak Cantonese, she speaks Mandarin. Her apartment is decorated with a plethora of kitschy Chinese idols and Maoist propaganda posters. When serving dumplings to Mr Lee, she provides a potted history of cannibalism in Chinese culture in an eerie disembodied voice-over commentary that is accompanied by the insistent beat of drums:

> Cannibalism should not even be considered immoral in China; it has existed since history began. Li's *Herbalist's Handbook* clearly stated that human flesh and organs are admissible ingredients for medieval recipes ... During famines, neighbours traded and cooked each other's children for survival ... Tales abound of caring sons and daughters, cutting off flesh for their parents' medicine. The classic *Water Margins* depicted heroes who savoured their enemies. One even served buns with a filling of human flesh ... Do you think we could have got through all those wars and famines without eating human flesh?

Although she cites various sources so as to normalise her own cannibalistic practices, Mei makes no explicit mention of the film's most significant intertextual reference here, namely Lu Xun's (1990 [1918]) story 'Diary of a Madman', in which the titular Madman hallucinates about involuntarily eating human flesh. Instead she quotes and misquotes from various canonical sources to prove the normalcy of cannibalism in Chinese culture. In *The Mouth that Begs: Hunger, Cannibalism and the Politics of Eating in Modern China*, Gang Yue (1999: 6) makes a case for the centrality of Lu Xun's text in Chinese cultural history with its persistent preoccupation with orality, hunger and cannibalism and 'the irreducible materiality of food and its metaphoric power'. Yue argues that historical sources and fictional texts alike identify anthropophagy, be it the ingestion of enemies or one's own children, 'as a powerful trope of negative totality in interpreting traditional Chinese culture and society' (Yue 1999: 4). Since 'Diary of a Madman' is told from the perspective of someone suffering from paranoia, the text remains ambiguous as to whether the alimentary perversions and cruel practices it describes, such as that of a daughter cutting her own flesh to nurture her sick mother back to health, are actually part of ancient China's anthropophagic morality or rather the horrifying projections of a deluded mind. However, as both Yue and Bachner (2018: 143) outline, the flesh-cutting practice of *gegouliaoqin* or *gegu*, to which Aunt Mei refers in the voice-over commentary, is frequently invoked as a model of '"civilized" cannibalism' and Confucian morality. It also features in Wayne Wang's cinematic adaptation of Amy Tan's best-selling novel *The Joy Luck Club* (1989, film 1993), in which a disavowed daughter carves a piece of flesh from her arm and boils it in a soup to transfer her own good health to her mother and thereby save her life. This act of filial piety represents a model of Confucian morality insofar as it seeks to preserve the life of a family elder through sacrificing one's own bodily integrity. Such self-sacrifice of the younger generation for the sake of their parents signifies, by extension, the sacrifice of the future for the sake of the past. The famous injunction at the very end of 'Diary of a Madman', 'save the children', has to be understood against the background of this Confucian practice.[14] However, when Aunt Mei cites these words, they take on a rather different meaning, representing an ironic inversion, not unlike Mei's above-mentioned ironic pun on the Chinese Communist Party slogan 'serve the people', first used by Chairman Mao in a speech in 1944.

The Hong Kong filmmaker Fruit Chan links cannibalism to the history of Mainland China, which is thus marked as primitive.[15] Its occurrence in Hong Kong represents, on the one hand, a form of cultural contamination while, on the other hand, functioning as a trope for excessive consumption and global commodity culture. As repeated tracking shots along the eclectic array of kitschy figurines in Aunt Mei's tiny flat, ranging from Chairman Mao through the Daoist goddess of nativity and mercy to the Virgin Mary, imply, she goes along with any ideology that suits her needs. She was as much part of China's past planned economy as she is now of China's new market economy. She has successfully adjusted to the new market forces by exploiting Chinese mainlanders who need to comply with the one-child policy and the wealthy Hong Kong elite, by 'processing the waste products of the former to capitalise on the desires of the latter for youth and beauty. Thoroughly adapted to the new market economy, she understands supply and demand and where there is desire there is snake oil' (Byron 2013: 139). The revolutionary songs she performs for her affluent clients are neatly integrated into her sales pitches, lending them a sense of Chinese local authenticity, which (as outlined in Chapter 3) is an effective strategy of exoticisation and the commodification of cultural difference. In *Dumplings*, purchasing power determines who stays young and who grows old. Only the super-rich can afford to partake in the youth-enhancing cannibalistic rituals. Thus, except for Aunt Mei, who lives on the diet from which she profits, all the other residents in the neglected housing estate where she runs her business are marked by old age and poverty.

The quest for eternal youth is first and foremost motivated by carnal desire. Both Mrs and Mr Lee succumb to cannibalism to stay young, desirable and, in the case of Mr Lee, virile. The ingestion of another body is the ultimate form of embodiment and one that simultaneously contains the Other in the Self and destroys it. Before seducing Mr Lee, Aunt Mei elaborates on the natural affinity between physical attraction and cannibalism, in another attempt to normalise the eating of human flesh: 'When two people are deeply in love all they desire is to be inside each other. Inside each other's skin, inside each other's guts.' The film neatly illustrates the intimate connection between cannibalism and sexual gratification. As soon as Mrs Lee has consumed the particularly potent dumplings, filled with the minced flesh of the five-month-old foetus, she rekindles her husband's passion for her and the couple make love to each other. Meanwhile, Aunt Mei and Mr Lee fornicate on the dining table immediately after he has devoured the dumplings. Indeed, such is the aphrodisiacal power of the dumplings, that even his unexpected discovery that Mei is thirty years older than her slim and shapely body and smooth skin suggest, does not dampen his desire for her. Asked if he will come back for more, he confirms the symbiotic relationship between cannibalism and carnal longing, replying: 'Yes, to eat your flesh.'

Conclusion

As this chapter demonstrates, exotic food films intermingle the culinary with the cultural and the corporeal, using cooking, eating and gustation as a trope for a multitude of human appetites and desires, be it a nostalgic longing for deep emotional bonds, a slower pace of life, a reawakening of the senses and sex. The displacement of erotic desires onto the fetishised depiction of exotic food has become increasingly prominent in response to the demands of political correctness. While the overt eroticisation of the exotic Other on screen used to be commonplace (witness the semi-nude temple dancer Seetha in Fritz Lang's *Der Tiger von Eschnapur* (The Tiger of Eschnapur, 1959), gyrating her hips underneath a gigantic statue of a full-bosomed Indian goddess), in contemporary global art cinema at least (though not in mainstream cinema), it has become 'non-pc'. Those who break this injunction, like Mira Nair in her explicit erotic-exotic fantasy *Kama Sutra: A Tale of Love* (1996), a voluptuous film inspired by the ancient Hindu compendium on the principles of lust and sexual pleasure, are harshly criticised.[16]

If exotic food must absorb these libidinal energies, then it is not surprising that the films under consideration here register intense bodily responses in the spectator, ranging from appetite to abjection, and are thus comparable to the 'body genres' (horror, porn, melodrama), theorised by Linda Williams (1991). Synaesthesia and visual spectacle, especially when combined, immerse the spectator in a world of sensorial opulence and excess that promises a release from the perceived atrophy of sensuous knowledge in late capitalist Western societies. Through portraying exotic foodways and, by implication, alternative ways of living, in highly appealing terms, *Eat Drink Man Woman*, *The Scent of Green Papaya*, *The Lunchbox* and *Ramen Shop* prompt transnational spectators to experience viscerally what it would be like to live more sensuously, pleasurably, slowly and intimately. In this way, the contact with the exotic Other in these films has the capacity to facilitate a process of transformation in the transnational spectator.

Yet the offer of a fantasy escape from the alleged anhedonia of dominant white culture is not the only reason for the broad transnational appeal of exotic food films. It is certainly no coincidence that many of the exotic (and ethnic) food films discussed in this chapter are made by diasporic filmmakers for whom embodied memories often serve as an important creative inspiration. Not only is the sensorium the locus of memory where the past crystallises in a sensation, waiting to be reawakened in a different place and time, but the heightened mobility, displacement and deterritorialisation experienced by people living in diaspora has fostered a yearning for proximity – to the homeland and the everyday rituals left behind – which lives on in the proximate senses. Diasporic filmmakers like Ang Lee, Tran Anh Hung and Fruit Chan are strategic and skilful brokers of alterity who know how to turn cultural difference into a valuable commodity in the global marketplace, being nominated for or winning prestigious awards at international film festivals and attracting sizeable audiences.[17]

Whether exotic food films are necessarily essentialist and reduce Other cultures to readily consumable commodities or whether they use exotic food and culinary rituals as a frame for exploring wider socio-cultural issues, has been the overarching question of this chapter. The discursive coupling of cultural critique and food, with its intimate connection to the body, serves as a prism to reflect upon and reassess Western and non-Western value systems and reveal that the material excess of late capitalism is unable to compensate for the lack of sensual pleasure, the hunger for deep emotional connections and the longing for stillness and contemplation. These are the values espoused through the fetishisation of exotic food, which (with the exception of the foetus-filled dumplings) represents a non-threatening form of Otherness. Admittedly, the idealisation of Other cultural values occasionally proves problematic in terms of its gender politics and ethnic essentialism. For example, the final sequence of *The Scent of Green Papaya* endorses Kuhyen's choice of the subservient and placid Asian woman over that of his thoroughly liberated, glamorous fiancée. Furthermore, it invokes a primitivist fecundity symbolism by linking the pregnant Mui with a bright yellow dress stretching over her round, pregnant belly to the ripe papaya. Ang Lee's *Eat Drink Man Woman*, on the other hand, avoids these pitfalls of exoticisation by using alimentary and gustatory tropes to reveal the cracks within the traditional Chinese immigrant family. The film makes a case for updating the traditional family structure, albeit not without upholding the affectionate bonds and values that ensure its stability. *Dumplings* stages the most explicit challenge to ethnic essentialism. By casting the female cannibals as our contemporary, urban Selves rather than as the primitive Other, Fruit Chan destabilises the dichotomy on which this enduring primitivist trope rests, suggesting that our excessive culture of consumption is the contemporary form of cannibalism.

Notes

1. Although the film is set in Taiwan, the protagonist, Mr Chu, is from Mainland China and has moved to Taiwan following the defeat of the Nationalist Party in a civil war with the Chinese Communist Party in 1949. His cuisine featured in the film is identifiably of Chinese origin.
2. After the emergence of the food film genre in the late 1980s, it took more than a decade before scholarly books on the topic were published, including Bower (2004), Keller (2006), Zimmerman (2010), Baron et al. (2014), Hertweck (2015) and Lindenfeld and Parasecoli (2017). Though some include chapters on food in world cinema, most focus on mainstream American films.
3. For a detailed analysis of these diasporic films, see Berghahn (2013: 113–15, 141–9).
4. See Rogov (2009) and Schütze (2014: 45–6) for detailed discussions of the regional and historical origins of these menu items.
5. According to Deppman (2001: 148), 'The title of the movie *Eat Drink Man Woman* (yin shi nan nu) refers to a popular classical characterization of basic needs: drink (yin), eat (shi), and sex (nan nu) are "irrepressible human desires" (ren chi ta yu)'; see also Dilley (2009).
6. As Forsdick (2000: 189–90) illustrates, for Victor Segalen synaesthesia and what he referred to as 'coloured hearing' was 'the aesthetic ideal' of exoticism.
7. In the history of cinema, several attempts have been made to reproduce smells in the auditorium, with the Odorama being one of the more effective devices; see Hediger and Schneider (2005) and Spence (2020).
8. As Spence et al. (2015: 8) illustrate, 'the relationship between the inducing taste and the concurrent colour in chromatic gustation synaesthesia is

unidirectional. That is, in every case . . . it was the taste (or flavour) of a food or drink that induced a particular colour concurrent, and not vice versa.' By contrast, 'the crossmodal correspondence between taste and colour', which is experienced by average, non-synaesthetic subjects, 'is bidirectional'.

9. 'Synesthesia is a condition present in 2%–4% of the population in which a sensory stimulus presented to one modality elicits concurrent sensations in additional modalities' (Brang and Ramachandran, 2011:1).
10. For Marks (2000), intercultural cinema is necessarily defined by scarcity, denoting its low production budgets and the deliberate avoidance of aesthetic opulence. It thus explicitly excludes exotic cinema although both share an intercultural dimension.
11. Like Ang Lee and Tran Anh Hung, Fruit Chan is a diasporic filmmaker. He was born in Guangdong, China, and moved with his family to Hong Kong when he was twelve years old.
12. The actress who plays the sixty-something Aunt Mei, the Chinese American Bai Ling, was thirty-eight years old when the film was released in 2004, and she appeared on the cover of *Playboy* a year later. Mrs Lee is played by the Cantopop singer Miriam Yeung Ching Wah, who was thirty years old at the time.
13. As Kilgour (1990), Barker et al. (1998), Lindenbaum (2004) and others have noted, cannibalism is deeply implicated in the colonial project. According to Lindenbaum (2004: 477), the colonial encounters between Europe and the New World, especially the Pacific, mark the beginnings of the discourse of cannibalism. 'As a prime symbol or signifier of "barbarism" the cannibal was central to the construction of the cultural "other", and to Enlightenment notions of refinement, modernity, and Western civilization.' In his study of literary representations of cannibalism in Chinese culture, Yue (1999: 28–30) distinguishes between 'hunger cannibalism', which existed in China and many other societies and 'ritual cannibalism', which is specifically linked to Indigenous cultures in Oceania and the Americas.
14. Bachner (2018: 1143) observes that the practice of *gegu* is widely cited as a form of '"civilized" cannibalism' but that 'there is some dispute over whether it was ever actually performed or belonged solely to the realm of the imagination.'
15. Torgovnick (1998: 189) proposes that the ritual human sacrifice is a form of cannibalism and one of the most persistent tropes which the West links to the primitive.
16. A review in *Variety* sums up the tenor of most others: 'A softcore feminist fantasy in the guise of a study of female empowerment, 16th-century style, "Kama Sutra: A Tale of Love" forces a historically set story through a narrowly modern prism. Mira Nair's look at sexual wiles and palace politics in Old India is graced by alluring undraped bods and sumptuous settings and costumes, but this hot-house melodrama is closer to "Dynasty" than to "Devi" and is not destined to be a critics' fave. A hard sell of sex and

exoticism to general, rather than arthouse, audiences is Trimark's best bet for generating some biz in domestic release early next year' (McCarthy 1996).
17. *Eat Drink Man Woman* was nominated for the Academy Awards and won the BAFTA for best non-English language film in 1995; it grossed USD7.3 million. worldwide. *The Scent of Green Papaya* won the Caméra d'Or at the Cannes Film Festival in 1993, the César Award (France's national film award) for the best debut feature and was nominated for the Academy Awards in the best foreign language film category; it grossed USD1.7 millon worldwide. *Dumplings* premiered in the Panorama section of the Berlin International Film Festival in 2004 and grossed close to USD800,000 as a stand-alone feature film and close to USD0.5 million as part of the *Three Extremes* release worldwide.

Filmography

Aguirre, the Wrath of God / Aguirre, der Zorn Gottes, Werner Herzog, 1972
All That Heaven Allows, Douglas Sirk, 1955
An All-Consuming Love / Chang Xiangsi, Zhaozhang He, 1947
The Assassin / Cike Nie Yin Niang, Hou Hsiao-Hsien, 2015
Atanarjuat: The Fast Runner / Atanarjuat, Zacharias Kunuk, 2001
Babette's Feast, Gabriel Axel, 1987
Bachna Ae Haseeno (trans. Watchout Beauties), Siddharth Anan, 2008
The Balanda and Bark Canoes, Rolf de Heer and Tania Nehme, 2006
Balzac and the Little Chinese Seamstress / Xiao cai feng, Sijie Dai, 2002
Before the Rains, Santosh Sivan, 2007
Belfast, Kenneth Branagh, 2021
The Best Exotic Marigold Hotel, John Madden, 2011
Big Night, Stanley Tucci and Campbell Scott, 1996
The Birth of Empire: The East India Company, BBC, 2014
Black Narcissus, Michael Powell and Emeric Pressburger, 1947
Black Venus / Venus Noire, Abdellatif Kechiche, 2010
Bride and Prejudice, Gurinder Chadha, 2004
Brief Encounter, David Lean, 1945
Calcutta, Louis Malle, 1969
Chinese Box, Wayne Wang, 1997
Chocolat, Claire Denis, 1988
Chocolat, Lasse Hallström, 2000
Couscous / La graine et le mulet, Abdellatif Kechiche, 2007
Dances with Wolves, Kevin Kostner, 1990
Darr (trans. Fear), Yash Chopra, 1993
Dil To Pagal Hai (trans. The Heart is Crazy), Yash Chopra, 1997
Dilwale Dulhania Le Jayenge (trans. The Bravehearted Will Take the Bride), Yash Chopra, 1995
Downton Abbey, ITV, 2010–15
The Drum, Zoltan Korda, 1938
Dumplings / Gau ji, Fruit Chan, 2004
Durian Durian, Fruit Chan, 2000
Earth, Deepa Mehta, 1998
Eat Drink Man Woman / Yin shi nan nu, Ang Lee, 1994
Eat Pray Love, Ryan Murphy, 2010

Embrace of the Serpent / El abrazo de la serpiente, Ciro Guerra, 2015
The English Patient, Anthony Minghella, 1996
Farewell My Concubine / Ba wang bie ji, Chen Kaige, 1993
Fire, Deepa Mehta, 1996
Fitzcarraldo, Werner Herzog, 1982
Flowers of Shanghai / Hai shang hua, Hou Hsiao-Hsien, 1998
The Four Feathers, Zoltan Korda, 1939
French Kiss, Lawrence Kasdan, 1995
Good Bye, Lenin! Wolfgang Becker, 2003
Gully Boy, Zoya Akhtar, 2019
Happy Feet, George Miller, 2006
Heading South / Vers le sud, Lauren Cantet, 2005
Heat and Dust, James Ivory, 1983
Hector and the Search for Happiness, Peter Chelsom, 2014
Hero / Ying xiong, Zhang Yimou, 2002
Hotel Salvation / Mukti Bhawan, Shubhashish Bhutiani, 2016
House of Flying Daggers / Shi Mian Mai Fu, Zhang Yimou, 2004
The Hundred-Foot Journey, Lasse Hallström, 2014
Indian Summers, Channel 4, 2015–16
Indochine, Régis Wargnier, 1992
In the Mood for Love / Fa yeung nin wah, Wong Kar-wai, 2000
Inuit Knowledge and Climate Change, Ian Mauro and Zacharias Kunuk, Isuma TV, 2010
The Jewel in the Crown, Granada Television, 1984
The Journals of Knud Rasmussen, Zacharias Kunuk and Norman Cohn, 2006
Ju Dou, Zhang Yimou, 1990
Kama Sutra: A Tale of Love, Mira Nair, 1996
Kuch Kuch Hota Hai (trans. Some Things Happen), Karan Johar, 1998
The Last of the Mohicans, Michael Mann, 1992
Lawrence of Arabia, David Lean, 1962
Le Grand Voyage (trans. The Great Journey), Ismaël Ferroukhi, 2004
Like Water for Chocolate / Como agua para chocolate, Alfonso Arau, 1992
The Lord of the Rings, Peter Jackson, 2001–3
The Lover / L'Amant, Jean-Jacques Annaud, 1992
The Lunchbox, Ritesh Batra, 2014
Lust, Caution / Se, jie, Ang Lee, 2007
Master and Commander, Peter Weir, 2003
M. Butterfly, David Cronenberg, 1993
Memoirs of a Geisha, Rob Marshall, 2005
The Mission, Roland Joffé, 1986
The Mistress of Spices, Paul Mayeda Berges, 2005
Moana, Robert Flaherty, 1926
Mohabbatein (trans. Love Stories), Aditya Chopra, 2000
Monsoon Wedding, Mira Nair, 2001

The Namesake, Mira Nair, 2007
Nanook of the North, Robert Flaherty, 1922
Nina's Heavenly Delights, Pratibha Parmar, 2006
Not One Less / Yi ge dou bu neng shao, Zhang Yimou, 1999
Notting Hill, Roger Michell, 1999
Once Were Warriors, Lee Tamahori, 1994
One Day in the Life of Noah Piugattuk, Zacharias Kunuk, 2019
Out of Africa, Sydney Pollack, 1985
Palm Trees in the Snow / Palmeras en la nieve, Fernando González Molina, 2015
Paradise: Love / Paradies: Liebe, Ulrich Seidl, 2012
A Passage to India, David Lean, 1984
Pather Panchali (trans. Pather Panchali: Song of the Little Road), Satyajit Ray, 1955
Phantom India / L'Inde fantôme, Louis Malle, 1969
Pushing Hands / Tui shou, Ang Lee, 1991
Queen, Vikas Bahl, 2013
Queen of the Desert, Werner Herzog, 2015
Rabbit-Proof Fence, Phillip Noyce, 2002
Raise the Red Lantern / Da hong deng long gao gao gua, Zhang Yimou, 1991
Ramen Shop / Ramen Teh, Eric Khoo, 2018
Red Sorghum / Hong gao liang, Zhang Yimou, 1988
Rhodes of Africa, Michael Balcon, 1936
The Road Home / Wo de fu qin mu qin, Zhang Yimou, 1999
Rouge / Yim ji kau, Stanley Kwan, 1987
Salaam, Bombay! (trans. Hello Bombay!), Mira Nair, 1988
Sanders of the River, Zoltan Korda, 1935
Sangam (trans. Confluence), Raj Kapoor, 1964
The Scent of Green Papaya / Mùi du du xanh, Tran Anh Hung, 1993
The Seawall / Un barrage contre le Pacifique, Rithy Panh, 2008
The Second Best Exotic Marigold Hotel, John Madden, 2015
The Sheik, George Melford, 1921
The Sheltering Sky, Bernardo Bertolucci, 1990
Slumdog Millionaire, Danny Boyle, 2009
Smoke Signals, Chris Eyre, 1998
Solino, Fatih Akin, 2002
Soul Food, George Tillman Jr, 1997
The Sound of Music, Robert Wise, 1965
Spring in a Small Town / Xiao cheng zhi chun, Fei Mu, 1948
Sweet Bean / An, Naomi Kawase, 2015
Tabu: A Story of the South Seas, Friedrich W. Murnau, 1931
Tampopo, Juzo Itami, 1985
Tanna, Martin Butler and Bentley Dean, 2015
Ten Canoes, Rolf de Heer and Peter Djigirr, 2006
Theeb, Naji Abu Nowar, 2014

Three . . . Extremes / Sam Gang 2, Fruit Chan, Park Chan-wook and Takashi Miike, 2004
Three Seasons, Tony Bui, 2000
Three Times / Zuihao de shiguang, Hou Hsiao-Hsien, 2005
The Tiger of Eschnapur / Der Tiger von Eschnapur, Fritz Lang, 1959
Timbuktu, Abderrahmane Sissako, 2014
Titanic, James Cameron, 1997
To Live / Huo zhe, Zhang Yimou, 1994
Tortilla Soup, Maria Ripoll, 2001
To the Ends of the Earth / Tabi no owari sekai no hajimari, Kiyoshi Kurosawa, 2019
Trishna, Michael Winterbottom, 2011
Tropical Malady / Sud pralad, Apichatpong Weerasethakul, 2004
Uncle Boonmee Who Can Recall His Past Lives / Loong Boonmee raleuk chat, Apichatpong Weerasethakul, 2013
Under the Hawthorn Tree / Shan zha shu zhi lian, Zhang Yimou, 2010
Vertigo, Alfred Hitchcock, 1958
Viceroy's House, Gurinder Chadha, 2017
Victoria and Abdul, Stephen Frears, 2017
Vivah (trans. Marriage/Wedding), Sooraj Barjatiya, 2006
Walkabout, Nicolas Roeg, 1971
Water, Deepa Mehta, 2005
The Wedding Banquet / Xi yan, Ang Lee, 1993
Whale Rider, Niki Caro, 2002
What's Cooking? Gurinder Chadha, 2000
When Harry Met Sally, Rob Reiner, 1989
The White Masai / Die weiße Massai, Hermine Huntgeburth, 2005
White Mischief, Michael Radford, 1987
White Shadows in the South Sea, W. S. van Dyke, 1928
The Wizard of Oz, Victor Fleming, 1939
Woman on Top, Fina Torres, 2000
The World of Suzie Wong, Richard Quine, 1960
Yellow Earth / Huang tu di, Chen Kaige, 1984
Zarafa, Rémi Bézançon and Jean-Christophe Lie, 2012
Zindagi Na Milegi Dobara (trans. You Only Live Once), Zoya Akhtar, 2011

Bibliography

Abbas, Ackbar (1997), *Hong Kong: Culture and the Politics of Disappearance*, Minneapolis: University of Minnesota Press.
Adorno, Theodor W. and Max Horkheimer (1997), *Dialectic of Enlightenment*, trans. John Cumming, London: Verso.
Agzenay, Asma (2015), *Returning the Gaze: The Manichean Drama of Postcolonial Exoticism*, Oxford and Bern: Peter Lang.
Ahmed, Sara (2000), *Strange Encounters: Embodied Others in Post-coloniality*, London and New York: Routledge.
Akomfrah, John (2012), '"De-Westernizing as Double Move": An Interview with John Akomfrah', in: *De-Westernizing Film Studies*, eds Saër Maty Bâ and Will Higbee, Abingdon: Routledge, pp. 257–74.
Allin, Michael (1998), *Zarafa: A Giraffe's True Story*, London: Headline.
Altglas, Véronique (2014), *From Yoga to Kabbalah: Religious Exoticisms and the Logics of Bricolage*, New York: Oxford University Press.
Andrew, Dudley (1997), 'Praying Mantis: Enchantment and Violence in French Cinema of the Exotic', in: *Visions of the East: Orientalism in Film*, eds Matthew Bernstein and Gaylyn Studlar, New Brunswick, NJ: Rutgers University Press, pp. 232–52.
_____ (2010), 'Time Zones and Jet Lag: The Flows and Phases of World Cinema', in: *World Cinemas, Transnational Perspectives*, eds Nataša Ďurovičová and Kathleen E. Newman, London and New York: Routledge, pp. 59–89.
Andrews, Nigel (2017), '*Hotel Salvation* – Wamth and Wisdom', *Financial Times*, 24 August, <https://www.ft.com/content/19f8aec0-88c6-11e7-8bb1-5ba57d47eff7> (last accessed 30 April 2021).
Appadurai, Arjun (1986), 'Introduction: Commodities and the Politics of Value', in: *The Social Life of Things: Commodities in Cultural Perspective*, ed. Arjun Appadurai, Cambridge: Cambridge University Press, pp. 3–63.
_____ (1996), *Modernity at Large: Cultural Dimensions of Globalization*, Minneapolis and London: University of Minnesota Press.
Appiah, Kwame Anthony (2005), *The Ethics of Identity*, Princeton, NJ: Princeton University Press.
_____ (2006), *Cosmopolitanism: Ethics in a World of Strangers*, London: Penguin.
Ashcroft, Bill (2001), *Post-colonial Transformation*, London and New York: Routledge.

Ashcroft, Bill, Gareth Griffiths and Helen Tiffin (2000), *Post-colonial Studies: The Key Concepts*, London and New York: Routledge.
Atunes, Luis R. (2016), *The Multisensory Film Experience: A Cognitive Model of Experiential Film Aesthetics*, Bristol: Intellect.
Bâ, Saër Maty and Will Higbee (2012), 'Introduction: De-Westernizing Film Studies', in: *De-Westernizing Film Studies*, eds Saër Maty Bâ and Will Higbee, Abingdon: Routledge, pp. 1–15.
Bachner, Andrea (2018), 'From China to Hong Kong with Horror: Transcultural Consumption in Fruit Chan's Dumplings', *Interventions: International Journal of Postcolonial Studies*, 20: 8, pp. 1137–52.
Badley, Linda, R. Barton Palmer and Steven Jay Schneider (eds) (2006), *Traditions in World Cinema*, Edinburgh: Edinburgh University Press.
Balassone, Merrill (2005), 'Stitching a Vision of China', *Los Angeles Times*, 25 August, <https://www.latimes.com/archives/la-xpm-2005-aug-25-wk-movies25-story.html> (last accessed 10 November 2022).
Barker, Francis, Peter Hulme and Margaret Iversen (eds) (1998), *Cannibalism and the Colonial World*, Cambridge: Cambridge University Press.
Barnes, Amy Jane (2009), 'From Revolution to Commie Kitsch: (Re-)Presenting China in Contemporary British Museums Through the Visual Culture of the Cultural Revolution', PhD Thesis, University of Leicester, School of Museum Studies.
_____ (2020), 'Chinese Propaganda Posters at the British Library', *Visual Resources*, 36: 2, pp. 124–47.
Baron, Cynthia, Diane Carson and Mark Bernhard (2014), *Appetites and Anxieties: Food, Film, and the Politics of Representation*, Detroit: Wayne State University Press.
Batchelor, David (2006), 'Chromophobia', in: *Colour: The Film Reader*, eds Angela Dalle Vacche and Brian Price, London and New York: Routledge, pp. 63–75.
Bauman, Zygmunt (1998), *Globalization: The Human Consequences*, Oxford: Polity Press.
Bazin, André (2005), 'Cinema and Exploration', in: *What Is Cinema?*, vol. 1, Berkeley: University of California Press, pp. 154–63.
Beeton, Sue (2005), *Film-Induced Tourism*, Bristol: Channel View Publications.
Berghahn, Daniela (2013), *Far-Flung Families in Film: The Diasporic Family in Contemporary European Cinema*, Edinburgh: Edinburgh University Press.
Berghahn, Daniela and Dieter Kosslick (2016), personal email correspondence, 19 October.
Berghahn, Daniela and Joseph J. Nako (2016), Skype interview with Joseph J. Nako, 29 July.
Bernstein, Matthew and Gaylyn Studlar (eds) (1997), *Visions of the East: Orientalism in Film*, New Brunswick, NJ: Rutgers University Press.
Berry, Chris (2007), 'Getting Real: Chinese Documentary, Chinese Postsocialism', in: *The Urban Generation: Chinese Cinema and Society at the Turn of the*

Twenty-First Century, ed. Zhang Zhen, Durham, NC: Duke University Press, pp. 115–34.

Berry, Chris and Mary Farquhar (2006), *China on Screen: Cinema and Nation*, New York: Columbia University Press.

Bessire, Lucas (2003), 'Talking Back to Primitivism: Divided Audiences, Collective Desires', *American Anthropologist*, 105: 4, pp. 832–8.

Bettinson, Gary (2015), *The Sensuous Cinema of Wong Kar-wai: Film Poetics and the Aesthetic of Disturbance*, Hong Kong: Hong Kong University Press.

Beugnet, Martine (2007), *Cinema and Sensation: French Film and the Art of Transgression*, Edinburgh: Edinburgh University Press.

Bhabha, Homi K. (1994), *The Location of Culture*, London and New York: Routledge.

_____ (1996) 'Unsatisfied: Notes on Vernacular Cosmopolitanism', in: *Text and Nation: Cross-disciplinary Essays on Cultural and National Identities*, eds Laura Garcia-Morena and Peter C. Pfeifer, Columbia, SC: Camden House, pp. 191–207.

_____ (2008), 'Foreword to the 1986 Edition' of Frantz Fanon, *Black Skin, White Masks*, trans. Charles Lamm Markmann, London: Pluto Press, pp. xxi–xxxvii.

Bharathi, D. (2018), '*Partition: 1947* or *Viceroy's House* Banned in Pakistan: Six Reasons to Know', *Ajanta News*, 28 August, <https://ajantanews.com/2017/08/28/partition-1947-or-viceroys-house-banned-in-pakistan-6-reasons-to-know/> (last accessed 25 May 2018).

Bhaumik, Kaushik (2006), 'Consuming "Bollywood" in the Global Age: The Strange Case of an "Unfine" World Cinema', in: *Remapping World Cinema: Identity, Culture and Politics in Film*, eds Stephanie Dennison and Song Hwee Lim, London: Wallflower Press, pp. 188–98.

Bhutiani, Shubhashish and Sanjay Bhutiani (2017), 'Q & A', included in the DVD *Hotel Salvation* Bonus Materials.

Bhutto, Fatima (2017) 'Fatima Bhutto on Indian Partition Film *Viceroy's House*: "I Watched This Servile Pantomime and Wept"', *The Guardian*, 3 March, <https://www.theguardian.com/film/2017/mar/03/fatima-bhutto-viceroys-house-watched-servile-pantomime-and-wept> (last accessed 23 April 2018).

Birus, Hendrick (2004), 'Goethes Idee der Weltliteratur. Eine historische Vergangenheitsbewältigung', *Goethezeitportal*, 19 January, <https://core.ac.uk/download/pdf/14509431.pdf> (last accessed 25 March 2019).

Blanchard, Pascal, Nicolas Bancel, Gilles Boetsch, Eric Deroo, Sandrine Lemaire and Charles Forsdick (eds) (2008), *Human Zoos: Science and Spectacle in the Age of Colonial Empires*, trans. Teresa Bridgeman, Liverpool: Liverpool University Press.

Blum-Reid, Sylvie (2003), *East–West Encounters: Franco-Asian Cinema and Literature*, London and New York: Wallflower Press.

Boetsch, Gilles and Pascal Blanchard (2008), 'The Hottentot Venus: Birth of a Freak (1815)', in: *Human Zoos: Science and Spectacle in the Age of Colonial*

Empires, eds Pascal Blanchard, Nicolas Bancel, Gilles Boetsch, Eric Deroo, Sandrine Lemaire and Charles Forsdick, trans. Teresa Bridgeman, Liverpool: Liverpool University Press, pp. 61–72.

Bongie, Chris (1991), *Exotic Memories: Literature, Colonialism, and the Fin de Siècle*, Stanford, CA: Stanford University Press.

Boorstin, Daniel J. (1961), *The Image: A Guide to Pseudo-Events in America*, New York: Harper & Row.

Booth, Robert (2020), 'Britain More Nostalgic for Empire than Other Ex-colonial Powers', *The Guardian*, 11 March, <https://www.theguardian.com/world/2020/mar/11/uk-more-nostalgic-for-empire-than-other-ex-colonial-powers> (last accessed 25 April 2020).

Bordwell, David (1989), *Making Meaning: Inference and Rhetoric in the Interpretation of Cinema*, Cambridge, MA: Harvard University Press.

Bower, Anne L. (2004), 'Watching Food: The Production of Food, Film, and Values', in: *Reel Food: Essays on Food and Film*, ed. Anne L. Bower, New York and London: Routledge, pp. 1–13.

Boym, Svetlana (2001), *The Future of Nostalgia*, New York: Basic Books.

Bradshaw, Peter (2016), '*The Assassin* Review – Captivatingly Hypnotic, if Impenetrable, *Wuxia* Tale', *The Guardian*, 21 January, <https://www.theguardian.com/film/2016/jan/21/the-assassin-review-captivatingly-hypnotic-if-impenetrable-wuxia-tale> (last accessed 25 January 2022).

Brang, David and V. S. Ramachandran (2011), 'Survival of the Synaesthesia Gene: Why Do People Hear Colors and Taste Words?', *PLoS Biology*, 9: 11, <https://journals.plos.org/plosbiology/article?id=10.1371/journal.pbio.1001205> (last accessed 15 May 2022).

Bredin, Marian (2015), '"Who Were We? And What Happened to Us?" Inuit Memory and Arctic Futures in Igloolik Isuma Film and Video', in: *Films on Ice: Cinemas of the Arctic*, eds Scott MacKenzie and Anna Westerstahl Stenport, Edinburgh: Edinburgh University Press, pp. 33–44.

Brook, Vincent (2003), 'To Live and Dye in China: The Personal and the Political in Zhang Yimou's *Judou*', *CineAction*, 60, pp. 21–9.

Bruzzi, Stella (1997), *Undressing Cinema: Clothing and Identity in the Movies*, London: Routledge.

Buckmaster, Luke (2015), '*Tanna* Review: Volcanic South Pacific Love Story Shot Entirely in Vanuatu', *The Guardian*, 5 November, <www.theguardian.com/film/2015/nov/05/tanna-review-volcanic-south-pacific-love-story-vanuatu> (last accessed 12 May 2016).

Bukatman, Scott (2006), 'Spectacle, Attraction and Visual Pleasure', in: *The Cinema of Attractions Reloaded*, ed. Wanda Strauven, Amsterdam: Amsterdam University Press, pp. 71–82.

Burgyone, Robert (2014), 'Colour in the Epic Film: *Alexander* and *Hero*', in: *The Return of the Epic Film: Genre, Aesthetics and History in the Twenty-First Century*, Edinburgh: Edinburgh University Press, pp. 95–109.

Byron, Glennis (2013), 'Cannibal Culture: Serving the People in Fruit Chan's *Dumplings*', in: *Globalgothic*, ed. Glennis Byron, Manchester: Manchester University Press, pp. 133–43.

Campbell, Duncan (2001), 'On Top of the World', *The Guardian*, 17 August, <https://www.theguardian.com/film/2001/aug/17/artsfeatures3> (last accessed 2 June 2020).

Campbell-Stephens, Rosemary (2020), 'Global Majority: We Need to Talk About Labels such as BAME', <https://www.linkedin.com/pulse/global-majority-we-need-talk-labels-bame-campbell-stephens-mbe> (last accessed 1 July 2022).

Carbonell, Ovidio (1996), 'The Exotic Space of Cultural Translation', in: *Translation, Power, Subversion*, eds Român Rodrâiguez Alvarez and Carmen Africa Vidal, Clevedon: Multilingual Matters, pp. 79–98.

Carew, Anthony (2016), 'Art with the Right Ingredients: *An* and the Films of Naomi Kawase', *Metro*, 188, pp. 48–54.

Célestin, Roger (1996), *From Cannibals to Radicals: Figures and Limits of Exoticism*, Minneapolis and London: University of Minnesota Press.

Chan, Felicia (2017), *Cosmopolitan Cinema: Imagining the Cross-cultural in East Asian Film*, London: I. B. Tauris.

Chaudhuri, Shohini (2005), *Contemporary World Cinema: Europe, The Middle East, East Asia and South Asia*, Edinburgh: Edinburgh University Press.

—— (2009), 'Snake Charmers and Child Brides: Deepa Mehta's *Water*, "Exotic" Representation, and the Cross-cultural Spectatorship of South Asian Migrant Cinema', *South Asian Popular Culture*, 7: 1, pp. 7–20.

—— (2014), *Cinema of the Dark Side: Atrocity and the Ethics of Film Spectatorship*, Edinburgh: Edinburgh University Press.

Childs, Elizabeth C. (2013), *Vanishing Paradise: Art and Exoticism in Colonial Tahiti*, Berkeley: Berkely University Press.

Chiu, Lily V. (2005), 'Camille's Breasts: The Evolution of the Fantasy Native in Régis Wargnier's *Indochine*', in: *France and "Indochine": Cultural Representations*, eds Kathryn Robson and Jennifer Yee, Lanham, MD and Oxford: Lexington Books, pp. 139–52.

Chow, Rey (1993), 'A Souvenir of Love', *Modern Chinese Literature*, 7: 2, pp. 59–78.

—— (1995), *Primitive Passions: Visuality, Sexuality, Ethnography, and Contemporary Chinese Cinema*, New York: Columbia University Press.

—— (2002), 'Sentimental Returns: On the Uses of the Everyday in the Recent Films of Zhang Yimou and Wong Kar-Wai', *New Literary History*, 33: 4, pp. 639–54.

—— (2007), *Sentimental Fabulations, Contemporary Chinese Films: Attachment in the Age of Global Visibility*, New York: Columbia University Press.

Ciafone, Amanda (2017), 'The Third Age in the Third World: Outsourcing and Outrunning Old Age to *The Best Exotic Marigold Hotel*', in: *Care Home

Stories: Aging, Disability, and Long-Term Residential Care, eds Sally Chivers and Ulla Kriebernegg, Bielefeld: Transcript-Verlag, pp. 155–73.
Ciment, Michel (2003), 'The State of Cinema', Address at the 46th San Francisco International Film Festival, <https://unspokencinema.blogspot.com/2006/10/state-of-cinema-m-ciment.html> (last accessed 2 June 2022).
Clark, Hazel (2000), *The Cheongsam*, Oxford: Oxford University Press.
Clarke, Roger (2016), '*The Assassin*', *Sight & Sound*, February, p. 68.
Clifford, James (1988), *The Predicament of Culture: Twentieth-century Ethnography, Literature, and Art*, Cambridge, MA: Harvard University Press.
_____ (1989), 'The Others Beyond the "Salvage Paradigm"', *Third Text*, 3: 6, pp. 73–8.
_____ (1992), 'Traveling Cultures', in: *Cultural Studies*, eds Lawrence Grossberg, Cary Nelson and Paula A. Treichler, London: Routledge, pp. 96–116.
_____ (2013), *Returns: Becoming Indigenous in the Twenty-First Century*, Cambridge, MA: Harvard University Press.
Cohen, Robin and Steven Vertovec (2002), 'Introduction: Conceiving Cosmopolitanism', *Conceiving Cosmopolitanism: Theory, Context, and Practice*, eds Robin Cohen and Steven Vertovec, Oxford: Oxford University Press, pp. 1–22.
Columpar, Corinn (2010), *Unsettling Sights: The Fourth World on Film*, Carbondale: Southern Illinois University Press.
Connell, John (2003), 'Island Dreaming: The Contemplation of Polynesian Paradise', *Journal of Historical Geography*, 29: 4, pp. 554–81.
Conrad, Joseph (1988 [1899]), *Heart of Darkness*, ed. Robert Kimbrough, New York and London: W. W. Norton & Company.
Cook, Pam (2005), *Screening the Past: Memory and Nostalgia in Cinema*, London: Routledge.
Cooke, Paul (2016), 'From "Auschwitz-land" to Banglatown: Heritage Conflicts, Film and the Politics of Place', in: *Screening European Heritage: Creating and Consuming History on Film*, eds Paul Cooke and Rob Stone, London: Palgrave Macmillan, pp. 235–55.
Corbin, Amy (2014), 'Travelling Through Cinema Space: The Film Spectator as Tourist', *Continuum: Journal of Media and Cultural Studies*, 28: 3, pp. 314–29.
Córdova, Amalia (2012), 'Towards an Indigenous Film Festival Circuit', in: *Film Festival Yearbook 4: Film Festivals and Activism*, eds Dina Iordanova and Leshu Torchin, St Andrews: St Andrews Film Studies, pp. 63–80.
Costa, Antonio (2006), 'Landscape and Archive: Trips Around the World as Early Film Topic (1896–1914)', in: *Landscape and Film*, ed. Martin Lefebvre, New York: Routledge, pp. 246–66.
Cousins, Mark (2004), 'The Asian Aesthetic', *Prospect Magazine*, 21 November, <https://www.prospectmagazine.co.uk/essays/56626/the-asian-aesthetic> (last accessed 23 February 2019).

Cross, Alice (1994), 'Portraying the Rhythm of the Vietnamese Soul: An Interview with Tran Anh Hung', *Cineaste*, 20: 3, pp. 35–7.
Cytowic, Richard E. (2002), *Synesthesia: A Union of the Senses*, 2nd edition, Cambridge, MA: MIT Press.
Damrosch, David (2003), *What Is World Literature?* Princeton, NJ: Princeton University Press.
D'Anglure, Bernard Saladin (2002), 'An Ethnographic Commentary: The Legend of Atanarjuat, Inuit and Shamanism', in: *Atanarjuat, the Fast Runner: Inspired by a Traditional Inuit Legend of Igloolik*, eds Paul Apak Angilirq, Zacharias Kunuk, Herve Paniak, Pauloosie Quilitalik, Norman Cohn and Bernard Saladin D'Anglure, Toronto: Coach House Books and Isuma Publishing, pp. 197–227.
D'Argenio, Maria Chiara (2018), 'Decolonial Encounters in Chiro Guerra's *El abrazo de la serpiente*: Indigeneity, Coevalness and Intercultural Dialogue', *Postcolonial Studies*, 21: 2, pp. 131–53.
Dariotis, Wei Ming and Eileen Fung (1997), 'Breaking the Soy Sauce Jar: Diaspora and Displacement in the Films of Ang Lee', in: *Transnational Chinese Cinemas: Identity, Nationhood, Gender*, ed. Sheldon Hsiao-peng Lu, Honolulu: University of Hawaii Press, pp. 187–220.
Davis, Therese (2007), 'Remembering Our Ancestors: Cross-cultural Collaboration and the Mediation of Aboriginal Culture and History in *Ten Canoes* (Rolf de Heer, 2006)', *Studies in Australasian Cinema*, 1: 1, pp. 5–14.
De la Garza, Armida, Ruth Doughty and Deborah Shaw (eds) (2020), *Transnational Screens: Expanding the Borders of Transnational Cinema*, London: Routledge.
De Luca, Tiago (2013), *Realism of the Senses in World Cinema: The Experience of Physical Reality*, London: I. B. Tauris.
De Luca, Tiago and Nuno Barradas Jorge (2016), 'Introduction: From Slow Cinema to Slow Cinemas', in: *Slow Cinema*, eds Tiago de Luca and Nuno Barradas Jorge, Edinburgh: Edinburgh University Press, pp. 1–21.
Dennison, Stephanie and Song Hwee Lim (2006a), 'Situating World Cinema as a Theoretical Problem', in: *Remapping World Cinema: Identity, Culture and Politics in Film*, eds Stephanie Dennison and Song Hwee Lim, London and New York: Wallflower Press, pp. 1–15.
_____ (eds) (2006b), *Remapping World Cinema: Identity, Culture and Politics in Film*, London and New York: Wallflower Press.
Deppman, Hsiu-Chuang (2001), 'Recipes for a New Taiwanese Identity? Food, Space, and Sex in the Works of Ang Lee', *American Association for Chinese Studies*, 8: 2, pp. 145–68.
Deshpande, Shekhar and Meta Mazaj (2018), *World Cinema: A Critical Introduction*, London and New York: Routledge.
Dharwadker, Vinay (2011), 'Diaspora and Cosmopolitanism', in: *The Ashgate Research Companion to Cosmopolitanism*, eds Maria Rovisco and Magdalena Nowicka, Farnham: Ashgate, pp. 125–44.
Diderot, Denis (2017 [1772]), *Supplément au Voyage de Bougainville*, Paris: Librairie Générale Française.

Dika, Vera (2003), *Recycled Culture in Contemporary Art and Film: The Uses of Nostalgia*, Cambridge: Cambridge University Press.

Dilley, Whitney Crothers (2009), 'Globalisation and Cultural Identity in the Films of Ang Lee', *Style*, 43: 1, pp. 45–64.

Dirlik, Arif (1996), 'The Global in the Local', in: *Global/Local: Cultural Production and the Transnational Imaginary*, eds Rob Wilson and Wimal Dissanayake, Durham, NC and London: Duke University Press, pp. 21–45.

Du Bois, W. E. B. (1903), *The Souls of Black Folk*, <https://www.gutenberg.org/files/408/408-h/408-h.htm#chap01> (last accessed 3 April 2022).

Dudrah, Rajinder (2012), *Bollywood Travels: Culture, Diaspora and Border Crossings in Popular Hindi Cinema*, Abingdon: Routledge.

Dunks, Glenn (2016), 'Isle-cross'd Lovers. Vanuatu's *Tanna* and the South Pacific on Film', *Metro Magazine*, 188, pp. 24–9.

Ďurovičová, Nataša and Kathleen E. Newman (eds) (2010), *World Cinemas, Transnational Perspectives*, London and New York: Routledge.

Dwyer, Michael D. (2015), *Back to the Fifties: Nostalgia, Hollywood Film and Popular Music of the Seventies and Eighties*, Oxford: Oxford University Press.

Dwyer, Rachel (2002), 'Landschaft der Liebe', in: *Bollywood: Das indische Kino und die Schweiz*, ed. Alexandra Schneider, Zürich: Edition Museum für Gestaltung, pp. 97–104.

Dyer, Richard (1996), *The Matter of Images: Essays on Representation*, 2nd edition, London and New York: Routledge.

—— (1997), *White*, London: Routledge.

—— (2007), *Pastiche*, London: Routledge.

El-Enany, Nadine (2020), 'Europe's Colonial Embrace and the Brexit Nostalgia for Empire Are Two Sides of the Same Coin', <https://blogs.lse.ac.uk/brexit/2020/04/29/europes-colonial-embrace-and-brexit-as-nostalgia-for-empire-are-part-of-the-same-story/> (last accessed 22 June 2021).

Elsaesser, Thomas (2005), *European Cinema: Face to Face with Hollywood*, Amsterdam: Amsterdam University Press.

—— (2009), 'World Cinema: Realism, Evidence, Presence', in: *Realism and the Audiovisual Media*, eds Lúcia Nagib and Cecilia Mello, Basingstoke: Palgrave Macmillan, pp. 3–19.

Embrace of the Serpent Press Kit, <http://press.peccapics.co.uk/Theatrical/Embrace%20Of%20The%20Serpent/Embrace%20of%20the%20Serpent%20Press%20Notes.pdf> (last accessed 15 August 2016; no longer valid).

Evans, Michael Robert (2010), *The Fast Runner: Filming the Legend of Atanarjuat*, Lincoln, NE and London: University of Nebraska Press.

Ezra, Elizabeth and Terry Rowden (eds) (2006), *Transnational Cinema: The Film Reader*, London: Routledge.

Fabian, Johannes (1983), *Time and the Other: How Anthropology Makes Its Object*, New York: Columbia University Press.

Fanon, Frantz (2008), *Black Skin, White Masks*, trans. Charles Lamm Markmann, London: Pluto Press.
Farley, David (2020), 'The Travel Ache You Can't Translate', *BBC Travel*, 24 March, <https://www.bbc.com/travel/article/20200323-the-travel-ache-you-cant-translate> (last accessed 25 March 2021).
Farquhar, Mary (2002), 'Zhang Yimou', *Senses of Cinema*, 20, May, <https://www.sensesofcinema.com/2002/great-directors/zhang/> (last accessed 20 April 2022).
Fee, Margery (1995), 'Who Can Write as Other?', in: *The Postcolonial Studies Reader*, eds Bill Ashcroft, Gareth Griffiths and Helen Tiffin, 2nd edition, London: Routledge, pp. 169–71.
Ferguson, Priscilla Parkhurst (2011), 'The Senses of Taste', *The American Historical Review*, 116: 2, pp. 371–84.
Fillitz, Thomas and A. Jamie Saris (2012), 'Authenticity Aujourd'hui', in: *Debating Authenticity: Concepts of Modernity in Anthropological Perspective*, eds Thomas Fillitz and A. Jamie Saris, Oxford and New York: Berghahn Books, pp. 1–24.
Fine, Robert and Robin Cohen (2002), 'Four Cosmopolitan Moments', in: *Conceiving Cosmopolitanism: Theory, Context, and Practice*, eds Robin Cohen and Steven Vertovec, Oxford: Oxford University Press, pp. 137–62.
Flanagan, Matthew (2008), 'Towards an Aesthetic of Slow in Contemporary Cinema', 16: 9, <http://www.16-9.dk/2008-11/side11_inenglish.htm> (last accessed 25 April 2022).
Flath, James (2004a), *The Cult of Happiness: Nianhua, Art and History in Rural China*, Vancouver: University of British Columbia Press and Seattle: Washington University Press.
_____ (2004b), '"It's a Wonderful Life": "Nianhua" and "Yuefenpai" at the Dawn of the People's Republic', *Modern Chinese Literature*, 16: 2, pp. 123–59.
Forsdick, Charles (2000), *Victor Segalen and the Aesthetics of Diversity: Journeys Between Cultures*, Oxford: Oxford University Press.
_____ (2001), 'Travelling Concepts: Postcolonial Approaches to Exoticism', *Paragraph*, 24: 3, pp. 12–29.
_____ (2003), 'Revisiting Exoticism: From Colonialism to Postcolonialism', in: *Francophone Postcolonial Studies: A Critical Introduction*, eds Charles Forsdick and David Murphy, London: Arnold, pp. 46–55.
_____ (2007), 'Exoticism', in: *Encyclopaedia of Erotic Literature*, eds Gaëtan Brulotte and John Phillips, New York: Routledge, pp. 440–2.
Forsdick, Charles and David Murphy (2003), 'Introduction: The Case for Francophone Postcolonial Studies', in: *Francophone Postcolonial Studies: A Critical Introduction*, eds Charles Forsdick and David Murphy, London: Arnold, pp. 1–14.
Foster, Karen Polinger (2020), *Strange and Wonderful: Exotic Flora and Fauna in Image and Imagination*, Oxford: Oxford University Press.

Foster, Stephen William (1982), 'The Exotic as Symbolic System', *Dialectical Anthropology*, 7: 1, pp. 21–30.
Friedberg, Anne (1993), *Window Shopping: Cinema and the Postmodern*, Berkeley: University of California Press.
Fusco, Coco (2012), '"There Is No Entirely Non-Western Place Left": De-Westernizing the Moving Image, an Interview with Coco Fusco', in: *De-Westernizing Film Studies*, eds Saër Maty Bâ and Will Higbee, Abingdon: Routledge, pp. 181–92.
Gabaccia, Donna R. (1998), *We Are What We Eat: Ethnic Food and the Making of Americans*, Cambridge, MA: Harvard University Press.
Gabriel, Teshome H. (1982), *Third Cinema in the Third World: The Aesthetics of Liberation*, Ann Arbor, MI: University of Michigan Research Press.
Galt, Rosalind (2011), *Pretty: Film and the Decorative Image*, New York: Columbia University Press.
Galt, Rosalind and Karl Schoonover (2010), 'Introduction: The Impurity of Art Cinema', in: *Global Art Cinema: New Theories and Histories*, eds Rosalind Galt and Karl Schoonover, Oxford: Oxford University Press, pp. 3–27.
Gao, Sally (2017), 'The Importance of Yin-Yang Philosophy in Chinese Food', *Culture Trip*, 23 January, <https://theculturetrip.com/asia/china/articles/the-importance-of-yin-yang-philosophy-in-chinese-cooking/> (last accessed 5 September 2021).
Geiger, Jeffrey (2005), 'Nanook of the North', in: *Film Analysis: A Norton Reader*, eds Jeffrey Geiger and R. L. Rutsky, New York: W. W. Norton & Co., pp. 118–37.
Giddens, Anthony (2002), *Runaway World: How Globalisation is Reshaping Our Lives*, 2nd edition, London: Profile.
Gilbert, Elizabeth (2006), *Eat Pray Love: One Woman's Search for Everything across Italy, India and Indonesia*, New York: Viking.
Gilman, Sander (1985), *Difference and Pathology: Stereotypes of Sexuality, Race and Madness*, Ithaca and London: Cornell University Press.
Gilroy, Paul (2004), *After Empire: Melancholia or Convivial Culture?* London: Routledge.
Ginneken, Jaap van (2007), *Screening Difference: How Hollywood's Blockbuster Films Imagine Race, Ethnicity and Culture*, Lanham, ML: Rowman & Littlefied.
Ginsburg, Faye (1995), 'Parallax Effect: The Impact of Indigenous Media on Ethnographic Film', *Visual Anthropology Review*, 11: 2, pp. 64–76.
────── (2003), '*Atanarjuat* Off-Screen: From "Media Reservations" to the World Stage', *American Anthropologist*, 105: 4, pp. 827–31.
Gopalan, Lalitha (2002), *Cinema of Interruptions: Action Genres in Contemporary Indian Cinema*, London: BFI Publishing.
Greenblatt, Stephen (1990), 'Stated Meeting Report: Resonance and Wonder', *Bulletin of the American Academy of Arts and Sciences*, 43: 4, pp. 11–34.
Griffiths, Alison (2002), *Wondrous Difference: Cinema, Anthropology, and Turn-of-the-century Visual Culture*, New York: Columbia University Press.

Griffiths, Gareth (1994), 'The Myth of Authenticity', in: *De-scribing Empire: Postcolonialism and Textuality*, eds Chris Tiffin and Alan Lawson, London: Routledge, pp. 70–85.

Grijp, Paul van der (2009), *Art and Exoticism: An Anthropology of the Yearning for Authenticity*, Berlin: Lit Verlag.

———— (2012), 'A Cultural Search for Authenticity: Questioning Primitivism and Exotic Art', in: *Debating Authenticity: Concepts of Modernity in Anthropological Perspective*, eds Thomas Fillitz and A. Jamie Saris, Oxford and New York: Berghahn Books, pp. 128–44.

Guillén, Michael (2016), '*Embrace of the Serpent*: An interview with Ciro Guerra', *Cineaste*, 41: 2, <www.cineaste.com/spring2016/embrace-of-the-serpent-ciro-guerra/> (last accessed 25 May 2016).

Gunning, Tom (2006), '"The Whole World Within Reach": Travel Images without Borders', in: *Virtual Voyages: Cinema and Travel*, ed. Jeffrey Ruoff, Durham, NC and London: Duke University Press, pp. 25–41.

———— (2010), 'Landscape and the Fantasy of Moving Pictures: Early Cinema's Phantom Rides', in: *Cinema and Landscape*, eds Graeme Harper and Jonathan Rayner, Bristol and Chicago: Intellect, pp. 31–70.

———— (2011), 'The Cinema of Attractions: Early Film, its Spectator and the Avant-Garde', in: *Critical Visions in Film Theory: Classic and Contemporary Readings*, Timothy Corrigan, Patricia White, with Meta Mazaj, Boston: Bedford/St Martins, pp. 69–76.

Hall, Sheldon and Steve Neale (2010), *Epics, Spectacle and Blockbusters*, Detroit: Wayne State University Press.

Hall, Stuart (1997), 'The Spectacle of the "Other"', in: *Representation: Cultural Representations and Signifying Practices*, ed. Stuart Hall, Milton Keynes: Open University Press, pp. 223–90.

Halle, Randall (2010), 'Offering Tales They Want to Hear: Transnational European Film Funding as Neo-Orientalism', in: *Global Art Cinema*, eds Rosalind Galt and Karl Schoonover, Oxford: Oxford University Press, pp. 303–19.

———— (2014), *The Europeanization of Cinema: Interzones and Imaginative Communities*, Urbana, IL: University of Illinois Press.

———— (2021), *Visual Alterity: Seeing Difference in Cinema*, Urbana, Chicago and Springfield: University of Illinois Press.

Hannerz, Ulf (1996), *Transnational Connections: Culture, People, Places*, London and New York: Routledge.

Harootunian, Harry (2002), 'Foreword: The Exotics of Nowhere', in: Victor Segalen, *Essay on Exoticism: An Aesthetics of Diversity*, trans. and ed. Yaël Rachel Schlick, Durham, NC and London: Duke University Press, pp. vii–xx.

Hartley, Julia Caterina, Wanrug Suwanwattana and Jennifer Yee (eds) (2022), *French Decadence in a Global Context: Colonialism and Exoticism*, Liverpool: Liverpool University Press.

Hartley, Leslie Poles (1953), *The Go-between*, London: Hamish Hamilton and The Book Society.

Hediger, Vinzenz and Alexandra Schneider (2005), 'The Deferral of Smell: Cinema, Modernity, and the Reconfiguration of the Olfactory Experience', in: *The Five Senses of Cinema*, eds Alice Autelitano, Valentina Re and Veronica Innocenti, Undine: Forum, pp. 241–64.

Held, David (2011), 'Cosmopolitanism, Democracy and the Global Order', in: *The Ashgate Research Companion to Cosmopolitanism*, eds Maria Rovisco and Magdalena Nowicka, Farnham: Ashgate, pp. 163–77.

Heldke, Lisa (2003), *Exotic Appetites: Ruminations of a Food Adventurer*, New York and London: Routledge.

Hertweck, Tom (ed.) (2015), *Food on Film: Bringing Something New to the Table*, Lanham and Boulder: Rowman & Littlefield.

Heung, Maria (1997), 'The Family Romance of Orientalism: From *Madame Butterfly* to *Indochine*', in: *Visions of the East: Orientalism in Film*, eds Matthew Bernstein and Gaylyn Studlar, New Brunswick, NJ: Rutgers University Press, pp. 158–83.

Higbee, Will and Song Hwee Lim (2010), 'Concepts of Transnational Cinema: Towards a Critical Transnationalism in Film Studies', *Transnational Cinemas*, 1: 1, pp. 7–21.

Hill, John, Pamela Church Gibson, Richard Dyer, E. Ann Kaplan and Paul Willemen (eds) (2000), *World Cinema: Critical Approaches*, Oxford: Oxford University Press.

Hillenbrand, Margaret (2012), 'Chromatic Expressionism in Contemporary Chinese Language Cinema', *Journal of Chinese Cinemas*, 6: 3, pp. 211–32.

Hinrichsen, Malte (2012), *Racist Trademarks: Slavery, Orient, Colonialism and Commodity Culture*, Münster: LIT Verlag, pp. 63–5.

Hirsch, Marianne (1997) *Family Frames: Photography, Narrative, and Postmemory*, Cambridge, MA and London: Harvard University Press.

Hjort, Mette (2010), 'On the Plurality of Cinema Transnationalism', in: *World Cinemas, Transnational Perspectives*, eds Nataša Ďurovičová and Kathleen E. Newman, London and New York: Routledge, pp. 12–33.

Hobson, Janell (2018), *Venus in the Dark: Blackness and Beauty in Popular Culture*, 2nd edition, London and New York: Routledge.

hooks, bell (2015), *Black Looks: Race and Representation*, New York: Routledge.

Hopgood, Fincina (2006), 'The Politics of Melodrama in Deepa Mehta's *Water*', *Metro*, 149, pp. 142–7.

Huggan, Graham (2001), *The Postcolonial Exotic: Marketing the Margins*, London and New York: Routledge.

Huhndorf, Shari (2003), '*Atanarjuat, The Fast Runner*: Culture, History, and Politics in Inuit Media', *American Anthropologist*, 105: 4, pp. 822–5.

Hung, Chiang-Tai (2000), 'Repainting China: New Year Prints (Nianhua) and Peasant Resistance in the Early Years of the People's Republic', *Comparative Studies in Society and History*, 42: 4, pp. 770–810.

Hunt, Leon and Leung Wing-Fai (eds) (2008), *East Asian Cinemas: Exploring Transnational Connections on Film*, London: I. B. Tauris.

Huppatz, Daniel J. (2009), 'Designer Nostalgia in Hong Kong', *Design Issues*, 25: 2, pp. 14–28.

Hutcheon, Linda (2009), 'Irony, Nostalgia, and the Postmodern', in: *The History on Film Reader*, ed. Marnie Hughes-Warrington, London and New York: Routledge, pp. 249–59.

Huyssen, Andreas (2006), 'Nostalgia for Ruins', *Grey Room*, 23, pp. 6–21.

Ide, Wendy (2015), '*The Assassin*', *The Times*, 22 May, <https://www.thetimes.co.uk/article/the-assassin-p2nlwff3bsn> (last accessed 20 August 2021).

Irani, Rashid (2018), 'Expect to Be Bored and Confused: *Viceroy's House* Review by Rashid Irani', *Hindustani Times*, 22 May, <https://www.hindustantimes.com/movie-reviews/expect-to-be-bored-and-confused-viceroy-s-house-review-by-rashid-irani/story-Auszwe7Y8PuUZhIeF5tTLK.html> (last accessed 3 June 2018).

Ives, Mike (2019), 'Mungau Dain, Villager Star in Pacific Island Film, Dies at 24', *The New York Times*, 10 January, <https://www.nytimes.com/2019/01/10/obituaries/mungau-dain-dead.html> (last accessed 15 March 2020).

Jameson, Fredric (1991), *Postmodernism or, the Cultural Logic of Late Capitalism*, Durham NC: Duke University Press.

Jay, Martin and Sumathi Ramaswamy (eds) (2014), *Empires of Vision: A Reader*, Durham, NC and London: Duke University Press.

Jeffries, Stuart (2015), 'The Best Exotic Nostalgia Boom: Why Colonial Style is Back', *The Guardian*, 19 March, <https://www.theguardian.com/culture/2015/mar/19/the-best-exotic-nostalgia-boom-why-colonial-style-is-back> (last accessed 4 August 2018).

Jones, Jonathan (2021), '"Paradise Exists!" Sebastião Salgado's Stunning Voyage into Amazônia', *The Guardian*, 21 June, <https://www.theguardian.com/artanddesign/2021/jun/21/paradise-exists-sebastiao-salgados-stunning-voyage-into-amazonia> (last accessed 23 June 2021).

Joyce, Hester (2009), 'Out from Nowhere: Pakeha Anxieties in *Ngati* (Barclay, 1987), *Once Were Warriors* (Tamahori, 1994) and *Whale Rider* (Caro, 2002)', *Studies in Australasian Cinema*, 3: 3, pp. 239–50.

Kaldis, Nick (2005), 'Compulsory Orientalism: Hou Hsiao-Hsien's *Flowers of Shanghai*', in: *Island on the Edge: Tawain New Cinema and After*, eds Chris Berry and Fei Lu Lu, Hong Kong: Hong Kong University Press, pp. 127–36.

Kamble, Jayashree (2015), 'All Work or All Play? Consumption, Leisure, and Ethics Under Globalization in *Zingdagi Na Milegi Dobara*', *South Asian Popular Culture*, 31: 1, pp. 1–14.

Kang, Inkoo (2017), '*Viceroy's House* Review: Whites are Burdened, Indians Contrived in Colonial Drama', *The Wrap*, 30 August, <https://www.thewrap.com/viceroys-house-review-manish-dayal-gillian-anderson/> (last accessed 15 May 2018).

Kapferer, Bruce (2013), 'How Anthropologists Think: Configurations of the Exotic', *Journal of the Royal Anthropological Institute*, 19: 4, pp. 813–36.

Kapferer, Bruce and Dimitrios Theodossopoulos (eds) (2016), *Against Exoticism: Towards a Transcendence of Relativism and Universalism in Anthropology*, Oxford and New York: Berghahn Books.
Kaplan, E. Ann (1997a), *Looking for the Other: Feminism, Film and the Imperial Gaze*, New York and London: Routledge.
―――― (1997b), 'Reading Formations and Chen Kaige's *Farewell My Concubine*', in: *Transnational Chinese Cinemas: Identity, Nationhood, Gender*, ed. Sheldon Hsiao-peng Lu, Honolulu: University of Hawaii Press, pp. 265–75.
Keller, James R. (2006), *Food, Film and Culture: A Genre Study*, Jefferson, NC: McFarland.
Kempley, Rita (1993), '*Indochine*', *The Washington Post*, 5 February, <https://www.washingtonpost.com/wp-srv/style/longterm/movies/videos/indochinepg13kempley_a0a35d.htm> (30 March 2022).
Kennedy, Harlan (1985), 'The Brits Have Gone Nuts', *Film Comment*, 21: 4, pp. 51–5.
Khoo, Olivia (2007), *The Chinese Exotic: Modern Diasporic Femininity*, Hong Kong: Hong Kong University Press.
Kiang, Jessica (2019), 'Film Review: *To the Ends of the Earth*', *Variety*, 15 October, <https://variety.com/2019/film/reviews/to-the-ends-of-the-earth-review-1203365770/> (last accessed 6 May 2021).
Kilgour, Maggie (1990), *From Communion to Cannibalism: An Anatomy of Metaphors of Incorporation*, Princeton, NJ: Princeton University Press.
King, Homay (2010), *Lost in Translation: Orientalism, Cinema, and the Enigmatic Signifier*, Durham, NC and London: Duke University Press.
Kirby, Lynne (1997), *Parallel Tracks: The Railroad and Silent Cinema*, Exeter: Exeter University Press.
Knellwolf, Christa and Iain McCalman (2002), 'Introduction', *Eigtheenth-Century Life*, Special Issue 'Exoticism and the Culture of Exploration', 26: 3, pp. 1–9.
Knopf, Kerstin (2008), *Decolonizing the Lens of Power: Indigenous Films in North America*, Amsterdam and New York: Rodopi.
Koepnick, Lutz (2002), 'Reframing the Past: Heritage Cinema and the Holocaust in the 1990s', *New German Critique*, 87, pp. 47–82.
Kracauer, Siegfried (1995), *The Mass Ornament: Weimar Essays*, Cambridge, MA: Harvard University Press.
Kristeva, Julia (1982), *Powers of Horror: An Essay on Abjection*, trans. Leon S. Roudiez, New York: Columbia University Press.
Krupat, Arnold (2007), '*Atanarjuat the Fast Runner* and Its Audiences', *Critical Inquiry*, 33: 3, pp. 606–31.
Kumar, Ranjit (2011), 'The Theory of Pleasure-Pauses: Making Sense of Interruptions in Indian Film Narrative', *Journal of Creative Communications*, 6: 1–2, pp. 35–48.
Lai, Linda Chiu-han (2001), 'Film and Enigmatization: Nostalgia, Nonsense, and Remembering', in: *At Full Speed: Hong Kong Cinema in a Borderless World*,

ed. Ching-Mei Esther Yau, Minneapolis: University of Minnesota Press, pp. 232–50.

Laine, Tarja (2005), 'Family Matters in *Eat Drink Man Woman*: Food Envy, Family Longing, or Intercultural Knowledge through the Senses?', in: *Shooting the Family: Transnational Media and Intercultural Values*, eds Patricia Pisters and Wim Staat, Amsterdam: Amsterdam University Press, pp. 103–14.

Laine, Tarja and Wanda Strauven (2009), 'Introduction: The Synaesthetic Turn', *New Review of Film and Television Studies*, 7: 3, pp. 249–55.

Lam, Adam (2005), 'Nostalgia and Dissatisfaction: Reading Zhang Yimou's *The Road Home* and *Not One Less* as Postmodern Texts', in: *Asian Futures, Asian Traditions*, ed. Edwina Palmer, Leiden and Boston: Brill, pp. 401–18.

Larsen, Jonas (2008), 'De-exoticizing Tourist Travel: Everyday Life and Sociality on the Move', *Leisure Studies*, 27: 1, pp. 21–34.

Lee, Christina (ed.) (2008), *Violating Time: History, Memory and Nostalgia in Cinema*, New York: Continuum.

Lee, Vivian P. Y. (2009), *Hong Kong Cinema Since 1997: The Post-Nostalgic Imagination*, Basingstoke: Palgrave Macmillan.

Leitch, Alison (2012), 'Slow Food and the Politics of "Virtuous Globalization"' in: *Food and Culture: A Reader*, eds Carole Counihan, Penny Van Esterik and Alice Julier, London: Routledge, pp. 409–25.

Leotta, Alfio (2011), *Touring the Screen: Tourism and New Zealand Film Geographies*, Bristol: Intellect.

Lévi-Strauss, Claude (2011 [1955]), *Tristes Tropiques*, trans. John and Doreen Weightman, London: Penguin Classics.

Levy, Daniel and Natan Sznaider (2011), 'Cosmopolitan Memory and Human Rights', in: *The Ashgate Research Companion to Cosmopolitanism*, eds Maria Rovisco and Magdalena Nowicka, Farnham: Ashgate, pp. 195–209.

Lewis, Simon (2014), 'What is Spectacle?', *Journal of Popular Film and Television*, 42: 4, pp. 214–21.

Lim, Song Hwee (2011), 'Transnational Trajectories in Contemporary East Asian Cinemas', in: *East Asian Cinemas: Regional Flows and Global Transformations*, ed. Vivian P. Y. Lee, Basingstoke: Palgrave, pp. 15–32.

—— (2014), *Tsai Ming-liang and a Cinema of Slowness*, Honolulu: University of Hawaii Press.

—— (2021), 'Re-orienting Screen Studies: A Preliminary Reflection', Keynote at the Screen Studies Conference 2021.

Lindenbaum, Shirley (2004), 'Thinking about Cannibalism', *Annual Review of Anthropology*, 33, pp. 475–98.

Lindenfeld, Laura and Fabio Parasecoli (2017), *Feasting Our Eyes: Food Film and Cultural Identity in the United States*, New York: Columbia University Press.

Lindstrom, Lamont (2015), 'Award-winning Film *Tanna* sets Romeo and Julia in the South Pacific', *The Conversation*, 5 November, <https://theconversation.com/award-winning-film-tanna-sets-romeo-and-juliet-in-the-south-pacific-49874> (last accessed 1 July 2020).

Locke, Ralph P. (2009), *Musical Exoticism: Images and Reflections*, Cambridge: Cambridge University Press.
Loti, Pierre (1887), *Madame Chrysanthème*, Paris: Calmann-Lévy.
Lu, Sheldon Hsiao-peng (1997a), 'Chinese Cinemas (1896–1996) and Transnational Film Studies', in: *Transnational Chinese Cinemas: Identity, Nationhood, Gender*, ed. Sheldon Hsiao-peng Lu, Honolulu: University of Hawaii Press, pp. 1–31.
―――― (1997b), 'National Cinema, Cultural Critique, Transnational Capital: The Films of Zhang Yimou', in: *Transnational Chinese Cinemas: Identity, Nationhood, Gender*, ed. Sheldon Hsiao-peng Lu, Honolulu: University of Hawaii Press, pp. 105–36.
―――― (2005), 'History, Memory, Nostalgia: Rewriting Socialism in Chinese Cinema and Television Drama', *Asian Cinema*, 16: 2, pp. 2–22.
Lu, Sheldon (2016), 'Space, Mobility, Modernity: The Figure of the Prostitute in Chinese-language Cinema', *Asian Cinema*, 27: 1, pp. 85–99.
Lu, Tonglin (2010), '*Dumplings* – New Diary of a Madam in Post-Mao Global Capitalism', *China Review*, 10: 2, pp. 177–200.
Lu, Xun (1990 [1918]), *Diary of a Madman and Other Stories*, Honolulu: University of Hawaii Press.
Lupton, Deborah (2005), 'Food and Emotion', in: *The Taste Culture Reader: Experiencing Food and Drink*, ed. Carolyn Korsmeyer, Oxford: Berg, pp. 317–24.
Lutz, Catherine A. and Jane L. Collins (1993), *Reading National Geographic*, Chicago and London: University of Chicago Press.
Ma, Sheng-mei (1996), 'Ang Lee's Domestic Tragicomedy: Immigrant Nostalgia, Exotic/Ethnic Tour, Global Market', *Journal of Popular Culture*, 30: 1, pp. 191–201.
MacCannell, Dean (1973), 'Staged Authenticity: Arrangements of Social Space in Tourist Settings', *American Journal of Sociology*, 79: 3, pp. 589–603.
―――― (2013), *The Tourist: A New Theory of the Leisure Class*, Berkeley: University of California Press.
MacKenzie, Scott and Anna Westerstahl Stenport (2015), 'Introduction: What Are Arctic Cinemas?', in: *Films on Ice: Cinemas of the Arctic*, eds Scott MacKenzie and Anna Westerstahl Stenport, Edinburgh: Edinburgh University Press, pp. 1–32.
Majer, Michele (2009/10), '*La Mode à la girafe*: Fashion, Culture, and Politics in Bourbon Restoration France', *Studies in the Decorative Arts*, 17: 1, pp. 123–61.
Manuel, George and Michael Posluns (1974), *The Fourth World: An Indian Reality*, New York: Free Press.
Marchetti, Gina (1993), *Romance and the "Yellow Peril": Race, Sex, and Discursive Strategies in Hollywood Fiction*, Berkeley: University of California Press.
Marks, Laura U. (2000), *The Skin of the Film: Intercultural Cinema, Embodiment, and the Senses*, Durham, NC: Duke University Press.

_____ (2006), 'Asphalt Nomadism: The New Desert in Arab Independent Cinema', in: *Landscape and Cinema*, ed. Martin Lefebvre, New York and London: Routledge, pp. 125–47.

Mason, Peter (1998), *Infelicities: Representations of the Exotic*, Baltimore and London: The John Hopkins University Press.

Masukor, Sarinah (2015), 'Old Recipe, New Flavour: Ritesh Batra's *The Lunchbox*', *Metro*, 183, pp. 70–3.

Matthews, Peter (2002), '*Atanarjuat: The Fast Runner*', *Sight & Sound*, 12: 3, pp. 35–6.

McCarthy, Todd (1996), '*Kama Sutra: A Tale of Love*', *Variety*, 21 October, <https://variety.com/1996/film/reviews/kama-sutra-a-tale-of-love-1200447209/> (last accessed 1 August 2022).

McClintock, Anne (1995), *Imperial Leather: Race, Gender and Sexuality in the Colonial Context*, New York and London: Routledge.

Meeuf, Russell (2007), 'Critical Localism, Ethical Cosmopolitanism and *Atanarjuat*', *Third Text*, 21: 6, pp. 733–44.

Mendes, Ana Christina (2010), 'Showcasing India Unshining: Film Tourism in Danny Boyle's *Slumdog Millionaire*', *Third Text*, 24: 4, pp. 471–9.

Meng, Jing (2020), *Fragmented Memories and Screening Nostalgia for the Cultural Revolution*, Hong Kong: Hong Kong University Press.

Mignolo, Walter D. (2011), 'Border Thinking, Decolonial Cosmopolitanism and Dialogues among Civilizations', in: *The Ashgate Research Companion to Cosmopolitanism*, eds Maria Rovisco and Magdalena Nowicka, Farnham: Ashgate, pp. 329–47.

Mishra, Vijay (2002), *Bollywood Cinema: Temples of Desire*, London and New York: Routledge.

Montaigne, Michel de (1877), *Essays of Michel de Montaigne*, trans. Charles Cotton, ed. William Carew Hazlitt, <https://www.gutenberg.org/files/3600/3600-h/3600-h.htm> (last accessed 2 September 2019).

Monteiro, Stephen (2014), 'Back to Bollystan: Imagined Space and Diasporic Identity in Contemporary Hindi Cinema', *Quarterly Review of Film and Video*, 31: 5, pp. 435–51.

Morcom, Anna (2015), 'How A. R. Rahman Brought Bollywood Soundtracks to the Western World', *The Conversation*, 14 August, <https://theconversation.com/how-a-r-rahman-brought-bollywood-soundtracks-to-the-western-world-44857> (last accessed 7 August 2020).

Mu, Aili (2003), 'Imaginary Constructs as Instruments of Critical Engagement: *Titanic* Reference in Zhang Yimou's *The Road Home*', *Asian Cinema*, 14: 2, pp. 35–54.

Muir, John Kenneth (2006), *Mercy in Her Eyes: The Films of Mira Nair*, New York: Applause.

Muldoon, James (2019), 'Academics, It's Time to Get Behind Decolonising the Curriculum', *The Guardian*, 20 March, <https://www.theguardian.com/education/2019/mar/20/academics-its-time-to-get-behind-decolonising-the-curriculum> (last accessed 15 August 2022).

Mulvey, James, Laura Rascaroli and Humberto Saldanha (2017), 'For a Cosmopolitan Cinema', *Alphaville: Journal of Film and Screen Media*, 14, pp. 1–15.

Mulvey, Laura (1975), 'Visual Pleasure and Narrative Cinema', *Screen*, 16: 3, pp. 6–18.

Naficy, Hamid (2001), *An Accented Cinema: Exilic and Diasporic Filmmaking*, Princeton and Oxford: Princeton University Press.

Naficy, Hamid and Teshome H. Gabriel (eds) (1993), *Otherness and the Media: The Ethnography of the Imagined and the Imaged*, Philadelphia and Reading: Harwood Academic.

Nagib, Lúcia (2006), 'Towards a Positive Definition of World Cinema', in: *Remapping World Cinema: Identity, Culture and Politics in Film*, eds Stephanie Dennison and Song Hwee Lim, London and New York: Wallflower Press, pp. 30–7.

_____ (2011), *World Cinema and the Ethics of Realism*, London and New York: Continuum.

_____ (2020), *Realist Cinema as World Cinema: Non-Cinema, Intermedial Passages, Total Cinema*, Amsterdam: Amsterdam University Press.

Nagib, Lúcia, Chris Perriam and Rajinder Dudrah (2012), 'Introduction', in: *Theorizing World Cinema*, eds Lúcia Nagib, Chris Perriam and Rajinder Dudrah, London and New York: I. B. Tauris, pp. xvii–xxii.

Nathan, Archana (2018), 'In Japan, Varanasi-set Film *Mukti Bhawan*, Starring Adil Hussain Is Winning Hearts', *Scroll.in*, 8 December, <https://scroll.in/reel/904769/varanasi-set-film-mukti-bhawan-starring-adil-hussain-is-winning-hearts-in-japan> (last accessed 12 April 2021).

Nava, Mica (2007), *Visceral Cosmopolitanism: Gender, Culture and the Normalisation of Difference*, Oxford: Berg.

Neale, Steve (2002), 'Colour and Film Aesthetics', in: *The Film Cultures Reader*, ed. Graeme Turner, London and New York: Routledge, pp. 85–94.

Nederveen Pieterse, Jan (2015), *Globalization and Culture: Global Mélange*, 3rd edition, Lanham, ML: Rowman & Littlefied.

Negra, Diane (2001), 'Romance and/as Tourism: Heritage Whiteness and the (Inter)national Imaginary in the New Woman's Film', in: *Keyframes: Popular Cinema and Cultural Studies*, eds Matthew Tinkcom and Amy Villarejo, London and New York: Routledge, pp. 82–97.

_____ (2002), 'Ethnic Food Fetishism, Whiteness, and Nostalgia in Recent Film and Television', *The Velvet Light Trap*, 50, pp. 62–76.

Nesselson, Lisa (2001), '*Atanarjuat: The Fast Runner*', *Variety*, May 14, <https://variety.com/2001/film/awards/atanarjuat-the-fast-runner-1200468334/> (last accessed 6 April 2020).

Ngai, Sianne (2012), *Our Aesthetic Categories: Zany, Cute, Interesting*, Cambridge, MA and London: Harvard University Press.

Nichols, Bill (1994), 'Discovering Form, Inferring Meaning: New Cinemas and the Film Festival Circuit', *Film Quarterly* 47: 3, pp. 16–30.

Noble, Jonathan (2000), '*Titantic* in China: Transnational Capitalism as Official Ideology?', *Modern Chinese Literature and Culture*, 12: 1, pp. 164–98.

Norindr, Panivong (1996), *Phantasmatic Indochina: French Colonial Ideology in Architecture, Film and Literature*, Durham, NC: Duke University Press.

Nowell-Smith, Geoffrey (ed.) (1996), *The Oxford History of World Cinema*, Oxford: Oxford University Press.

Pang, Laikwan (2012), 'Colour and Utopia: The Filmic Portrayal of Harvest in Late Cultural Revolution Narrative Films', *Journal of Chinese Cinemas*, 6: 3, pp. 263–82.

Papastergiadis, Nikos (2011), 'Cultural Translation, Cosmopolitanism and The Void', *Translation Studies*, 4: 1, pp. 1–20.

Parker, Ol and Deborah Moggach (2009), *The Best Exotic Margigold Hotel*. Based on the Book *These Foolish Things* by Deborah Moggach, London: Blueprint Pictures, 22 June.

Petrini, Carlo (2003), *Slow Food: The Case for Taste*, trans. William McCuaig, New York: Columbia University Press.

Polan, Dana B. (1982–83), '"Above All Else to Make You See": Cinema and the Ideology of Spectacle', *boundary 2*, 11: 1–2, pp. 129–44.

Ponzanesi, Sandra (2014), *The Postcolonial Cultural Industry: Icons, Markets, Mythologies*, Basingstoke: Palgrave Macmillan.

Porter, Roy (1990), 'The Exotic as Erotic: Captain Cook at Tahiti', in: *Exoticism in the Enlightenment*, eds George Sebastian Rousseau and Roy Porter, Manchester: Manchester University Press, pp. 117–43.

Prasch, Thomas (2016), '*Embrace of the Serpent*. Film Review', *Film & History*, 46: 2, pp. 93–5.

Pratt, Mary Louise (2008), *Imperial Eyes: Travel Writing and Transculturation*, 2nd edition, London and New York: Routledge.

Prins, Harald E. L. (1997), 'The Paradox of Primitivism: Native Rights and the Problem of Imagery in Cultural Survival Films', *Visual Anthropology*, 9, pp. 243–66.

Probyn, Elspeth (2000), *Carnal Appetites: FoodSexIdentities*, London: Routledge.

Proust, Marcel (1999 [1913]), *À la recherche du temps perdu*, Paris: Gallimard.

Putcha, Rumya Sree (2020), 'After *Eat, Pray, Love*: Tourism, Orientalism, and Cartographies of Salvation', *Tourism Studies*, 20: 4: pp. 450–66.

Rabinovitz, Lauren (2006), 'From Hale's Tours to Star Tours: Virtual Voyages, Travel Ride Films, and the Delirium of the Hyper-Real', in: *Virtual Voyages: Cinema and Travel*, ed. Jeffrey Ruoff, Durham, NC and London: Duke University Press, pp. 42–60.

Raheja, Michelle H. (2007), 'Reading Nanook's Smile: Visual Sovereignty, Indigenous Revisions of Ethnography, and *Atanarjuat (The Fast Runner)*', *American Quarterly*, 59: 4, pp. 1159–85.

Ramaswamy, Sumathi (2014), 'Introduction: The Work of Vision in the Age of European Empires', in: *Empires of Vision: A Reader*, eds Martin Jay and Sumathi Ramaswamy, Durham, NC and London: Duke University Press, pp. 1–22.

Rancière, Jacques (2000), *The Politics of Aesthetics: The Distribution of the Sensible*, trans. and intro. Gabriel Rockhill, London and New York: Continuum.
Rangarajan, Padma (2014), *Imperial Babel: Translation, Exoticism and the Long Nineteenth Century*, New York: Fordham University Press.
Rawle, Steven (2018), *Transnational Cinema: An Introduction*, London: Palgrave.
Rayns, Tony (2015), *In the Mood for Love*, London: BFI Publishing.
_____ (2022), 'One Second', *Sight & Sound*, 32: 9, p. 78.
Reiss, Hans (ed.) (1970), *Kant's Political Writings*, Cambridge: Cambridge University Press.
Richardson, Michael (2010), *Otherness in Hollywood Cinema*, New York: Continuum.
Rist, Peter (2002), 'Zhang Yimou's *The Road Home*', *Offscreen*, 6: 8, <https://offscreen.com/view/road_home> (last accessed 13 April 2022).
Robinson, Andrew (2011), *The Apu Trilogy: Satyajit Ray and the Making of an Epic*, London: I. B. Tauris.
Roesch, Stefan (2007), *The Experiences of Film Location Tourists*, Bristol: Channel View Publications.
Rogov, Daniel (2009), 'Two Reflections on a Film: *Eat Drink Man Woman*', *Wine Lovers* Discussion Forum, 12 September, <http://forums.wineloverspage.com/memberlist.php?mode=viewprofile&u=3440> (last accessed 9 May 2022).
Rony, Fatimah Tobing (1996), *The Third Eye: Race, Cinema, and Ethnographic Spectacle*, Durham, NC and London: Duke University Press.
Rooney, David (2015), '*Tanna*. Venice Review', *Hollywood Reporter*, 9 August, <http://www.hollywoodreporter.com/review/tanna-venice-review-820900> (last accessed 1 July 2020).
Root, Deborah (1996), *Cannibal Culture: Art, Appropriation, and the Commodification of Difference*, New York: Routledge.
Rosaldo, Renato (1989), 'Imperialist Nostalgia', *Representations*, 26, pp. 107–22.
Rosario, Kennith (2017), '*Viceroy's House* Review: A Soapy Political Saga', *The Hindu*, 17 August, <https://www.thehindu.com/entertainment/movies/viceroys-house-review-a-soapy-political-saga/article19510228.ece> (last accessed 15 May 2018).
Rovisco, Maria (2012), 'Towards a Cosmopolitan Cinema: Understanding the Connection between Borders, Mobility and Cosmopolitanism in the Fiction Film', *Mobilities*, 8: 1, pp. 148–65.
Roy, Sanip (2010), 'The New Colonialism of *Eat Pray Love*', *Salon*, 14 August, <https://www.salon.com/2010/08/14/i_me_myself/> (last accessed 3 July 2022).
Rushdie, Salman (1992a), *Imaginary Homelands: Essays and Criticism 1981–1991*, London: Granta Books in association with Penguin.
_____ (1992b), *The Wizard of Oz*, London: BFI Publishing.
Russell, Catherine (2020), 'Amazon Cinema: Vegetal Storytelling', in: *Cinema of Exploration: Essays on an Adventurous Film Practice*, eds James Leo Cahill and Luca Caminati, New York: Routledge, pp. 229–43.

R. V. (2017), '"*Viceroy's House*" Is an Antidote to Colonial Triumphalism', *The Economist*, 7 March, <https://www.economist.com/prospero/2017/03/07/viceroys-house-is-an-antidote-to-colonial-triumphalism> (last accessed 17 May 2018).

Said, W. Edward (2003 [1978]), *Orientalism*, reprinted with a new Preface, London: Penguin.

Salgado, Sebastião (2020), 'We Are on the Eve of Genocide: Brazil Urged to Save Amazon Tribes from Covid-19', *The Guardian*, 3 May, <https://www.theguardian.com/world/2020/may/03/eve-of-genocide-brazil-urged-save-amazon-tribes-covid-19-sebastiao-salgado> (last accessed 5 May 2020).

Saluja, Supreet and Richard J. Stevenson (2018), 'Cross-modal Associations between Real Tastes and Colors', *Chemical Senses*, *43*: 7, pp. 475–80.

Santaolalla, Isabel (ed.) (2000), *"New" Exoticisms: Changing Patterns in the Construction of Otherness*, Amsterdam: Rodopi.

Schmidt, Benjamin (2018), *Inventing Exoticism: Geography, Globalism, and Europe's Early Modern World*, Philadelphia: University of Pennsylvania Press.

Schneider, Alexandra (2002), '"Home Away from Home" oder warum die Schweiz im indischen Kino (k)eine Rolle spielt', in: *Bollywood: Das indische Kino und die Schweiz*, ed. Alexandra Schneider, Zürich: Edition Museum für Gestaltung, pp. 136–45.

Schou, Solvej (2012), '*Best Exotic Marigold* Director John Madden on Filming in India', *EW*, <https://ew.com/article/2012/12/10/best-exotic-marigold-hotel-john-madden-india/> (last accessed 15 August 2021).

Schütze, Irene (2014), 'Kochen als Kunst im Kino: *Eat Drink Man Woman*, (1994) / Regie: Ang Lee', in: *Kulinarisches Kino: Interdisziplinäre Perspektiven auf Essen und Trinken im Film*, ed. Daniel Kofahl, Bielefeld: Transcript Verlag, pp. 45–59.

Scott, A. O. (2002), 'Film Festival Review: A Far-off Inuit World in a Dozen Shades of White', *The New York Times*, 30 March, <https://www.nytimes.com/2002/03/30/movies/film-festival-review-a-far-off-inuit-world-in-a-dozen-shades-of-white.html> (last accessed 15 June 2020).

Segalen, Victor (2002 [1955]), *Essay on Exoticism: An Aesthetics of Diversity*, trans. and ed. Yaël Rachel Schlick, Durham, NC and London: Duke University Press.

Sexton, Jamie (2017), 'The Allure of Otherness: Transnational Cult Film Fandom and the Exoticist Assumption', *Transnational Cinemas*, 8: 1, pp. 5–19.

Shapiro, Ron (2000), 'In Defence of Exoticism: Rescuing the Literary Imagination', in: *"New" Exoticisms: Changing Patterns in the Construction of Otherness*, ed. Isabel Santaolalla, Amsterdam: Rodopi, pp. 41–9.

Sharkey, Heather J. (2015), '*La Belle Africaine*: The Sudanese Giraffe Who Went to France', *Canadian Journal of African Studies / Revue Canadienne des études africaines*, 49: 1, pp. 39–65.

Sharpe, Jenny (1993), *Allegories of Empire: The Figure of the Woman in the Colonial Text*, Minneapolis: University of Minnesota Press.

Shaviro, Steven (1993), *The Cinematic Body*, Minneapolis: University of Minnesota Press.

Shaw, Deborah (2016), 'Falling into *The Embrace of the Serpent*', *Mediático*, 21 July, <https://reframe.sussex.ac.uk/mediatico/2016/07/21/embrace-of-the-serpent/> (last accessed 15 August 2016).

—— (2018), 'Transnational Cinema: Mapping a Field of Study', in: *The Routledge Companion to World Cinema*, eds Rob Stone, Paul Cooke, Stephanie Dennison and Alex Marlow-Mann, London and New York: Routledge, pp. 290–8.

Sheppard, William Anthony (2019), *Extreme Exoticism: Japan in the American Musical Imagination*, New York: Oxford University Press.

Shohat, Ella and Robert Stam (1994), *Unthinking Eurocentrism: Multiculturalism and the Media*, London: Routledge.

Simons, John (2012), *The Tiger That Swallowed the Boy: Exotic Animals in Victorian England*, Faringdon: Libri Publishing.

Singh, Maanvi (2019), 'Dior Perfume Ad Featuring Johnny Depp Criticized over Native American Tropes', *The Guardian*, 31 August, <https://www.theguardian.com/fashion/2019/aug/30/diors-fragrance-ad-draws-criticism-for-featuring-native-american-tropes> (last accessed 8 January 2022).

Singh, Raghubir (1987), *Banaras: Sacred City of India*, London: Thames and Hudson.

Skrbiš, Zlatko and Ian Woodward (2013), *Cosmopolitanism: Uses of the Idea*, Los Angeles and London: Sage.

Slater, Candance (2002), *Entangled Eden: Visions of the Amazon*, Berkeley: University of California Press.

Smith, Iain Robert (2017), 'Theorising Cult Cosmopolitanism: The Transnational Reception of Bollywood as Cult Cinema', *Transnational Cinemas*, 8: 1, pp. 20–34.

Smith, Linda Tuhiwai (2012), *Decolonizing Methodologies: Research and Indigenous Peoples*, London: Bloomsbury Academic.

Sobchack, Vivian (2004), *Carnal Thoughts: Embodiment and Moving Image Culture*, Berkeley: University of California Press.

—— (2006), 'Cutting to the Quick: Techne, Physis and Poiesis and the Attractions of Slow Motion', in: *The Cinema of Attractions Reloaded*, ed. Wanda Strauven, Amsterdam: Amsterdam University Press, pp. 337–53.

Sontag, Susan (1979), *On Photography*, London: Penguin.

Spence, Charles (2020), 'Scent and the Cinema', *i-Perception*, 11: 6, pp. 1–22.

Spence, Charles, Xiaoang Wan, Andy Woods, Carlos Velasco, Jialin Deng, Jozef Youssef and Ophelia Deroy (2015), 'On Tasty Colours and Colourful Tastes? Assessing, Explaining and Utilizing Crossmodal Correspondences between Colours and Basic Tastes', *Flavour*, 4: 23, <https://flavourjournal.biomedcentral.com/articles/10.1186/s13411-015-0033-1> (last accessed 16 May 2022).

Spengler, Christine (2009), *Screening Nostalgia: Populuxe Props and Technicolour Aesthetics in Contemporary American Film*, Oxford: Berghahn Books.

Sperb, Jason (2016), *Flickers of Film: Nostalgia in the Time of Digital Cinema*, New Brunswick, NJ: Rutgers University Press.

Spivak, Gayatri Chakravorty (1995), 'Can the Subaltern Speak?', in: *The Postcolonial Studies Reader*, eds Bill Ashcroft, Gareth Griffiths and Helen Tiffin, London and New York: Routledge, pp. 28–37.

Stam, Robert (2019), *World Literature, Transnational Cinema, and Global Media: Towards a Transartistic Commons*, London and New York: Routledge.

Staszak, Jean-Francois (2009), 'Other/Otherness', in: *International Encyclopaedia of Human Geography*, eds N. J. Thrift and Rob Kitchen, Amsterdam and London: Elsevier, pp. 43–7.

Stephanson, Anders and Fredric Jameson (1989), 'Regarding Postmodernism: A Conversation with Fredric Jameson', *Social Text*, 21, pp. 3–30.

Stoler, Ann Laura (1997), 'Making Empire Respectable: The Politics of Race and Sexual Morality in Twentieth-century Colonial Cultures', in: *Dangerous Liaisons: Gender, Nation, and Postcolonial Perspectives*, eds Anne McClintock, Aamir Mufti and Ella Shohat, Minneapolis and London: University of Minnesota Press, pp. 344–73.

Stone, Jon (2016), 'British People Are Proud of Colonialism and the British Empire, Poll Finds', *The Independent*, 19 January, <https://www.independent.co.uk/news/uk/politics/british-people-are-proud-of-colonialism-and-the-british-empire-poll-finds-a6821206.html> (last accessed 21 May 2018).

Stone, Rob, Paul Cooke, Stephanie Dennison and Alex Marlow-Mann (eds) (2018), *The Routledge Companion to World Cinema*, London and New York: Routledge.

Stors, Natalie, Luise Stoltenberg, Thomas Frische and Christoph Sommer (2019), 'Tourism and Everyday Life in the Contemporary City: An Introduction' in: *Tourism and Everyday Life in the City*, eds Natalie Stors, Luise Stoltenberg, Thomas Frische and Christoph Sommer, London: Routledge, pp. 1–23.

Sund, Judy (2019), *Exotic: A Fetish for the Foreign*, London: Phaidon Press.

Tan, Amy (1989), *The Joy Luck Club*, London: Heinemann.

Tanna Press Kit, <http://distribution.paradisbio.dk/log/film/Tanna/tanna%20presskit%20(for%20web).pdf> (last accessed 20 March 2016).

Tasker, Yvonne (ed.) (2004), *Action and Adventure Cinema*, London: Routledge.

Ten Canoes Press Kit, <https://encodeur.movidone.com/getimage/A9fSjViIzmg9AesaAWQjOyul3J7VpL91PrLX_G3Tr3QkJAY6uDoxZcBG2UrPRvHkswFnxZX8vNMA1XkoFK-SYBjn-CUvwVMQOWZTq_E_yt4fdo3rRcH90A8ZpUTKPAEHv3ZluhyLJ-wG-5Q8XGoYv6U_h4RqnJBSNR9ct-pvUsfR6_A8_LFfosrLnSw8_kuhdveP5ZXKj-i4-hflS79OgjPV> (last accessed 1 August 2020).

Teo, Stephen (2005), *Wong Kar-wai*, London: BFI Publishing.

Thorpe, Vanessa (2017), 'British Film with a Punjabi Heart: Director's Personal Take on Partition', *The Guardian*, 16 January, <https://www.theguardian.com/film/2017/jan/16/viceroys-house-tells-bloody-truth-of-partition> (last accessed 17 May 2018).

Todorov, Tzvetan (1993), *On Human Diversity: Nationalism, Racism, and*

Exoticism in French Thought, trans. Catherine Porter, Cambridge, MA: Harvard University Press.
Torgovnick, Marianna (1998), *Primitive Passions: Men, Women and the Quest for Ecstasy*, Chicago: Chicago University Press.
Tzanelli, Rodanthi (2007), *The Cinematic Tourist: Explorations in Globalization, Culture and Resistance*, London and New York: Routledge.
Udden, James (2017), *No Man an Island: The Cinema of Hou Hsiao-hsien*, Hong Kong: Hong Kong University Press.
Urry, John (1995), *Consuming Places*, London and New York: Routledge.
Urry, John and Jonas Larsen (2011), *The Tourist Gaze 3.0*, Los Angeles and London: Sage.
Valck, Marijke de (2007), *Film Festivals: From European Geopolitics to Global Cinephilia*, Amsterdam: Amsterdam University Press
Vann, Michael G. (2008), '*Indochine*', *Asian Studies, Asian Educational Media Service*, 13: 1, pp. 63–5, <https://www.asianstudies.org/wp-content/uploads/indochine.pdf> (last accessed 21 March 2022).
Venuti, Lawrence (2018), *The Translator's Invisibility: A History of Translation*, 3rd edn, London: Routledge.
Viatori, Maximilian (2009), 'Re-imagining Amazonia', *Focaal: European Journal of Anthropology*, 53, pp. 117–22.
Viceroy's House Press Kit (2017), Transmission Films, Australia, <https://www.transmissionfilms.com.au/uploads/media/Viceroys_House_-_Transmission_Press_Kit.pdf> (last accessed 17 May 2018).
Vieira, Patrícia (2020), 'Rainforest Sublime in Cinema: A Post-Anthropocentric Amazonian Aesthetics', *Hispania* 103: 4, pp. 533–43.
Virdi, Jyotika (2017), 'A National Cinema's Transnational Aspirations? Considerations on Bollywood', *South Asian Popular Culture*, 15: 1, pp. 1–22.
Wang, Robin (2012), *Yingyang: The Way to Heaven and Earth in Chinese Thought and Culture*, Cambridge: Cambridge University Press.
Werbner, Pnina (2006), 'Vernacular Cosmopolitanism', *Theory, Culture & Society*, 23: 2–3, pp. 496–8.
Whitehead, Neil L. (2002), 'South America / Amazonia: The Forest of Marvels', in: *The Cambridge Companion to Travel Writing*, eds Tim Youngs and Peter Hulme, Cambridge: Cambridge University Press, pp. 121–38.
Wiegman, Robyn (1998), 'Race, Ethnicity and Film', in: *The Oxford Guide to Film Studies*, eds John Hill and Pamela Church Gibson, Oxford: Oxford University Press, pp. 158–68.
Williams, Linda (1991), 'Film Bodies: Gender, Genre, and Excess', *Film Quarterly*, 44: 4, pp. 2–13.
Windsor, D. A. (1998), 'Nargis, Ray, Rushdie and the Real', *South Asia: Journal of South Asian Studies*, 21: 1, pp. 229–42.
Wong, Ka F. (2011), 'From National Allegory to Global Commodity: The Cinematic Images of Gong Li', in: *Transnational Asian Identities in Pan-Pacific*

Cinemas: The Reel Asian Exchange, eds Philippa Gates and Lisa Funnel, London: Routledge, pp. 147–60.

Young, Deborah (2015), '*The Assassin*: Cannes Review', *The Hollywood Reporter*, 20 May, <https://www.hollywoodreporter.com/review/assassin-cannes-review-797267> (last accessed 25 January 2022).

Young, Robert C. (1995), *Colonial Desire: Hybridity in Theory, Culture and Race*, London and New York: Routledge.

Yue, Gang (1999), *The Mouth That Begs: Hunger, Cannibalism and the Politics of Eating in Modern China*, Durham, NC and London: Duke University Press.

Zeng, Li (2009), 'The Road to the Past: Socialist Nostalgia in Postsocialist China', *Visual Anthropology*, 22: 2–3, pp. 108–22.

Zhang, Emma Yu (2018), 'Enchanting World of Crafts: Handmade and Homemade Things, Affective Labor and Orality in *The Road Home*', *Journal of Chinese Cinemas*, 12: 1, pp. 1–19.

Zhang, Yingjin (2002), *Screening China: Critical Interventions, Cinematic Reconfigurations, and the Transnational Imaginary in Contemporary Chinese Cinema*, Ann Arbor: Center for Chinese Studies.

Zimmerman, Steve (2010), *Food in the Movies*, Jefferson, NC and London: McFarland.

Žižek, Slavoj (1991), *Looking Awry: An Introduction to Jacques Lacan through Popular Culture*, Cambridge, MA and London: MIT Press.

_____ (2006), 'Guilty Pleasures', *Film Comment*, 42: 1, pp. 12–13.

Index

Note: Page references in *italic* refer to illustrations. n refers to notes.

Abbas, Ackbar, 154, 172n, 173n
abjection, 200–1
Adorno, Theodor W., 109
Adventures of Tintin, The, 116
aesthetic/aesthetics
  of art cinema, 9, 12, 43, 131
  category, 4, 13, 101, 123
  of decontextualisation, 20
  of diversity, 21–2
  ethnographic, 67, 78, 79, 84
  of exoticism, 14, 17n, 21, 30, 44, 45, 50–2, 54, 159, 207n
  mode of perception, 13, 22, 53, 65, 104–5, 125, 135
  of sensuous indulgence, 14, 48, 159–61, 170, 177, *195*, 197
  pleasure, 28, 105–6, 135, 153, 160, 170
  realism/realist, 17n, 43, 64, 68, 105, 107, 129
  theories, 123
  transnational, 41, 79
  value, 22, 79
  see also cinematography; colour; exoticism; iconography
Aguirre, the Wrath of God/Aguirre, der Zorn Gottes (Werner Herzog), 89
Agzenay, Asma, 16n
Ahmed, Sara, 1
Akhtar, Zoya, 106, 127–8
Akomfrah, John, 10
All-Consuming Love, An/Chang Xiangsi (Zhaozhang He), 158

All That Heaven Allows (Douglas Sirk), 158
alterity, 2, 4, 14, 28, 32, 34, 43, 53, 54, 60, 65, 73, 78, 79, 80, 94, 99n, 108, 113, 141, 199, 206; *see also* cultural difference; Otherness/ the Other
Amazonia, 80, 89–90
Amazônia (exhibition), 89, 99n
Amazonian Indigenous peoples, 83, 89
Amazonian mythology, 92
Amiens International Film Festival, 70
Andrew, Dudley, 8, 11, 17n, 34
Angiliriq, Paul Apak, 68
Anti-Rightist Campaign, 162, 173n
Appiah, Anthony Kwame, 67, 98n
Appadurai, Arjun, 171–2
Apu Trilogy (Satyajit Ray), 45–6
Ashcroft, Bill, 41, 52, 57n
Ashizawa, Akiko, 133
Assassin, The/Cike Nie Yin Niang (Hou Hsiao-Hsien), 43, 49–50
Atanarjuat: The Fast Runner/ Atanarjuat (Zacharias Kunuk), 13, 60, 67–79, 82, 83, 84, 96, 98n
audiences/spectators
  global, 43, 82, 83, 140, 141, 156, 157, 159, 161, 164, 167, 168, 171, 179, 190
  local, 11, 70, 140, 157, 168, 171
  transnational, 13, 17n, 42, 44, 60, 68, 72, 73, 80, 84, 96, 106, 131, 154, 161, 167, 169, 171, 189, 196, 198, 206

Australian Academy of Cinema and Television Awards, 71
authenticity, 32, 54, 73, 75, 106
  cult of, 62, 63
  cultural, 53, 59, 78, 106, 141
  Indigenous art and, 64
  local, 13, 60, 61, 64, 67, 68, 74, 75, 78–80, 85, 95–6, 114, 190, 204
  and nostalgia, 164
  performance of, 63
  quest for, 61–5
  staged, 84–6
autoethnographic salvage, 75–6; *see also* ethnographic salvage
autoethnography, 4, 19, 31, 35, 36, 37, 40, 52, 53, 63, 68, 198
  and world cinema, 39

Bâ, Saër Maty, 6, 15
Baartman, Saartje (aka 'Hottentot Venus'), 55n
Babette's Feast (Gabriel Axel), 179
Bachna Ae Haseeno (Watchout Beauties, Siddharth Anan), 126
Bachner, Andrea, 203–4, 208n
Bai, Ling, 208n
Balanda and Bark Canoes, The (Rolf de Heer and Tania Nehme), 75
Balzac and the Little Chinese Seamstress/Xiao cai feng (Sijie Dai), 164–5
Banks, James, 30
Bao Shi, 162
Barclay, Barry, 59
Bardem, Javier, 137n
Barnes, Amy Jane, 167–8
Batchelor, David, 123
Batra, Ritesh, 189–90
Bauman, Zygmunt, 110–11, 113
Bazin, André, 64, 90
Beeton, Sue, 102
Before the Rains (Santosh Sivan), 145
Beijing Film Academy, 9
Belfast (Kenneth Brannagh), 165

Berlin International Film Festival/Berlinale, 12, 61, 98, 174n, 209n
Berry, Chris, 164
Bessire, Lucas, 78
Best Exotic Marigold Hotel, The (John Madden), 14, 101, 102, 111, 116–24, 129, 135
Bhabha, Homi, 23, 29, 31, 36, 37
Bhutiani, Sanjay, 132
Bhutiani, Shubhashish, 14, 124, 129–32
Bhutto, Fatima, 154
Big Night (Stanley Tucci and Campbell Scott), 181–2
Birth of Empire: The East India Company (BBC documentary series), 150
black activism, *négritude* movement, 69
black identity, 36–7
Black Narcissus (Michael Powell and Emeric Pressburger), 115
Black Venus/Venus Noire (Abdellatif Kechiche), 55n
Bride and Prejudice (Gurinder Chadha), 113
Blanc, Charles, 123
Blixen, Karen, 121, 145–6
Bollywood, 40, 109–10, 113
Bongie, Chris, 21, 87, 141, 143
Bonneville, Hugh, 151
Boorstin, Daniel, 110
Bougainville, Antoine de, 29, 30, 90
Bower, Annie, 178–9
Boyle, Danny, 45, 106, 107, 138n
Boym, Svetlana, 142, 161, 173n
Branagh, Kenneth, 165
Brief Encounter (David Lean), 158
Burton, Richard (British explorer), 30
Butler, Martin, 13, 80, 82, 90, *91*
Byron, Glennis, 202

cabinets of curiosities (*Wunderkammern*), 20
Calcutta (Louis Malle), 46

INDEX

Cannes Film Festival, 50, 68, 71, 79, 166
cannibal, 29, 199, 208n
cannibalism, 178, 198–205
　civilised, 204, 208n
　endocannibalism, 201
　fascinating, 87
　gegu, 204, 208n
　hunger vs ritual, 208n
capitalism, global, 14, 59, 60, 88, 128, 164, 170, 177, 183
Carbonell, Ovidio, 56n
Caro, Niki, 83
Célestin, Roger, 44–5, 125
Césaire, Aimé, 23
Chadha, Gurinder, 14, 113, 140, 150, 151–4, 181, 182
Chan, Felicia, 97n
Chan, Fruit, 15, 58n, 198, *201*, 202, 204, 206, 207, 208
Chang, William, 159
Chaudhuri, Shohini, 131
Chelsom, Peter, 14
Chen Kaige, 39, 55
cheongsam, 155–8, 159
Cheung, Maggie, 155–6, 157, 159, 172
China/Chinese
　Communist regime, 154, 162, 164, 167–8
　Cultural Revolution, 162, 164–5
　film censorship, 165, 166
　food culture, 176, 202, 203, 207
　medicine, 176, 187, 188, 203
　postsocialism, 140
　and primitivism, 204
　see also Chinese cinema
Chinese Box (Wayne Wang), 30
Chinese cinema
　cultural appropriation of, 42
　Fifth Generation, 3, 9, 39–40, 55
　postsocialist nostalgia films, 161–8, 171
Chinese New Year prints (*nianhua*), 167–8, 174n

chinoiserie, 23
Chocolat (Claire Denis), 145
Chocolat (Lasse Hallström), 178, 179
Chow, Rey, 4, 36, 38, 39, 40, 44, 52, 55, 57n, 167
Ciment, Michel, 198
cinema
　art, 3, 12, 43, 60, 89, 129, 198
　of attractions, 103, 107
　early cinema travelogues, 34, 103
　mainstream, 11, 14, 40, 80, 98n, 101, 102, 129, 135, 161, 177, 178, 205, 207n
　slow, 183, 197–8
　and spectacle, 34–5, 107
　see also global art cinema; Bollywood; transnational cinema; world cinema
cinematography, 130, 159
　black-and-white, 76, 80, 122, 163
　camera angle, 122, 152, 175
　colour, 51, 54, 69, 78, 122, 130–1, 160, 200
　cinéma verité style, 46
　image composition, 49, 153, 197
　light/lighting, 46, 47, 51, 78, 130, 197, 200, 202
　painterly style, 47, *49*, 51, 159, 197
　slow motion, 160
Claude Glass, 104–5
Clifford, James, 59n, 69, 79, 96n
Cohen, Robin, 98n
Cohn, Norman, 68–9, 76–7, 78
Cole, Nat King, 159, 160, 172
Collee, John, 80
Collins, Jane, 105
Columpar, Corinn, 97n
colonialism, 20, 21, 22, 36, 68, 94, 128, 141, 145, 173n
　and civilising mission, 29, 88, 115–16
　and colonial desire, 145, 181
　and the family trope, 149
　and postimperial melancholia, 151

colonialism (*cont.*)
   and power, 27–8, 35, 36, 144, 145, 146
   and sexuality, 144–5
   see also imperialist nostalgia films; neo-colonialism; Orientalism
colour, 21, 51, 69, 122–4, 130–1, 160, 168, 196, 200
   and chromophobia, 123
   and exoticism, 44, 47, 54, 101, 122, 123–4, 131, 136, 153, 163
   and synaesthesia, 48, 196–7, 207–8n
   see also cinematography
Confucianism, 185, 204
Conrad, Joseph, 89
contact zone, 15, 20, 39, 42, 128
Cook, James, 29, 30, 56n
cosmopolitanism, 65–8, 82
Couscous/La graine et le mulet (Abdellatif Kechiche), 181, 182
Cronenberg, David, 58n
Cruz, Penelope, 177
culinary film festivals, 179
culinary tourism, 181
cultural appropriation, 42, 76, 83, 180–1, 188
cultural difference
   commodification of, 21, 79, 101, 114–15, 135, 204
   domestication of, 20, 21, 31, 32, 43, 53, 61, 80, 131, 159
   fetishisation of, 14, 36, 52, 63, 106, 108, 177, 205, 206
   spectacle of, 44, 101, 107, 108, 136, 143
   see also alterity; Otherness/the Other
cultural translation, 13, 31–2, 38, 40, 41–2, 53–4, 56n, 57n, 73, 79, 83, 159, 196–7
   world cinema, 9, 38–43
   see also autoethnography; exoticism; self-exoticism

Dai, Sijie, 165
Dain, Mungau, 80, 84, 85, *91*
Damrosch, David, 38
Dances with Wolves (Kevin Kostner), 60
D'Anglure, Bernard Saladin, 74
Darr (Fear, Yash Chopra), 124
Dean, Bentley, 13, 80, 82, 90, *91*
decoloniality, 128
decolonising, 40, 76
   film studies, 1, 5–6, 10, 15n
   the gaze/the lens, 3, 13, 55, 70, 94, 95
de Heer, Rolf, 13, 71–2, 76, 77
Deleuze, Gilles, 192
Deneuve, Catherine, 147
Dennison, Stephanie, 11, 16n, 40
Deppman, Hsiu-Chuang, 207n
Deshpande, Shekhar, 11, 16n
diasporic filmmaker, 9, 165, 181, 197, 198, 205, 208n
Dil To Pagal Hai (The Heart is Crazy, Yash Chopra), 126
Dilwale Dulhania Le Jayenge (The Bravehearted Will Take the Bride, Yash Chopra), 125–7
Depp, Johnny, 97n
Dior, 97n
Djigirr, Peter, 13, *74*, 77, 98n
documentaries, ethnographic, 64, 74
double consciousness, 37
Downton Abbey (television drama series), 151
Doyle, Christopher, 159–60, 200, 202
Drum, The (Zoltan Korda), 144
Du Bois, W. E. B., 4, 36, 37
Dumplings/Gau ji (Fruit Chan), 15, 178, 198–205, 207, 209n
Duras, Marguerite, 146
Durian Durian (Fruit Chan), 58n
Dyer, Richard, 28, 99n, 111, 144, 171

Earth (Deepa Mehta), 138n
Eat Drink Man Woman/ Yin shi nan nu (Ang Lee), 175–7, 183–8, 206

Eat Pray Love (Ryan Murphy), 14, 102, 110–15, 119–22, 134, 135
Eckhout, Albert, 26, *27*, 88
Elsaesser, Thomas, 39
embodied memories *see* memory/memories
embodied perception, 47, 48, 160, 196
embodied spectatorship, 191–2
Embrace of the Serpent/El abrazo de la serpiente (Ciro Guerra), 10, 13, 43, 67, 79–96, 97n
empire, films of, 144
English Patient, The (Anthony Minghella), 145
enigmatisation, 140, 157
eroticism, 30, 51, 56n, 58n, 165, 178, 179–81; *see also* sexuality
Esquival, Laura, 179
ethnographic documentaries, 64, 74
ethnographic films, 35–6, 97n, 198
ethnographic gaze, 1, 35, 38, 55n, 78
ethnographic salvage, 59, 77, 86–7, 180
ethnography, 26, 34, 39, 51, 74
Eurocentrism, 28, 38, 52, 120–1, 125, 146
exotic, origins and definition, 19–20, 21
exotic gaze, 4–5, 20, 43, 51, 53, 104–8, 125, 141
  as déjà vu, 47, 104, 125, 135, 136n, 171
  legacies of European colonialism, 2, 66, 128
  and the Oriental's orientalism, 41, 52, 55
  reversal of, 41, 93–4, 128
  and the third eye, 37–8, 41
  seeing themselves through Western eyes, 5, 10, 40, 55
  see also ethnographic gaze; imperial gaze; tourist gaze

exotic nostalgia films, 141, 154–6, 161–9, 170–1
exoticism
  aesthetic principles of, 44, 46–7, *49*, 50–4, 78, 92, 159, 197–8
  and aesthetics of decontextualisation, 20
  as autoethnography, 35–40, 63
  and colour, 44, 47, 54, 101, 122, 123–4, 131, 136, 153, 163
  conceptualisation of, 4–5, 11, 19–23, 87, 113, 142, 143
  contestations surrounding, 2, 4, 13, 22, 44, 53, 54, 135
  and cosmopolitanism, 65–8, 82, 87, 91, 95
  as cultural translation, 31–2, 42–3, 53, 56n, 57n, 83, 159
  decentred, 3, 6, 8, 11, 19, 53, 54, 61, 85, 93, 124
  and domesticating Otherness, 20, 21, 32, 43, 44, 53, 61
  and eclecticism, 20, 26, *27*, 54, 114, 137n, 204
  and emphatic visuality, 33–5, 54
  and Eurocentrism, 2, 85, 121, 125, 128
  and hermeneutic circuit, 43, 125
  and hermeneutic deficit, 5, 45, 49, 54, 73, 171
  imperialist vs exoticising, 143
  and multisensorial pleasure of, 28, 47, 160–1, 177, 197
  and nostalgia, 22, 58n, 139, 141–3, 169–70
  and Orientalism, 3, 13, 19, 23–9, 40, 52, 53, 56n, 118, 149
  of place, 118–21
  and primitivism, 53, 87–8, 142, 191
  as salvage project, 62, 87, 89, 142
  spatial trajectory of, 143
  strategic performance of, 41, 52, 55, 68, 128, 131

exoticism (*cont.*)
　and utopianism, 29–30, 90, 169
　see also autoethnography; cultural translation; self–exoticism
exotisme, 23

Fabian, Johannes, 59, 96n
Fanon, Frantz, 4, 23, 36–7
Farewell My Concubine / Ba wang bie ji (Chen Kaige), 50
Farquhar, Mary, 169
Fei Mu, 158
female sexuality and colonialism, 144–5
Ferguson, Priscilla Parkhurst, 191, 193
Fernweh, 143
Ferroukhi, Ismaël, 129
film festivals, 2, 10, 12, 39, 42, 45, 47, 70, 71, 82, 85, 86, 98n, 132, 166, 167, 174n, 179, 209n; *see also* specific film festivals
film funding
　EU schemes, 8, 131
　film festival funds, 10
　Indigenous filmmaking, 69, 77
　transnational, 10, 41, 58n, 131
　World Cinema Fund, 61
films from elsewhere, 5, 8, 11, 49; *see also* global art cinema; transnational cinema; world cinema
Finch Hatton, Denys, 121
Fine, Robert, 98n
Fire (Deepa Mehta), 138n
Fitzcarraldo (Werner Herzog), 89
Flaherty, Robert, 64, 73, 75, 90, 99–100n
Flath, James, *The Cult of Happiness*, 167
Flowers of Shanghai / Hai shang hua (Hou Hsiao-Hsien), 50, 51–2, 55, 58n
food films
　emergence of genre of, 178–9

　exotic, 15, 177–8, 180, 181–3, 188–92, 196, 206
　ethnic, 180, 181–3, 206
　familial bonds, 183, 185–6, 188
　taste and smell, 177, 191–3, 195–7, 201, 207–8n
　see also synaesthesia
Forsdick, Charles, 23, 93, 141, 207n, 216
Foster, Stephen William, 56n
Foucault, Michel, 27
Four Feathers, The (Zoltan Korda), 144
Fourth Cinema, 59
Fourth World, 97n
Frankfurt School, 108
French Kiss (Lawrence Kasdan), 120–1
Freud, Sigmund, 108
Fusco, Coco, 9

Gabaccia, Donna, 181
Gabriel, Teshome, 40
Gallego, David, 80, 92
Galt, Rosalind, 4, 12 109, 123
Gauguin, Paul, 29–30, 90
Gérôme, Jean-Léon, 24–5, *24*, 26
Giddens, Anthony, 183
Gilbert, Elizabeth, 111–13
Gilroy, Paul, 151
giraffe, as diplomatic gift, 21
giraffomania (*la mode à la girafe*), 21
global art cinema, 8, 12, 17n, 32, 41, 43, 44
globalisation, 8, 18, 65, 85, 95, 125, 170, 172, 183
Global Majority, 6, 16n
Goethe, Johann Wolfgang von, 38
Gong Li, 168–9, 174n
Good Bye, Lenin! (Wolfgang Becker), 165
Gopalan, Lalitha, 109, 137n
Grand Tour, 104
Grand Voyage, Le (The Great Journey), 129

Greenblatt, Stephen, 56n
Griffiths, Alison, 35–6, 97n
Griffiths, Gareth, 62–3
Grijp, Paul van der, 56n
Grimoin-Sanson, Raoul, 34
Guajajara, Sonia, 90
Guerra, Ciro, 10, 13, 80, *81*, 83, 86, 89, 92, 94, 100n
Gully Boy (Zoya Akhtar), 106
Gulpilil, David, 71

Hale, George C., 34
Hale's Tours and Scenes of the World, 34
Halle, Randall, 41, 99n, 131
Hallström, Lasse, 138n, 177, 178
Hannerz, Ulf, 65, 82
Happy Feet (George Miller), 80
haptic visuality, 160–1, 197; *see also* embodied perception; intermodality; synaesthesia
Hartley, L. P., 141
Heading South/Vers le sud (Lauren Cantet), 137n
Heart of Darkness, 88–9
Heat and Dust (James Ivory), 144
Hector and the Search for Happiness (Peter Chelsom), 14, 102, 111, 115–16, 120, 122
Heine, Heinrich, 142
Heldke, Lisa, 177
heritage cinema, 47, 143, 152, 154, 157, 159, 172n
Hero/Ying ziong (Zhang Yimou), 17n
Herzog, Werner, 89, 136n, 140
Higbee, Will, 6, 9, 16n
Hillenbrand, Margaret, 123–4
Hindi cinema (popular) *see* Bollywood
Hinduism, 46
Hinrichsen, Malte, 57n
Hirsch, Marianne, 173n
Hitchcock, Alfred, 158
Hjort, Mette, 8, 9
Hofer, Johannes, 172n
Hong Kong, 157, 173n, 202–3

Hong Kong nostalgia films, 140–1, 154–6, 157–9
hooks, bell, 180–1
Horkheimer, Max, 109
Horner, James, 163
horror films, Asian, 199
Hotel Salvation/Mukti Bhawan (Shubhashish Bhutiani), 102, 124, 129–32
Hou Hsiao-Hsien, 12, 43, *49*, 51–2
House of Flying Daggers/Shi Mian Mai Fu (Zhang Yimou), 17n
Huggan, Graham, 62, 108, 143
human zoos, 20, 34, 54
Hundred-Foot Journey, The (Lasse Hallström), 138n, 177, 182–3
Hutcheon, Linda, 169
Huwiler, David, 130
Huyssen, Andreas, 139, 164

iconography, 80, 90, 199
 of 'Chineseness', 167–8
 of exoticism, 37, 43, 91, 94, 119, 124, 136n
 of India, 118
 of Noble Savage, 81
 of Orientalism, *24*
 of revolutionary *nianhua*, 167–8
 of 'savagery', 60, 88
 of South Sea Paradise, *91*
Ide, Wendy, 50
Igloolik Isuma production company, 68, 69, 70
Ihimaera, Witi, 83
imaginary geographies, 104, 125, 128, 135
imagineNATIVE Film + Media Arts Festival, 70
Imedin people, 80, 85
imperial gaze, 35, 40, 55
 Imperial Eye, 121, 122, 135–6
imperialist nostalgia films, 143–54, 170
India
 Holi festival, 47, 124

India (*cont.*)
  lunchbox delivery system, 189–90
  Partition (1947), 151–3
  poverty, 45–6, 107
  spirituality, 46, 129, 131, 136
Indian Summers (Channel 4 television series), 145, 150
Indigènitude, 69
Indigenous filmmaking/films, 68–79
  workshops and projects, 69–70
Indigenous peoples
  art and authenticity, 64
  collective memory, 86–7
  and the New World, 26
Indochine (Régis Wargnier), 14, 99n, 140, 146–50, 161, 170, 171, 174n
intermodality, 160; *see also* embodied perception; haptic visuality; synaesthesia
In the Mood for Love/ Fa yeung nin wah (Wong Kar-wai), 14, 43, 139, 140, 141, 154–61, 170, 172, 173n
Inuit Knowledge and Climate Change (Ian Mauro and Zacharias Kunuk), 98n
Inukitut language, 70
Iranian New Wave, 43

Jacob, Gilles, 166
James Bond franchise, 102
Jameson, Fredric, 139, 149
Japan, 132, 188–9
japonisme, 23
Jardin des Plantes, Paris, 21
Jay, Martin, 33
Jewel in the Crown, The (Granada Television series), 145
Jones, Ian, 77
Journals of Knut Rasmussen, The (Zacharias Kunuk and Norman Cohn), 98n
Ju Dou (Zhang Yimou), 39, 52, 166, 168, 169, 171

Kaldis, Nick, 52
Kama Sutra: A Tale of Love (Deepa Mehta), 30, 205
Kant, Immanuel, 66, 98n, 109
Kawase, Naomi, 15, 188–9
Kechiche, Abdellatif, 55n
Kennedy, Harlan, 153
Khoo, Eric, 188, 206
Khoo, Olivia, 2, 3, 131
Kiarostami, Abbas, 12
Knellwolf, Christa, 118
Koch-Grünberg, Theodor, 81, 94
Korda, Zoltan, 144
Kosslick, Dieter, 61
Kristeva, Julia, 200–1
Kuch Kuch Hota Hai (Some Things Happen, Karan Johar), 113
Kumar, Ranjit, 109
Kunuk, Zacharias, 68, 70, 72–3, 98n
Kunzle, David, 157
Kurosawa, Akiri, 12
Kurosawa, Kiyoshi, 14, 102, 129, 128–36
Kwan, Stanley, 158

Lai, Linda Chiu-han, 140–1, 157
Laine, Tarja, 192
Lam, Adam, 173n
Lang, Fritz, 205
Last of the Mohicans, The (Michael Mann), 60
Latin American Indigenous People's Film Festival, the, 70
Lawrence of Arabia (David Lean), 136n
Lean, David, 136n, 144, 158
Lee, Ang, 15, 30, 175, 177, 183, *184*, 188, 206, 207, 208n
Lee, Lilian, 198
Lee, Vivian, 154
Le Grand Voyage (The Great Tour, Ismaël Ferroukhi), 129
Lelord, François, 115
Leotta, Alfio, 102

Lévi-Strauss, Claude, 21, 74, 89
Levy, Daniel, 87
Like Water for Chocolate/Como agua para chocolate (Alfonso Arau), 43, 178, 179–80
Lim, Song Hwee, 9, 11, 15n, 40, 56n, 197–8
Lindenfeld, Laura, 181
Lindstrom, Lamont, 85–6
Li, Shizen, 203
Liu Li-Chang, 161
local authenticity, 190; *see also* authenticity
Locarno International Film Festival, 12
Lord of the Rings, The (Peter Jackson), 102
Loti, Pierre, 30, 51
Lover, The/L'Amant (Jean-Jacques Annaud), 145, 146
Lu, Sheldon Hsiao-peng, 42
Lu, Tonglin, 199
Lu, Xun, 203, 204
Lumière brothers, 34
Lunchbox, The, 15 (Ritesh Batra), 189–90, 206
Lupton, Deborah, 202
Lust, Caution/Se, jie (Ang Lee), 30, 140
Lutz, Catherine, 105
Lyon, Captain George, 75–6

Ma, Sheng-mei, 186
MacCannell, Dean, 84
Madame Chrysanthème, 51
Madden, John, 14, 117, *119*, 124
Maeda, Atsuko, 132, 133–4
Malle, Louis, 46
Manuel, George, 97n
Mao Zedong, Chairman, 165, 167, 204
Māori culture, 60, 83, 97n, 99
Marks, Laura, 137n, 160–1, 176, 192, 197

Mason, Peter, 18, 20, 56n
Master and Commander (Peter Weir), 80
Mazaj, Meta, 11, 16n
M. Butterfly (David Cronenberg), 58n, 140
McCalman, Iain, 118
McClintock, Anne, 149
McCurry, Steve, 46, 57n, 131, 137n
McSweeney, Michael, 130
Meeuf, Russell, 78
Mehta, Deepa, 43, 45, 47, *48*, 57n, 58n, 130, 131, 138n
melancholia, 96, 151, 173n
Melanesia, 60, 85, 99n
Memoirs of a Geisha (Rob Marshall), 30, 58n
Memmi, Albert, 23
memory/memories, 75, 94, 145, 155, 157, 160, 161, 165, 173n, 186
  collective, *81*, 86–7, 95, 96, 149, 162, 164, 172
  cosmopolitan, 87
  cultural, 13, 60, 61, 64, 68, 77, 95, 135, 141, 154
  embodied, 48, 160, 192–8, 206
  of past objecthood, 4, 40
  and postmemory, 173n
  Rushdie on, 163
Mendes, Ana, 106
Merlau-Ponty, Maurice, 192, 196
Micronesia, 99n
Miike, Takashi, 199
Mission, The (Roland Joffé), 89
Mistress of Spices, The (Paul Mayeda Berges), 178
Mitscherlich, Alexander and Margarete, 151
Moana (Robert Flaherty), 90
Mohabbatein (Love Stories), Aditdya Chopra, 124
Monsoon Wedding (Mira Nair), 113
Montaigne, Michel de, 29
Morelia Film Fest, 70

Mulvey, Laura, 35, 104
Murnau, Friedrich W., 90, 99–100n
Murphy, David, 23
Murphy, Ryan, 14, *120*
musical scores
   Earth, 138n
   Eat Pray Love, 113–14
   To the Ends of the Earth, 135
   Fire, 138n
   The Hundred-Foot Journey, 138n
   In the Mood for Love, 159
   The Road Home, 162–3
   Slumdog Millionaire, 138n
   Titanic, 163
   Viceroy's House, 138n
   Water, 138n

Nabokov, Vladimir, 143
Nagib, Lucía, 11, 16n, 17n
Nair, Mira, 45, 46–7, 107, 113, 124, 204
Nako, J. J., 82, 84, 85
Namesake, The (Mira Nair), 113
Nanook of the North (Robert Flaherty), 64, 73, 75, 97n, 99n
National Geographic, 33, 46, 105, 131
Native American Film and Video Festival, 70
nativism, 62, 64
Negra, Diane, 120–1, 180
négritude movement, 69
neo-colonialism, 112, 117, 131, 143
Ngai, Sianne, 4
nianhua (Chinese woodblock prints), 167–8, 174n
Nichols, Bill, 42–3
Nina's Heavenly Delights (Pratibha Parmar), 181, 182–3
Noble Savage, 13, 29, 81, 88
nostalgia
   armchair, 172
   and exoticism, 22, 58n, 139, 141–3, 169–70
   and ecological consciousness, 88, 92
   for familial bonds, 183
   imperialist, 92, 143–4, 151
   origins and definition, 139, 172n
   reflective vs restorative, 161, 173n
   spatial trajectory of, 142–3
   see also nostalgia films
nostalgia films, 140–1, 143
   exotic, 14, 140, 141, 154–6, 161–9, 170–1
   Hong Kong, 140–1, 154, 158
   imperialist, 140, 143–54, 170
   postsocialist, 161–8, 171
Not One Less/ Yi ge dou bu neng shao (Zhang Yimou), 166, 173n
Notting Hill (Roger Michell, 199), 120–1
Nunavut, Canada, 69

Once Were Warriors (Lee Tamahori), 98n
One Day in the Life of Noah Piguattuk (Zacharias Kunuk), 98n
Orientalism, 3, 13, 19, 41, 52, 56n, 156, 169
   and exoticism, 23–9, 53, 56n, 118
   geographical scope of, 23–4
   iconography of, *24*–5, 119
   neo-Orientalism, 113, 149, 176
   Oriental's orientalism, 41, 52, 55
   and power hierarchies, 26–7, 53, 118
   see also Otherness/the Other; primitivism
Otherness/the Other, 2, 3, 4, 5, 15, 16n, 17n, 18, 19, 20, 28, 29, 30–1, 39, 41, 46, 47, 50, 53, 54, 59, 65, 66, 93, 94, 99n, 102, 108, 113–14, 118, 120, 171, 158, 197
   and ambivalence, 28–9, 32
   commodification of, 52, 180–1
   desire for, 30–1, 78, 135, 180, 181
   and the Self, 1, 26, 33, 36, 38, 126, 205

see also alterity; cultural difference; exoticism; Orientalism; primitivism
Out of Africa (Sydney Pollack), 121–2, 144, 145–6
Ozu, Yasujiro, 12

Palm Trees in the Snow/Palmeras en la nieve (Fernando González Molina), 140
Pang, Laikwan, 174n
Panh, Rithy, 146
Paradise: Love/Paradies: Liebe (Ulrich Seidl), 137n
Parasecoli, Fabio, 181
Paris Exposition (1900), 34
Park Chan-wook, 199
Parry, William Edward, 75
Partition (1947), 151–3
Partition: 1947 (Indian release title of *Viceroy's House*), 151
Passage to India, A (David Lean), 144, 145
pastiche, 38, 168, 171, 172
Pather Panchali (Pather Panchali: Song of the Little Road, Satyajit Ray), 45
Phantom India/L'Inde fantôme (Louis Malle), 46
photography, 33, 35, 46, 54, 57n, 76, 80, 86, 89, 95, 103, 104–6, 131, 150
Piaf, Edith, 135
Ping-bin, Mark Lee, 49–50, 159–60
pleasure
  and exoticism, 26, 27–8, 54, 88, 108, 135, 161, 192
  guilty, 107–9, 136
  see also eroticism; spectacle
Polan, Dana, 108
Polynesia, 22, 29, 99n
Ponzanesi, Sandra, 109
Posluns, Michael, 97n
postcolonial, 23, 57n, 69, 141
  cinema, 40

guilt, 95, 149, 170
resistance, 44, 55, 60
transformation, 41, 52, 54, 57n
visuality, 198
writers and critics, 23, 36, 143
postcolonialism, 2, 57n
postcoloniality, 23
postsocialist nostalgia films, 161–8, 171
Pratt, Mary Louise, 15n, 20, 36, 39, 121
primitivism, 23, 25, 26, 29, 87–8, 142, 178, 191, 204, 207
Prince Philip Movement, The, 100n
Prins, Harald, 68
Probyn, Elspeth, 177
Proust, Marcel, 193
Puccini, Giacomo, 51, 114
Pushing Hands/Tui shou (Ang Lee), 183

Queen (Vikas Bahl), 127
Queen of the Desert (Werner Herzog), 136n, 140
Qulitalik, Paul, 70

Rabbit-Proof Fence (Phillip Noyce), 60, 77
Rahman, A. R., 137–8n, 152
Raise the Red Lantern/Da hong deng long gao gao gua (Zhang Yimou), 39, 50–1, 166, 168, 169
Raj revival films, 139–40, 144, 145, 150–4
Ramaswamy, Sumathi, 33
Ramen Shop/Ramen The (Eric Khoo), 188, 206
Ramingining Aboriginal people, 71, 72, 75
Rancière, Jacques, 13
Ray, Satyajit, 45–6
Rayns, Tony, 154
Red Sorghum/Hong gao liang (Zhang Yimou), 166, 168, 169, 171

Red Trilogy (Zhang Yimou), 166, 168, 171
Regnault, Félix, 29
Rhodes of Africa (Michael Balcon), 144
rituals and cultural Otherness, 44, 45, 46, 47, 78, *79*, 84, 113–14, *120*, 125, 168, *184*, 193, 198, 204, 206
Road Home, The / Wo de fu qin mu qin (Zhang Yimou), 140, 161–9
Roberts, Julia, 137n
Rocha, Glauber, 12
Roesch, Stefan, 102
Rony, Fatimah Tobing, 36, 37, 43, 87, 97n
Root, Deborah, 16n, 76
Rosaldo, Renato, 92, 143–4
Rouge / Yim ji kau (Stanley Kwan), 158
Rousseau, Henri, *25*–6, 30
Rovisco, Maria, 64, 67
Roy, Sanip, 112
Rushdie, Salman, 37, 60, 85, 122–3, 141, 163

Said, Edward, 23–4, 26–7, 118
Salaam, Bombay! (Mira Nair), 45, 46–7, 107, 124
Salaam Balak Trust (NGO), 45
Salgado, Sebastião, 80, 89–90
San Bao, 162–3
Sanders of the River (Zoltan Korda), 144
Sangam (Confluence, Raj Kapoor), 138n
Santaolalla, Isabel, 2
Sartre, Jean-Paul, 23
Scent of Green Papaya, The / Mùi du du xanh (Tran Anh Hung), 15, 43, 177, 192–8, 206–7
Schamus, James, 183
Schmidt, Benjamin, 33
Schoonover, Karl, 12, 17n
Schultes, Richard Evans, 81, 94
Seawall, The / Un barrage contre le Pacifique (Rithy Pan), 99n, 146, 173n
Second Best Exotic Marigold Hotel, The (John Madden), 116, 117–18
Segalen, Victor, 21–3, 29–30, 78, 90, 161
self-exoticism, 5, 37, 39, 41, 50, 51, 52, 54, 55, 128, 131; *see also* autoethnography; cultural translation; exoticism
sense memory *see* embodied memories
sexuality, 26, 56n, 90, 144–5, 181, 186, 205; *see also* eroticism
Shanghai, 154, 155, 156, 164
Shanghai Tang, 156–7
Shapiro, Ron, 2
Sharpe, Jenny, 145
Shaviro, Steven, 192
Shaw, Deborah, 8, 93
Sheik, The (George Melford), 136n
Sheltering Sky, The (Bernardo Bertolucci), 136n
Shohat, Ella, 3, 11, 28, 35, 136n
Singh, Raghubir, 46, 57n, 131
Sirk, Douglas, 158
Sissel, Sandi, 46
slow cinema, 183, 197–8
slow food movement, 176, 183, 189
slum tourism, 57n, 106–7
Slumdog Millionaire (Danny Boyle), 45, 106, 138n
smell and taste, 191–2, 193; *see also* synaesthesia
Smith, Linda Tuhiwai, 61, 62
Smithsonian Institution's Native American Film and Video Festival, The, 70
Smoke Signals (Chris Eyre), 98n
Sobchack, Vivian, 160, 192, 195
Solino (Fatih Akin), 181
song-and-dance sequences, 126
Sontag, Susan, 105–6, 111
Soul Food (George Tillman Jr), 181–2

soundtrack, 135, 198; *see also* musical scores
spectacle
  ethnographic, 20, 37
  human zoos, 20, 34, 54
  and colour, 47, 95, 101, 123
  and cultural difference, 14, 28, 35, 60, 78, 101, 102, 108, 110, 113, 140, 166
  and exoticism, 34–5, 47, 66, 78, 96, 160
  and nature, 90, 91
  and pleasure, 28, 44, 107–9, 136, 197
  Western distrust of, 44, 109, 136
Spence, Charles, 207n
Spivak, Gayatri Chakravorty, 23, 112
Spring in a Small Town/Xiao cheng zhi chun (Fei Mu), 158
Stam, Robert, 3, 11, 28, 35, 136n
Staszak, Jean-Francois, 128
Stoler, Ann Laura, 144
Strauven, Wanda, 192
sublime, 68, 91, 102, 136
Sundance, 70
Sweet Bean/An (Naomi Kawase), 188–9
synaesthesia, 177, 192, 196, 207n; *see also* embodied perception; haptic visuality; intermodality
Sznaider, Natan, 87

Tabu: A Story of the South Seas (Friedrich W. Murnau), 90
Tampopo (Juzo Itami), 178
Tan, Amy, 204
Tanna (Martin Butler and Bentley Dean), 13, 43, 60, 67, 79–88, 90–4, 96, 100n
taste and smell, 191–2, 193; *see also* embodied memory; haptic visuality; intermodality; synaesthesia
television

  drama series, 145, 150, 151
  food programmes, 179
  travel shows, 104
Ten Canoes (Rolf de Heer and Peter Djgirr), 13, 60, 67, 71–9, 82–4, 92
Teo, Stephen, 10, 155
Theeb (Naji Abu Nowar), 137n
Third Cinema, 40, 41
Thomson, Donald, 76
Three ... Extremes/Sang Gang 2 (Fruit Chan, Park Chan-wook and Takashi Miike), 209n
Three Times/Zuihao de shiguang (Hou Hsiao-Hsien), 58n
Tiger of Eschnapur, The/Der Tiger von Eschnapur (Fritz Lang), 205
Timbuktu (Abderrahmane Sissako), 137n
Titanic (James Cameron), 162, 163
To Live/Huo zhe (Zhang Yimou), 165
To the Ends of the Earth/Tabi no owari sekai no hajimari (Kiyoshi Kurosawa), 14, 102, 129, 128–36
Todorov, Tzvetan, 5, 22, 29, 30, 110
Torgovnick, Marianna, 208n
Tortilla Soup (Maria Ripoll), 177, 181–2
tourism/tourist industry, 102–3, 104, 106–7, 112, 115, 119, 129, 132, 137n, 181
tourist films, 132–5
tourist gaze, 102–8, 119, 125, 131, *134*
  Kurosawa on, 133, 134
  see also exotic gaze
tourists, 110–11
Tran Anh Hung, 9, 15, 177, 192–8, 206, 208n
transnational
  audiences/spectators, 13, 17n, 42, 44, 60, 68, 72, 73, 80, 84, 96, 106, 131, 154, 161, 167, 169, 171, 189, 196, 198, 206

transnational (*cont.*)
  audience appeal, 4, 35, 44, 45, 68, 128, 158, 168, 174, 177, 206
  cinema, 1, 3, 5, 6, 8–10, 12, 16–17n, 32, 41, 97, 101, 172n
  circulation, 4, 5, 12, 38, 53, 157
  exhibition, 39, 70, 132
  imaginary, 176, *184*
  production, 10, 41, 58, 165
  reception, 11, 17, 19, 38, 41, 42, 43, 53, 68, 141, 166, 171
  see also film funding; world cinema
travel, mass cultural practice of, 103
travellers, 110
travelogues, 34
Trishna (Michael Winterbottom), 30
Tropical Malady / Sud pralad (Apitchatpong Weerasethakul), 43
Tzanelli, Rodanthi, 102

Udden, James, 58n
Umebayashi Shigeru, 159
Uncle Boonmee Who Can Recall His Past Lives / Loong Boonmee raleuk chat (Apitchatpong Weerasethakul), 43
Under the Hawthorn Tree / Shan zha shu zhi lian (Zhang Yimou), 165
United Nations Declaration of the Rights of Indigenous Peoples, 69
Urry, John, 103–4, 106, 119
Uzbekistan, 132, 133

vagabonds, 110–11
Venice Film Festival / La Biennale de Venezia, 12, 85, 131, 132
Venuti, Lawrence, 31–2, 56n
Vertigo (Alfred Hitchcock), 158
Viceroy's House (Gurinder Chadha), 14, 138n, 140, 141, 150–4, 161, 170, 174n
Victoria and Abdul (Stephen Frears), 140, 150
Vieira, Patrícia, 100n

Vivah (Marriage/Wedding, Sooraj Barjatiya), 113
Vogt, Carl, 29

Walkabout (Nicolas Roeg), 60
Wallis, Samuel, 29
Wang, Wayne, 204
Wargnier, Régis, 140, 146–*47*
Water (Deepa Mehta), 43, 45, 47–8, 57n, 58n, 124, 130, 131
Wawa, Marie, 84, 85, *91*
The Wedding Banquet / Xi ya (Ang Lee), 183
wedding films, 113–14
Weerasethakul, Apichatpong, 43
Wen-Ying Huang, 49
Whale Rider (Niki Caro), 60, 83
What's Cooking? (Gurinder Chadha), 181, 182
When Harry Met Sally (Rob Reiner), 178
White Masai, The / Die weiße Massai (Hermine Huntgeburth), 137n
White Mischief (Michael Radford), 145
white privilege, 14, 111–16, 135
White Shadows in the South Sea (W. S. van Dyke), 90
wild animals, domestication of, 20–1
Williams, Linda, 192, 206
Winterbottom, Michael, 30
Wizard of Oz, The (Victor Fleming), 122–3
Woman on Top (Fina Torres), 177, 178
women
  allegorical narratives of Chinese, 166, 169
  erotic encounters with exotic, 30, 51, 56n, 58n
  and colonialism, 99n, 144–5
Wong Kar-wai, 10, 14, 123, 139, 140, 154–6, 158–61, 171–2
world cinema, 32
  and the contact zone, 39, 128

INDEX 253

world cinema (*cont.*)
   cultural translation, 38–43, 196
   decoded as exotic, 43–52
   self-exoticism, 39
   transnational circulation and reception of, 4, 5, 12, 14, 19, 35, 38, 39, 43, 53, 68, 70, 97n, 141, 158, 196
World Fair, Paris *see* Paris Exposition (1900)
World of Suzie Wong, The (Richard Quine), 58n, 156

Yakel people, 82, 85–6
Yellow Earth/Huang tu di (Chen Kaige), 39
Yeung, Miriam Ching Wah, 208n
yinyang, 187–8
Yolngu people, 71, 72, 76, 77
Young, Robert, 145
Yue, Gang, 203–4

Zarafa, 21, 53
Zarafa (Rémi Bézançon and Jean-Christophe Lie), 56n
Zhang, Emma Yu, 163
Zhang Yimou, 12, 17n, 39, 50–1, 140, 161, 55, 123, *163*, 164–5, 166–7, 168, 173n
Zhou Xuan, 158, 159
Zindagi Na Milegi Dobara (You Only Live Once, Zoya Akhtar), 124, 127–8
Žižek, Slavoj, 109, 165–6

EU representative:
Easy Access System Europe
Mustamäe tee 50, 10621 Tallinn, Estonia
Gpsr.requests@easproject.com

www.ingramcontent.com/pod-product-compliance
Lightning Source LLC
Chambersburg PA
CBHW070323240426
43671CB00013BA/2351